OIL, POLITICS AND VIOLENCE: NIGERIA'S MILITARY COUP CULTURE (1966–1976)

OIL, POLITICS AND VIOLENCE: NIGERIA'S MILITARY COUP CULTURE (1966–1976)

Max Siollun

Algora Publishing
New York

Library of Congress Cataloging-in-Publication Data —

Siollun, Max.
    Oil, Politics and Violence: Nigeria's Military Coup Culture (1966–1976) / Max
Siollun.
        p. cm.
    Includes bibliographical references and index.
    ISBN 978-0-87586-708-3 (trade paper : alk. paper) — ISBN 978-0-87586-709-0
(hard cover: alk. paper) — ISBN 978-0-87586-710-6 (ebook) 1. Coups d'etat—Nigeria—
History—20th century. 2. Military government—Nigeria—History—20th century. 3.
Nigeria—Politics and government—1960- I. Title.

    DT515.8.S54 2009
    966.905'3—dc22

                                2008053756

Front Cover: (from top left, clockwise)
Homes and Market Near Lagoon, Lagos, Nigeria, © Paul Almasy/CORBIS
Lt. Colonel Odumegwu Ojukwu, leader of secessionist Biafra, © Bettmann/CORBIS
Niger Delta - The Curse of Black Gold — Mr. Esau Goldsmith, 57, in the fishing village
of Nembe, in Bayelsa state.... In the background is a Shell pipeline.© Ed Kashi/Corbis, June
16, 2006
Lagos, March 12, 1984, © William Campbell/Sygma/Corbis

Printed in the United States

Location of Major Ethnic Groups

ABOUT THE AUTHOR

Max Siollun is a historian and commentator on Nigerian political and governmental issues, specializing in Nigerian history and the Nigerian military's participation in politics. Although born in Nigeria, he was educated in England and is a graduate of the University of London. For the past decade has been a well known columnist for several publications on Nigerian history and contemporary affairs. His balanced critiques on Nigerian history and the Nigerian military's intervention in politics has given him a reputation as one of the most renowned scholars on Nigeria's post independence history, and has gained him unprecedented access to documentary and eyewitness sources regarding Nigeria's history.

TABLE OF CONTENTS

Preface

Sometimes referred to as the "Giant of Africa," with a population of over 140 million, Nigeria is Africa's most populous country; a quarter of all Africans are Nigerian. Nigeria is located in west Africa, just north of the equator and south of the Sahara desert. Its southern coastline dips into the Atlantic Ocean. Nigeria is the United States' largest trading partner in sub-Saharan Africa, with annual trade between the two countries in 2009 valued at approximately $30 billion.

Nigeria exports more than one million barrels of crude oil a day to the United States (representing nearly 50% of Nigeria's daily crude oil production), and it is projected that by 2015, Nigeria will provide 25% of the United States' oil supply.[1] With the United States' frequently strained relations with Arab countries, Nigeria is increasingly viewed in Washington as an alternate dependable crude oil supplier.

Nigeria's gross domestic product (GDP) is larger than the combined GDP of its fifteen neighboring west African countries that make up the Economic Community of West African States (ECOWAS). It is a regional economic, political and military superpower in west Africa, is blessed with abundant wealth from crude oil and natural gas, has the best educated workforce in Africa, and enjoys a vibrant free press with over one hundred privately owned newspapers and magazines.

Its nationals are leaders in arts, science, finance and literature. Professor Wole Soyinka is Africa's most distinguished playwright and was the first African to win the Nobel Prize for literature. Nigeria's former Finance Minister Ngozi Okonjo-Iweala is a Managing Director of the World Bank. Dr. Augustine Njoku-Obi developed a cholera vaccine. Despite having all the prerequisites to become a superpower, Nigeria staggers from one crisis to another. After ten military coups, three heads of government assassinated, three ruinous decades of military dictatorship, and a civil war that claimed a million lives, Nigeria is still struggling to fulfill its vast potential.

---

1 Speech of Nigerian Minister of Foreign Affairs, Chief Ojo Maduekwe, at the Southern Center for International Studies, Atlanta, Georgia, entitled, *"Old Ties in New Times: Nigeria and the next USA Administration."*

Under military rule, the country abandoned its traditionally agriculture-based economy and adopted a dangerously polarized oil-dominant economy that is extremely susceptible to fluctuations in oil prices. Nigeria became almost totally dependent on earnings from its crude oil exports which currently account for over 90% of its foreign exchange earnings. Since Nigeria's oil is exclusively located in the south of the country, this also polarized the country on ethnic and religious lines, with the mainly Christian inhabitants of the oil producing southern areas bitterly resenting that the revenue from oil drilled from their land is used to develop non-oil producing areas.

Oil is obtained from only 9 of Nigeria's 36 states.[1] Approximately 75% of Nigeria's oil and over 50% of its earnings are obtained from just three of these oil producing states.[2] Despite producing the overwhelming majority of Nigeria's wealth, the inhabitants of the oil communities do not have the political strength to resist control of their resources by Nigeria's federal government.

Nigeria's crude oil wealth paradoxically became an impediment to its democratic development, as it incentivized the country's military to seize and retain political power. Within 18 months of seizing power, the Nigerian military threatened the corporate existence of the country as two different factions of the army attempted to secede, replicated Nigeria's political and societal cleavages within itself, and plunged the country into the brutal famine ravaged Biafran civil war that claimed over a million lives, and presented Western viewers for the first time, with their now prototypical imagery of the emaciated and starving African child. The excesses of the Nigerian military were largely ignored by Western governments which were anxious not to interrupt a generous supply of crude oil. Nigeria's "Bonny Light" crude oil is highly attractive to its Western importers as it has a low sulfur content and is easy to refine. Therefore Western relations with Nigeria are largely dictated by economic interests rather than by any sense of altruism or adherence to democratic principles.

It is often said that history is written by victors. In many cases in Nigeria, history is not written at all. A combination of official reluctance to divulge combustible past events in a country permanently poised on an ethnic and religious powder keg, and the determination of the *dramatis personae* to avoid having their misdeeds exposed, means that early Nigerian post-independence history is in many places a collection of folk tales and fables. This has also caused Nigeria to be greatly misunderstood and misrepresented overseas, especially in the area of the Nigerian military's pivotal interference in the politics and governance of Nigeria. Nigerians are aware that their military ruled them for 30 out of the country's first 40 years after independence. Yet there is little situational awareness of how the military became so politically powerful. Even though ostensibly democratic today, Nigeria is still dominated by the same military cabal that over four decades sporadically overthrew democratically elected governments, fought the Biafran civil war and imposed an economic blockade that caused famine and a million deaths, recklessly squandered the country's oil wealth, and played the greatest role in disrupting the country's political evolution.

The decade between 1966 and 1976 was the most politically explosive decade of Nigeria's history during which it almost disintegrated, and Nigerian governments mastered the art of taking their country to the edge of an abyss and pulling back at the last moment. Most of the prior books on this time period were written by the protagonists, and their accounts are sometimes tainted by their embittered personal

---

1 Akwa Ibom, Bayelsa, Cross River, Delta, Edo, Rivers, Abia, Imo, and Ondo states.
2 Bayelsa, Delta and Rivers states.

experiences and grievances. There is a substantial readership that desires a balanced, impartial and full account of that crisis racked decade. This book seeks to educate the reader about the dynamic that existed within the military and which influenced its conduct and interference in Nigerian politics. Rather than giving the sanitized version of coups that is in other books, the author has deliberately given extremely graphic accounts of events in order for the reader to appreciate the ruthless brutality that often accompanies military coups d'états.

Nigeria's return to civilian democratic rule in 1999 has encouraged greater freedom of expression and political debate regarding topics that were considered taboo in the days of military rule. This has presented a welcome opportunity to discuss previously taboo topics, in order that future generations can learn from them and avoid the mistakes of the past. Those that do not heed history are doomed to repeat it.

Major Nigerian Languages

Source: Eghosa E. Osaghae, *Crippled Giant: Nigeria Since Independence.*

Map of Nigeria, 1966, Four-Region Structure

Source: Eghosa E. Osaghae, *Crippled Giant: Nigeria Since Independence.*

Map of Nigeria, 1967–1976, Twelve-State Structure

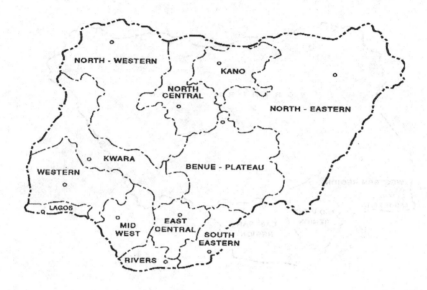

Source: Eghosa E. Osaghae, *Crippled Giant: Nigeria Since Independence.*

Map of Nigeria, 1976–1987, Nineteen States

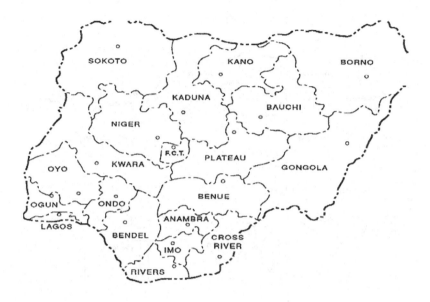

Source: Eghosa E. Osaghae, *Crippled Giant: Nigeria Since Independence.*

Map of Nigeria, 1991–1996, Thirty States

Source: Eghosa E. Osaghae, *Crippled Giant: Nigeria Since Independence.*

Map of Nigeria, 1996–Present, Thirty-Six States

Source: Nigerian Embassy – Australia.

Africa and Nigeria

Source: Brighter Day Charities

CHAPTER 1. THE PRE-COUP DAYS: POLITICS AND CRISIS

When it gained independence from the UK in 1960, hopes were high that, with mineral wealth and the most educated workforce in Africa, Nigeria would become Africa's first superpower and a stabilizing democratic influence in the region.

However, these lofty hopes were soon dashed and the country lumbered from crisis to crisis, with the democratic government eventually being overthrown in a violent military coup in January 1966. From 1966 until 1999, the army held onto power almost uninterrupted (except for a short-lived return to democracy between 1979 and 1983) under a succession of increasingly authoritarian and corrupt military governments and army coups. Military coups and military rule (which began as an emergency aberration) became a seemingly permanent feature of Nigerian politics.

Nigeria has been democratic since 1999. The period from 1999 till the present is the longest period that Nigeria has ever gone without suffering a military coup. Despite being ruled by the military for most of their post-independence history, the majority still insist that democracy is their preferred method of governance.

INDEPENDENCE

An army officer named Captain David Ejoor commanded the army guards at the midnight flag raising ceremony on Nigeria's Independence Day on October 1, 1960. Little did Ejoor know then what a pivotal role he and his army colleagues would play in their country's political destiny. The causes and origins of military intervention in Nigerian politics are so complex that they cannot be separated from the prevailing political situation at the time. After Nigeria gained independence from the UK on October 1, 1960, its domestic politics *tried* to emulate those of its former colonial master by adopting a Westminster-style parliamentary democracy. There the similarities ended.

The political culture of the UK is one of refined debate and sophisticated party maneuvering by comparison to Nigeria's politics, fragmented as it is along regional and ethnic lines. The country was artificially created by a colonial power without the consent of its citizens. Over 250 ethnic groups were arbitrarily herded together into an unwieldy and non-consensual union by the UK. Nigeria was so ethnically, religiously and linguistically complex that even some of its leading politicians initially doubted it could constitute a real country. It was infamously referred to as "the mistake of 1914."[1] During one of Nigeria's early constitutional conferences, future Prime Minister Tafawa Balewa stated that Nigeria "existed as one country only on paper. It is still far from being united. Nigerian unity is only a British intention for the country." Another prominent politician stated that "Nigeria is not a nation; it is a mere geographic expression. There are no 'Nigerians' in the same sense as there are English or Welsh or French. The word 'Nigeria' is merely a distinctive appellation to distinguish those who live within the boundaries of Nigeria from those who do not."[2]

The largest ethnic groups in the north of country were the Muslim, traditional and socially conservative, Hausa and Fulani ethnic groups. Intermarriage and cultural assimilation had blurred the distinction between the two ethnicities and Nigerians refer to them in compound form as the "Hausa–Fulani." The south was dominated by two competing ethnic groups: the proud and culturally rich Yorubas in the south-west, and the energetic and vibrant Igbos in the south-east. The British carved the country into three regions broadly corresponding to the location of these three largest ethnic groups. Hemmed in between them were approximately another 250 disparate ethnicities. Some were millions strong and others had only a few hundred members. Most of these groups had nothing in common with each other outside of their mutual suspicion and hostility.

The differences between them were accentuated by religion. The south of the country is predominantly Christian and the north predominantly Muslim. The general outlook of the people in the north and south is so different as to give them practically nothing in common and to make physical confrontation between them a virtual certainty. There is less difference between an Englishman and a Spaniard, with their shared Latin-derivative languages and culture, than there is between a Muslim northerner and a Christian southerner, with their diametrically opposed religions, language, food, manners, dress and culture. The cultural differences between the ethnic groups made it virtually impossible for Nigerians to have any commonality of purpose.

Party politics (and political parties) took on the identity and ideology of each of the three geo-political regions in the north, south-east and south-west. The dominant and largest political party in the Northern Region was the Northern People's Congress (NPC), whose motto of "One North, One People" gave an entirely accurate description of its objectives. It was unashamedly a regional party, did not bother to field candidates outside the Northern Region and was dismayed that it did not receive reciprocal treatment from southern parties. The NPC also resisted attempts by southern parties to field candidates in the Northern Region, and regarded southern parties' campaigning in the Northern Region as assaults on its territorial sovereignty. Southerners viewed the NPC as the party of the Hausa–Fulani ethnic group. The Western Region's dominant party was the Yoruba-led Action Group (AG) and the Eastern Region was dominated by the National Council of Nigerian Citizens (NCNC), which was controlled by the Igbos. These regional based parties assured two things: firstly that none of the parties could govern Nigeria on its own, and secondly that ethnic conflict was only a matter of time away.

---

1 Ahmadu Bello, referring to the amalgamation of southern and northern Nigeria in 1914.
2 Obafemi Awolowo, *Path to Nigerian Freedom.*

The different regions began jostling each other even before Nigeria gained independence from the UK. In 1953 the southern AG and NCNC parties tabled a motion in the federal House of Representatives calling for Nigeria's independence in 1956 (the motion was tabled by Anthony Enahoro). Northerners were apprehensive as they felt the Northern Region did not yet have an administration and educated workforce capable of operating independently of the British colonial rulers. AG and NCNC delegates walked out when the Northern majority in the House diluted the motion by removing the reference to "1956" and substituted it with a more modest goal of attaining independence when practicable. The NPC leader, the Sardauna of Sokoto, Ahmadu Bello, regarded the 1956 date as "an invitation to commit suicide." When they left the House, Northern delegates were jeered and harassed by southern mobs in Lagos for their reluctant approach to independence. This humiliation rankled long in the Northern memory.

After independence in 1960 the NPC took control of the federal government with the NCNC as the junior partner in a shaky coalition. The NPC's deputy leader, Tafawa Balewa, became the Prime Minister and the NCNC's eloquent leader Dr. Nnamdi Azikiwe took the ceremonial role of Governor-General until 1963, when the country became a republic, upon which his title was changed to "President." The AG formed the opposition with the energetic Obafemi Awolowo as Leader of the Opposition. The Yoruba were left out in the cold while the Igbo and Hausa–Fulani parties (the NCNC and NPC respectively) colluded. The constitution of the government was odd.

The NPC's immensely powerful leader, the Sardauna of Sokoto Alhaji, Sir Ahmadu Bello, could have become Prime Minister but chose to instead become Premier of the Northern Region, and handed over the Prime Minister's chair to his deputy, Tafawa Balewa. The Sardauna was only interested in matters pertaining to the south to the extent they had consequences in the Northern Region. Bello's comment that "I would rather be called Sultan of Sokoto than President of Nigeria" summed up his outlook. Bello was doubtless the most powerful politician in the country by virtue of being the leader of its biggest party in Parliament, and by being Premier of the Northern Region, and was an inspirational figure for Nigeria's Muslim population. However, while Balewa was regarded as a humble man, with integrity, he was also — rightly or wrongly — viewed by many southern politicians as Bello's puppet. Southerners resented the fact that the government was being ruled by proxy by a regional ruler and viewed Bello as the real power behind the throne. This perception was not helped when Bello referred to Balewa his "lieutenant in Lagos." This may have encouraged the southern politicians' disrespectful attitude toward Balewa and the Northern Region. The fact that many of the southern politicians, such as Azikiwe and Awolowo, were extremely erudite intellectuals, while Balewa and Sardauna did not have university degrees, made some southern politicians feel that the Northern politicians were not intellectually fit to rule the country.

Northern leaders feared that a Yoruba and Igbo alliance from the south could swamp them, threatening their way of life and their political dominance. Bello expressed these fears: "A sudden grouping of the eastern and western parties (with a few members from the north opposed to our party) might take power and endanger so endanger the north. This would, of course be utterly disastrous."[1] Bello's fear was not without justification and Northerners for their part resented the condescending

---

1 Schwartz, *Nigeria*, page 152.

attitude of southerners. Some southerners regarded Northerners as backward, un-educated and unsophisticated, and some Northerners felt southerners were no more than ill-mannered infidels.

The Northern Region had threatened to secede unless it was given half the seats in the post-independence Parliament. It was eventually given more seats in Parlia-ment than the two southern regions put together. This meant that no meaningful governmental decision affecting Nigeria could be taken without the consent of the Northern political leaders. Southern rulers belatedly began to appreciate that North-ern politicians were not as backward as they had thought and that the lopsided Parliament meant that Northern politicians would control Nigeria's politics forever. Northerners felt vulnerable due to the overwhelming educational advantage of the south. At independence, Northerners accounted for just 10% of primary school enrol-ments, and of over one thousand students at the University of Ibadan, just over fifty were Northern. Despite the fact that the Northern Region constituted two thirds of Nigeria's land mass, the number of secondary schools in the south outnumbered those in the Northern Region by a ratio of over twenty to one.

Concerned that the better educated southerners might gobble up the best jobs in the Northern Region, the Premier of the Northern Region, Sir Ahmadu Bello, em-barked upon a "northernization" program with the aim of filling job vacancies in the Northern Region with Northern candidates. Where no qualified Northern candidate was available, expatriates were hired in preference to southerners. This antagonized many southerners.

In 1963 a census revealed that the population of the south was greater than that of the Northern Region. Each region's census results determined its share of seats in the Parliament, and each region was widely assumed to have inflated its population count. The results from the south showed a preposterously high rate of population growth, unprecedented in the history of mankind. The Prime Minister ordered a veri-fication of the results, after which an additional eight million people were "found" in the Northern Region. The verification exercise showed that the Northern Region did after all have a larger population than the south. The census figures caused mutual bitterness between the Northern Region and south, with each region accusing the other of massively distorting the census figures. It also carved a huge rift in the NPC–NCNC coalition and leaders from both parties publicly traded insults. The United States noted that:

> The facts of geography and population assure that under the constitution, the federal government will continue to be dominated by the party representing the tradition-bound Moslems of the north, who are generally contemptuous of the south and unsympathetic to its problems. The southern regions, which are deeply divided along tribal, regional, and party lines, resent northern domination.[1]

The tragedy which subsequently occurred was based on mutual fear. The south feared that the Northern Region would use numerical advantage to suppress the south. The Northern Region feared that southerners would use superior academic qualifications to dominate the Northern Region.

Meanwhile the political leadership of the AG was tearing apart at the seams. Un-like the loyal and cordial relationship between the leader and deputy of the NPC, the AG's leader and deputy did not see eye to eye. The party leader, Awolowo, favored

---

1 Memorandum from Robert W. Komer of the National Security Council Staff to the President's Special Assistant for National Security Affairs, Washington, January 2, 1965.

maintaining the AG as an effective opposition and alternative to what he believed was a conservative government. However, his deputy Chief Samuel Akintola (also the Premier of the Western Region) was not impressed with the liberal socialist rhetoric of Awolowo's supporters. He advocated forging closer links with the federal government as he saw little to be gained in staying in opposition; a hostile federal government would use its power to punish the AG.

The disagreement between Awolowo and Akintola led a faction within the AG to attempt to dismiss Akintola. On May 25, 1962, the Western Region House of Assembly met to debate a motion of no confidence in Akintola. In what many believe was a pre-meditated disturbance orchestrated by Akintola supporters to prevent a discussion on the motion, Mr. E.O. Oke (member for Ogbomosho South-West) jumped up and flung a chair across the chamber. Mr. F. Ebubeduike (member for Badagry East) then seized the speaker's mace and tried to club the speaker with it. The mace was smashed on the speaker's table. Mr. S.A. Adeniya (member for Oro East) then hit Mr. K.S.Y. Momoh (Minister of Trade and Industry) over the head with a chair. A free-for-all fight erupted inside the chamber with chairs thrown and tables broken. Order was temporarily restored when baton- and tear-gas-wielding police entered. When the meeting reassembled hours later, with police inside the chamber, Akintola's supporters led by J.O. Adigun and Chief S.A. Tinubu again disrupted proceedings by smashing and throwing chairs. The speaker adjourned the meeting.

In a suspiciously prompt move the federal government imposed a state of emergency in the Western Region and appointed the Prime Minister's personal friend and physician, Dr. Moses Koyejo Majekodunmi, as the Administrator of the Western Region. Majekodunmi's aide-de-camp (ADC) was a young army officer named Murtala Muhammed.

The lopsided federal structure was a stick of dynamite waiting to be detonated. Unable to influence policy by means of the ballot box, it became apparent to southerners that the only way for them to alter the Northern Region's control of the country was via a constitutional amendment (unlikely, since politicians from the Northern Region controlled the Parliament) . . . or violence. The conviction and imprisonment of the AG leader Chief Obafemi Awolowo for treason seemed to suggest that some southerners had chosen the latter option. In a controversial trial Awolowo and several of his AG supporters were convicted of plotting to overthrow the federal government by force of arms. The convicted men included Lateef Jakande and Anthony Enahoro (who first brought the motion for Nigeria's independence). The prosecution's case was that Awolowo and his party supporters had been training fighters in Ghana and that they tried to bribe army officers to rebel against the government. Some of the evidence claimed that an attempt was made to recruit a Yoruba army officer named Samuel Ademulegun into the plot. Although Awolowo's supporters claimed that the suspects were framed and that the whole affair was a show trial aimed at eliminating the opposition, a genuine plot to overthrow the government did exist and was infiltrated by Special Branch police officers.[1] Although it was initiated by civilians, the Awolowo treason trial may be regarded as the culmination of Nigeria's first coup plot. Decades later during a workshop on Nigerian history, one of Awolowo's co-accused (who escaped from Nigeria rather than face trial), the AG General Secretary

---

1 The Special Branch of the Nigerian police was then headed by the Irishman John O'Sullivan. John Lynn (another Irish police officer) headed the investigation into the plot and was a key prosecution witness. Lynn was the head of the police's Criminal Investigation Department.

Samuel Ikoku, publicly confessed that the plot was real and that they had attempted to overthrow the federal government by extra-constitutional means:

> We were fed up with the way the Nigerian system, the Nigerian state and the Nigerian government were operating, we were deeply committed to a change of government and we saw that waiting for elections would not produce any solution to the problem. This is what we did. We started preparations for it and the preparations had gone very far and I believe we would have pulled it off. But unfortunately for us, our leader was so kind to the Nigerian police that he had a police informant among his planners and so the police knew every move we were making. And so it was easy to trip us up. Well, after the act, people have been saying, there was no coup because we went to court, there was no plan to overthrow the government. Naturally, if you catch me over a coup plot and take me to court, I have to enter a plea of not guilty, I did not do it. This is normal. ... Our leader even became the number two citizen in the country. I felt it was time to tell the country the truth, so that our history would be correct. So, all I am saying is that, yes, there was an attempt to overthrow the govern-ment. Yes, I took part in the attempt. Yes, it failed, thanks to people like M.D. Yusuf and Co.[1]

Awolowo's incarceration was followed by the perpetuation in the Western Region of an unpopular government led by Chief Samuel Akintola of the NNDP. The Western Region proved to be the battleground for political fighting at the federal level and in an attempt to further weaken the opposition a new Mid-Western Region was carved out of the Western Region in 1963. An Igbo Mid-Westerner Dr. Dennis Osedebay became the Premier of the new region. Till today it is still the only demo-cratically created region or state in Nigeria's history. All of the 36 Nigerian states which exist today were created by the military.

IGBOS

Out of Nigeria's ethnic matrix, Igbos distinguished themselves by becoming the most prominent and commercially successful. They were educated, adventurous and hard working. When the expatriate British workers departed, Igbos moved quickly to fill their clerical, administrative and technical jobs. In the impoverished Northern Region, the Igbos' commercial success, Christianity, and Westernized manner did not endear them to some of their Northern neighbors. Northerners grumbled about, and bitterly resented, the presence of huge numbers of Igbo migrants who in their view were taking all the best jobs. The Sardauna's policies were belatedly creating a Northern educated class. However, when young Northerners completed school they would find the best jobs already occupied by Igbos, who were generally far better educated (little attention was paid to the fact that the Northern Region did not have enough skilled or educated workers to fill all these posts). As a successful economic migrant population, like other economically successful migrant ethnicities in other countries, they were resented and cast in the role of scapegoats. They were even re-ferred to as "the Jews of Africa." The title was not fanciful, as many Igbos did regard themselves as a special or "chosen" race and valued personal achievement highly. Igbos were exceptionally intelligent, innovative and resourceful, and they knew it. However, their confidence in their abilities sometimes crossed over into outbursts

---

1 National Workshop on the Events, Issues and Sources of Nigerian History, 1960–1970, held at State House, Kawo, Kaduna, 7–9 June 1993, and reproduced in Bala Usman, *Inside Nigerian History* pages 43–44.

of chest-thumping pride that antagonized other ethnic groups. Addressing the Igbo State Union in 1949, Dr. Nnamdi Azikiwe declared that "The God of Africa has specially created the Igbo nation to lead the children of Africa from the bondage of the ages." Such statements fuelled fears in other regions that Igbo leaders wanted "to build up the Igbo as a master race."[1] Some stereotyped and caricatured Igbo characteristics doubtless played a part in increasing the animosity towards them. They were satirized as arrogant, clannish and money grabbing. Some Northerners used a pejorative term ("Nyamiri") to refer to Igbos.

The events of January 15, 1966 gave Northerners an opportunity to vent their frustrations. A bloody past event should have served as a warning of the dangers in the increasing anti-Igbo sentiment. In May 1953 a delegation from the AG, the leading Yoruba party, had scheduled a visit to the northern city of Kano. NPC leaders bitterly opposed the visit and regarded it as a territorial violation. The NPC's Mallam Inuwa Wada raised the stakes by uncompromisingly declaring that "Having abused us in the south, these very southerners have decided to come over to the north to abuse us. . . . We have therefore organized about a thousand men ready in the city to meet force with force." Inevitably, violence ensued — but not between Yorubas and Hausa–Fulanis, as might have been expected. Northern mobs instead attacked and murdered scores of the most visible and vulnerable southerners in the Northern Region: Igbos. The transferred malice that led to this pogrom was a small taste of what lay ahead for Igbos.

Corruption

Corruption among government ministers was also rife. The ostentatious lifestyle of prominent ministers such as Chief Festus Okotie-Eboh raised eyebrows, to say the least. Okotie-Eboh's original surname was "Edah" but he altered it to that of a more powerful family. Ministers were accused of taking "kickbacks" for large government contracts. As many civil servants lacked experience and training in governmental, constitutional and parliamentary practice and affairs, they could easily be manipulated (wittingly or unwittingly) as pawns in ministers' corrupt practices.

The name of the Finance Minister Chief Festus Samuel Okotie-Eboh was frequently mentioned in the corruption allegations. A former colonial officer said that Okotie-Eboh was:

> a fat, jovial character. . . . Those who disliked the Minister referred to him as "festering Sam." . . . Okotie-Eboh's name had become synonymous with corruption in Lagos. . . . Okotie-Eboh was a gross squalid crook who dragged Nigeria down to his own level. . . . He had dragged Nigeria into the sewer, but because of his corruption Nigeria has no sewers. The money to pay for them is still in Swiss banks.[2]

1964 Federal Elections

At federal level, the fragile coalition between the NPC and the NCNC was breaking down and the NCNC instead allied itself with the opposition AG to form the United Progressive Grand Alliance (UPGA). The NNDP retained its close links with the NPC, and the two parties formed the Nigerian National Alliance (NNA). As the

---

1 Awolowo, *Awo.*
2 Harold Smith, *A Squalid End to Empire: British Retreat from Africa.*

NNA and UPGA prepared for a mammoth federal election showdown in 1964, there were rumblings of a possible military coup. The treatment of Awolowo demonstrated that no party could afford to be in opposition for long, and the supremacy that could be enjoyed by a victorious party in government. Thus political parties regarded elections as a do or die affair. Tension reached unprecedented levels during the heated federal election campaign. Many of the politicians were little more than ethnic champions uninterested in a national outlook. The campaign was conducted not on platforms of policy or ideology, but on the basis of personal abuse and vitriolic ethnic chauvinism. A declassified diplomatic wire from the US State Department archives accurately described the position:

> ... [v]ery complicated African politics, in which tribes, religions and economics all play a part, are involved in the situation. The Northern Premier is at odds with the Eastern Premier in whose region large oil deposits have been discovered. In the heat of the election campaign, there have been threats of secession by the east; threats of violence "that would make Congo look like child's play" from the north.[1]

The scandalous corruption, malpractices and wild speeches by politicians on both sides which marred the election campaign led the President, Dr. Azikiwe to make a dramatic appeal to the parties, stating that:

> If they have decided to destroy our national unity ... it is better for us and for our many admirers abroad that we should disintegrate in peace and not in pieces. Should the politicians fail to heed this warning, then I will venture the prediction that the experience of the Democratic Republic of Congo will be child's play if it ever comes to our turn to play such a tragic role. ... From the blind passion of those who worship power, may Allah save our republic.

Underestimating the win-at-all-costs mentality of the NNA, the UPGA unwisely decided to boycott the election on the ground that the NNA was planning to rig it. The NNA went ahead with the election regardless and increased its parliamentary majority by winning unopposed in many districts. The boycott was successful only in the Eastern Region. Due to the widespread electoral malpractices, President Azikiwe refused to call Balewa to form a new government following the elections. For several days, Nigeria teetered on the edge of an abyss as the President and Prime Minister tried to scheme each other out of power. President Azikiwe summoned the heads of the army (Major-General Welby-Everard), navy (Commodore Joseph Wey) and police (Louis Edet) to remind them of their oath of loyalty to him in his position as commander-in-chief of the country's armed forces. The President and Prime Minister jockeyed for control and loyalty of the army, as many thought that Azikiwe might use the army to intervene to break the political deadlock.

In a move that was either an attempt to give a semblance of order, or at intimidation, Balewa announced that the army would make a country-wide tour to "give the people an opportunity to see their army." In Lagos, troops paraded in battle order. The General Officer Commanding (GOC) the army Major-General Welby-Everard announced that this was in order "to show the people of Lagos that the army is ready in case of trouble."[2] Welby-Everard obtained legal advice from Professor Gower (Dean of Law, University of Lagos), who advised him that in the event of conflicting

---

1 Memorandum from Samuel E Belk of National Security Council Staff to the President's Special Assistant for National Security Affairs, Washington, December 30, 1964.

2 Ojiako, *Nigeria Yesterday, Today and ?*, page 204.

orders from the President and the Prime Minister, the Prime Minister's orders were to be obeyed. The British Cypriot judge of the Nigerian Supreme Court, Sir Vahe Bairamian, also approached Welby-Everard and urged him to keep the army out of the crisis. After meeting with both Azikiwe and Balewa, the armed forces service chiefs advised Azikiwe that in the event of conflicting orders from the President and Prime Minister, they would obey the Prime Minister's orders.

Welby-Everard circulated a memorandum to his senior officers confirming this stance. Azikiwe also obtained legal advice which indicated that the service chiefs were right to declare their willingness to take orders from the Prime Minister only. This, allied to the fact that the NPC were planning to depose Azikiwe as President by having him declared medically incapacitated, convinced Azikiwe to call on Balewa to form a new government after several days of perilous uncertainty. The new government was a coalition featuring ministers from the NPC, NCNC and NNDP.

The Wild West

The Western Region elections of 1965 were marred by even more spectacular rigging, voter and candidate intimidation, arson, murder and thuggery. Although it is likely that all parties were engaged in some form of electoral malpractice, the NNDP seemed to be the grand masters of voting irregularities. Akintola was described as the "high priest of election rigging."[1] The stigma of vote rigging that followed the NNDP was not alleviated when some NNDP officials barely bothered to conceal their intentions, declaring in advance that they would "win" the election even if people did not vote for them.

The plan to foreclose any chance of an electoral victory for the NNDP's opponents was multi-faceted. Opposition candidates and voters were often intimidated or prevented from filing nomination papers or voting. Even where opposition candidates managed to stand for election and win in results declared at polling stations, radio announcements would announce a different set of results with NNDP candidates being declared "unopposed" winners. The NNDP was shockingly declared the winner of the election against all expectations. Many westerners could not understand how a party they loathed and voted against could have possibly gained a legitimate victory. Akintola's retention of power led to even greater violence in the Western Region. Protests, arson and murders placed many parts of the Western Region into a state of near anarchy, which earned the region the nickname of the "wild west." There was great consternation that the federal government (which in 1962 had declared a state of emergency due to a fight in the regional legislature) refused to declare another state of emergency now that murder and violence of infinitely greater intensity were the order of the day. Cynics pointed out that the federal government declined to declare a state of emergency as it did not want to threaten the rule of its ally Chief Akintola. Akintola was ruling over a population that was largely in revolt against him and many parts of which felt that he had been imposed on them irrespective of their vote for a different party. It seemed as if the people of the Western Region would never be able to remove Akintola from power via the ballot box. The country now had two governments that were the product of illegitimate elections. The federal government was in power despite a partially boycotted and flawed election in 1964, and now the Western Region's government under Akintola was in power after

---

1 Schwartz, *Nigeria*, page 199.

a spectacularly rigged election. The entire political system was corrupted from the federal to the regional level.

Chapter 2. The Nigerian Army: The Way Things Were

The Nigerian army of the mid 1960s was a small, light, colonial army numbering no more than 10,000, which, it was presumed, would be engaged primarily in internal security and peacekeeping operations as opposed to involvement in sustained warfare or political matters.

Nigerianization

In the lead up to, and the years following Nigerian independence, the government embarked upon a "Nigerianization" exercise to transfer command of the army from British to Nigerian soldiers. The British instructors and senior officers were concerned that the Nigerianization program was proceeding too quickly and feared that Nigerian soldiers were not yet ready to independently command the army. However, the federal government brushed aside their concerns and proceeded with the program, leading to accelerated promotions in the army.

To rapidly create a Nigerian officer corps, well-educated senior Nigerian NCOs already serving under British officers in the army were sent for six-month courses at the Officer Cadet Schools at either Eaton Hall, in Chester, or Mons at Aldershot, both in the United Kingdom. Mons trained armored corps and artillery cadets, while cadets in other army services attended Eaton Hall. After attending such courses, Nigerian NCOs were given short service commissions as officers of the army.

The first Nigerian to be so commissioned was Louis Victor Ugboma, in 1948. "Duke" Bassey, Sey (originally from Ghana), Johnson Aguiyi-Ironsi and Samuel Ademulegun followed soon thereafter, in 1949. Ralph Shodeinde was commissioned in 1950 and Wellington in 1952. To further enable indigenous officer proliferation, slots were also reserved for Nigerians at the elite Royal Military Academy at Sandhurst in the UK. Prior to attending Sandhurst, Nigerian cadets would be sent on a preparatory course at the Regular Officers Special Training School (ROSTS) in Teshie, Accra, Ghana. In 1953 the first Nigerian Sandhurst-trained officers were commissioned: Zakariya Maimalari and Umar Lawan. Later that year, two NCOs Babafemi Ogundipe and Robert Adebayo also underwent short service commission officer training and became officers. Sey resigned in 1952, Wellington and Ugboma left in 1953 and Umar Lawan was discharged, leaving Bassey as the most senior Nigerian officer remaining. This led to Bassey being given the army number N/1 and created a myth that ran for decades holding that he was the first Nigerian officer to be commissioned into the army.[1]

The Nigerian Defense Academy (under the command of the Indian Brigadier M.R. Varma) was opened in 1964 to train officer cadets and it produced its first officers in 1967. The officers from this first intake who later rose to prominence include Donaldson Oladipo Diya, Joshua Dogonyaro, Aliyu Mohammed Gusau, Salihu Ibrahim, Allison Madueke, Ishola Williams, Bello Kaliel, and Mamman Kontagora.[2]

The Nigerianization program unwittingly stratified the army on ethnic lines. By the mid 1960s the army's most senior officers were career soldiers who had originally enlisted as NCOs and then risen through the ranks. Most of these were Yoruba (Samuel Ademulegun, Babafemi Ogundipe, Ralph Shodeinde, Robert Adebayo). Immediately behind them in seniority were the first Sandhurst-trained generation of Nigerian officers. These men were largely Kanuri Muslims from the north (Zakariya Maimalari, Umar Lawan, Kur Mohammed). Johnson Aguiyi-Ironsi was the only member of the army's top stratum that was not Yoruba or Kanuri. The lt-colonels were ethnically diverse (e.g., Ejoor, Ojukwu, Kurubo), but many of the majors were Sandhurst-trained Igbos and most junior officers like lieutenants and NCOs were Northerners who had been encouraged to join the army's infantry by an army recruitment campaign by Northern politicians. This meant that when the senior strata of the army officer hierarchy ended their careers, their successor commanders would inevitably emerge from the middle-grade officer ranks dominated by the Igbos. These Igbos would be directly commanding mostly Northern subordinates. The psychology of this relationship was later to prove fatal.

THE FIRST GOC

Before indigenous soldiers took control of Nigeria's army, the four most senior officers of Nigerian origin were Brigadiers Johnson Aguiyi-Ironsi, Samuel Ademulegun, Babafemi Ogundipe, and Zakariya Maimalari. Each man was markedly different in temperament. Aguiyi-Ironsi was the most senior and genial but not universally respected, Ademulegun was the most capable but also the most unpopular, Ogundipe the most apolitical but also the least conspicuous, and Maimalari was the best trained but also the least experienced.

The contract of the army's British expatriate General Officer Commanding (GOC), Major-General Christopher Earle Welby-Everard, was to expire in 1965. Major-General Robert Exham, appointed in 1956, had been the first GOC of the Nigerian army; he was succeeded by Major-General Norman Forster in 1960. Forster handed over to Welby-Everard in 1962. Another British officer, Brigadier Frank Goulson, filled in on an interim basis during the handover from Forster to Welby-Everard. Goulson was

---

1 Bassey was later superseded in seniority by other officers, but he became the first commander of the Federal Guards in 1962.
2 Diya later became the Chief of General Staff and narrowly missed being executed after being sentenced to death for his role in a military coup in 1997. Aliyu Mohammed became Chief of Army Staff, National Security Adviser and head of military intelligence. Dogonyaro became commander of the west African ECOMOG peacekeeping operation in Liberia. Ibrahim became Chief of Army Staff and Kontagora later became Minister of the Federal Capital Territory.

later killed in a car crash while traveling from Enugu to Lagos. Welby-Everard was an Oxford University graduate (Corpus Christi College) and had been injured during the Second World War. Prior to his posting as Nigeria's GOC, he held a prestigious position at NATO, based in Norway as the Chief of Staff to the Commander-in-Chief, Allied Forces, Northern Europe. He was from an aristocratic family with a fine military tradition.[1] During his tenure Welby-Everard appointed the first indigenous Nigerian army Quartermaster-General and Adjutant-General. These were Lt-Colonels Ojukwu and Gowon respectively.

Welby-Everard was due to leave Nigeria in February 1965 to mark the completion of the army's "Nigerianization." The trio of Aguiyi-Ironsi, Ademulegun, and Maimalari were perceived as favorites to succeed him. The issue of choosing the first indigenous GOC became an unofficial political campaign among the officer corps and generated much debate and gossip in the officers' mess. The issue was not defused by the fact that Aguiyi-Ironsi, Ademulegun and Maimalari did not see eye to eye with each other. Most officers presumed that Aguiyi-Ironsi and Ademulegun were favorites due to their seniority in age and experience. Both were former NCOs who rose up through the ranks. Opposing camps developed within the officer corps. Officers who were close to politicians went so far as to give their recommendations to their political contacts. Both camps were unaware that they were backing the wrong horse. While Ademulegun hoped that his political contacts would get him the job, Aguiyi-Ironsi showed little interest in the "campaign."

Maimalari

Brigadier Maimalari was a notoriously ferocious disciplinarian and intimidating character who would not tolerate any disobedience. He "feared nobody," "exacted unqualified discipline from all his subordinates and would brook no insubordination."[2] Like his military colleagues from the north, Colonel Kur Mohammed and Lt-Colonels Pam and Largema, he was an alumnus of the famous Government College (now Barewa College) in Zaria. He and Umar Lawan were the first officers in the history of the Nigerian army to graduate from the world famous Sandhurst Royal Military Academy in the United Kingdom. Maimalari was widely respected within the army (especially among Northern soldiers, who viewed him as a role model) and was tipped to become a future GOC. After being commissioned into the army in 1953, he had an extraordinarily rapid rise through the ranks. It took him eight years to become a major, but after that took only two further years to reach the rank of brigadier (a promotion of three ranks) and found himself commanding an entire brigade, and in the same rank as, or outranking, men who had entered the army a decade before him. The only officers of equal rank to him were Aguiyi-Ironsi, Ogundipe and Ademulegun.

Ademulegun

Brigadier Ademulegun was another stickler for discipline and was the most controversial of the brigadiers. The son of a tailor and farmer, he was also a keen horse rider and had worked as a teacher prior to joining the army. Although a Christian, his wife Latifat was a Muslim. For most of his career he held equal seniority with

---

1 His brother Phillip and nephew Roger were both officers in the Royal Navy, and his son Hugh became a colonel in the British army and is the Adjutant-General of the British army's principal personnel office.

2 Gbulie, *Nigeria's Five Majors*, page 54.

Aguiyi-Ironsi and the pair were promoted to brigadier simultaneously. He also served in the Congo as part of the United Nations (UN) peacekeeping force and met future Congo head of state Joseph Mobutu. While acknowledged as "a first class soldier"[1] who could walk the walk and talk the talk, he was personally unpopular in the army, especially among junior officers. Some accused him of being "pro Akintola." His open friendship with the Sardauna of Sokoto, Premier of the Northern Region, won him few friends in the army and accepting a gift from the Sardauna (a horse) irritated many junior officers (who ignored the fact that Ademulegun was not really in a position to refuse gifts from the most powerful politician in the land). Ironically, Ademulegun felt that his political links would land him the job of GOC. He may have been a little overconfident about his chances of securing the job. Some literature has claimed that he was the most politicized of the senior officers and identified with NNA politicians. However, he was not one-dimensionally an NNA man in his political associations, as he was friendly with the head of the Ibadan grammar school who was also the AG's chaplain.

AGUIYI-IRONSI

Brigadier Johnson Aguiyi-Ironsi was the most decorated of the three. Nicknamed "Johnny Ironside," he had attended school in Calabar and Kano and could speak all four of Nigeria's main languages (English, Igbo, Hausa and Yoruba). Although a tall, broad, and physically imposing man who looked every inch a soldier, he was easy going and spoke in a slow, measured tone. He had been the premier soldier of his generation and was considered good enough to command a UN peacekeeping force in the Congo. During his first stint in the Congo in 1960, he was commander of the Nigerian contingent of the UN peacekeeping force there. He returned to Congo in 1964 as the commander of the entire UN peacekeeping force (the first African to command a UN peacekeeping force). While Aguiyi-Ironsi was in the Congo, he took on the rank of major-general (thus becoming the first African to attain that rank), but reverted to brigadier when he returned to Nigeria. He was also awarded a medal for gallantry by the Austrian government for the role he played in rescuing Austrian hostages during the Congo peacekeeping mission. During the same mission Aguiyi-Ironsi sent Maimalari (who was then two ranks below him) home to Nigeria after a disagreement over the circumstances in which Nigerian troops should be permitted to open fire.

OGUNDIPE

Brigadier Ogundipe was a veteran who had served in Burma and India during the Second World War. His personality was easier going than those of Brigadiers Ademulegun and Maimalari. He fought in India and Burma as a member of the British army and re-enlisted (this time into the RWAFF) after the Second World War. He also served as Chief of Staff during the Congo UN peacekeeping operation.

The author has obtained a copy of a top secret memorandum written by the outgoing British GOC Major-General Welby-Everard to the Ministry of Defense permanent secretary in September 1964 outlining his recommendations for his successor.[2] In this memorandum, Welby-Everard noted that of the army's four Brigadiers, the

---

1 Ibid., page 53.
2 Top secret memorandum from Major-General Welby-Everard to Permanent Secretary dated 14 September 1964.

contenders to replace him were Brigadiers Aguiyi-Ironsi, Ademulegun and Ogundipe. Welby-Everard noted, "I consider [Brigadier Maimalari] to be too young at present and not sufficiently mature." It would take several years for Maimalari to be ready, and thus the older brigadiers had to keep the seat warm for him.

Considering each of the three other brigadiers in turn, Everard noted the following:

Brigadier Aguiyi-Ironsi: "Ironsi has been away from Nigeria and consequently out of direct contact with the army for the past 3 years, first as military adviser in London, then as a student at the Imperial Defense College and finally for the first 6 months of this year as commander of the United Nations force in the Congo. He has never commanded a brigade in Nigeria and has only been a battalion commander for about 6 months in 1960/61. He has therefore been out of direct touch with recent developments and is not as familiar with the careers of officers in the army as are other senior officers. As he has never served under my command it is difficult for me to assess accurately his professional ability." Welby-Everard doubted whether Aguiyi-Ironsi would make a good GOC.

Brigadier Ademulegun was said to have "a wide and up to date knowledge of the army and its current problems and his professional military knowledge is good. He is a forceful leader but somewhat intolerant in his opinions and hasty in his judgment. For this reason he has a good many critics, not to say enemies, in the army. There is no doubt in my opinion that he has the professional ability to make a good GOC and also has the necessary leadership qualities, but I fear that he might not command the unswerving loyalty of all the officers. This would not apply to the same extent if Ironsi was Chief of Defense Staff."

Brigadier Ogundipe. Everard noted that Ogundipe "commanded the Nigerian brigade in the Congo as well as currently commanding 2 brigade in Lagos. Whilst Chief of Staff in the Congo he earned high praise for his military ability, fine character and powers of organization. His professional knowledge is good and he possesses a sound and well balanced judgment. He has an equitable temperament and is universally respected by all ranks in the army." Contrary to popular perception (which believes that Welby-Everard recommended Ademulegun or Maimalari), Everard went on to recommend Brigadier Ogundipe as his successor, as in his opinion Ogundipe had "the military ability, leadership qualities and the personal characteristics to make a good GOC. . . . My opinion is that Ogundipe would make the best GOC, because I consider that he would be more likely to command the loyalty of the whole army than either of the other two, and there would be less likelihood of opposing factions springing up within the officer corps."

Welby-Everard also considered appointing a Chief of Defense Staff above the GOC. If his recommendation of Ogundipe was accepted, he suggested that Aguiyi-Ironsi could be appointed the Chief of Defense Staff, otherwise he "would have to leave the army and be found other employment." A job for Ademulegun could be found outside Nigeria, such as the post of Nigeria's military adviser in London or Washington, or possibly a role with the Organization of African Unity (OAU). In the scenario of Ogundipe as GOC, Everard recommended appointing Maimalari and Colonel Adebayo as the brigade commanders in Kaduna and Lagos respectively. Colonel Kur Mohammed would be sent to attend a course at the Imperial Defense College with Lt-Colonel Njoku taking his place as deputy commandant of the Nigerian Defense Academy. In that scenario Everard felt that Lt-Colonel Pam "would be very suitable" as Chief of Staff at army headquarters. The Chief of Staff post was created by Welby-Everard to offload some of his administrative burden during his tenure as GOC.

Everard acknowledged that his recommendation might not be accepted and suggested the following alternative postings if Aguiyi-Ironsi or Ademulegun were instead appointed GOC:

Scenario 2 — Ademulegun as GOC:
Aguiyi-Ironsi would either be appointed Chief of Defense Staff, or would have to leave the army and be found other employment.
1 brigade Kaduna, Maimalari
2 brigade Lagos, Adebayo
Chief of Staff (Army), Lt-Colonel Njoku or Pam

Scenario 3 — Aguiyi-Ironsi as GOC:
Ogundipe would attend the Imperial Defense College, and there would be no Chief of Defense Staff.
1 brigade Kaduna, Maimalari
2 brigade Lagos, Ademulegun
Chief of Staff (Army), Colonel Adebayo

The federal government did not accept Welby-Everard's recommendation. Despite being the outgoing GOC's choice, Ogundipe was not well known in official circles. Ademulegun and Aguiyi-Ironsi were more prominent personalities. Ademulegun's friendship with the Sardauna meant he was well known in Kaduna political circles, and Aguiyi-Ironsi's high-profile appointments to the UN and the UK made him conspicuous to high ranking officials. NCNC politicians canvassed Aguiyi-Ironsi's case. The Prime Minister was anxious not to upset his Igbo coalition partners in the NCNC by bypassing Aguiyi-Ironsi, the most senior brigadier.

However, the Sardauna bitterly opposed Aguiyi-Ironsi's candidacy. The Sardauna and most NPC ministers favored Ademulegun, whom they knew. The Prime Minister sent Maitama Sule to convince the Sardauna to agree to Aguiyi-Ironsi's appointment as GOC. After several hours of persuasion, the Sardauna acquiesced with reluctance.[1] The federal government ignored the advice of its GOC, went with Scenario 3 and gave the top job to Aguiyi-Ironsi when Welby-Everard's contract expired on 11 February 1965. Welby-Everard returned to the UK and entered the private sector, working for the security firm Securicor and holding a number of other charitable and local positions.

THE ARMY UNDER AGUIYI-IRONSI

In January 1966 the army had only two brigades and five battalions. The battalions in the south (first, second and fourth) were under the operational command of Brigadier Maimalari's 2 brigade in Lagos, while the third and fifth battalions were under the operational command of the 1 brigade, which was headquartered in Kaduna and commanded by Brigadier Ademulegun. After losing out in the race to be the first GOC, Ogundipe was one brigadier too many and had to be kept busy. He was therefore posted to the UK as Nigeria's military attaché. Table 1 of Appendix 1 shows the rank and background of the Nigerian military's high command as at January 14, 1966.

---

1 Clark, *A Right Honorable Gentleman*, page 714.

CHAPTER 3. SOLDIERS AND POLITICS

The pertinent question is how an apolitical professional army with less than fifty indigenous officers at independence in 1960 became politicized and overthrew its country's government less than six years later. The officer corps became politicized due to a number of factors including the introduction into the army of university graduates, the politicians' unwise meddling in army affairs, and the government's use of the army to solve political crises created by it. Although the federal government's use of the army to suppress civil disturbances (which required political solutions rather than an iron fist) was partially successful, it also radicalized some of the officers that took part in those operations.

Although ostensibly multi-ethnic and meritocratic, the method of recruitment into the army had created an ethnic stratification time bomb, and made intra-military conflict inevitable. Most of the officers were southern and their subalterns and NCOs were mostly Northern. Northerners typically enlisted in combat units while southerners tended to enter technical units. This created a regional dichotomy with well-educated southern officers dominating the officer corps and technical units, although they were not always the best infantry soldiers. In contrast Northern soldiers were by temperament comfortable in infantry units, although they were not as educated as southern officers. All this also fit effortlessly with Northern and southern stereotypes, Northerners seeing themselves as tough warriors and southerners seeing themselves as erudite and sophisticated.

Igbo soldiers tended to score very highly in the entrance exam for the army, and left unchecked could have used their superior education to totally dominate the officer corps. At independence Igbos constituted over 60% of the army's officer corps. With a civilian government dominated by Northerners, and the army's officer corps dominated by Igbos, there was an ever present risk of future conflict if one day the interests of the government and army diverged. Northern ministers were sufficiently concerned about Igbo predominance in the officer corps that they tried to block Igbo soldiers from filling army posts vacated by departing British officers. The Northern Region's Governor Sir Kashim Ibrahim claimed that the Prime Minister had remarked to his colleagues, "Well, we are all surrounded by Igbo officers; if anything happens they are going to kill us."[1]

The former colonel commandant of the Royal West African Frontier Force (RWAFF) and an honorary colonel of the army, General Sir Lashmer Whistler, was unsympathetic to Northern complaints about Igbo domination of the officer corps. "Bolo" Whistler considered Northern leaders to be architects of the problem, having resisted all attempts by British authorities to achieve greater penetration of Western education in the Northern Region, and for not putting educated Northern candidates forward for officer admission.[2] "Bolo" Whistler was acquainted with other British officers that served in Nigeria such as Major-Generals Exham and Welby-Everard. Major-General Exham was Bolo Whistler's Chief of Staff in the Western Command and the former Nigerian Governor-General Sir James Robertson was Bolo's friend.

Rather than wait for large numbers of suitably qualified Northern officers to emerge, the Defense Minister (a Northerner) shifted the goalposts, and lowered the educational bar for officer admission. Northern concern over Igbo presence in the officer corps led to the introduction of a regional quota system into the army recruitment process. This quota system allocated a percentage of army recruitments to each region, with the Northern Region being guaranteed 50% of officer admissions, and the Eastern Region and Western Region each having 25%. The educational requirements for officer admission were also reduced, thus making it easier for less educated Northerners to enlist. This raised a debate between Northerners and southerners as to which of mental or physical dexterity should be the primary determinant in army admission. Northern political interference in the military process was possible because the four most senior posts in the Ministry of Defense were occupied by Northerners. The Defense Minister, Minister of State for the Army, Ministry of Defense permanent secretary and deputy permanent secretary were all Northern (Inuwa Wada, Ibrahim Tako Galadima, Sule Kolo and Ahmadu Kurfi respectively). Northern politicians seized on the quota system as a way of guaranteeing a sizeable Northern representation in the army and made great efforts to encourage young Northern students to enlist in the army. This act of great political foresight by the Northern leaders bore fruit for decades to come. The students they encouraged to enlist were to play decisive roles in Nigeria's political destiny.

Ibrahim Babangida, Abdulsalam Abubakar, Mamman Vatsa, Garba Duba, Gado Nasko, Sani Bello, Mohammed Magoro[3] and Sani Sami[4] were students at the Government College in Bida in the early 1960s when army recruiters showed up. The recruiters were accompanied by the federal government's Minister of State (Army) Ibrahim Tako Galadima and paraded a smartly-uniformed young Northern army officer before Babangida, Abubakar and their classmates. The students were told that if they worked hard, one day they could be army officers too. The young officer presented to them was called "Jack" Gowon.[5] Elsewhere in the Northern Region, at Barewa College, a similar scenario was played out when Zak Maimalari came to the college to deliver a talk on the benefits of an army career. One of the students at Barewa College at the time was named Murtala Muhammed.

---

1 Akinjide Osuntokun, *Power Broker: A Biography of Sir Kashim Ibrahim*, page 101.
2 Smyth, Sir John, *Bobo Whistler. The Life of General Sir Lashmer Whistler*, page 230.
3 Later became Minister of Internal Affairs.
4 Currently the Emir of Zuru.
5 Maier, *This House Has Fallen*, page 50.

Although the quota system increased Northern recruitment into the officer corps, some established officers feared that it would lead to a degradation in service standards. The lowering in educational entrance standards particularly antagonized some southern officers who feared that the Northern-led government was trying to expand its political dominance of the country to the army and was sacrificing merit for the sake of increasing Northern numerical representation in the officer corps.

Among the officers who enlisted after the introduction of the quota and lowering of educational entrance standards were B. S. Dimka and S. Abacha. The quota system continued to cause disaffection among certain southern officers for years and was a grievance held by some of the officers that executed Nigeria's first military coup. There are several accounts that Northern ministers on occasion intervened directly to waive minimum academic requirements for Northern cadets, or overruled cadet instructors by ordering the recruitment of academically unqualified Northerners. Such accusations were made regarding future Northern officers (and future coup plotters) Nuhu Nathan, Isa Bukar and Pam Mwadkon.[1]

Additionally an unofficial "caste" system was developing between the officers with regular combatant commissions from Sandhurst and the former NCOs who became officers after short service officer training. The officers with regular combatant commissions were regarded as the elite of the officer corps and some of them did not respect the professional competence of their senior officers, most of whom had risen up through the ranks without training at elite military academies. Some of the better educated Sandhurst officers and graduate officers felt that the older senior officers were pro-establishment, unimaginative and not fit to command the army.

The 1964 election crisis during which Azikiwe and Balewa courted senior military figures sensitized some officers to the potentially pivotal political role that the army could play. The above factors, combined with inter-officer tensions regarding recruitment and promotion, created fertile ground for increasing officer politicization. Tensions existed between Sandhurst alumni and the non-Sandhurst soldiers, senior officers and middle grade officers, and the accelerated promotions of the Nigerianization program created unrealistic career expectations among some junior officers who were impatient for promotions and seemingly wanted to become generals overnight. There was also residual bad blood from the rivalry to be the first GOC. Brigadiers Ademulegun and Maimalari did not fully cooperate with Aguiyi-Ironsi. Ademulegun believed he would have been a better GOC and was not shy about pointing out the inadequacies of the man picked in preference to him. Both he and Maimalari were skeptical of Aguiyi-Ironsi's ability. There was an unusual concentration of southern officers in the Northern Region, and Northern officers in the south, which gave a precarious military balance. Brigadier Maimalari (a Northerner) headed the brigade based in the south, and the 4th battalion in Ibadan, army headquarters Chief of Staff and Adjutant-General in the south were also Northerners. Meanwhile the northern brigade was commanded by Brigadier Ademulegun (a southerner), and the two northern battalions in Kaduna and Kano and the Nigerian Military Training College (NMTC) in the Northern Region were also commanded by southerners.

---

1 All three were former students at the Nigerian Military School in Zaria. Nathan and Mwadkon were classmates, as was Tunde Idiagbon, and they were two years ahead of Bukar.

THESE BOOKISH PEOPLE

The ideological circle of Nigeria's first coup seems to have consisted primarily of officers who embarked upon military careers after completing university degrees. Hassan Katsina once commented on the presence of some "bookish people" who had joined the army for rather different reasons from the normal military crowd. Katsina was probably referring to the graduates that had begun to enlist in the army. These graduates may have been exposed to the left-wing political doctrine which was sweeping across much of Africa, Asia, and South America at the time. Some of them, such as Lt-Colonel Banjo and Majors Ademoyega and Ifeajuna, also had links with radical left-wing intellectuals in Lagos and at the University of Ibadan who were largely pro-UPGA. These acquaintances included Wole Soyinka, Christopher Okigbo and J.P. Clark. The University of Ibadan was generally regarded as a hotbed of radical student activism. Lt-Colonel Banjo and Major Ifeajuna were old acquaintances from their student days there.

Chukwuemeka Ojukwu was the first university graduate to obtain a combatant commission in the Nigerian army. Olufemi Olutoye was the second. By January 1966, the Nigerian army had seven graduates with combatant commissions: Lt-Colonels "Emeka" Ojukwu and Victor Banjo, and Majors Olufemi Olutoye, Adewale Ademoyega, Emmanuel Ifeajuna, Emmanuel Udeaja and Oluwole Rotimi.[1] All seven were southerners and either Igbo (Ojukwu, Ifeajuna, Udeaja) or Yoruba (Banjo, Olutoye, Ademoyega, Rotimi). Three or four of these graduates were involved conceptually, or physically, in Nigeria's first military coup. Banjo and Ifeajuna were students together at the University of Ibadan. Banjo and Udeaja had degrees in Mechanical Engineering from the Royal Military College of Science, Shrivenham, UK. Ojukwu had a degree in History from Lincoln College, Oxford University.

The GOC Major-General Aguiyi-Ironsi noticed the increasing political sophistication of his men and moaned, "I asked for soldiers and am being given politicians dressed in uniform."[2] Some of the graduates displayed a great deal of intellectual arrogance towards their superiors and colleagues. Northern politicians were suspicious of the entrance of southern graduates in the army and the Sardauna ordered Defense Minister Inuwa Wada to stop recruiting them.[3]

Southern officers were more likely to be politicized than their Northern counterparts. This is not to say that Northern officers were immune to political influence. However, they were less inclined to resort to a violent outlet for their political ideals since the politicians in power were their fellow Northerners. Northern officers tended to identify with and be supportive of the Northern politicians whose relaxation of army recruitment policies and direct encouragement and intervention had allowed many of them to find careers in the army. There was also a kinship and synergy amongst Northern officers on one hand, and between Northern officers and Northern politicians on the other. Northerners could readily form such social support groupings due to the small number of academic institutions in the Northern Region. Thus Northern politicians and soldiers were more likely than their southern counterparts to have graduated from the same institutions. The presence of Sandhurst-trained Northern officers in the army was a source of pride for Northern politicians and a vindication of their policies. They tracked and encouraged the career progression of Northern officers. For example the Northern Region's Governor Sir Kashim Ibrahim

---

1 The army also had graduates in non-combat units such as Colonel Austen-Peters and Henry Adefope of the medical corps, and Charles Ndiomu of the education corps.

2 Muffett, *Let Truth Be Told*, page 173.

3 Akinjide Osuntokun, *Power Broker: A Biography of Sir Kashim Ibrahim*, page 101.

(a Kanuri) was a former schoolteacher of Brigadier Maimalari. He was also in contact with other officers from the Borno area of north-eastern Nigeria such as Colonel Kur Mohammed, Lt-Colonel Largema and Major Mohammed Shuwa.

The more politically sophisticated southern officers were sympathetic to the UPGA and opposed the continued imprisonment of Awolowo, whom they admired for his intellectual energy and political ideals. These southern officers were disillusioned at the government's corruption and unfailing ability to create, but not to solve, crisis after crisis. Some of them felt that the system had been so thoroughly corrupted that it could not be changed by an election. Major Nzeogwu declared that "it is impossible to vote out a Nigerian minister" because "elections are always rigged." However, the affinity between politicians and officers that prevailed in the Northern Region was absent in the south, perhaps due to the fact that southern civilians haughtily regarded soldiery as a career for the poorly educated. These stereotypes began to dissipate when many openly began to call for the army to intervene to break the political deadlock. The political crisis was a frequent topic of conversation among radical southern intellectuals, academics and their army acquaintances. The civilians would often urge their army colleagues to take drastic action to change the situation. At times it was barely veiled incitement. Second Lieutenant Cyril Azubuogu recalls that:

> Any army officer was being harangued by civilians because of the state of the nation. People felt that the army should do something, that the country should be salvaged. . . . Most army officers at that time had the same problem of people coming to us, saying, what are you doing? The country is on fire. Why don't you do something about it?[1]

Disgusted by the political mess the country was in after only six years' independence and by the corruption, avarice and selfishness of politicians, a group of politically radical army officers took the bait. They decided that the only means out of the political impasse was to execute a military revolution to overthrow the government. At the core of this thinking was a group of young, mostly Sandhurst-trained army officers in the rank of major. They were a combination of graduates and officers with links to radical academics in the south west area of Nigeria. Their plan was to overthrow the government, release opposition leader Obafemi Awolowo from prison, and install him as the president.

THE INNER CIRCLE

According to a Special Branch report prepared by the police, Majors Ifeajuna and Okafor and Captain Oji were the original members of the conspiratorial group and came up with the idea of Nigeria's first military coup in August 1965. While Major Emmanuel Ifeajuna was certainly one of the originators of the plot, the participants have admitted that they had discussed the idea of a coup for several years before 1965. Even the federal government-produced pamphlet *Nigeria 1966* concedes that the same group of officers who executed the coup in 1966 had originally planned to execute it in 1964. Nigeria 1966 claims that:

> As far back as December 1964, a small group of army officers mainly from the Ibo ethnic group of the Eastern Region dissatisfied with political developments within the Federation began to plot, in collaboration with some civilians, the overthrow of what was then the Government of the Federation of Nigeria and the eventual assumption of power in the country.[2]

---

1 *Daily Independent* Online, October 3, 2003.
2 The pamphlet claims that the chief plotters were Majors Nzeogwu, Ifeajuna, and Okafor, and Captain Nwobosi, and that others connected with the plot were Captain Oji, Majors

The plotters (including Major Nzeogwu) had definite plans for a coup during an army shooting competition in 1964. Their plan was to neutralize senior army officers by sedating them during the competition.[1] The plan is well known in military and political circles and was even mentioned in a US diplomatic cable which claimed that "strong rumors of an impending Army coup purportedly planned for the annual Army Shooting competition were also heard in political circles."[2] The plot was cancelled when senior officers failed to attend the competition. Then Brigadier Aguiyi-Ironsi was also alleged to have tipped off the Prime Minister about the plot.[3]

The original core of conspirators was broader than Ifeajuna, Okafor and Oji. It also included Major Christian Anuforo. Most of the original core conspirators were based in the south, and they began to seek co-conspirators stationed in the Northern Region. This led Major Anuforo to bring his former schoolmate and boyhood friend Major Nzeogwu into the plot. Nzeogwu was based in Kaduna in the Northern Region. Both Anuforo and Nzeogwu were Igbos, raised in the north and fluent Hausa speakers. Nzeogwu in turn recruited the flamboyant sports car driving Major "Wale" Ademoyega, his colleague at the Nigerian Military Training College (NMTC). Nzeogwu had also been Ademoyega's instructor when the latter was a cadet. Of the foregoing insiders, Major Ademoyega (Yoruba) was the only non-Igbo. Although the ethnic composition of the group may not have been deliberate, ethnic ties may have been unconsciously present in so far as was necessary to facilitate plot secrecy, communication and shared political outlook.

These insiders sought to recruit other like-minded officers. All attempts to recruit members of the 4th battalion failed. The Majors instead had to rely on the commanding officer of the 2 Field Battery in Abeokuta Captain Nwobosi to travel to Ibadan to carry out the coup there. Nwobosi was not brought into the conspiracy until around 48 hours before its execution. However, his status as a former schoolmate of Majors Nzeogwu and Anuforo meant that he was trusted and could be relied on at short notice. Nwobosi's deputy at the 2 Field Battery was Captain Domkat Bali. The plotters also later claimed that they recruited the commander of the 2nd Recce squadron in Abeokuta, Major John Obienu. Obienu was an outstanding officer who won an award for being the best overseas cadet in his graduating class at Sandhurst in 1962. The plotters were tied together as a loose coalition by their grievances against senior political and/or military figures. Majors Nzeogwu, Anuforo, Ademoyega and Ifeajuna were certainly motivated by a desire to overthrow the corrupt order of the politicians. However, among the other participants, it was not solely about politics. The coup may have served as an outlet for some of their professional frustrations and fears about the direction the army was being taken by Northern officials in the Ministry of Defense. In his book,[4] Captain Gbulie complained vehemently that the dilution of officer admittance procedures disproportionately advantaged the Northern Region and lowered the caliber of officers that were being recruited. Major Okafor was also

---

Anuforo, Chukwuka, Onwuatuegwu and Ademoyega, Lieutenant Oyewole, and Second-Lieutenants Azubuogu, Juventus Chijioke Ojukwu and Wokocha. The list of 1964 conspirators is over-inclusive. Some of the conspirators named (such as Nwobosi and Ojukwu) were not involved in the plot as far back as 1964.

1 See Nigeria 1966, and Madiebo, *The Nigerian Revolution and The Biafran War*, page 19.

2 Memorandum from Samuel E Belk of National Security Council Staff to the President's Special Assistant for National Security Affairs, Washington, December 30, 1964.

3 Luckham, *The Nigerian Military: A Sociological Analysis of Authority and Revolt*, page 243.

4 *Nigeria's Five Majors: Coup d'Etat of 15th January 1966, First Inside Account*.

said to be upset that the Federal Guards (which had formerly served as a ceremonial unit) was being used to provide security for the Prime Minister and he had an out-standing grievance with Brigadier Maimalari, too, after the Brigadier overruled his handling of a disciplinary matter involving a soldier in the Federal Guards named Corporal Magaji Birnin-Kebbi. The only way such disgruntled officers could change the military structure of which they disapproved was to topple Nigeria's political and military system.

There was also a puritanical element within the coup plotters and among some junior officers who were not impressed by the enthusiastic drinking culture among their superior officers such as Aguiyi-Ironsi, Maimalari, Ademulegun, Ogundipe, Kur Mohammed and Largema.

Some of the plotters may have been politically radicalized after having front row seats in the major political events of the time. Major Nzeogwu served as an intel-ligence officer during Awolowo's treason trial and Majors Anuforo, Ademoyega and Onwuatuegwu all served in the army units that were used to quell the Tiv upris-ing (and they sympathized with the grievances of the Tiv rioters and disapproved of the manner in which they were suppressed). Another soldier who served during the Tiv disturbances and later came to prominence was an NCO from the Tarok ethnic group, John Shagaya. One of Captain Nwobosi's close friends (a corporal) was killed on duty during the government's military crackdown in the Western Region.

METHOD OF RECRUITMENT

The Majors' *modus operandi* for recruitment into the plot was to vehemently criti-cize the government in the presence of other officers. If another officer joined in the criticism they would explore the depth of the officer's dissatisfaction with the gov-ernment. The topic would be quickly changed if their intended target for recruitment showed no interest or was supportive of the government. Then Major Alex Madiebo recalls that, during lunch on one occasion with Major Ifeajuna, Ifeajuna voiced his opinion that the only solution for the political impasse was a military coup. When Madiebo expressed skepticism that a coup could succeed, Ifeajuna changed the topic and never brought it up again.[1] A former colleague of Nzeogwu, Theophilus Danjuma noted that:

> Nzeogwu spoke to me, we were very good friends. Nzeogwu was a very charm-ing person. He had his method; he would start by criticising government and then watch your reaction. . . . if you joined him in criticising the government. . . . Then he would say well, we would [sic] fix them one day. That's how he recruited.[2]

Major Tim Onwuatuegwu bought Nzeogwu's anti-government line. An accom-plished boxer who had won medals during his training at Sandhurst, Onwuatuegwu was an Igbo from Nnewi and another colleague of Major Nzeogwu at the NMTC, where Onwuatuegwu was also an instructor. Onwuatuegwu was tagged a dull, pa-rade ground "goody two shoes" type by one of his own course-mates at Sandhurst, but fell under Nzeogwu's spell and was convinced enough to break into the house of, and shoot, a brigade commander during the first coup. One officer who seems to have been unaffected by Nzeogwu's political rhetoric was Salihu Ibrahim, an outstanding

---

1 Madiebo, *The Biafran Revolution and the Nigerian Civil War*, page 16.
2 *Newswatch*, November 2, 1992.

cadet, top of his class at the NDA, and who by all accounts matured into a thoroughly professional officer who abhorred military participation in government.[1]

However, apart from the commander of the Federal Guards, Major Donatus Okafor, the plotters were unable to recruit much beyond a narrow base of junior officers and failed to conscript from any of the well armed infantry battalions where the vast majority of the gun carrying troops were Northerners. Okafor was born in the northern city of Kaduna and was another fluent Hausa speaker. His father had a building business in Kano and one author claims that his mother was a Tiv from the Northern Region.[2] He was a former instructor in the army's education corps and his participation was essential for the plotters because of the strategic role he held as the commander of the Federal Guards, the army unit responsible for providing security for the Prime Minister and for ceremonial army displays. Okafor personally knew the Prime Minister and his staff, and his familiarity with the Prime Minister's routine, domestic staff and residence layout was crucial for the plotters. He was virtually regarded as a member of the Prime Minister's household.

Of the officers who eventually executed the coup, not all were in the conspiratorial group from the beginning. In an effort to prevent the plot from leaking, most of the junior soldiers who took part were not taken into confidence until a day or two before the coup, or in many cases were not informed of their mission until the coup was already in progress. There were broadly three concentric circles in the plot:

The "core" group of majors who planned and led the operation. In this category were Majors Ifeajuna, Nzeogwu, Ademoyega, Anuforo, Chukwuka, Onwuatuegwu and Okafor.

A group of officers who were not in the original ideological circle of the coup, but who were brought in a day or two before the coup's execution. In this category is Captain Nwobosi.

Junior officers who were ordered to guard or man strategic locations during the coup, and who simply obeyed orders without realizing that they were facilitating a military coup.

By late 1965, the core conspirators had been assembled. The table below profiles the inner circle of the plotters:

Name	Origin/ Training	Year of Commission	Post
Major Christian Anuforo*	Sandhurst	1959	General Staff Officer (Grade II), Army Headquarters, Lagos
Major Chukwuma Kaduna Nzeogwu*	Sandhurst	1959	Chief Instructor, Nigerian Military Training College, Kaduna

---

1 Ibrahim retired from the Nigerian army in 1993 after rising to the rank of Lt-General, and serving as Chief of Army Staff. Strangely, for a man who disliked military governments, he served nine consecutive years in military governments, first as a member of Major-General Buhari's Supreme Military Council, 1984–85, then in General Ibrahim Babangida's Armed Forces Ruling Council 1985–1993.

2 Trevor Clark, *A Right Honorable Gentleman: The Life and Times of Alhaji Sir Abubakar Tafawa Balewa.*

Major Donatus Okafor	NCO	1959	Commanding Officer, Federal Guards, Lagos
Major Emmanuel Ifeajuna	Mons Officer Cadet School, Aldershot, UK	1960	Brigade Major, 2 Brigade, Lagos
Major Humphrey Chukwuka	Sandhurst	1960	Deputy Adjutant-General, Army Headquarters — Lagos
Major Timothy Onwuatuegwu	Sandhurst	1961	Instructor, Nigerian Military Training College, Kaduna
Major Adewale Ademoyega	Mons Officer Cadet School, Aldershot, UK	1962	Nigerian Military Training College (sub-unit), Abeokuta
Captain Ben Gbulie	Sandhurst	1961	Commander, Army Engineers — Kaduna
Captain Ogbonna Oji	Short Service Commission	1961	Army Headquarters, Lagos

Major Ademoyega was the only one of the insiders that was not Igbo. The plotters had similar backgrounds and most of them were prototypical young Igbos of their generation: urbane, educated, arrogant, well travelled and polyglot fluent Hausa speakers born and raised in the north. They were all young, aged between 28 and 35. The plotters were successful at infiltrating and recruiting officers working at the NMTC in Kaduna, and staff officers at army headquarters in Lagos, where several of the core conspirators overlapped with each other in various postings. Major Nzeogwu worked with Majors Onwuatuegwu and Ademoyega at the NMTC and all three had been former members of the 5th battalion in Kano. Majors Anuforo and Chukwuka and Captain Oji were all staff officers working at army headquarters in Lagos. The table below shows how the plotters had successfully infiltrated army headquarters. The italicized names were among the plotters.

ARMY HEADQUARTERS, LAGOS. MILITARY POSTINGS AS AT JANUARY 14, 1966:

NAME	POST
Colonel Kur Mohammed	Chief of Staff at Army Headquarters (acting, in place of Colonel Robert Adebayo)
Lt-Colonel James Pam	Adjutant-General
Lt-Colonel Arthur Unegbe	Quartermaster-General
Major Patrick Anwunah	General Staff Officer, Grade I
*Major Christian Anuforo**	General Staff Officer, Grade II
Captain Ogbonna Oji	General Staff Officer, Grade III
Major Humphrey Chukwuka	Deputy Adjutant-General

On the periphery of the Majors were a group of more senior officers, who although not physically involved in the coup, morally supported its aims. Lt-Colonels Ojukwu and Banjo had been accused of showing a greater than average interest in political matters. Security reports concerning coup plotting by Banjo were passed to Prime Minister Balewa, but no further action was taken. Both Lt-Colonels Ejoor and Gowon claimed that during the 1964 election crisis, Lt-Colonel Ojukwu approached them with a plan to replace the government with a military regime.[1] Major Ademoyega claimed that the Majors floated the idea of a coup to Lt-Colonels Hilary Njoku and Francis Fajuyi. According to Ademoyega, the two Lt-Colonels were not opposed to a military coup, but declined to be physical participants to it. They instead promised to support the plotters if they succeeded.[2] None of the Lt-Colonels became physically involved when the Majors eventually struck and two (Njoku and Ojukwu) actually played a role (to varying degrees) in crushing the coup, while Fajuyi and Ojukwu became military governors in Nigeria's first military administration.

Some senior officers such as Brigadier Ademulegun and Colonel Shodeinde were quizzed by their junior officers on the country's deteriorating political situation. These junior officers were frustrated by their superiors' disinterest in political affairs and insistence on the army's neutrality. Those junior officers were probably "flying a kite" to assess the likely disposition of their superiors in the event of a coup. This was to present the Majors with their most controversial choice in the execution of the coup. Given that their superior officers were virtually certain to oppose a coup and stand in their way, the Majors knew that they could not successfully execute a coup unless those superior officers could somehow be neutralized. The decision taken by the Majors as to how to deal with their superiors proved tragic.

Major Emmanuel Arinze Ifeajuna was the Brigade Major of 2 brigade in Lagos. Contrary to some literature which erroneously claims he was from the Mid-West, Ifeajuna was an Igbo from Onitsha in the Eastern Region, where he attended the illustrious Dennis Memorial Grammar School. He was also a graduate of the University of Ibadan (where he showed early signs of subversiveness by taking part in a student protest). His peers at university included Emeka Anyaoku (later Secretary-General of the Commonwealth). He was also an international athlete of some repute and at the 1954 Commonwealth Games, became the first black African to win a Commonwealth gold medal, setting a new Commonwealth record for high jumping in the process. This might be the success that turned Ifeajuna's head and gave him a sense of self importance. One of his colleagues said that "Ifeajuna was a very interesting character, extremely well read and very politically conscious."[3] Ifeajuna was the ideological inspiration behind Nigeria's first coup and wrote a manuscript explaining why he felt a military coup was necessary. This manuscript has never been published.

A Man Called Kaduna

Major Patrick Chukwuma Kaduna Nzeogwu was a promising, charismatic and strong-willed officer who worked as the chief instructor of the NMTC in Kaduna. Nzeogwu was born in the Northern Region's capital of Kaduna to Igbo immigrant parents from the Mid-West Region. Such was his family's affinity to the city of Nzeogwu's birth that they and his military colleagues called him "Kaduna." When

---

1 Ejoor, *Reminiscences*, page 33.
2 See Ademoyega *Why We Struck*, page 51.
3 Abiodun Adekunle, *The Nigeria–Biafra War Letters: A Soldier's Story*.

not in his army uniform he wore northern mufti and frequently referred to himself as "a Northerner." Nzeogwu spoke fluent Hausa (the *lingua franca* of the Northern Region) like a native. In fact Nzeogwu's command of Hausa was better than his Igbo. He was an exceptionally devout Catholic who attended mass daily, a teetotaller, a non-smoker, and despite being a bachelor, unlike many men of his age he did not spend much time chasing women. Yet he was prepared to kill in a military coup that he believed to be just. From an early age he had a voracious appetite for reading books, not all of which had any immediate relevance to his studies. His favored books concerned politics and guerrilla warfare. Even his detractors were prepared to admit that he "was an incorruptible idealist without ambitions of power . . . in many ways a man born before his time."[1] He was also the first Nigerian army officer to be trained in military intelligence and in this role was exposed to sensitive information on politicians and soldiers that most others were not privy to. A colleague observed that:

> Any officer (or, for that matter, civilian) who knew him could tell you that this man was a pure nationalist who burned within with the love of his country. . . . He gave scant regard to the place of origin of his countrymen, having been born in Kaduna and raised in an era of nationalistic consciousness. He was sophisticated in his analysis of history and of political events in the country.[2]

So what possessed a puritanical, bible-thumping young man to murder the nation's most powerful politician in the middle of the night? Nzeogwu's thought process is chilling in its simplicity:

> We had a short list of people who were either undesirable for the future progress of the country or who by their positions at the time had to be sacrificed for peace and stability.[3]

Nzeogwu had demonstrated a rebellious streak even in his youth and was suspended from school for his part in a student protest. He had also harbored anti-government sentiment for several years before 1966. Over time he developed a pathological hatred of corruption and ethnic chauvinism. Nzeogwu had been reported for disseminating anti-government rhetoric to junior officers and for allegedly telling them, "Wait until the day you will look at the senior officers through the sights of your rifle." These reports were passed to his boss at the NMTC Colonel Ralph Shodeinde, and to Brigadier Ademulegun. Shodeinde did not take punitive action against Nzeogwu but noted that "There is never smoke without fire, even if it is smouldering fire."[4] Brigadier Ademulegun was sufficiently concerned to write a report mentioning that Nzeogwu was "a young man in a hurry" who "should be closely watched."

The Awolowo Factor

What were the Majors' objectives? The imprisoned leader of the opposition Obafemi Awolowo seemed to be the problem and the solution to Nigeria's first military coup. Awolowo's imprisonment made him a martyr to his admirers. The Western Region crisis, Awolowo's detention and the federal government's alliance with the unpopular vote rigging regime of Akintola caused great disaffection among Yorubas and other southerners. Having been incarcerated after leading the opposition against a government the Majors detested, Chief Awolowo seemed to the Majors to

1 DJM Muffett, *Let Truth be Told.*
2 Abiodun Adekunle, *Nigeria–Biafra War Letters: A Soldier's Story.*
3 Dennis Ejindu, interview with Major Nzeogwu, *Africa and the World*, May 1967.
4 Obsasanjo, *An Intimate Portrait of Chukwuma Kaduna Nzeogwu*, page 83.

have been victimized by the government. To them he was a credible alternative who shared their left-wing socialist ideology. Major Nzeogwu said that:

> Neither myself nor any of the other lads was in the least interested in governing the country. We were soldiers and not politicians. We had earmarked from the list known to every soldier in this operation who would be what. Chief Obafemi Awolowo was, for example, to be released from jail immediately and to be made the executive provisional President of Nigeria. We were going to make civilians of proven honesty and efficiency who would be thoroughly handpicked to do all the governing.[1]

Majors Ifeajuna and Ademoyega, and Captains Gbulie and Nwobosi all confirmed that they intended to release Awolowo and install him as Nigeria's new leader.[2] Nwobosi went so far as to say that the Majors had more faith in Awolowo than they did in the President Nnamdi Azikiwe:

> We planned that after the coup, none of us was going to be the Head of State . . . Awolowo was in Calabar prison and in our own minds, this was the man we wanted to put at the helm of affairs of the federal government. . . . We wanted to put somebody who was sincere. . . . Awolowo was our man, our man for the job; I don't think he was even the best friend of the Igbo. He wasn't, but we wanted a job done and we knew that the man who would do it well was Awolowo. You know Zik? Zik is from next door to my place, from my town Obosi, but I wouldn't trust Zik to do that type of thing we had in mind. I'm telling you the honest truth.[3]

Awolowo's secretary Odia Ofeimun confirmed that the Majors intended to release Awolowo:

> The plan of the coup makers was to release Awolowo from jail and make him their own leader. . . . They were comfortable with Awolowo's ideas and believed they would help the nation. . . . People were told that it was an Igbo coup but that is not correct. It is a very interesting part of the Nigerian story. In the first place, there have been many serious lies that have been told by our leaders. . . . Our leaders have not been bold enough to tell us the truth. But the point is that the average Yoruba man could never really believe that some Igbo would plan a coup and hand over power to Awolowo because that is not the way Nigeria is seen.[4]

An air force officer (Major Nzegwu) and Captain Udeaja were briefed to fly to Calabar to release Chief Awolowo from prison after the coup.

A negotiated settlement to the Western Region crisis might have pre-empted the subsequent coup. However rather than addressing the underlying causes of dissatisfaction by seeking a compromise involving Awolowo's release, conducting fresh, credible elections, or redeeming its image by severing its alliance with Akintola's regime, the federal government ordered the army to suppress volatile political dissatisfaction. The Ibadan-based 4th battalion of the army (commanded by Lt-Colonel Abogo Largema) was deployed to restore order in the anarchic Western Region. Most of the soldiers in the 4th battalion were of Northern origin and their allegedly pro-Akintola conduct during the operation made 4th battalion soldiers unpopular with the local population as some of them were perceived to be biased towards the NNDP. The NPC government decided to authorize an even more severe and massive

---

1 *Nigerian Tribune*, July 2, 1967
2 Ibid., Ademoyega, *Why We Struck*, pages 68–69, and Gbulie, *Nigeria's Five Majors*.
3 Momoh, *The Nigerian Civil War 1967–1970: History and Reminiscences*, pages 737 and 739.
4 *Guardian*, May 6, 2007.

military crackdown, crudely codenamed "Operation No Mercy," to curb the lawlessness in the Western Region. To carry out the operation, the government first had to reshuffle the upper echelons of the security forces. The Inspector-General of Police, Louis Edet, was sent on leave and replaced by Kam Selem (a Northerner). Edet was Nigeria's first indigenous Inspector-General of Police after the departure of British officer John .E. Hodge. The army's Igbo GOC Major-General Johnson Aguiyi-Ironsi was also to be sent on indefinite leave and replaced by Brigadier Maimalari (a Northerner) or Brigadier Ademulegun, and the Igbo commanding officer of the Lagos-based 1st battalion Lt-Colonel Hilary Njoku was also to be replaced by another Northerner (Lt-Colonel Gowon). These reshuffles may have been routine, but by accident or design, would result in the replacement of officers from the NCNC power base of the Eastern Region by Northerners. Aguiyi-Ironsi's departure would probably have been window dressed by giving him a decorative "promotion." At the time there was discussion of creating an African high command, and senior army officers from Nigeria and Ghana were enthusiastic about the idea. As Africa's most decorated soldier, Aguiyi-Ironsi was the obvious candidate to head the African high command.

Additionally, the Tiv people, who inhabited the lower part of the Northern Region, were in a state of open revolt and wanted to rid themselves of Hausa–Fulani domination. Again the federal government turned to the army. An army unit led by Lt-Colonel James Pam[1] was sent to quell the rebellion under the codename "Operation Administration." Pam may have been chosen for this role as, like the Tiv, he was a Christian from a minority ethnic group (Birom). Pam had once been ADC to the Northern Region's former Governor Sir Bryan Sharwood-Smith. His father Rwang Pam was the Sarkin Jos (Chief of Jos) and he also had brothers serving in the air force and in the police.

UNHEEDED WARNINGS

Both the Special Branch of the police and the army high command were aware that a coup was being plotted. Special Branch was headed by T.A. Fagbola who was its first indigenous head after the departure of Irishman John O'Sullivan (the last British head of Nigeria's Special Branch). Fagbola forwarded intelligence reports regarding a coup plot to both the federal and regional governments. It was alleged that the reports specifically mentioned Majors Ifeajuna and Nzeogwu by name, and that Nzeogwu's name had been on Special Branch's files since he received intelligence training in the UK.[2] Commissioner of Police Mohammed Dikko Yusuf (popularly known as "M.D.") later claimed that Fagbola warned the government: "Soldiers are going to strike, but we don't know when." Yusuf also claimed that Brigadier Ademulegun warned at an intelligence committee meeting, that the plotters had fixed, then changed, the date for their coup.[3]

Senior officers in the army hierarchy like Aguiyi-Ironsi, Ademulegun and Maimalari were aware that a coup was being planned (although it is not clear whether they knew exactly who was behind the plot and when it would be executed). As noted above Brigadier Ademulegun and Colonel Shodeinde long before documented their concerns regarding Major Nzeogwu's rebellious streak. The Minister of Information

---

1 The Rwang Pam stadium (home of Nigerian football club Mighty Jets) is named after Pam's father.

2 Clark, *A Right Honorable Gentleman*, page 747.

3 Ayo Opadokun, *Aristocratic Rebel*.

Ayo Rosiji urged Brigadier Ademulegun to utilize his access to the Sardauna to warn the Sardauna to be careful. In unguarded conversation with other officers, Brigadier Maimalari cryptically alluded to bloodshed on the horizon. He went so far as to confide his concerns to his Kanuri kinsman and former school teacher Sir Kashim Ibrahim. Maimalari warned Kashim that unless urgent action was taken, the senior officers and politicians would soon be dead.[1] Aguiyi-Ironsi was so concerned that he decided to travel to Bauchi to warn the Prime Minister (where the Prime Minister was on leave). He passed a warning to the Prime Minister's secretary Stanley Wey, which Wey relayed up the defense hierarchy to Defense Minister Inuwa Wada. Wada was nonchalant; he felt that a military coup was not possible in Nigeria. He informed Aguiyi-Ironsi that it was not necessary for him to travel to Bauchi and that he (Wada) would inform the Prime Minister when the Prime Minister returned.[2]

In over five years of lurching from one crisis to another, senior politicians had probably become accustomed to security scares and threats, and thus may have become desensitized to what they regarded as conspiracy theories. One politician who was not taking a *laissez-faire* attitude to the coup rumors was Akintola. Akintola travelled to Kaduna on Friday January 14, 1966 to warn the Sardauna of an impending coup. Lt-Colonel Largema of the 4th battalion also attended that meeting. Frustrated that his warnings failed to elicit the required degree of urgency from the Sardauna, Akintola returned to Ibadan. After the meeting Largema was sent to Lagos to brief Aguiyi-Ironsi. He never got to deliver the message. Brigadier Ademulegun also sought an audience with the Sardauna on January 14. Since all four men (Sardauna, Akintola, Ademulegun and Largema) died the next day, the entire truth about what was discussed in Kaduna on January 14 may never be known.

The NPC Minister of Works Alhaji Shehu Shagari approached Balewa to warn him of rumors of a coup plot. Balewa was unfazed and told Shagari there was no cause for alarm. When Shagari urged Balewa to take the matter more seriously, he was irritated and asked Shagari to leave him alone, but not before telling Shagari that Akintola had been to Kaduna earlier in the day with "another scare story" for the Sardauna. Balewa said he told the Sardauna not to take Akintola's claims seriously.[3]

Prior to the coup, Nzeogwu gave cryptic clues about his intentions. On one occasion while discussing Brigadier Ademulegun, Nzeogwu told Major Alex Madiebo to "go easy with the Brigadier, for when a strong wind blows, all the grass bends low to allow it to pass."[4] Madiebo did not immediately appreciate the significance of what Nzeogwu told him, but on January 15, 1966, Nzeogwu made his intentions explicitly clear. However, it was to be a case of good intentions and dreadful consequences.

1 Akinjide Osuntokun, *Power Broker: A Biography of Sir Kashim Ibrahim*, page 100.
2 Ibid., page 106.
3 Ibid., page 118.
4 Madiebo, *The Nigerian Revolution and the Biafran War*, page 12.

CHAPTER 4. ENTER "THE FIVE MAJORS"

Major Ifeajuna was the leader of the Lagos operations. Majors Nzeogwu and On-wuatuegwu were to lead the operations in the Northern Region, Captain Nwobosi was in charge of Ibadan, and Lieutenant Jerome Oguchi was to stage the coup in Enugu. The neutralization of key government personnel was a key component of the plot. According to the Special Branch report, the plotters planned to arrest the following Ministers:

Alhaji Sir Abubakar Tafawa Balewa	Prime Minister
Chief Festus Okotie-Eboh	Finance Minister
Alhaji Sir Ahmadu Bello	Premier, Northern Region
Dr. Michael Okpara	Premier, Eastern Region
Dr. Dennis Osedebay	Premier, Mid-West Region
Chief Samuel Ladoke Akintola	Premier, Western Region
Dr. Kingsley Ozumba Mbadiwe	Minister of Trade
Taslim Olawale Elias	Attorney-General
Jaja Wachuku	Minister of Aviation
Inuwa Wada	Minister of Defense
Waziri Ibrahim	Minister of Economic Development
Richard Akinjide	Minister of Education
Moses Adekoyejo Majekodunmi	Minister of Health
Ayo Rosiji	Minister of Information
Shehu Shagari	Internal Affairs
Matthew Mbu	Minister of State (Navy)

It appears that some discussion did take place between the Majors as to whether or not to kill the target personalities. There was a divergence of opinion; some wanted a clean sweep of the Augean stable and for all targets to be shot without exception, and a second group insisted that no blood should be shed. Captain Gbulie revealed that "we could not come into agreement on whether some people should be killed. This issue was therefore left to the judgment of officers to use the situation on the ground to determine whether to kill or not."[1] As will be shown later, that proved unwise. It seems extraordinary that for such a sensitive operation a huge decision such as whether or not to take or spare lives was left to the discretion of individual soldiers. Executing such an operation without strict predetermined parameters would inevitably result in haphazard execution, leading to the appearance of sectional killings. Some within the plot remained consistent in their approach.

In the category of those who made predetermined decisions to kill their targets seem to be Majors Anuforo and Nzeogwu, and those who did not wish to harm their targets include Lieutenant Oguchi. As will be shown later, Major Onwuategwu and Captain Nwobosi were inconsistent in their approach.

Towards the First Coup

During a brigade conference in the week ending January 14, 1966, a note signed by Major-General Aguiyi-Ironsi was circulated to the officers attending. The note warned that some army officers were planning to "cause trouble."[2] The officers in attendance were asked to reinforce security and be vigilant when they returned to their posts. It does not appear that the senior officers appreciated the scale of the "trouble" afoot. The coup's timing caught many of the army's high command and Ministry of Defense officials by surprise as many of them were away from their posts. The Defense Minister Alhaji Inuwa Wada was overseas, as was the permanent secretary in the Ministry of Defense, Alhaji Sule Kolo. Of the five battalions, only Lt-Colonel Ojukwu's 5th battalion in Kano was not in flux. Command of the first battalion in Enugu had just been transferred from Lt-Colonel Francis Fajuyi to Lt-Colonel David Ejoor (who was attending the brigade conference in Lagos), so it was being temporarily commanded by the deputy commander Major Gabriel Okonweze. Command of the Lagos-based 2nd battalion was also in transition from Lt-Colonel Hilary Njoku to Lt-Colonel Gowon who was returning from a course overseas. The commanding officer of the 3rd battalion in Kaduna Lt-Colonel Kurubo suddenly travelled to Lagos on the eve of the coup, leaving his deputy Major Okoro in charge. The commander of the Ibadan based 4th battalion Lt-Colonel Largema had travelled first to Kaduna, and then to Lagos. His deputy Major Macaulay Nzefili was in charge of the 4th battalion while Largema was away. Thus in the absence of their commanders, the first, third and fourth battalions were being temporarily commanded by their deputy commanders, all of whom were Igbo (Majors Okonweze, Okoro and Nzefili respectively) and the 5th battalion was under the command of its substantive commander Lt-Colonel Ojukwu, who was also Igbo. Therefore on the night of January 14, 1966, all five battalions of the army were temporarily under Igbo commanders (albeit for a period of 24 hours only).

---

1 Gbulie was speaking at the Human Rights Violations Investigations Commission.
2 Ejoor, *Reminiscences*, page 21.

January 14 1966: Friday Night Party at Brigadier Maimalari's House, 11 Thompson Avenue, Lagos

On the night of January 14, 1966, many of the army's senior officers were attending a party in honor of the Lagos-based 2 brigade's commander Brigadier Maimalari, who had remarried. Maimalari's first wife had been shot dead in a bizarre accident involving a hunting rifle. Some of the officers attending that party (including Maimalari himself) were murdered a few hours after that party. The party was attended by some of the coup plotters themselves (their absence would have been suspicious) and most senior officers in Lagos. The guests included several dignitaries and government ministers such as the NPC's national legal adviser Alhaji Abdul-Ganiyu Folorunso Abdulrazaq, and Jacob Obande. Military guests included the GOC Major-General Aguiyi-Ironsi, Colonel Kur Mohammed, Lt-Colonels Gowon, Largema, Pam, Njoku and Ejoor, Majors Ifeajuna, Anuforo, Okafor and Obienu, and the military attaches of the US and the UK. Brigadier Ogundipe, Colonel Adebayo and Lt-Colonel Nwawo were absent as they were abroad.

After this party, the Special Branch report states that the following officers attended a meeting at Ifeajuna's house: Majors Ifeajuna, Anuforo, Ademoyega, Chukwuka, Okafor, Captains Oji and Adeleke, Lieutenants Godfrey Ezedigbo, Fola Oyewole, Godwin Onyefuru and Second-Lieutenants Emmanuel Nweke, Boniface Ikejiofor, Kuku Wokocha, and Ozoemena Igweze. The report goes on to state that:

> Major Ifeajuna addressed the meeting on the subject of the deteriorating situation in western Nigeria to which, he contended, the politicians had failed to find a solution. He added that as a result the entire country was heading towards chaos and disaster. He next acquainted the junior officers with the inner circle's plans and asked them if they were prepared to assist to put an end to this state of affairs. From there they moved out to get men and arms after which they fanned out in three groups for their targets.

Apart from the parley at Ifeajuna's house and the men assisting Nzeogwu in Kaduna, it does not appear that all the junior ranks and NCOs acting under the Majors were fully briefed that, or were aware that, they were participating in a military coup. Most of the junior officers and NCOs were simply told that they were proceeding on an "internal security" exercise, and they obeyed orders from the Majors, issued arms and ammunition, and only later realized that they were taking part in a plot to overthrow the government.

Saturday Morning, January 15, 1966: "Plenty Plenty Palaver"

Lt-Colonels David Ejoor and Abogo Largema were guests of the Ikoyi hotel on the night of Friday 14. When Ejoor went downstairs the following morning to check out, he noticed a trail of bloodstains leading from the staircase into the hotel lobby. His driver then ran into the hotel in terrific agitation to incoherently warn him: "Sir, big trouble. Prime Minister dem don take away. I sleep for Federal Guard. No sleep. My weapon don take away. Plenty plenty palaver."[1] To compound matters, when Ejoor went back upstairs he saw spent shell casings outside Largema's room. He began to realize that something cataclysmic had occurred overnight.

---

1 Ibid.

EVENTS OVERNIGHT

Kaduna — Northern Region

In the weeks leading up to January 15, Majors Nzeogwu and Onwuatuegwu carried out reconnaissance on the official lodge of the Sardauna. Some accounts claim that the Sardauna was aware that he was being watched. Nzeogwu often took his men on a night-time training exercise known as "Exercise Damisa." His men were unaware that the military exercise they were participating in was actually a practice run for a military coup to overthrow the government. As the chief instructor at the NMTC, Nzeogwu could bring troops out at night-time without arousing suspicion or giving the impression of unusual activity. The commander of the 1 brigade in Kaduna Brigadier Ademulegun had reprimanded Nzeogwu and warned him to keep his military exercises a safe distance away from the Sardauna's lodge. Although Ademulegun complained about the commotion, he took no further action as he was unaware of the exercise's real purpose. In the early hours of January 15, 1966, Nzeogwu turned "Exercise Damisa" into a full-blown coup. Nzeogwu led a group of soldiers into a bush close to the Sardauna's lodge. Once there, Nzeogwu informed the men of their real mission:

> On Saturday morning the other officers and men thought they were going out only on a night exercise. It was not until they were out in the bush that they were told the full details of the plan. . . . Any man had the chance to drop out. More than that, they had bullets. They had been issued with bullets but I was unarmed. If they disagreed, they could have shot me. . . . Most of the other ranks were northerners but they followed. . . . It was a truly Nigerian gathering. Only in the army do you get true Nigerianism.[1]

Among the men accompanying Nzeogwu in "Exercise Damisa" were Second-Lieutenants John Atom Kpera and Harris Eghagha.[2] None of the men accompanying Nzeogwu objected, and most even enthusiastically supported the idea. Nzeogwu, assisted by three Northern sergeants, Musa Manga[3] (from Zuru), Duromola Oyegoke (from Ilorin) and Yakubu Adebiyi (an instructor in the NMTC's tactical wing), subjected the Sardauna's house to such an intensely sustained burst of fire with an anti-tank weapon that it burst into flames. Manga, Oyegoke and Adebiyi were from the Northern Region. Nzeogwu personally conducted a search of the residence, hunting for the Sardauna. While he searched the compound other officers including Second-Lieutenant Samson Omeruah deployed soldiers from the 3rd battalion around the outer perimeter wall of the Sardauna's compound.

After losing his temper at his initial failure to locate him, Nzeogwu found the Sardauna hiding with his wives and domestic staff near his car park. The Sardauna was shot dead by Nzeogwu. The Sardauna's faithful bodyguard Zarumi, who came to defend him with a sword, was also shot dead, as well as one of his wives (Hafsatu) who refused to be parted from her husband and tried to shield him with her body. Hafsatu was the daughter of the Waziri of Sokoto. Two of the Sardauna's other

---

1 *New Nigerian*, 18th January 1966.
2 Later Brigadier and commander of the Nigerian army's engineers.
3 Manga joined the army in 1954 and worked under Nzeogwu at the NMTC. Manga was later arrested for his role in the coup but was released after July 1966 and returned to army duties till he retired as a Sergeant-Major in 1981. He died in May 1994. His relative Mohammed Manga was also in the army and later became a Colonel.

wives were also present but were not harmed. The attack on the Sardauna's lodge raised an alarm which was connected to the house of the Senior Assistant Secretary for Security Ahmed Ben Musa. Musa drove to the Sardauna's lodge to ascertain the cause of the alarm. When he arrived he was shot dead inside his car before he had a chance to disembark and investigate. Kaduna residents had become so accustomed to the night-time training exercises that they were not perturbed when they heard gunshots in the middle of the night.

Northerners awoke the next morning to see the smouldering ruins of the dead Sardauna's lodge. Some looting took place as a throng of civilians came to see the ruins and investigate the rumors. The Sardauna was later buried in Kaduna. Nzeowgu's roommate Major Olusegun Obasanjo had been on a course overseas during the coup and returned to home to hear that some politicians and soldiers had been killed. Totally unaware that his roommate was culpable, Obasanjo innocently asked which country the soldiers who killed the politicians were from.

BRIGADIER ADEMULEGUN

Nzeogwu's co-conspirator in Kaduna, Major Tim Onwuatuegwu, personally led a detachment of soldiers to Brigadier Ademulegun's house. Onwuategwu made his way up to the Brigadier's bedroom, where he was lying beside his wife. According to the Majors' version of events, Ademulegun reached for a drawer beside his bed, and as he did so, Onwuategwu shot him and his wife dead. Ademulegun had attended a piano recital the previous day and his terrified young children were in the house when their father was shot. They were initially comforted by their housemaid Gbelle, but they had become orphans overnight. After their father's murder, Aguiyi-Ironsi's wife Victoria took the Ademulegun children away from Kaduna and had them housed in Lagos. They were given government scholarships to university degree level. Ademulegun's then six-year-old daughter Solape later worked as a journalist and now owns a school. Ademulegun's son Frank later became a group captain in the air force but is now deceased.

When he received reports of gunfire at the Sardauna's lodge, the commander of the 1st Reconnaissance Squadron Major Hassan Katsina ordered Corporal John Shagaya and Sergeant Dantsoho Mohammed to drive into town, carry out reconnaissance and report back on the disturbances. The two young soldiers saw the corpses of policemen at the Sardauna's lodge and the bullet riddled corpses of Brigadier Ademulegun and his wife still in their bedroom. The coup soldiers at Brigadier Ademulegun's house had distastefully permitted other soldiers to enter and view the corpses of the Brigadier and his wife. The gruesome scene was not forgotten by those soldiers.

COLONEL SHODEINDE

The head of the NMTC Colonel Ralph Shodeinde was also killed. The manner of his death is unclear. His wife (who was present when he was killed) testified that he was shot by several soldiers including Majors Nzeogwu and Onwuategwu. Other accounts claim that a grenade was tossed at him. It is not clear whether Nzeogwu could have been involved in Shodeinde's death since presumably he was pre-occupied at the time with killing the Sardauna. Responsibility for Shodeinde's murder certainly lies with Onwuategwu. The Majors' bloodlust, in some cases, and failure to kill in others is puzzling. The same Major Onwuatuegwu who shot a senior officer and his wife in their bedroom went on to arrest, but did not harm, the Governor of the Northern Region: Sir Kashim Ibrahim. Ibrahim was treated with utmost respect by the men who abducted him, and Nzeogwu saluted Kashim and apologized to him for having him placed under arrest. Ironically some of the junior Northern soldiers guarding Kashim wanted him executed for being an accomplice to a corrupt government. Onwuatuegwu vehemently disagreed and vowed that Kashim would not be harmed under any circumstances. Kashim asked to be taken to his home town of Maiduguri and an aircraft was brought to take him home.[1]

STRATEGIC LOCATIONS

Separately troops under the command of the Sandhurst-trained Captain Ben Gbulie were taking over strategic locations and facilities in Kaduna. Gbulie's group was compartmentalized as follows: (i) Broadcasting facilities: Lieutenant Edwin Okafor and Second-Lieutenant John Atom Kpera were in charge of seizing control of the headquarters of the Nigerian Broadcasting Corporation, while Second-Lieutenant Ezedinma was to do the same at the radio and TV stations (ii) Second-Lieutenants Ben Iloabuchie and Second-Lieutenant Patrick Ibik were to take control of the P & T Telephone Exchange (iii) while Second-Lieutenant Harris Eghagha and Sergeants Bernard and Fonkat were to mount roadblocks at strategic locations.

Ibadan — Western Region

In Ibadan the Premier of the Western Region Chief Samuel Akintola had been forewarned that soldiers were coming to get him. His deputy Chief Remi Fani-Kayode was first arrested by the plotters. Fani-Kayode (nicknamed "Fani Power") was not killed but was instead taken by his captors to the Federal Guard barracks in Lagos, where he was later discovered by loyal troops and eventually released on the orders of Lt-Colonel Gowon, and then taken to a safe house in Ikoyi. Fani-Kayode's young son Femi witnessed his father's arrest that night. Femi Fani-Kayode later became Nigeria's Aviation Minister. After this arrest, Kayode's wife telephoned Akintola to inform him of what had happened. Akintola thus had the advantage of having prior notice of the impending arrival of uninvited guests. Shortly afterward a detachment of soldiers led by Captain Emmanuel Nwobosi arrived at Akintola's residence. Nwobosi drove to Ibadan from the Abeokuta garrison. Nwobosi stood in the middle of Akintola's courtyard and shouted at Akintola to submit himself for arrest. When Akintola did not comply, the soldiers tried to arrest him, upon which Akintola opened fire on them with his shotgun, lightly wounding a few of them including Captain Nwobosi. After bravely fighting for his life and engaging Nwobosi and Second-Lieutenants Bob Egbikor and Ambrose Chukwu in a gunfight (according to the Special Branch report), Akintola was shot dead. His nephew was also killed by the soldiers. Akintola's sons, daughter-in-law Dupe (wife of Akintola's oldest son Yomi) and grandchildren were present in the house. Dupe and her son were wounded. Akintola's son Tokunboh (a school student at Eton in the UK) was present, having come home to visit his father during his school holidays. Some have claimed that Akintola's life might have been spared had he (like Fani-Kayode) given himself up, and that he may have been provoked the soldiers into killing him by shooting at them. However, in a subsequent interview, Nwobosi gave the impression that Akintola's murder was premeditated,

---

1 Osuntokun, *Power Broker: A Biography of Sir Kashim Ibrahim*, page 103.

and that the plotters never intended to harm Fani-Kayode.[1] Nwobosi exhibited a puzzling mix of brutality and compassion during the coup. The Special Branch report mentions that shortly before killing Akintola, he had taken a detour from his assignment to help a pregnant woman who had gone into labor to get to a hospital.

Lagos — Federal Capital

Arrest of the Prime Minister and Finance Minister

The Lagos branch of the coup was led by Major Emmanuel Ifeajuna. The key officers assisting Ifeajuna in Lagos were Majors Wale Ademoyega, Don Okafor, Chris Anuforo and Humphrey Chukwuka. Between 2 a.m. and 3 a.m. Ifeajuna and some Lieutenants made their way to Prime Minister Abubakar Tafawa Balewa's residence on King George's road. A few hours earlier the Prime Minister had finished a meeting with three of his cabinet ministers K.O. Mbadiwe (Minister of Trade), Raymond Njoku (Minister of Communications) and Taslim Elias (Attorney-General). It was the last time he would see his ministers. The intruders overpowered (but did not kill) the police officers on guard duty, and forced the domestic aide-de-camps (ADCs) to lead them to the Prime Minister's living quarters at gunpoint. The Madaki of Bauchi Alhaji Muhammadu was in the Prime Minister's residence but was not seen by the intruders. He later claimed that the Major who led the operation at the Prime Minister's residence was Major Okafor. This was almost certainly a case of mistaken identity. The physical characteristics that the Madaki described (light skin and thin moustache) are consistent with Major Ifeajuna, as recorded by all other accounts. Okafor was well known among the Prime Minister's domestic staff and would have been recognized. They did not so identify him. The Prime Minister had two ADCs, one Hausa and the other Igbo (Kaftan Topolomiyo and Maxwell Orukpabo respectively). Kaftan was born in the Republic of Chad but moved to Nigeria as a child. He had served in the army but found himself hopelessly outgunned and outnumbered by the younger intruders. The ADCs initially tried to sell a dummy to the soldiers by claiming that they did not know where the Prime Minister slept nor did they have keys to his bedroom. Nonetheless the intruders forced them up the stairs at gunpoint to the Prime Minister's bedroom. The Prime Minister opened his bedroom door to find Major Ifeajuna brandishing a gun. Ifeajuna saluted and informed the Prime Minister that he was under arrest. The Prime Minister asked for, and was given, time to say his prayers before being led out wearing a white gown, white trousers and slippers (the Prime Minister's attire will become relevant later). When they got downstairs Major Ifeajuna ordered the other soldiers to salute the Prime Minister, and they complied. Kaftan pleaded that the Prime Minister was his elderly mother's only son and that her heart would be broken if he came to any harm. As the Prime Minister was led out of his residence and down the road on foot, Kaftan followed, demanding to know where they were taking him. Kaftan continued to follow on foot, and remonstrate on the Prime Minister's behalf until the Prime Minister told him to restrain himself and go back. The Prime Minister was put into a waiting army vehicle and driven away along Awolowo road. He was told by his captors that he would not be harmed and that the trouble going on in the country was not his fault.

Concerned for the Prime Minister's safety, Balewa's domestic staff telephoned the Lagos Commissioner of Police Hamman Maiduguri to inform him that the Prime

---

1 Momoh, *The Nigerian Civil War 1967–1970, History and Reminiscences*, page 737.

Minister had been kidnapped by soldiers. They also placed another call to the army's GOC Major-General Aguiyi-Ironsi. The alarm had been raised. Maiduguri in turn contacted the acting Inspector-General of Police Alhaji Kam Selem, and around 3 a.m., the two went to the residence of the deputy permanent secretary in the Ministry of Defense, Ahmadu Kurfi, to break the news of the Prime Minister's abduction.[1]

In the absence of the Defense Minister Alhaji Inuwa Wada and Ministry of Defense Permanent Secretary Alhaji Sule Kolo, Kurfi was now the most senior ministry of defense civil servant still in the country. In a carbon copy of British tradition, the Prime Minister lived next door to the Finance Minister. After arresting Balewa, soldiers led by Second-Lieutenant Godfrey Ezedigbo went next door and arrested the Finance Minister Chief Festus Okotie-Eboh. Okotie-Eboh's arrest was particularly aggressive and eyewitnesses say that the soldiers who arrested him tossed him into their army Land Rover "like a sack." The corruption allegations against Okotie-Eboh may have led the soldiers to single him out for special treatment.

STRATEGIC LOCATIONS

Soldiers led by Major Ademoyega set up roadblocks and occupied strategic locations including the control room of the police headquarters at Lion Building, the P & T telephone exchange and the Nigerian External Communications building. Major Ademoyega personally addressed the employees at these locations and ordered them not to connect any calls.

Ikoyi Hotel

Lt-Colonel Abogo Largema was a guest at the Ikoyi Hotel on the night of the coup. As a cadet Largema had been an athlete of some prowess and represented Sandhurst at boxing and athletics. Despite the fact that Largema was away from his post, and that Largema was not allotted to him, Major Ifeajuna made his way to the hotel and forced the desk clerk, at gunpoint, to inform Largema that he had a "phone call." When Largema emerged from his room to take the bogus "phone call," he walked straight into an ambush as Ifeajuna and Second-Lieutenant Ezedigbo emerged from their hiding place in the corridor and shot him dead.

Back to 11 Thompson Avenue: Brigadier Maimalari's House

A group of Federal Guard soldiers led by their commanding officer Major Don Okafor and Captain Oji, went to 11 Thompson Avenue, the residence of the commander of the Lagos-based 2 brigade, Brigadier Maimalari. Okafor tried to bluff his way past Maimalari's guards by claiming he had come to take over guard duties from them. As the plotters were trying to access his compound, the Brigadier's phone rang. He came downstairs to answer it, but as soon as he picked up the receiver, he heard a burst of machine gun fire. It was the sound of the intruders engaging his guards in a gunfight. A member of Maimalari's guards was killed. One of the intruders was also arrested. When he heard the gunfire, Maimalari dropped the receiver and ran out of the house into the road. Major Okafor's attempts to track down Maimalari were unsuccessful. As Maimalari was escaping on foot, he came across the car of his Brigade Major, Emmanuel Ifeajuna, who was en route to the Federal Guard barracks

---

1 Kurfi, *The Nigerian General Elections, 1959 and 1979 and the Aftermath.*

with the captured Prime Minister. Recognizing Ifeajuna, Maimalari waved down the car, and was promptly shot dead by Ifeajuna and Second-Lieutenant Ezedigbo. In the crossfire, Ezedigbo was accidentally injured by Major Ifeajuna. The whole incident would have been witnessed by the Prime Minister, who was still held captive, and was present in Ifeajuna's car at this time.

One question that merits further investigation is who placed the call that caused Brigadier Maimalari's phone to ring as the mutineers were arriving to get him. Could it have been Aguiyi-Ironsi or Pam, trying to warn him? Pam's wife later said she telephoned Brigadier Maimalari as the coup was in progress.

THE GOC IN TOWN

Meanwhile the army's GOC, Major-General Aguiyi-Ironsi, was leading a charmed life. After leaving Brigadier Maimalari's party he went on to another party on board the Elder Dempster flagship *Aureol* at Apapa Wharf.[1] While he was attending the second party, soldiers led by Major Don Okafor showed up at his house at 1 Glover Road in Ikoyi.[2] The experienced head of Aguiyi-Ironsi's guards became suspicious when the soldiers explained that they had come to take over guard duty from them. This was the same pretext used by Okafor as he was trying to access Brigadier's Maimalari's residence. Aguiyi-Ironsi's guard chief challenged the unscheduled visitors and responded that in his 15 years of army service, he had never heard of guards being switched in the middle of the night.[3] Aguiyi-Ironsi was absent and the plotters left empty handed.

When Aguiyi-Ironsi returned from the second party he received two telephone calls: one from the Prime Minister's residence and another from Lt-Colonel James Pam, whose house at number 8 Ikoyi Crescent was being attacked by soldiers under the command of Major Humphrey Chukwuka (who was a colleague of Pam at army headquarters).[4] Other soldiers assisting Chukwuka included Second-Lieutenant Godwin Onyefuru and Sergeant Donatus Anyanwu. The plotters shot out the tires of Pam's car, which was parked outside his house, and abducted Pam in the presence of his wife Elizabeth, who was nursing a newborn baby. Chukwuka was a regular guest at Pam's house and thus Elizabeth knew him personally. Chukwuka promised her that her husband would not be harmed. After being allowed to take an overcoat to keep himself warm, Pam was taken alive to the officers' mess at the Federal Guard barracks.

Lt-Colonel Unegbe and Colonel Kur Mohammed were also accosted at their homes at number 7 Point Road and number 1 Park Lane, respectively. Unegbe was shot dead in the presence of his pregnant wife. She later gave birth but not without complications. Unegbe was the only Igbo killed during the coup. Popular misconceptions claim that Unegbe (due to his Igbo ethnicity) was not initially a target of the Majors, but was killed only because he refused to hand over the keys to the armory. However at the time of the coup, Unegbe was the Quartermaster-General of the Nigerian army at army headquarters in Lagos. The Quartermaster-General is the officer

---

1 Schwartz, *Nigeria*, page 194.

2 This house is now known as Flagstaff House and is the official residence of the head of the Nigerian army.

3 David Ejoor, *Reminiscences*, page 23.

4 Lt-Colonel Ejoor met with Aguiyi-Ironsi a few hours later and confirmed that Aguiyi-Ironsi informed him that he was telephoned by both Pam and staff at the Prime Minister's residence. Ibid page 25.

responsible for procurement and army supplies such as uniforms, boots and helmets. Not being in command of a combat unit, Unegbe had no access to any armory keys. As soldiers, the Majors would have known this. Also, the fact that Unegbe was *shot* at his house demonstrates that the Majors were already armed when they got to him. Unegbe's home would also be a very odd place to obtain armory keys, as soldiers are not in the habit of storing them under their pillows when they go to bed at night. It seems incoherent that the Majors would apprehend Unegbe at his house in order to obtain the keys for an armory they had already accessed. Additionally, the mutineers in other units outside Lagos managed to get access to weapons without resorting to killing the respective quartermasters of their various units. What is more probable is that Unegbe was killed because he was known to be close to Brigadier Maimalari and was not interested in a coup.

After the telephone calls he had received from the residences of the Prime Minister and Lt-Colonel Pam, Aguiyi-Ironsi instructed his guards not to let anyone in (Lance Corporal Clement Abayilo was the second in command of Aguiyi-Ironsi's guards that night), left home, and headed for the Federal Guard barracks (which was in the same neighborhood, in Ikoyi). The guards said Aguiyi-Ironsi left home shortly after 3:00 a.m. When he arrived, he put the Federal Guard soldiers on alert, told them to be battle ready and instructed the Regimental Sergeant Major (RSM), RSM Tayo not to take orders from any officer other than him. He told RSM Tayo to refuse orders from even his own commanding officer Major Okafor. The officers in the Federal Guards at that time included Lieutenant Paul Tarfa[1] and Captain Joseph Garba. However, at the time Garba was out of the country serving as a member of the United Nations Military Observer Mission in India/Pakistan. He was to play a prominent role in subsequent coups and became a Nigerian diplomat. Aguiyi-Ironsi was beginning to cause problems for the Majors. When Major Okafor re-appeared at the Federal Guard barracks, he discovered that his men were now hostile, having been turned against him on Aguiyi-Ironsi's orders. Okafor complained to his fellow plotter Major Ademoyega:

> I just spoke to my RSM just now, and he nearly shot me. He said the GOC had been to the barracks.... He [Aguiyi-Ironsi] commanded the troops not to take any orders from me, and none of them would obey me now. In fact they were ready to shoot me.[2]

3:30 a.m.

Sometime between 3:20 a.m. and 4:00 a.m. Aguiyi-Ironsi was seen driving his Jaguar staff car (easily recognizable with its official "NA1" GOC license plates) to the police headquarters at Lion Building in Obalende, Lagos. Unbeknownst to Aguiyi-Ironsi, Major Ademoyega had been at Lion Building and departed only minutes earlier.

Aguiyi-Ironsi entered the lobby with his pistol drawn and saw two soldiers[3] (the soldiers had been posted there by Major Ademoyega). When the soldiers could not give him a satisfactory explanation as to what they were doing there, he ordered them to return to their barracks immediately and informed them that he was going to rouse the 2nd battalion to attack some soldiers who were "engaged on unlawful opera-

---

1 Later became commander of the Federal Guards.
2 Ademoyega *Why We Struck*, pages 74-75.
3 Corporal D. Ohazuruike and Corporal S. Esonu.

tions in Lagos."[1] On his way Aguiyi-Ironsi came across a checkpoint on Carter Bridge manned by the plotters under an armed Captain Ogbo Oji (who, like Aguiyi-Ironsi, was from Umuahia). Aguiyi-Ironsi was told to put his hands up, but instead roared, "Get out of my way!"[2] Aguiyi-Ironsi managed to face down the men at the checkpoint and continued his journey. He even managed to bully them into saluting him before he left. The young officers at the checkpoint lost their nerve when confronted by the intimidating presence of their GOC (whom they probably were astonished to see still alive).

For the third time in the space of two hours Aguiyi-Ironsi emerged unscathed from the clutches of the coup plotters. First, he was absent when Major Okafor's original hit squad came for him at his house. He then came across a different section of the plotters in the police headquarters at Lion Building, and came eyeball to eyeball with Captain Oji, but was lucky for a third time and managed to escape to rouse the Federal Guards and 2nd battalion for a counter-attack against the Majors. Some accounts also claim that at some point during the night Aguiyi-Ironsi went to, or at the very least tried to reach, the Prime Minister's residence, having been informed of his abduction.

2nd Battalion, Ikeja, Lagos

Next, Aguiyi-Ironsi drove to the 2nd battalion headquarters at Ikeja. Once again he bypassed the officers and turned to the unit's RSM. He ordered the RSM Garuba Mohammed to tell all officers to report. A bugler alarm was rung to alert the officers. The battalion's command was convoluted due to its being in transition from Lt-Colonel Hilary Njoku to Lt-Colonel Gowon. Njoku had been in command of the battalion for three years, headed it when it was originally stationed in Abeokuta, and remained in charge when it was moved to Ikeja. Contrary to claims elsewhere that Njoku refused to vacate his command in favor of Gowon, or that the handover was delayed to ensure the presence of an Igbo commander during the coup, Njoku later revealed that it was Brigadier Maimalari who ordered a slight delay in the handover, against his own personal desire to immediately hand over to Gowon.[3] Aguiyi-Ironsi telephoned Njoku and explained that some soldiers had taken up arms against the government. Despite his longstanding command and association with Aguiyi-Ironsi, Njoku was suddenly no longer trusted. Aguiyi-Ironsi asked Njoku, "Are you with us or against us?" and ordered him to immediately report to 2nd battalion headquarters if he was still loyal. When Njoku arrived and approached Aguiyi-Ironsi, the apprehensive Aguiyi-Ironsi drew his pistol and warned Njoku to keep his distance. Having assured Aguiyi-Ironsi of his loyalty, Njoku telephoned the battalion's Adjutant Major Martin Adamu and told him to report to headquarters.

With Maimalari, Kur, Largema and Pam all dead, Lt-Colonel Gowon was now the most senior surviving Northern officer in the Nigerian army. Gowon was staying at the barracks, having just returned from a course in England and was woken by the commotion as the GOC was rousing the officers. He joined Aguiyi-Ironsi and Njoku to plan a counter-attack against the Majors. The 2nd battalion became a beehive of activity as more and more officers showed up (including Lt-Colonel Kurubo). Kurubo was the battalion commander in Kaduna, the city where Nzeogwu had just struck.

---

1 Special Branch report.
2 Forsyth, *The Biafra Story*, page 40
3 Njoku, *A Tragedy Without Heroes*, page 21.

Very conveniently he suddenly travelled to Lagos on the eve of the coup and was out of harm's way when Nzeogwu struck. This suggests that the plot might have leaked to a wider circle of officers than first thought.

However, as the most senior officers, Aguiyi-Ironsi, Njoku and Gowon took charge. According to Njoku, the agitated Aguiyi-Ironsi continually muttered his dis- approval of the Majors' adventurism, repeatedly exclaiming "These boys! These boys!" Njoku observed that: "In all my association with him, it was the first time I saw him frightened and shaky."[1] When Aguiyi-Ironsi regained his composure, he gave orders for the arrest of Major Ifeajuna, Captain Oji and Lieutenant Wokocha.[2] He also or- dered that if arrest was not possible, they should be shot. It is not clear how Aguiyi- Ironsi knew that these men were among the mutineers. He may have been alerted to Chukwuka's involvement by the earlier telephone call he received from Lt-Colonel Pam's wife. Aguiyi-Ironsi was likely alerted to Ifeajuna's involvement by the distress call he received from the Prime Minister's residence. He might have been made aware of Okafor's involvement by his guards, who turned Okafor away earlier in the night when Okafor came to arrest him. Alternatively, he could have been tipped off by someone who knew of the plot.

Back to the Federal Guard Barracks — Lagos

At the Federal Guard officers' mess the plotters under Majors Ifeajuna, Ademoye- ga, Anuforo, Chukwuka and Okafor met as pre-arranged with their captives in tow: the Prime Minister, the Finance Minister, Colonel Kur Mohammed and Lt-Colonel Pam. When Chukwuka arrived with Pam, Major Anuforo scolded him for bringing Pam to the mess alive. Chukwuka argued that he was not prepared to spill any blood, and that he had promised Pam's wife that her husband would not come to any harm.[3] All bar one of the plotters' key targets in Lagos were either under arrest or dead. Piv- otally, Major-General Aguiyi-Ironsi had eluded his would be captors and was not among the captives brought to the Federal Guard officers mess. When asked by his colleagues where Aguiyi-Ironsi was, Major Okafor complained: "I went to his house to arrest him. I found that he was not there. . . . He had been to another party after Maimalari's party."[4] Major Ademoyega confirmed the situation that confronted the Majors as follows:

> (Major) Okafor came along with his bad news that General Ironsi had not been found at home when he went there. He was said to have gone to another party after Maimalari's. But he had since resurfaced at the Dodan Barracks and suc- ceeded in raising troops against us. . . . After that, he was said to have driven to the 2nd Battalion barracks at Ikeja to raise more troops against us. . . . The news of Ironsi's escape came as a shock to all of us.[5]

The Majors left the Federal Guard barracks in a convoy, taking their captives with them. At a point on the way Pam was told to step out of the vehicle. When he left the vehicle he was shot dead by Major Chris Anuforo. Anuforo and Pam had served together less than two years earlier during the army's operations to quell the Tiv uprising and were also colleagues working together at army headquarters in Lagos.

---

1 Ibid., page 20.

2 Ibid., page 19, and Barrett, *Danjuma: The Making of a General*.

3 See transcript of statement by Lieutenant Godwin Onyefuru in Njoku, *A Tragedy Without Heroes*, p. 180

4 Ademoyega *Why We Struck*, page 75.

5 Ibid., page 75.

Pam's then baby boy Yusuf is today a lawyer, and later became the Commissioner of Justice and Attorney General of Plateau State. He made an unsuccessful attempt to become the Peoples Democratic Party (PDP) governorship candidate in Plateau state in 2007 but lost to Jonah Jang (a former air force officer) in the PDP's primaries. One of Lt-Colonel Pam's other children is Dr. Ishaya Pam — the Chief Medical Director of the University of Jos Teaching Hospital. Ishaya and Yusuf's older sister is a High Court Judge.

Of the plotters, Anuforo was the most ruthless in the use of his firearm on the night of January 15. According to the Special Branch report, Anuforo personally shot dead Lt-Colonels Pam and Unegbe, Colonel Kur Mohammed and the Finance Minister Chief Festus Okotie-Eboh.

2 Brigade Headquarters, Apapa — Lagos

By early morning on Saturday 15, news that something untoward had occurred overnight spread to other army units including the 2 brigade headquarters in Apapa, Lagos. The officers at brigade headquarters included Majors Murtala Muhammed, Christian Ude, John Kweti (a Togolese officer), and Captains T.Y. Danjuma, Ahmadu Yakubu, and Musa Usman of the air force. Even some officers who were not supposed to be in Lagos and who were not members of Lagos military formations suddenly showed up there. These included Major Mobolaji Johnson and Lt-Colonel Fajuyi. Some angry officers who were impatient for more information decided to conduct their own investigation into what was going on. They arrested and interrogated soldiers who were not in the barracks when news of the coup broke. The leading figures behind these interrogations at Apapa included Majors Murtala Muhammed, Martin Adamu and Captain Yakubu Danjuma. At one point an enraged Muhammed cocked his pistol and interrogated the detained men at gunpoint. Major Ude tried in vain to restrain Murtala. Some of the detainees were beaten up badly and confessions were extracted from them. A similar exercise was simultaneously being conducted at the 2nd battalion headquarters in Ikeja by Majors Henry Igboba, Provost Marshal Ibanga Ekanem and Captain Godwin Ugoala. The detainees (including Lieutenant Godwin Onyefuru) gave the names of the officers who ordered them out on an "internal security operation." The detainees were released from their angry captors into official custody only after persuasion from Lt-Colonel Gowon. The commander of the 2nd reconnaissance squadron at Abeokuta Major John Obienu was one of those that showed up late to the 2nd battalion on the morning of January 15. Major Igboba wanted to arrest him but was restrained from doing so. Obienu pacified his squadron and they joined the anti-coup officers under Aguiyi-Ironsi.

At this point, the idea of forming a military government was not being discussed and the focus was on suppressing the revolt. Armed with orders from Aguiyi-Ironsi, soldiers from the 2nd battalion (including units commanded by Lt-Colonel Gowon and Major Hans Anogho) mobilized loyal troops to re-capture key installations. The anti-coup soldiers fanned out into Lagos to secure key location including the Parliament building, Prime Minister's residence, Post & Telecommunications building and NBC building. The soldiers were ordered not to allow anyone in or to allow any broadcasts without authorization from Aguiyi-Ironsi or Gowon. The counter-attack did not go through without incident. Firstly Lieutenant William Walbe (one of the officers dispatched by Aguiyi-Ironsi to counter the mutiny) was mistakenly arrested by another group of soldiers on the same mission. Walbe was released on the orders of his Angas kinsman Lt-Colonel Gowon. Two soldiers (one southern, the other

Northern) under the command of Major Anogho, who had been sent to counter-at-
tack the plotters, did not see eye to eye and the Northerner Second-Lieutenant Tijani
Katsina ended up settling the argument by shooting his colleague Second-Lieutenant
James Odu dead.[1]

Back to Abeokuta — Western Region

When the plotters in Lagos realized that the "GOC was in town," still alive and
mobilizing troops to counter-attack them, some of them began to flee. Those brave
enough to return to metropolitan Lagos found that the troops they had posted to
strategic locations had either been dismissed, arrested or replaced with new troops
loyal to Aguiyi-Ironsi and with orders to hunt down the Majors. When the Lagos
plotters began assembling at their pre-arranged rendezvous point at the Federal
Guard barracks, they found it under the control of hostile troops that had been
briefed by Aguiyi-Ironsi and told to ignore their orders. The soldiers posted at the
P & T telephone exchange and the Nigerian External Communications building by
Major Ademoyega faithfully remained in their positions until the following morning
when, worried that Major Ademoyega had not returned, they departed and made
their way back to their units. They were arrested when they returned to their units.
By the following morning many of the Lagos coup plotters in Lagos had either been
driven out from Lagos or arrested.

Enugu and Benin — Eastern Region and Mid-West Region

Contrary to popular myth, a coup was attempted in Enugu and Benin. Overnight
Major Ifeajuna sent orders to the 1st battalion in Enugu asking them to deploy soldiers
to take over key installations and arrest government ministers in Enugu and Benin.
As there was no military formation in the Mid-West Region, no soldiers could be
deployed directly from the region. For several hours the officers in Enugu mulled over
the strange but seemingly legitimate order. Finally they took position at the Enugu
airport in the early hours of the morning. A different company of soldiers under Captain Joseph Ihedigbo also headed to the Mid-West Region's capital of Benin.[2] The
Igbo Premier of the region Dennis Osadebay was placed under house arrest. Com-
mentators have subsequently speculated that the life of the Eastern Region's Premier Dr. Michael Okpara may have been spared because the head of state of Cyprus,
Archbishop Makarios, was his guest at the time of the coup. A more plausible reason
for Okpara's survival is that the officer assigned to arrest him (Lieutenant Oguchi)
was one of those who advocated a bloodless coup.[3] As soon as Makarios departed to
return to Cyprus, Okpara was arrested.

In Enugu, a radio broadcast was interrupted as armed soldiers burst into the
broadcasting room live on air, and bemused listeners heard the terrified broadcaster
announce in real time that he was being surrounded by armed soldiers who were
ordering him to stop his normal broadcast. Some easterners feared that the federal
government had launched a military crackdown on the Eastern Region. The 1st battalion's new commander Lt-Colonel Ejoor was in Lagos when the coup occurred. When
he first reported to Aguiyi-Ironsi in Lagos, Aguiyi-Ironsi could not determine which

---

1 See account of Major Anogho in Iloegbunam, *Ironside*, page 8.
2 Ejoor, *Reminiscences*.
3 Gbulie, *Nigeria's Five Majors*, page 136.

of his men he could trust and which officers were for or against the coup. Clutching a pistol Aguiyi-Ironsi asked Ejoor, "David, are you with me or against me?"[1] Having tactfully assured Aguiyi-Ironsi of his loyalty, Ejoor was ordered to fly to Enugu and take charge of the 1st battalion there. Ejoor arrived just before midday on January 15 with Lieutenants Yohanna Kure[2] and Agada. Ejoor had previously been serving as the GSO(I) at army headquarters in Lagos. He was succeeded as GSO(I) by Major Patrick Anwunah.

Quickly taking control of the 1st battalion from Major Okonweze, Ejoor ordered the soldiers who had departed for various installations on Major Ifeajuna's orders to return to barracks. A separate group of troops under Lieutenant Kure was ordered to intercept any attempt to release Awolowo from prison. Ejoor also ordered the battalion's Adjutant, Lieutenant S.M. Yar'Adua to arrest Lieutenant Aloysius Akpuaka — the officer who relayed Ifeajuna's orders to the battalion.[3] By late night on the 15th, the unit under Captain Ihedigbo that travelled to Benin had returned to base in Enugu.

Kano — Northern Region

Although he may have wanted an end to the NPC government, the commanding officer of the 5th battalion in Kano Lt-Colonel Ojukwu was not playing ball with the Majors. He was at the parade ground when he received a telegram informing him of the coup. Ojukwu disarmed his soldiers, locked the armory, and sent the armory keys to a relative in Kano for safekeeping before he dared to share the news with his men. Ojukwu briefed his friend the Emir of Kano Alhaji Ado Bayero of events, and the two men rode together in the same car through the streets of Kano and made a radio appeal for calm in orchestrated acts of solidarity. Ojukwu took Bayero to the battalion for his protection. Ojukwu also received "orders" from 1 brigade in Kaduna, purportedly from Brigadier Ademulegun. Ojukwu was not fooled and ignored the "orders." When Nzeogwu came out into the open and later asked Ojukwu to release funds for his soldiers to be paid, Ojukwu refused. One of Nzeogwu's aides, Captain Ude, was dispatched to Kano, but was arrested on Ojukwu's orders when he arrived.

Back to Kaduna — Northern Region

In Kaduna, Major Nzeogwu was in full control and was facing none of the problems encountered by his co-conspirators in the south. In the early afternoon of January 15, 1966, Nzeogwu made a radio broadcast declaring martial law over the Northern Region. Nzeogwu declared that the aim of the revolution was "to establish a strong, united and prosperous nation free from corruption and internal strife." In that broadcast he uttered the following spine-chilling words which have acquired near legendary status in Nigeria:

> Our enemies are the political profiteers, the swindlers, the men in high and low places that seek bribes and demand 10 percent; those that seek to keep the country divided permanently so that they can remain in office as ministers or VIPs at least, the tribalists, the nepotists, those that make the country look big for nothing before international circles, those that have corrupted our society and put the Nigerian political calendar back by their words and deeds.

---

1 Ejoor, *Reminiscences*, page 25.
2 Kure later became a member of a coup tribunal in 1985.
3 *New Soja* magazine, 2nd edition, 2005.

Chapter 5. From Civilian to Military Rule: History in the Making

Reaction to the Coup

Coincidentally, the army's last British GOC Major-General Welby-Everard was on a return visit to Nigeria when the coup occurred. He returned to the UK at short notice. Within the army (outside the circle of plotters) many soldiers initially thought that the disturbances were either an internal army mutiny or an extension of the political troubles between the government and opposition parties. Until bullet riddled bodies and bloodstains were discovered, many thought that the attacks on soldiers may have been acts of political sabotage by thugs and agents of political parties who had unwisely bitten off more than they could chew. Residents of Lagos woke up to find that their phone lines were not working and that their electricity had been cut. When they found out the reason for these outages, they were ecstatic. Once it became clear that what had occurred was a military coup, public opinion welcomed it with jubilation.

Saturday January 15, 1966

Of over 300 parliamentarians, fewer than 40 felt brave (or were foolhardy) enough to show up for work following the coup. They were met by stern looking soldiers and dispersed before long, as they did not have a quorum. The terrified surviving NPC and NCNC ministers met separately. The NPC ministers met at the house of the Kanuri Transport Minister Zanna Bukar Dipcharima (who was now the most senior NPC minister in the absence of Balewa and the Sardauna) at 1B Bourdillon Road in Ikoyi, while NCNC ministers met at the home of the Minister of Trade Dr. Kingsley Mbadiwe (who had met with the Prime Minister only a few hours before he was kidnapped). Mbadiwe returned to the Prime Minister's residence on Saturday morning and was seen weeping after being informed that the Prime Minister had been kidnapped and was still missing.

9–10 a.m., 2nd Battalion Headquarters, Ikeja — Lagos

On Saturday morning senior police officers including the acting Inspector-General of police Kam Selem and two British expatriate police officers Leslie Marsden and Commissioner of Police, Force Headquarters M.V. Jones arrived at the 2nd battalion headquarters in Ikeja. They asked for, and Aguiyi-Ironsi granted them permission to reconnect the telephone lines which had been severed. They also informed Aguiyi-Ironsi that the Minister of State (Army) Alhaji Tako Galadima, wanted to see him at the police headquarters.

Police Headquarters, Moloney Street, Obalende — Lagos

At the police headquarters Aguiyi-Ironsi found not just Galadima but a virtual war cabinet including several security officials such as the acting Inspector-General of Police Alhaji Kam Selem, Theophilus Fagbola of the police Special Branch, Marsden, the military attaches of the UK and the US Messrs Berger and Hunt, Lagos Commissioner of Police Hamman Maiduguri, the senior defense civil servant Alhaji Ahmadu Kurfi, and other Special Branch police officers.

When the Prime Minister's domestic staff alerted the police that the Prime Minister had been abducted, Selem and Maiduguri relayed the information to Kurfi. More bad news followed for Kurfi when he discovered that Maimalari, Kur, Pam and Largema had all been murdered overnight. He had attended Government College, Zaria, with all four of them. On arrival Aguiyi-Ironsi was at first treated with suspicion by some of the Northerners who thought that he might have been an accomplice to the coup. However, while he was talking to them, news of the Sardauna's murder arrived, and the suspicion of Aguiyi-Ironsi eased when he wept on hearing the news and explained that, as the crisis unfolded, he did not know which of his officers to trust.

Midday

The shaken surviving members of the Council of Ministers tried to call an ad-hoc cabinet meeting inside the police headquarters. Most of the cabinet ministers were too afraid to attend. In the end they managed to muster a threadbare "cabinet meeting" in the police headquarters attended by Galadima, Dipcharima, Shehu Shagari (Minister of Works), Stanley Wey (the Prime Minister's Secretary), Maitama Sule (Minister of Mines and Power), Taslim Elias (Attorney-General), Nuhu Bamali (Foreign Minister), Chief H.O. Davies (Minister of State, Industries), Chief Abiodun Akerele (Minister of State, Information), and Mbadiwe. Aguiyi-Ironsi, the British High Commissioner Sir Francis Cumming-Bruce, and Marsden were also in attendance.

The ministers gave Aguiyi-Ironsi written orders to locate the Prime Minister and suppress the rebellion. The order was signed by Galadima in his role as acting Minister of Defense (in the absence of the substantive Minister of Defense Inuwa Wada). Aguiyi-Ironsi was also told to protect the Parliament building as the ministers feared that it might be destroyed by the coup plotters. Aguiyi-Ironsi and the NPC ministers asked for British military assistance to suppress the rebellion. The British were willing to assist but insisted that the request must be submitted in writing by the Prime Minister. With the Prime Minister missing there was no one who could submit the request in writing to the UK. Therefore the NPC ministers travelled to the home of the Igbo acting Senate President Dr. Nwafor Orizu and asked him to appoint Dip-charima as acting Prime Minister. While the NPC ministers were at Orizu's house, Major-General Aguiyi-Ironsi showed up. He spoke to Orizu and to Dipcharima, and reiterated the need to appoint an acting Prime Minister that could issue orders to the army. The 1964 crisis and standoff between President Azikiwe and Prime Minister Balewa had taught him that only the Prime Minister could issue valid orders to the army. Orizu informed the other ministers that he was unable to appoint an acting Prime Minister at that time as he wanted to confer with NCNC members to ascertain whether they would support Dipcharima's appointment. He advised the ministers to return to their homes and await an update from him.

Ademoyega and Anuforo on the Loose

Meanwhile Majors Ademoyega and Anuforo were still on the loose and seeking a way to scheme their way past the loyal troops now guarding key points in Lagos. Due to Major Obienu's failure to show up at the rendezvous point with them, they decided to head for Obienu's headquarters in Abeokuta to check for him. Before they could do so they had to get rid of the cargo of corpses they were carrying in their vehicles. The captive Finance Minister Okotie-Eboh was also with them and still alive. They drove out of Lagos in a convoy towards Abeokuta. Assistant Superintendent of Police Ibrahim Ahmed Babankowa was manning a police checkpoint in Sango Otta when their convoy passed him. The convoy did not arouse Babankowa's suspicions as he presumed that the soldiers were engaged on an internal security operation in an effort to calm the lawlessness in the Western Region. A few kilometers after Babankowa's checkpoint, the convoy stopped and the corpses were dumped in the bush. According to the Special Branch report, Okotie-Eboh was then asked to step down from the vehicle he was in by Major Anuforo, led into the bush by Majors Anuforo and Ademoyega, and shot dead by Anuforo. It seems that the murder of Okotie-Eboh and Balewa may have been afterthoughts and not part of the original plan.

Majors Ademoyega and Anuforo then headed to the 2nd Recce squadron in Abeokuta to look for Obienu. When they arrived, Obienu was nowhere to be found. Anuforo was the former commander of the 2nd Recce squadron and he was personally acquainted with many men in the unit. He used his familiarity with the unit to commandeer armored vehicles and headed back toward Lagos along with a few junior officers including Lieutenants Pam Mwadkon and Kasaba. These young officers did not know Ademoyega and Anuforo's real mission. As the convoy of vehicles stopped to refuel, the young officers overheard the following radio announcement on behalf of the Council of Ministers:

> In the early hours of this morning, 15 January 1966, a dissident section of the Nigerian army kidnapped the Prime Minister and the Minister of Finance and took them to an unknown destination. The General Officer Commanding the Nigerian army and the vast majority of the Nigerian army remain completely loyal to the Federal Government and are already taking all appropriate measures to bring the situation under control. All essential public services continue to function normally. The Federal Government is satisfied that the situation will soon return to normal and that the ill-advised mutiny will be brought to an end and that law and order in the few disturbed areas of the country will soon be restored. All public buildings and establishments in the federal territory are being guarded by loyal troops.

Upon hearing the announcement, Lieutenant Mwadkon realized that he was in the company of the mutineers and immediately turned his armored vehicle around and drove off. He was pursued by Anuforo but Anuforo stood down when Mwadkon pointed a gun at him and threatened to shoot if he did not back off. The experience of being duped severely embittered Mwadkon and would come back to haunt the Majors six months later. The loss of the armored vehicles was the final nail in the coffin for the Lagos coup.

SATURDAY JANUARY 15–SUNDAY JANUARY 16, 1966

The surviving senior military officers scheduled an emergency meeting at the police headquarters. The author has not been able to confirm the exact time of this meeting but it took place sometime between Saturday evening/night and early afternoon on Sunday.[1] According to Lt-Colonel Njoku the meeting was attended by Major-General Aguiyi-Ironsi, Commodore Wey, Lt-Colonels Banjo, Fajuyi, Gowon, Kurubo and Njoku, and Major Anwunah.[2]

At this stage further unrest could potentially have emerged from two sources in the restive army. Firstly some over-zealous junior soldiers who did not quite understand their role sought to extract their own "entitlements" as members of the army by setting up impromptu roadblocks, harassing civilians and looting. They had to be brought to heel and sent back to the barracks with the help of officers including Lieutenants Ibrahim Babangida and Garba Duba. The second problem was that Major Nzeogwu remained in control of the Northern Region and was threatening to march south to complete the job. Nzeogwu compelled air force officers including Captain John Yisa Doko and Second-Lieutenant Godfrey Ikechukwu Amuchienwa to conduct reconnaissance flights from the air force base in Kaduna to other Northern cities such as Jebba, Jos, Kano, and Makurdi.

Aguiyi-Ironsi faced a stark choice. If the status quo under civilian rule was restored, another coup could occur within hours or days. A further coup could come from either within the original circle of conspirators or from the Majors' other sympathizers who were lurking. There were other officers outside the immediate coup circle who shared the Majors' wish to be rid of the government (though they may not have approved of the Majors' violent *modus operandi*). These included Lt-Colonels Fajuyi, Banjo, Ojukwu and Njoku, and Major Madiebo. Several other junior officers may have also been motivated to emulate the Majors by staging their own coup. In the view of officers attending the meeting, these circumstances were not conducive to the continuation of civilian rule. Against this backdrop, many officers advocated that the army should take over the government. This, they argued, was the only way to avoid further bloodshed and a violent confrontation with Nzeogwu, as no one could be sure whether the troops would remain loyal to the government. Lt-Colonel Banjo was one of those in favor of a military takeover. In a subsequent letter to Aguiyi-Ironsi, Banjo claimed he told Aguiyi-Ironsi:

> I had spent a considerable time with you [Aguiyi-Ironsi] in the attempt to persuade you that in order to save Nigeria from the awful event of a civil war the

---

1 According to Lt-Colonel Njoku, the meeting took place on the evening of Saturday January 15 (see *A Tragedy Without Heroes, page 25*). Lt-Colonel Banjo's recollection was that the meeting occurred at midday on Sunday January 16 (see letter from Banjo to Aguiyi-Ironsi dated June 1, 1966 as reproduced in *A Break in the Silence: Lt-Colonel Victor Adebukunola Banjo* by Ogunsheye, F. Adetowun).

2 Njoku, *A Tragedy Without Heroes*, page 25.

army should take over government under yourself. . . . I had by word and deed rallied support for yourself [Aguiyi-Ironsi] and a military take-over of government among a large number of officers all over Nigeria. . . . I was present at the meeting of senior officers of the army with yourself at noon on Sunday 16th January at which I spoke first and spoke for a military government under yourself.

Banjo's account is corroborated by Lt-Colonel Njoku, who also attended that meeting. According to Njoku:

> Victor Banjo said that he was in touch with Kaduna and some of the boys. He was very emphatic that the cabinet then headed by Zana Bukar Dipcharima capitulated [*sic*] to the army."[1]

Njoku also advocated a military takeover of the government. He told Aguiyi-Ironsi:

> We must stop the confusion and suspicion and get together and salvage the nation. The only course open to the House of Representatives and the Senate was to interpret their letter to the GOC[2] into the language both the army and the politicians understood and save the country, i.e. through constitutional transfer of political power to the Army to restore law and order.[3]

Commodore Wey gave his views on which officers should be appointed to the military government.[4]

SUNDAY EVENING, JANUARY 16, 1966, CABINET OFFICE — LAGOS

On Sunday, January 16, the surviving members of the shaken Council of Ministers were asked to report to the cabinet office for another emergency meeting at 6:30 p.m. When the NPC ministers arrived, they found the GOC Major-General Aguiyi-Ironsi already sitting with Dipcharima and the acting Minister of Defense, Ibrahim Tako Galadima. The NCNC ministers initially refused to attend for fear of their safety. The NPC's legal adviser and Minister for Railways Alhaji Abdulrazaq asked Aguiyi-Ironsi to delay starting the meeting until the NCNC ministers arrived. Abdulrazaq[5] did not want it to appear as if the NPC had sidelined their junior coalition partners by meeting with Aguiyi-Ironsi without them. Aguiyi-Ironsi dispatched his ADC to collect the NCNC ministers, while the already present ministers tensely waited.

Eventually a dishevelled Mbadiwe was brought to the cabinet office by armed troops along with the other NCNC ministers. A total of seventeen ministers from the coalition cabinet were brave enough to show up for the meeting (including Dipcharima, Mbadiwe, Galadima, Shehu Shagari, Abdulrazaq, Taslim Elias, Nuhu Bamali, Ali Monguno, and Minister of Education Richard Akinjide). The Prime Minister was still missing and his chair was left empty as a mark of respect. The head of the navy, Commodore Joseph Wey, and the acting Inspector-General of Police, Alhaji Kam Selem, were also present. The mood was very different from the cabinet meeting the previous day at police headquarters. On this occasion it was Aguiyi-Ironsi issuing instructions. He briefed the ministers on the cataclysmic events that had just occurred and told them that the army was pressing him to take power. An irritated Aguiyi-

---

1 Ibid., page 26.

2 This is a reference to the written orders given to Aguiyi-Ironsi earlier by the surviving cabinet ministers.

3 Njoku, *A Tragedy Without Heroes*, page 26.

4 Confirmed by Commodore Wey during meeting of Nigeria's military leaders at Aburi in Ghana in January 1967.

5 Abdulrazaq was the first Northerner to qualify as a lawyer.

Ironsi criticized the ministers for their army recruitment policy, which he claimed forced politically radical university graduates on him. Aguiyi-Ironsi felt that such officers were not real soldiers and were more interested in politics than they were with soldiering.[1] Some of the Northern politicians present vouched that Aguiyi-Ironsi seemed genuinely upset by, and wept at, the death of his military colleagues. Among those present at the historic meeting was Shehu Shagari, who was then the Minister of Works and later became Nigeria's President. He described events as follows:

> Major-General Ironsi admitted to us that he had been unable to suppress the rebellion, which he said was getting out of hand. He stated that the mutineers were in control of Kaduna, Kano and Ibadan, and had killed two regional premiers, Sir Ahmadu Bello and Chief Akintola. They had also murdered a number of his best officers, including Brigadiers Maimalari and Samuel Adesujo Ademulegun, the Commander 1st Brigade Headquarters in Kaduna. Ironsi was full of emotion and even shed some tears. When we asked him about the whereabouts of Sir Abubakar and Chief Okotie-Eboh, he said he still did not know but averred efforts were being made to locate them. At this stage, Mbadiwe broke down and kept crying, "Please, where is the Prime Minister?" When we reminded Major-General Ironsi if he needed to avail himself of the British pledge of assistance, he replied it was too late as the army was pressing him [Ironsi] to assume power. Indeed, he confessed his personal reluctance to take over because of his ignorance of government; but insisted the boys were adamant and waiting outside. He advised it would be in our own interest, and that of the country, to temporarily cede power to him to avert disaster. Accordingly, we acceded to his request since we had no better alternative. Ironsi then insisted that the understanding be written.[2]

Shagari's account was corroborated by Abdulrazaq, who took notes as Aguiyi-Ironsi spoke. Abdulrazaq recalled that "I was the only one who took notes at that meeting. He [Ironsi] told us that Major Nzeogwu had taken over power and threatened that if we didn't cooperate with them they would kill all of us."[3]

At this tense meeting, the Council of Ministers agreed to abdicate power to the armed forces. The politicians were in such a state of disarray that the handover statement was scribbled on a piece of paper by Abdulrazaq. The statement in manuscript was endorsed by the other ministers. The ministers agreed to later have the statement typed. The statement which was eventually signed by Dipcharima and Mbadiwe read as follows:

> The council of ministers, meeting on 16th January 1966, have asked us to convey to you their unanimous decision to transfer voluntarily the government to the armed forces of the republic and wish the armed forces success to bring about peace and stability in Nigeria, and that the welfare of our people shall be their paramount task.[4]

A New Political Order

Ten minutes before midnight on Sunday, January 16, 1966, the acting President, Dr. Nwafor Orizu, made a nationwide broadcast stating that:

---

1 See next chapter. Aguiyi-Ironsi also separately complained that he "asked for soldiers" but was instead "given politicians dressed in uniform."

2 Shehu Shagari, *Beckoned to Serve*, page 118.

3 *This Day*, November 12, 2007.

4 Kingsley Mbadiwe, *Rebirth of a Nation*, page 186.

I have tonight been advised by the council of ministers that they had come to the unanimous decision voluntarily to hand over administration of the country to the armed forces of the republic with immediate effect. All ministers are assured of their personal safety by the new administration. I will now call upon the General Officer Commanding the Nigerian army, Major-General Aguiyi-Ironsi to make a statement to the nation on the policy of the new administration. It is my fervent hope that the new administration will ensure the peace and stability of the Federal Republic of Nigeria and that all citizens will give them their full cooperation.[1]

Shortly afterward and on behalf of the military, Aguiyi-Ironsi accepted this offer:

The government of the federation of Nigeria having ceased to function, the Nigerian armed forces have been invited to form an interim military government for the purposes of maintaining law and order, and of maintaining essential services. This invitation has been accepted, and I, General J.T.U. Aguiyi-Ironsi, the General Officer Commanding the Nigerian army, have been formally vested with authority as head of the Federal Military Government and Supreme Commander of the Nigerian armed forces.[2]

The full text of Aguiyi-Ironsi's inaugural broadcast is reproduced in Appendix 2. The bluff and uncomplicated 42-year-old Major-General Johnson Aguiyi-Ironsi accepted the government's "invitation" to take over power and became Head of State and leader of the first military government in Nigeria's history. He was a man with limited educational achievements, but he possessed great courage and had the Anglophile manner of a British drill sergeant. His new job would require not just courage but a deft touch and a great deal of mental dexterity. As well as becoming Head of State, Aguiyi-Ironsi was elevated from army GOC to "Supreme Commander" of the Nigerian armed forces and was now in overall command of all armed forces services: the army, air force, navy and police. Aguiyi-Ironsi was no stranger to politically illustrious company. He had served as former Governor-General Sir John Macpherson's first African ADC, and as equerry to Queen Elizabeth II during her visit to Nigeria in 1956. He was sent to Buckingham Palace to learn his duties for the latter assignment. There was considerable myth behind the man, too. Aguiyi-Ironsi carried with him at all times, and used as a swagger stick, a stuffed crocodile mascot called "Charlie" which also acquired mythological status. Apocryphal stories claimed that the crocodile mascot made Aguiyi-Ironsi invulnerable and was used to help him dodge or deflect bullets in the Congo. Perhaps the most famous photograph of Aguiyi-Ironsi was that of him beaming, on the steps of an airplane as he was leaving the UN peacekeeping mission in Congo, waving goodbye while clutching "Charlie." Despite the stories, the crocodile mascot probably had something to do with the fact that the name "Aguiyi" translates into "crocodile" in Igbo. The words of retired Major-General Ike Nwachukwu (then a Second Lieutenant) indicate Aguiyi-Ironsi's stature at the time. Nwachukwu said that the first time he saw Aguiyi-Ironsi "was at a training operation in Kachia, Kaduna State. When the GOC landed, it was like seeing a God. And he was indeed the God of us all soldiers."[3]

There is some confusion regarding Aguiyi-Ironsi's paternal parentage, with some reports erroneously stating that his father was an Igbo from Sierra Leone. A report on him published in *West Africa* magazine stated that his father was a train driver

---

1 Government Notice, No. 147/1966.
2 Federal Ministry of Information Release and Government Notice No. 148/1966.
3 *Tell* Magazine (No.33) August 12, 1996.

stationed at Kano.[1] This was an error mixed in with factual content and was picked up and repeated in other publications such as Miners' *The Nigerian Army*.[2] However, Aguiyi-Ironsi's father Mazi Ezeugo was an Igbo from Umuahia and:

Aguiyi-Ironsi lived in Kano as a young boy.

Aguiyi-Ironsi served in Sierra Leone during his early days in the army.

As a youngster, Aguiyi-Ironsi lived with his older sister Anyamma and her husband Theophilus Johnson — giving strangers the impression that Johnson was his father.

Aguiyi-Ironsi's *brother-in-law* Theophilus Johnson was a Sierra Leone national.

Although the handover from the civilians to the army was presented as a "voluntary" decision of the Council of Ministers, several years later Alhaji Ali Monguno and Alhaji A.G.F. Abdulrazaq of the NPC, and Richard Akinjide of the NNDP subsequently gave the impression that Aguiyi-Ironsi took power from the Council of Ministers by force.

Did Aguiyi-Ironsi coerce the Council of Ministers or did they willingly hand over power to him? The question remains unclear, as it was Akinjide who released an effusive statement on behalf of the NNDP to herald the advent of the military regime and to wish it well. The other members of the Council of Ministers have never articulated this interpretation of events, and neither did Commodore Wey or Kam Selem who accompanied Aguiyi-Ironsi to the fateful handover. The lack of clarity is compounded by the ostensibly consensual wording of both the handover note given by the Council of Ministers to the army and the subsequent broadcast by Orizu. However, it seems that a faction of surviving senior officers had already resolved to take power by the time Aguiyi-Ironsi, Wey and Selem met with the Council of Ministers on the evening of Sunday January 16. If this is true, then perhaps Aguiyi-Ironsi did not meet with the Council of Ministers to *request* power, but to *inform* them of a military takeover — a polite consultation by senior officers with the surviving federal ministers in order to communicate the armed forces' decision to take over the government. Setting aside the conceptual issue as to whether the Council of Ministers had the legal authority to abdicate to the armed forces, the most likely scenario seems to be that the Council of Ministers consented to the handover, but did so because they felt that refusing to hand over was not a genuine option available to them. On Sunday evening, most of the coup plotters were still on the loose and Major Nzeogwu was in control of the Northern Region, having made a spine-chilling broadcast threatening physical punishments against, or elimination of, the corrupt old order. Most ministers were terrified that the plotters or rogue elements in the army would drop by at any moment to eliminate them. The politicians were also intimidated by the presence of armed soldiers at key installations and outside the cabinet office where they were meeting with Aguiyi-Ironsi, Wey and Selem. In these circumstances they would accede to any request by the military, regardless of their genuine feelings.

The position is perhaps best captured by the following passage from a book written by Taslim Elias and Richard Akinjide (two of the ministers that were present at the handover and who later expressed skepticism as to the consensual nature of the handover):

> Those summoned were too frightened and panicky to say "No" to Major-General J.T.U. Aguiyi-Ironsi's firm declaration of intent to take power immediately,

1 *West Africa*, 21 January 1967.
2 Miners, *The Nigerian Army 1956–66*, page 242.

and this amidst the rattle and the whir of military engines in and around the cabinet premises on that awesome night.[1]

However, the "handover" by the Council of Ministers to the armed forces was a legal fiction because the Nigerian constitution did not have any provisions authorizing the government to abdicate its governing responsibilities to the military. Additionally, given that no acting Prime Minister was appointed or presided over the meeting, it is doubtful that the surviving Council of Ministers had convened a valid meeting at which legally binding resolutions could be made. After Aguiyi-Ironsi's broadcast to the entire country proclaiming the new military government, Lt-Colonel Ejoor made a broadcast to the Eastern Region reiterating the same and stating that he would be the military government's representative in the Region. Lt-Colonel Ojukwu made a similar broadcast to the Northern Region and another broadcast was made to the Western Region. Lt-Colonel Ejoor went so far as to meet with Eastern civil servants to introduce himself. The announcements and introductions made to the various regions were confusing as the officers who made them were soon redeployed and assigned to regions other than those to which they had made their announcements.

Meanwhile, Major Nzeogwu was still in control in the Northern Region. However, he was getting no cooperation from Lt-Colonel Ojukwu of the 5th battalion in Kano. Additionally Aguiyi-Ironsi had managed to subdue his colleagues in the south, and Nzeogwu's only choices were either to engage in a confrontation with Aguiyi-Ironsi (which Nzeogwu was likely to lose, as the bulk of the army would obey Aguiyi-Ironsi's orders rather than his) or risk the institution of two rival military governments. Officers in Lagos demanded that he be brought down to Lagos, dead or alive. Before long, Major Nzeogwu found himself isolated, confused and feeling betrayed.

> I am anxious to hand over command to a superior officer, but none has appeared. We have let it be known that we will grant safe conduct to any high ranking officer who wishes to speak to us. We think that some staff officers are not passing on our messages to the Supreme Commander. We wanted to change the government for the benefit of everybody also. We were concerned with what was best for Nigeria. Our action made the Supreme Commander and he should recognize us.[2]

Nzeogwu was however scathing about the performance of his colleagues in the south:

> Both of us in the north[3] did our best but the other three stationed in the south failed because of incompetence and misguided considerations in the eleventh hour. The most senior among them [Major Ifeajuna] was in charge of a whole brigade and had all the excuse and opportunity in the world to mobilize his troops anywhere, anyhow and any time. He did it badly. In Lagos, even allowing for one or two genuine mistakes, the job was badly done. The mid-west was never a big problem. But in the east, our major target, nothing practically was done. . . . He and the others let us down.[4]

Despite Nzeogwu's harsh denunciation of his colleagues, the Majors' coup probably failed because they simply did not have enough men and transport at their disposal to complete their operation of arresting and guarding leading political figures and senior army officers, disrupting communications networks, setting up roadblocks,

1 Elias, Akinjide, *Africa and the Development of International Law*, page 114.
2 *New Nigerian*, 18th January 1966.
3 Nzeogwu and Major Onwuatuegwu.
4 Ejindu, interview with Major Nzeogwu, *Africa and the World*, May 1967.

defending themselves against counter-attacking forces and taking over broadcasting facilities. They did not even have enough military vehicles and some of them resorted to using civilian vehicles. Rather than launch simultaneous attacks on all the targets or assigning one team to each target, the Majors were so undermanned that they had to sequentially move from one target to the next. For example Major Ifeajuna arrested the Prime Minister, then set out for the Ikoyi Hotel, shot Brigadier Maimalari along the way and then later shot Lt-Colonel Largema at the Ikoyi Hotel. This sequential execution is what allowed warning to reach Major-General Aguiyi-Ironsi and enabled him to organize a counter-attack. Additionally the need for secrecy meant that a rehearsal of the coup was not possible. Major Nzeogwu was the only participant who was able to rehearse (under the guise of a military training exercise). The failure of Major Okafor to accomplish any of the tasks allotted to him was also crucial in the coup's failure. He failed to arrest either Major-General Aguiyi-Ironsi or Brigadier Maimalari (who was later shot when he inadvertently ran into a separate group of the plotters under Major Ifeajuna).

After a few days of negotiations, during which Aguiyi-Ironsi used Nzeogwu's friends such as Majors Madiebo and Obasanjo, and Lt-Colonel Nwawo, as intermediaries, Nzeogwu agreed to submit to the authority of Aguiyi-Ironsi. Nzeogwu explained his decision as follows:

> I was being sensible. The last thing we desired was unnecessary waste of life. If I had stuck to my guns there would have been a civil war, and as the official head of the army, he would have split the loyalty of my men. Again you must remember that the British and other foreigners were standing by to help him. Our purpose was to change the country and make it a place we could be proud to call our home, not to wage war.[1]

On January 17, 1966, wearing his trademark white scarf, Major Nzeogwu appeared for a joint press conference and handed over control of the Northern Region to Aguiyi-Ironsi's appointed designee: the newly promoted Lt-Colonel Hassan Katsina. He was flown down to Lagos, escorted by Lt-Colonel Conrad Nwawo (an officer whom Nzeogwu trusted). The only other passengers on the plane carrying Nzeogwu and Nwawo were the wife and children of Lt-Colonel Njoku, who were returning to Lagos after a trip to Kaduna.

Many claim that Nzeogwu and Aguiyi-Ironsi struck a deal whereby Aguiyi-Ironsi promised that the Majors would not be punished. Whatever the deal was, Nzeogwu and his fellow conspirators found themselves locked up at the notorious Kiri-Kiri prison in Lagos. After his arrival in Lagos on January 19, Nzeogwu was initially admitted to the Lagos Teaching Hospital for treatment for wounds he sustained during his assault on the Sardauna's lodge. A day after his arrival he was arrested by Majors Henry Igboba and Murtala Muhammed and taken into custody. Over one hundred junior soldiers and NCOs were also arrested and joined the Majors in detention. After the coup failed, and having dumped their victims' corpses in the bush, some of the conspirators such as Majors Ademoyega, Onwuatuegwu, and Captain Gbulie returned to their posts and went back to work as if nothing had happened. This group managed to stay free for a few weeks (some until February 1966) until their role in the coup was revealed under interrogation by the NCOs and other officers already under arrest. They too were apprehended and sent to Kiri-Kiri. Not all of the culprits were arrested. For unknown reasons some of the non-Igbo participants

---

1 Ibid.

such as Captain John Swanton, and Second-Lieutenants Kpera, Eghagha, Ibik and Waribor, were not arrested.

With the help of his friend, the poet *cum* radical political intellectual Christopher Okigbo, Major Ifeajuna fled to Ghana where he was received by Ghana's President Kwame Nkrumah, who housed him with Samuel Ikoku. Ikoku was the former AG General Secretary and had fled to Ghana after being charged as an accomplice during the Awolowo treason trial in 1962. Ghana's role in the whole affair has not been fully revealed. One author claims that a member of Nkrumah's presidential guard (Colonel David Zanlerigu) personally accompanied Ikoku to pick up Ifeajuna.[1] Zanlerigu later became Ghana's Minister of Works and Housing. Nkrumah swiftly announced his recognition of the new Nigerian military government even though no official request for recognition had been sent to Ghana from Nigeria. Within weeks Nkrumah was overthrown in a military coup and replaced as head of state by Lt-General Joseph Ankrah of the Ghanaian army. Ironically, one of the officers that staged the Ghanaian coup (Akwasi Amankwa Afrifa) was a course mate of Major Nzeogwu at Sandhurst and the two men were even in the same company. Afrifa later became Ghana's head of state. When he was a cadet, Afrifa trained at the ROSTS in Ghana with other Nigerian officers including Joe Akahan, Festus Akagha, Alphonsus Keshi, David Ogunewe, Christian Ude, and Louis Chude-Sokei. That famous cadet class also included future Ghanaian head of state Lt-General Fred Akuffo. Ifeajuna later unwisely returned to Nigeria after being promised amnesty. The promise was not kept and he was arrested and thrown into prison with the other plotters when he returned. The fallout from the coup's failure later led Ifeajuna and Ademoyega to attempt to apportion blame by engaging each other in a fistfight.[2]

Thursday, January 20, 1966: A Grisly Discovery

Meanwhile, the Prime Minister was still missing. Aguiyi-Ironsi told the press that the Prime Minister's whereabouts were still unknown but that searches were being conducted for him. A few days later Assistant Superintendent of Police Ibrahim Babankowa visited a clinic to get medication for himself. While he was there he overheard a conversation between two other patients about a mysterious unpleasant smell in their neighborhood. Babankowa recalled the convoy of army vehicles that had passed his checkpoint on the morning of January 15 (as detailed above). Babankowa led his police team on a search of the area the patients came from, and they discovered the decomposing bodies of Balewa and Lt-Colonel Largema in a bush along the Lagos–Abeokuta road. Balewa's body was propped up at the foot of a tree. Babankowa left some of his men by the bush to guard the location and went to the Ikeja provincial police headquarters to report his macabre discovery. When Babankowa arrived, he reported his discovery to Chief Superintendent of Police Alhaji Kafaru Tinubu,[3] and from there telephoned and briefed the acting Inspector-General of police Alhaji Kam Selem. Selem in turn passed on the news to Aguiyi-Ironsi and told Babankowa to come to the police headquarters at Lion Building, which Aguiyi-Ironsi was now using as his office since he no longer felt safe working in army units. When Babankowa arrived at Lion Building, an astonished Aguiyi-Ironsi asked him,

---

1 Willard Scott Thompson, *Ghana's Foreign Policy, 1957–1966: Diplomacy, Ideology, and the New State*, pages 387-388.

2 Ademoyega *Why We Struck*, page 101.

3 Tinubu's nephew Bola Ahmed Tinubu later became the Governor of Lagos State.

in Hausa, whether it was really true that he had found the Prime Minister's body. Babankowa confirmed his discovery in person to Selem and Aguiyi-Ironsi.[1]

FRIDAY JANUARY 21, 1966

A convoy of vehicles (including a vehicle carrying several coffins) ferried the Prime Minister's ADC Kaftan and the Madaki of Bauchi Alhaji Muhammadu to the location where Babankowa found the bodies. Recollection of the crisis in some quarters was subsequently tainted by the deep conviction of an Igbo conspiracy. The Madaki later claimed that "all" of the people present in the convoy were Igbo. This is not accurate as many non-Igbos (including Northerners) such as Babankowa, Commissioner of police Timothy Omo-Bare, Balewa's ADC Kaftan, Colonel Austen-Peters (head of the army medical corps) and the Madaki of Bauchi himself were present in the convoy. The Madaki was an in-law of the Prime Minister and was in the Prime Minister's residence the night he was abducted. Babankowa arrived to find his men still faithfully standing guard over the bodies. The Prime Minister's corpse was identified by the white embroidered gown he was wearing when he was arrested by Major Ifeajuna. The new military government publicly announced the discovery of the Prime Minister's body and flew flags at half mast for three days. The Prime Minister was buried in his family compound in Bauchi. Acting Inspector-General of Police Kam Selem and the Lagos Commissioner of Police Hamman Maiduguri represented the new military government at the funeral. It appears that, while the arrest of the Prime Minister was part of the plot, his murder may not have been, and Ifeajuna and his co-conspirators may have exceeded their orders by killing him. In the aftermath of the coup, Nzeogwu rattled off a list of names that were on the Majors' hit list. He mentioned the usual unsurprising suspects such as the Sardauna, Azikiwe, Okpara, Orizu, Okotie-Eboh and Akintola, but Balewa's name was conspicuously absent. Sir Kashim Ibrahim (who was detained and in Nzeogwu's presence at the time) pointedly recalled Nzeogwu's failure to mention Balewa.[2]

Balewa was not killed until it was clear that the coup was doomed to fail. Those who hoped that the Prime Minister was alive all along or that the plotters would use his release as a bargaining chip were disappointed. Why such violent attacks by the Majors on their targets? Perhaps to forestall any chance of the former leaders ever returning to power. Major Nzeogwu reasoned that: "We wanted to get rid of rotten and corrupt ministers, political parties, trade unions and the whole clumsy apparatus of the federal system. We wanted to gun down all the bigwigs on our way. This was the only way. We could not afford to let them live if this was to work."[3]

---

1 *Weekly Trust*, March 20 2004.
2 Akinjide Osuntokun, *Power Broker: A Biography of Sir Kashim Ibrahim*, pages 103–104.
3 *Daily Telegraph*, 22nd January 1966.

Chapter 6. A New Type of Government

The new military government was welcomed with a massive outpouring of jubilation and goodwill. The vast majority of the public had never been in close contact with soldiers before, and thus held them in a mixture of awe and fear. Having seen the ease with which the soldiers dispatched politicians they did not like, many civilians looked at soldiers as invincible and fearsome creatures. The soldiers' crisply starched uniforms, peaked caps, Sandhurst honor and impeccable British accents (gained from their training by British instructors) reinforced positive public perceptions of them. The Nigerian army was essentially a stepchild of the British army, having adopted its doctrinal and social ethos. Nigerian officers personified this with their ramrod postures, swagger sticks and British parade ground and mess vocabulary. Having distinguished itself during the UN peacekeeping mission in the Congo, the army was the only national institution that had not been tainted by the corruption and anarchy of the post-independence years. Soldiers were also regarded as disciplined, honest and patriotic and the public generally trusted that they would always act in the national interest and without succumbing to the temptations of corruption and avarice that so many of the politicians fell into. It is a measure of public exasperation with politicians, and yearning for good leadership, that the public were willing to put so much faith and optimism in a group of soldiers with moderate education and no political experience.

Governing Organs of the Military Government

Aguiyi-Ironsi appointed military governors in each of the country's four regions. They replaced the deposed civilian Premiers. Two of the four military governors were graduates of Sandhurst. His choice of Lt-Colonel Hassan Katsina (the son of the Emir of Katsina, Usman Nagogo) to be the military governor of the Northern Region was politically astute. Katsina was a Sandhurst-trained, polo-playing officer of Northern blue blood stock and considered a member of the Northern "establishment." The son of an Igbo millionaire and business tycoon, Lt-Colonel Chukwuemeka Ojukwu was appointed military governor of the Eastern Region. Although Igbo by parentage,

Ojukwu was born in Zungeru in the Northern Region and had attended Nigeria's most prestigious school Kings College before later graduating with a degree in History from Lincoln College, Oxford University (where he joined the communist party) in the UK prior to joining the Nigerian army. He attended Oxford at the same time as future federal civil servants Phillip Asiodu and Allison Ayida. The three men all also attended Kings College. Intellectually, Ojukwu was in a different league to many of his peers. His appointment to be the Eastern Region's military governor was also ironic as he had spent very little of his life in that region. For most of his life he lived either in other parts of Nigeria or overseas.

The respected Lt-Colonel Francis Fajuyi (who won a medal for bravery during the peacekeeping operation in Congo) was appointed for the Western Region, and the Sandhurst-trained Lt-Colonel David Ejoor was appointed to govern the Mid-West Region. Although Fajuyi was doubtless an excellent soldier, a more educated officer such as Major Rotimi or Major Olutoye may have been a better choice for the intellectual challenges of governance. Another Sandhurst alumnus, the affable Lt-Colonel "Jack" Gowon (who had just returned from a course he was attending overseas), succeeded Colonel Kur Mohammed as the Chief of Staff at army headquarters. During the crisis, he was the officer in greatest proximity to Aguiyi-Ironsi and was acting as his virtual second in command.

The story of how Gowon acquired his nickname of "Jack" is an instructive example of the patronizing attitude of colonialists towards Africans. During a training exercise conducted when Gowon was a cadet at Sandhurst, Gowon was asked for his name by a British drill sergeant-major. On hearing that Gowon's first name was "Yakubu," the drill sergeant-major decided that he could not pronounce (or could not be bothered to try to pronounce) "Yakubu" and started referring to Gowon as "Jack."[1] The name stuck.

REACTION TO THE NEW REGIME

Although they are now loath to admit it, civilians enthusiastically welcomed the new military government with open arms. Even the ousted parties and politicians supported the new regime. The NPC issued a statement stating that:

> The party gives its unqualified support to the military regime and to the Major-General in particular. We call on all our party members and supporters to co-operate with the military regime and to give the new administration unflinching support in its great task of bringing peace and stability to Nigeria. . . . We pray that the Almighty God may help Major-General J.T.U. Aguiyi-Ironsi, in the execution of the difficult national duties thrust upon him by the present circumstances.[2]

Alhaji Dauda Adegbenro, Kolawale Balogun and Richard Akinjide of the AG, NCNC and NNDP respectively issued similar statements of support for Aguiyi-Ironsi on behalf of their parties. Apocryphal gossip claimed that the new regime was lining up and summarily executing policemen who took bribes. An expatriate resident in Nigeria at the time said that "It was a good time to be alive. There was an enormous sense of relief, even of elation, and an air of expectancy for a week or two in which everyone worked hard at his own job, anxious to prove his allegiance to the spirit of the revolution. Few if any bribes were offered or taken, long distance telephone

---

1 See Alex Madiebo, *The Nigerian Revolution and the Biafran War*, pages 52 and 54.
2 Statement signed by Alhaji Hashim Adaji and reproduced in *Daily Times* January 19 1966.

calls were put through in an instant, and people even drove their cars with more care."[1] Newspapers similarly opened with wildly jubilant headlines and triumphant exclamations of celebration at the overthrow of the government. *Time* Magazine ran a feature on the coup headlined "The Men of Sandhurst" which claimed that "The raids were brilliantly planned, precisely executed (murmured one resident Englishman: 'Sandhurst training certainly leaves its mark')."

In a remarkably succinct conclusion on the coup and the problems ahead, the *Time* article concluded:

> Nigerians fell in immediately behind their new regime. Businessmen and labor unions cheered, university students paraded through the streets of Lagos bearing a coffin and a banner proclaiming "Tyranny Has Died." All political parties—including the deposed Northern People's Congress—swore their allegiance. Editorialized the West African Pilot: "This great country has every reason to be proud of the military, which has taken over the fumbling feudal and neocolonialist regime. Today, independence is really won." That still remained to be seen. For while the joy was obviously genuine in the south, it was just as obviously mixed in the north. . . . The assassination of the Sardauna of Sokoto raised a possibility that southerners have long feared: a Moslem holy war of reprisal. Besides, it was far from clear that the power struggle within the army itself had been fully resolved.[2]

With uncannily accurate foresight, US intelligence were asking the right questions and foresaw the potential issues ahead. Three days after the coup an intelligence memorandum asked, "What would happen if Ironsi was assassinated?" and correctly assessed that "If Nigeria could fall victim to military takeover, then it could happen anywhere in Africa."[3]

From England, the convalescing President Azikiwe issued a statement expressing his dismay at the violent nature of the coup:

> Violence has never been an instrument used by us, as founding fathers of the Nigerian Republic, to solve political problems. . . . I consider it most unfortunate that our 'Young Turks' decided to introduce the element of violent revolution into Nigerian politics No matter how they and our general public might have been provoked by obstinate and perhaps grasping politicians, it is an unwise policy. . . . As far as I am concerned, I regard the killings of our political and military leaders as a national calamity.

The new Federal Military Government (FMG) was empowered to make laws for the "peace, order and good government of" Nigeria. It also suspended several parts of the constitution (mostly those parts dealing with party politics) abolished the posts of Prime Minister and President,[4] and formed a new a Supreme Military Council (SMC) consisting of the following:

---

1 John Oyinbo, *Crisis and Beyond*, page 42.

2 *Time* Magazine — Friday, January 28, 1966.

3 Both quotes taken from Memorandum dated January 18, 1966 from the Deputy Director for Coordination, Bureau of Intelligence and research (Koren) to the Director of the Bureau.

4 Constitution (Suspension and Modification) Decree.

SUPREME MILITARY COUNCIL, JANUARY 1966

Name	Position	Region/ Ethnicity
Major-General Johnson Aguiyi-Ironsi	Supreme Commander, Nigerian Armed Forces and Head of State	East: Igbo
Brigadier Babafemi Ogundipe	Chief of Staff, Nigerian Armed Forces[1]	West: Yoruba
Commodore Joseph Wey	Commanding Officer — Nigerian Navy	Mixed Yoruba/ eastern minor-ity ethnicity
Lt-Colonel Yakubu "Jack" Gowon	Chief of Staff, Army	North: Angas
Lt-Colonel George Kurubo	Commanding Officer — Nigerian Air Force	East: Ijaw
Lt-Colonel Chukwuemeka Ojukwu	Military Governor, Eastern Region	East: Igbo
Lt-Colonel Hassan Usman Katsina	Military Governor, Northern Region	North: Fulani
Lt-Colonel David Ejoor	Military Governor, Mid-West Region	Mid-West: Urhobo
Lt-Colonel Francis Fajuyi	Military Governor, Western Region	West: Yoruba

[1] The title of this post was later changed to "Chief of Staff, Supreme Headquarters".

The acting Inspector-General of Police, Alhaji Kam Selem, was later added to the SMC, and Major Mobolaji Johnson[1] was later appointed the military governor of Lagos (but was not an SMC member). Attorney-General Gabriel Onyuike was also subsequently allowed to attend SMC meetings in an observatory capacity. Onyuike was the Eastern Region's former Director of Public Prosecutions and replaced Taslim Elias who resigned to be the Dean at the University of Lagos' law faculty. The SMC replaced the Parliament as Nigeria's highest legislative organ. A new cabinet known as the Federal Executive Council replaced the Council of Ministers (the previous cabinet under Balewa's government). In a gross distortion of the separation of pow-ers doctrine, the SMC members were also members of the FEC, as was the deputy Inspector-General of Police. Aguiyi-Ironsi suddenly had several jobs. As well as his elevation from army GOC to Head of State, he was now Supreme Commander of the armed forces (in overall charge of the army, air force and navy), and chairman of the SMC and the FEC. After a few weeks he moved into State House in Lagos (Azikiwe's former residence).

Aguiyi-Ironsi appointed the following ministers to the FEC.

---

1 Johnson was a former student of Methodist Boys High School in Lagos. The school also pro-duced other famous military officers: Air Marshal Nureini Yusuf (former Chief of Air Staff), Commodore Adekunle Lawal, and Vice-Admiral Babatunde Elegbede.

FEC Members

Name	Portfolio	Region of Origin
G. Ige	Agriculture and Natural Resources	North
C.O. Lawson	Communications	West
Alhaji Musa Daggash	Defense	North
Allison Ayida	Economic Development	Mid-West
S.S. Waniko	Education	East
T. Eneli	Establishments	East
Edwin O. Ogbu	External Affairs	North
Abdul Aziz Atta	Finance	North
B.N. Okagbue	Health	East
Philip Asiodu	Industries	Mid-West
Grey Eronmosele Longe	Information	Mid-West
Alhaji A. Mora	Internal Affairs	North
M.A. Tokunbo	Labor and Welfare	Mid-West
H.A. Ejeyuitchie	Mines and Power	Mid-West
Alhaji Abdulrahman Howeidy	Special Duties (Internal Affairs)	West
Alhaji Sule Kolo	Trade	North
H.O. Omenai	Transport	Mid-West
S.O. Williams	Works and Housing	West
Alhaji Sule Katagum	Chairman of the Federal Public Service Commission (civil service)	North
A.E. Howson-Wright	Chairman of the Nigerian Railway Corporation	Mid-West
A.I. Obiyan	Chairman of the Nigerian Ports Authority	Mid-West

Only two members of the entire FEC (Okagbue and Eneli) were Igbo.

Legal and Constitutional Basis of Military Rule

The curious reader may wonder how a military government can legally exist and rule in a constitutional federal republic such as Nigeria, which has a constitution with provisions for multi-party democracy, and government by elected officials, and does not recognize any form of government other than an elected one. Many Nigerian pro-democracy activists and human rights advocates incorrectly argue that military rule is illegal. This is not always accurate. A military coup can establish a new government if it is effective and results in an abrupt and complete elimination of the previous constitutional and governmental framework. The legal basis for military rule in Nigeria can be found in two sources: (i) the Constitution (Suspension and Modification) Decree, and (ii) the Federal Military Government (Supremacy and Enforcement of Powers) Decree.

After coming to power in January 1966, Major-General Aguiyi-Ironsi's government had a reality problem as it was ruling a country whose constitution did not recognize governance by the armed forces. To address this anomaly Aguiyi-Ironsi's government promulgated the Constitution (Suspension and Modification) Decree which decreed Aguiyi-Ironsi's regime into existence and suspended certain parts of the Constitution (mainly those parts dealing with civilian governance and terms of office of elected officials). The FMG presumed that this decree gave it the power to enact any law or measures it wished without regard to the constitution or interference from the courts.

However, the military's presumption that it derived legal legitimacy from the fact that it had been "invited" to form a government by the rump cabinet in January 1966 involuntarily limited its own powers. In the famous court case of *Lakanmi v. Attorney-General of the Western Region* in 1970, the Supreme Court voided the FMG's Forfeiture of Assets (Validation) Decree 1968 which had forcibly forfeited the properties of certain persons that had been acquired by corrupt means. The court not only voided the decree but also ruled that the fact that the military government had been *invited* to form a government by the previous democratically elected civilian government meant that the military government was not an extra-constitutional or revolutionary regime and therefore still had to act in accordance with the *unsuspended* parts of the constitution.

The military were not going to accept judicial oversight over their actions and later nullified the *Lakanmi* verdict by enacting the Federal Military Government (Supremacy and Enforcement of Powers) Decree 1970 (the "Supremacy Decree"), which is explicit on the supremacy of military authority and gave the military government sweeping powers to enact Decrees whose legality could not be questioned by the courts even if the Decree conflicted with an *unsuspended* part of the constitution. The Supremacy Decree reversed the previous trend, and established that the legal basis of military rule derived not from the handover to Aguiyi-Ironsi by the rump cabinet on Sunday, January 16, 1966, but directly from the violent overthrow of the civilian government by the Majors on the previous day. The January 15 coup is specifically referenced in the preamble to the Supremacy Decree.

The preamble of the Supremacy Decree stated that "The military revolution which took place on 15 January 1966 effectively abrogated the whole pre-existing legal order in Nigeria." In other words, a revolution occurred in Nigeria on January 15 and the previous civilian constitutional structures in place were eliminated even before Major-General Aguiyi-Ironsi met with the Council of Ministers the next day. There had been no need for him to ask the Council of Ministers to hand over power because they were already out of power. Subsequently every single military government in Nigeria's history has re-enacted the Constitution (Suspension and Modification) Decree and the Federal Military Government (Supremacy and Enforcement of Powers) Decree and used them as the legal basis of its rule.

Applying the logic of the *Lakanmi* judgment, the military regimes which began in January 1966 with Major-General Aguiyi-Ironsi's regime and ended in 1979 with General Obasanjo's regime were all legal governments since each derived its authority from the Majors' overthrow of the government in January 1966 and not from the Council of Ministers' handover to Major-General Aguiyi-Ironsi.

Military Governance

Although the January coup succeeded in replacing Nigeria's political leaders, the underlying issues that the coup intended to solve still remained. The new regime of Major-General Aguiyi-Ironsi went vigorously to work on these issues. It declared itself a "corrective" government and arrested and detained politicians from the past regime (except those of the NPC). The detainees included Kingsley Mbadiwe, Michael Okpara, Dennis Osedebay and Chiefs Theophilus Owolabi Shobowale Benson and M.N. Ugochukwu. A number of commissions of inquiry were created to investigate allegations of corruption and mismanagement in several public bodies including the Nigerian Railways Corporation, the Lagos city council and the Electricity Corporation of Nigeria (ECN). The General-Manager of the ECN happened to be Dr. Ademola Banjo, the older brother of Lt-Colonel Victor Banjo.

The military governors took to public office in swashbuckling style. Lt-Colonel Fajuyi dismissed and arrested several officials and ministers appointed by the former regime of Akintola.[1] Hassan Katsina dubbed Fajuyi as an "Action Grouper" in sarcastic reference to Fajuyi's treatment of NNDP opponents of the AG. Fajuyi also ordered the completion of water supply systems which allegedly, had been deliberately delayed by Akintola's regime as punishment for districts that did not vote for him. Lt-Colonels Ejoor and Ojukwu of the Mid-West and Eastern Regions respectively were seemingly engaged in a competition to outdo each other. Ejoor locked out civil servants who showed up to work late, paraded them in the Oba's square, and upbraided them for their lack of punctuality. Ojukwu ordered portraits of former President Azikiwe and former Prime Minister Balewa to be removed from government buildings. The military governor of the Northern Region Lt-Colonel Katsina decreed a reduction in food prices.

Despite the new military regime's attempts to delineate itself from the former discredited civilian government, it acknowledged its own limitations by retaining the former civilian governors of each region to act as advisers to the inexperienced and newly appointed military governors.[2] There was also administrative continuity as the former secretary to the Balewa government, Stanley Olabode Wey, retained his post, albeit in a re-designated title of Secretary to the Federal Military Government. Wey was also the brother of Commodore Wey (head of the navy).

Many southerners welcomed the military's entrance into politics as an excellent opportunity to finally abrogate the country's lopsided constitutional arrangement and Parliament which effectively gave the Northern Region a perpetual veto on southern political initiatives. There had been fevered debate as to which consti-

---

1 All those arrested were members of Akintola's NNDP regime: Chief Remi Fani-Kayode, Richard Akinjide (former federal Education Minister and NNDP General-Secretary), J.O. Adigun (former Minister of Land and Housing and one of those who caused the 1962 fight inside the Western Region House of Assembly that was the catalyst for a state of emergency in the region), Claudius Akran (former Finance Minister), Babatunde Olowofoyeku (former Minister of Justice and Attorney-General), Okunola Adebayo (former Minister of Home Affairs), Salawu Fajinmi (former Minister of Transport), Nathaniel Kotoye (former Minister of Trade and Industry), Adebiyi Adeyi (former Minister of Works), Alhaji Busari Obiesesan (former speaker of Western Region House of Assembly), Emmanuel Olakanmi (former chairman of the Housing Corporation), Lekan Salami (former executive director of the Development Corporation), Dr. S.D. Opabunmiro.

2 The former civilian governors were: Sir Kashim Ibrahim (Northern Region), Sir Odeleye Fadahunsi (Western Region), Sir Samuel Jereton Mariere (Mid-West Region) and Sir Francis Akanu Ibiam (Eastern Region).

---

tutional structure the country should adopt. Many felt that the regionalized federa-tion exacerbated ethnic tension, encouraged regional insularity and prevented the country from meshing into a true union. However, some Northerners were not par-ticularly enthusiastic about forging closer links with the south and regarded regional autonomy as a protection mechanism against southern infiltration. A Constitutional Review Study Group was appointed to formulate and submit proposals on Nigeria's future constitutional framework. The study group was headed by the most famous lawyer in Nigeria's history Chief Rotimi Williams. Its proposals would be submitted to a Constituent Assembly, which would be subject to ratification in a referendum prior to being implemented. A commission on economic planning was also appointed, headed by Chief Simeon Adebo (Yoruba), Nigeria's former representative at the UN. One of the commission's members was Dr. Pius Okigbo, the former economic adviser to the federal government. He later went on to work for the World Bank.

The most controversial administrative appointment was that of Francis Nwoke-di as sole commissioner to review the feasibility of unifying the country's regional public services. Nwokedi was Igbo and prior to his appointment was a permanent secretary in the ministry of foreign affairs. To non-Igbos, Nwokedi's appointment had the appearance of cronyism as he had worked with and became acquainted with Aguiyi-Ironsi during the UN operation in Congo. Critics immediately questioned why he alone was appointed to head this project. This appointment continues to rankle in some quarters, even today, but in fact it was unremarkable as several of the other study groups had sole commissioners, such as Mr. Justice Stephen Peter Thomas (judicial services), M.O. Ani (statutory corporations), A.I. Wilson (informa-tion services), and Alhaji Yusuf Gobir (prisons and police). None of the foregoing was Igbo and therefore their appointments as sole commissioners in their respective fields did not raise any alarms. Nonetheless the Nwokedi issue caused such a furor that Aguiyi-Ironsi appointed a second non-Igbo commissioner (Michael Ani), from the Mid-West, to assist Nwokedi.

UNIFICATION DECREE

In May Lt-Colonel Katsina returned from an SMC meeting in Lagos and enigmat-ically told reporters to "Tell the nation that an egg will be broken tomorrow." Clearly, something dramatic was being planned. In May 1966, Aguiyi-Ironsi issued perhaps the most controversial Decree in Nigeria's history: the "Unification Decree."[1] Under the Decree Nigeria would cease to be called "The Federal Republic of Nigeria" but would instead be referred to as "The Republic of Nigeria." The former regions were now "groups of provinces," and the military governors would govern groups of prov-inces which corresponded exactly to the former regions, whose territorial contiguity was also unaffected. The Federal Military Government was renamed the "National Military Government," the Federal Guards were renamed the "National Guards," and so on. Additionally, in an attack on "tribalism" (which Aguiyi-Ironsi identified as one of Nigeria's biggest ills) Aguiyi-Ironsi also abolished all the political parties and over 100 tribal and cultural associations including the powerful Igbo State Union, which at that time was the most powerful Igbo umbrella organization.

Most controversial of all, the Decree unified the previously separate civil services of each region. Hitherto the civil service had been regionalized, with each region hav-ing its own separate civil service. A separate civil service had always been an in-built

---

1 Decree 34 of 1966.

protection for Northerners from the energetic and pushy Igbos. Northerners feared that unifying the civil service would expose the Northern Region's civil service to competition from the better educated southerners (especially Igbos), who could swamp them and replace Northern civil servants. With one Decree, the Sardauna's northernization program had been terminated.

The Decree was actually less dramatic than it seemed and merely gave legal basis for the factual state of affairs that existed since Aguiyi-Ironsi became head of state. From the outset of military rule in January, Nigeria was *de facto* being administered under a unified system of governance. The presence of military governors for each region was misleading because the military governors were militarily junior to Aguiyi-Ironsi and were unlikely to enact regional measures that were not approved by him. Although the Decree came as a shock to many, it should have been anticipated. As far back as February, Aguiyi-Ironsi had declared that "all Nigerians want an end to regionalism." The Unification Decree's promulgation seems to have been premeditated as far back as March when the Nwokedi Commission went to work. Nwokedi's remit was to consider the feasibility of unifying the civil service. In other words, unification was already under consideration *before* the Commission was inaugurated.

A popular misconception is that the Decree was unilaterally enacted by Aguiyi-Ironsi without debate at the SMC. Gowon alleged that Decree 34 was discussed by the SMC but was suddenly issued without warning before the SMC concluded its debate.[1] However Attorney-General Gabriel Onyuike (who was present during SMC debates regarding it) disagreed with Gowon and alleged that the Decree was unanimously adopted by the SMC:

> The Decree was the unanimous decision of the Supreme Military Council. . . . It was not a decision taken at only one meeting of the SMC. The draft of Decree No. 34 was considered at various meetings of the SMC and amendments by way of additions and deletions were made…The meeting of the Supreme Military Council at which the draft Decree was approved was held on a Saturday…I remember that it was Lieutenant Colonel Hassan Katsina (as he then was) who suggested that and it was agreed that the promulgation of the Decree would be delayed until the Military Governors had returned to their capitals.[2]

Whatever its origin, the Decree split southern and Northern public opinion. Aguiyi-Ironsi's political reforms were considered pedestrian in the south, and too radical in the Northern Region. Some Northerners claimed that recent Igbo graduates were swamping Northern institutions with job applications and would soon head northward to colonize the Northern Region and permanently relegate Northerners to menial work. The manner in which the Decree was promulgated without extensive consultations also caused disillusion. Having been in power since independence, politicians from the Northern Region were not accustomed to major governmental changes being implemented without their consent. Any trend toward centralization that was not initiated by a Northern leader would inevitably cause uproar in the Northern Region.

THE MAY 1966 RIOTS

Northern reaction to the Decree was swift and violent. Northern mobs took to the streets and protested, chanting "down with the military government" and, more tellingly, "Araba" (a Hausa word meaning "let us separate"). Serious disturbances

---

1 Momoh, *The Nigerian Civil War, 1967–1970: History and Reminiscences*, page 542.
2 Iloegbunam, *Ironside*, page 126.

broke out in the Northern Region and several hundred Igbos (by conservative esti-
mates — the death toll was probably much higher) were attacked and murdered by
Northern mobs. Some had their properties looted and burned.

Aguiyi-Ironsi was shaken and belatedly began to appreciate the depth of the
wounds caused by the January coup. The SMC held an emergency all night meeting to discuss the rioting. Aguiyi-Ironsi upbraided Katsina for not keeping a lid on
the disturbances. Katsina came to the meeting with files and copies of inflammatory
press articles that denigrated the memory of the dead Sardauna. He also brought a
memorandum from the Northern Emirs who demanded the repeal of the Unification
Decree or an assent to the Northern Region's secession. Lt-Colonel Kurubo took the
minutes of that SMC meeting.[1] In their public pronouncements after the meeting
Aguiyi-Ironsi and the military governors took great pains to explain that the Decree
was largely a change in nomenclature and entirely a transitional measure that was
without prejudice to the ongoing constitutional review. They also reassured the public that no major constitutional changes would be implemented without a referendum. Hassan Katsina found himself in a conflict of interest as a Northerner and in
his position as a member of the government. Although he felt a duty of loyalty to the
government and its policies, he personally found it difficult to reconcile these with
the pressure being put on him by his fellow Northerners. He joined other members of
the SMC in justifying the Decree:

> The unification Decree is not intended to give advantage to any section of the
> community. . . . The measures introduced are interim and temporary until civil-
> ian administration is once again restored. We in the army have got a unified
> command and it is the method we are used to. . . . Until the return of civilian
> rule, we have got to work with the methods we are used to. . . . The permanent
> arrangements for the government of Nigeria cannot be made without the fullest
> consultation with the people.[2]

However, he later admitted,

> I knew of the May riot. I knew very well there was going to be those riots . . .
> underneath, I was happy it had happened. To be honest to you, because we did
> not want unification. . . . Outwardly I had to show I am for the government. But
> underneath I was happy it had happened because I knew the Decree will be
> soon demolished.[3]

Aguiyi-Ironsi appointed a tribunal of inquiry to investigate the anti-Igbo pogroms. The tribunal was impeccably balanced: its chairman was a British Judge of
the Nigerian Supreme court Sir Justice Lionel Brett, and it had four other members
from each region of the country: Dr. Eni Njoku (Eastern Region), Justice Ayo Gabriel Irikefe (Mid-West Region),[4] Dr. Russell Aliyu Dikko (Northern Region) and
Justice Oyemade (Western Region). The tribunal's balanced composition did not
alter Northern perceptions and the tribunal was opposed by Northerners. To them
the speed with which it was created smacked of double standards as the SMC had
failed to put the January Majors on trial for six months, yet was able to swiftly set

---

1 Confirmed by Hassan Katsina during the National Workshop on the Events, Issues and
  Sources of Nigerian History, 1960–1970, held at State House, Kawo, Kaduna, 7-9 June 1993.
  Also see Bala Usman, *Inside Nigerian History*, 1950–1970, page 119.

2 *Morning Post*, June 10, 1966.

3 Katsina was speaking at the National Workshop on the Events, Issues and Sources of Nigerian
  History, 1960–1970, held at State House, Kawo, Kaduna, 7-9 June 1993. These quotes are
  also reproduced in *Inside Nigerian History*, 1950–1970, pages 118 and 119.

4 Later became Chief Justice.

up a tribunal to investigate disturbances in the Northern Region which had occurred just weeks earlier.

The SMC did not do a very good job of "marketing" the Decree in advance as a purely administrative measure, as opposed to a drastic constitutional change (which is how it was perceived). Aguiyi-Ironsi implemented the Decree first, then tried to explain its rationale afterwards (rather than the other way round). With hindsight, the problem was probably not the Unification Decree itself, but the fact it was enacted by the much distrusted and feared Igbos. Successive Northern led governments operated a system of governance more unitary than anything the Decree, or Aguiyi-Ironsi, ever envisaged. The timing of the Decree was also crucial. In the initial days of the military government, such was the jubilation among the population that the government could have pushed through any radical measures without much opposition. Most of the population were simply glad to be rid of the previous government and would accept any alternative. Aguiyi-Ironsi may have got away with the Unification Decree had he capitalized on the enormous momentum and outpouring of goodwill that greeted his rise, by enacting it in the opening days or weeks or his regime. He had been urged by southern intellectuals to pursue a unitary constitutional structure. However, as the FMG became increasingly gripped by inertia and fear of further alienating Northerners following the January coup, the euphoria that greeted its ascent to power began to dissipate, at least in the Northern Region. A sober critique of the FMG's performance turned increasingly hostile in the Northern Region when recalled in conjunction with the violent January coup. Aguiyi-Ironsi had the right ideas, but implemented them at the wrong time. By the time Aguiyi-Ironsi decided to seize the bull by the horns and push through dynamic reforms, it was too late. His honeymoon period had passed. The momentum had already been lost. Northerners began asking questions about January: why was it that no Igbo politician had been killed? Why was it that only one Igbo soldier had been killed? (and even then popular folklore erroneously believed that he had been shot inadvertently when he refused to hand over the keys to the armory). Why was it that Aguiyi-Ironsi managed to survive the January coup and emerge as head of state? Why were the Northern Region's two most prominent politicians and four highest ranking soldiers killed? To the casual observer these were innocent coincidences caused by the mobility of unit commanders, politicians and a brigade conference in Lagos. To others, they were evidence of a Machiavellian Igbo plot.

Fear of an Igbo Planet

Although the January coup may not have been *intended* as an Igbo takeover, it inevitably bore the appearance of one. By merely emerging as an Igbo head of state after a coup staged by mostly Igbo soldiers, Aguiyi-Ironsi's every move (no matter how innocent or well intentioned) was interpreted as a furtherance of an Igbo plot to dominate the country. The overwhelming majority of the January plotters were Igbo, most of their victims were non-Igbo, the Igbo GOC emerged unscathed and became head of state, the Igbo President was conveniently overseas when the coup took place, and the Igbo Premiers of the Eastern and Mid-West Regions were unharmed while the non-Igbo Premiers of other two regions were murdered. These factors coupled with the simple arithmetic of the January coup's casualties and survivors would inevitably lead even the most neutral observer to the inescapable conclusion that the whole affair was an Igbo inspired plot.

After seeing the Northern Region's political and military leaders murdered by Igbos, and an Igbo leader enacting decrees that were consistent with the ideology of the party identified with Igbos (the NCNC), this conclusion would most readily be reached in the Northern Region. For Northerners, things could hardly be worse. The in-built constitutional protection they enjoyed through a lopsided federal Parliament had been removed by Aguiyi-Ironsi's assumption of power, and now he was issuing decrees favored by their enemies. Igbos may have been similarly aggrieved and paranoid if Northern soldiers had murdered the two most powerful politicians (Doctors Azikiwe and Okpara), and the four most senior army officers (Major-General Aguiyi-Ironsi, and Lt-Colonels Ime Imo, Hilary Njoku and Emeka Ojukwu), from the Eastern Region. The fact that the Igbo President of the country Dr. Nnamdi Azikiwe was overseas when the January coup occurred was interpreted by some Northerners as evidence that he had foreknowledge of the coup and arranged to be out of harm's way when it occurred. Little attention was paid to the fact that Azikiwe travelled out of the country to receive medical treatment for a lung infection (with the prior knowledge and agreement of Prime Minister Balewa). He was given medical advice to take a lengthy convalescence. During his convalescence, Azikiwe embarked upon on a Caribbean cruise, which bizarrely saw him visit Haiti's then dictator "Papa Doc" Duvalier. However, some of the plotters suspected that Major Ifeajuna leaked the plot to Azikiwe. Several years later Captain Nwobosi revealed that:

> I have, and most of us had, the firm belief that Ifeajuna tipped Zik that these things were happening. . . . I cannot tell you for sure I know but we had the suspicion all through that Ifeajuna tipped Zik.[1]

Azikiwe's desire to promptly return to Nigeria after the coup gave the impression that his absence may not have been entirely due to his ill health. Considering the same issue, then Commissioner of Police M.D. Yusuf later observed that the police had no evidence to suggest Azikiwe was involved in the coup, but could not determine whether or not he was tipped off.[2]

Northern media began to replay speeches by the Sardauna and Balewa, both of whom were now being recalled with increasing nostalgia and heroism. The hostility and contempt for the politicians who had caused the crisis leading to the coup were suddenly forgotten and their reputations redeemed. The only political conversation worth holding were those regarding the dreaded Igbos. The mental distinction that existed in January between the "rebel" Majors and the "loyal" units of the army headed by Aguiyi-Ironsi disappeared and the roles of Aguiyi-Ironsi, the Majors and all other Igbos military and civilian, were mentally sublimated to create the myth of a gigantic Igbo plot to impose "Igbo hegemony" on the rest of the country. These theories presupposed that every Igbo man, woman and child, whether military or civilian, was an accomplice and shared guilt with the Majors. The irony was that the prominent Igbos who were so vilified as part of the "conspiracy" were more Northern than they were Igbo. They were all fluent Hausa speakers born and/or raised in the Northern Region. Azikiwe, Ojukwu, Nzeogwu, and Okafor were all born in the Northern Region, and both Anuforo and Nwobosi grew up in the Northern Region. Even Aguiyi-Ironsi had lived in Kano as a child and he too was a fluent Hausa speaker.

---

1 Momoh, *The Nigerian Civil War, 1967–1970: History and Reminiscences*, page 740.
2 National Workshop on the Events, Issues and Sources of Nigerian History, 1960–1970, held at State House, Kawo, Kaduna, 7-9 June 1993. Also see Bala Usman, *Inside Nigerian History*, 1950–1970, pages 43-44.

In private jocular moments he referred to his fellow Igbos by their Northern pejorative term "Nyamiri."[1]

Was Aguiyi-Ironsi an Accomplice?

The Majors' failure to arrest or kill the GOC Major-General Johnson Aguiyi-Ironsi, has led some to believe that he was part of, or was at the very least tipped off about, the January coup. Depending on whose story one believes, Aguiyi-Ironsi was either: (i) in on the plot and an ally of the Majors (ii) was on the Majors hit list but managed to escape due to being tipped off by Igbo participants within the coup circle. Even Brigadier Ogundipe suspected that Aguiyi-Ironsi had foreknowledge of the coup.[2] Some Northerners confronted Aguiyi-Ironsi and he emotionally denied complicity in face to face meetings with prominent Northerners such as the Sultan of Sokoto, Sir Kashim Ibrahim, Hassan Katsina and M.D. Yusuf. Nzeogwu's comments in his famous *Africa and the World* "interview" with Dennis Ejindu are instructive. Nzeogwu said of the coup plot:

> We got some but not all. *General Ironsi was to have been shot.* But we were not ruthless enough. As a result he and the other compromisers were able to supplant us.[3] (Author's emphasis.)

Many years later Captain Ben Gbulie also revealed that "An attempt was made [to arrest or kill Aguiyi-Ironsi], but someone alerted him and he fled."[4] Captain Nwobosi added to this theme by confirming that "Ironsi was to be killed that night. Ironsi was against us."[5] If Aguiyi-Ironsi was part of the coup plot, it would be odd for the Majors to plan to kill him. Aguiyi-Ironsi's decision to appoint three Northerners to investigate the Majors' coup would also be an extremely foolhardy move if he really was an accomplice, since the Northerners (who had been the primary victims of the January coup) would not hesitate to compile a trail of evidence leading back to him. Some of the Majors could barely conceal their contempt for Aguiyi-Ironsi. Nzeogwu was unwilling to give him significant professional praise. When asked what he thought of Aguiyi-Ironsi as a soldier, Nzeogwu replied, "I am afraid I cannot tell you that." The most complimentary thing he had to say of Aguiyi-Ironsi was to admit that "as a person he was very well liked and as the Supreme Commander, his orders were promptly carried out," before rounding off by disrespectfully adding that Aguiyi-Ironsi "joined the army as a tally clerk and was a clerk most of the time." In his book Captain Ben Gbulie was even more critical of Aguiyi-Ironsi and described him as "inept and inefficient — hardly the caliber of officer to command an army. In fact, the coup planners considered him unfit to command even a funeral detail."[6] It would be odd for the Majors to bring into their plot, someone they held in such contempt.

Aguiyi-Ironsi's survival may have owed more to good fortune than to him being privy to the coup plot (as well as the Majors tactical mistake in arresting or killing other senior officers before they got hold of Aguiyi-Ironsi). Their professional disre-

---

1 Robert Melson and Howard Wolpe, *Nigeria: Modernization and the Politics of Communalism*, page 382.

2 Personal communication with a member of Brigadier Ogundipe's family.

3 *Daily Telegraph*, 22nd January 1966

4 Captain Gbulie was giving testimony at the Justice Chukwudifu Oputa chaired Human Rights Violations Investigations Commission in 2001.

5 Momoh, *The Nigerian Civil War, 1967–1970: History and Reminiscences*, page 737.

6 Gbulie, *Nigeria's Five Majors*, page 53.

spect for Aguiyi-Ironsi may have led them to underestimate him and think that he could not stop them, and instead focused their attention on officers such as Maimalari and Ademulegun whom they appeared to think posed far greater threats to their plans. The Majors overlooked the fact that Aguiyi-Ironsi was the only officer in the entire Nigerian army with the authority to enter any army unit and issue orders to any soldier. Although his role on January 15 has been incorrectly presented as that of an indolent drunk, as was shown above Aguiyi-Ironsi was very active throughout the night and day. He managed to outwit the Majors despite them having the advantages of surprise, numerical strength and a head start of several hours.

Aguiyi-Ironsi may have been tipped off by one of the conspirators while the coup was in progress. If this theory is true, then the most likely informant is Major John Obienu. Captain Ben Gbulie is convinced that their accomplice Major Obienu leaked the coup and turned on them. He claimed Obienu had been observed nervously "drinking like a fish" at Brigadier Maimalari's party the night before the coup, failed to show up for the pre-coup meeting at Major Ifeajuna's house and failed to play any part in the coup even though he had promised to turn up and support the plotters with armored cars. Obienu was in Lagos on January 15 and was one of the officers that rallied round to put the coup down. However, unlike the other conspirators, he was not arrested and detained. This may have been because he reported the plot. Aguiyi-Ironsi's actions throughout the coup and its aftermath suggest that he was taken genuinely by surprise. Moreover even the Northerners who were present with, or met him during this time (such as Gowon) have admitted that even they do not believe he was part of the Majors' plot. Joe Garba later came to the same conclusion. Gowon revealed that "I think it will be unfair to accuse him [Ironsi] of ethnicity. I do not think I had ever known him to be ethnic."[1] Future head of state Olusegun Obasanjo also later conceded that "Ironsi was not the sort of person to plan a conspiracy"[2] [sic]. Whatever his faults were, Aguiyi-Ironsi was no great actor. It would be incredible if a bluff, straight talking, simple soldier like Aguiyi-Ironsi was part of such an elaborate and Machiavellian conspiracy when everything about his demeanor, background and temperament suggests a man who is incapable of pulling off something so subtle.

Provocation in the North

Northerners were appalled at southern indifference to the murder of their political and military leaders. Such affront to Northern sensitivities was reinforced by some particularly tactless articles in the southern press which welcomed the January coup with jubilation. The June 1966 issue of *Drum* magazine caused great offense in the Northern Region. This issue contained an article by a columnist named Caz Idapo with photos and passages about the dead Sardauna and his ancestry that Muslim Northerners considered almost blasphemous. Idapo was not Igbo but Igbos nevertheless took the blame. They had worn out their welcome to the extent that all offense caused by southerners became synonymous with Igbos.

It was the uneducated classes on both sides that were sowing the seeds of further conflict. These classes did not appreciate the complex military and political dynamic at play and tended to simplify the crisis by portraying the January coup as either an Igbo plot or an Igbo triumph. Flashpoints inevitably arose where these opposing camps came into frequent contact. Northerners accused Igbo traders in the Northern

---

1 Elaigwu, Gowon: *The Biography of a Soldier–Statesman*, page 54.
2 Obasanjo, *An Intimate Portrait of Chukwuma Kaduna Nzeogwu*.

Region of taunting them about the January coup, provocatively displaying photos of Major Nzeogwu, and of playing a gramophone song with bursts of gunfire in the background that reminded Northerners of the January coup. With their triumphant reaction to the coup, Igbos in the Northern Region were unwittingly sensitizing Northern fears of an Igbo conspiracy, and simultaneously digging Aguiyi-Ironsi's grave. Northerners would find such behavior deeply offensive in normal times, let alone at a time when they were shattered after the death of their leaders. In response Aguiyi-Ironsi passed Decree 44 which made it an offense "to display or pass on images, songs, instruments, or words which are likely to provoke any section of the country." An Igbo journalist and a number of others were arrested pursuant to this decree.

Although the January coup was the pretext for the anti-Igbo hostility, the real reasons were more deep rooted and went back several years. The coup extracted long held prejudices and negative stereotypes about Igbos. Ibrahim Haruna (then a Lt-Colonel and the Chief Ordnance Officer) later revealed his belief that:

> ...Igbos constituted only 15 percent of Nigeria's population. They were dominant and in control of most of the sectors of the country's public and private commercial life. They were everywhere, and freely doing anything. This however was not necessarily because of their dynamism and adaptability... . . . but because of their nature of being overbearing, unduly aggressive, ethnocentric and inward-looking. They had, after 1960 Nigeria's independence, one ambition left to be realized: federal political power.[1]

Igbos were also blamed for worsening economic conditions and rising food prices, as many of them were traders and Northerners reflexively attributed their worsening economic situation to the Igbo traders who had "control" of commerce and prices. Igbos had always predominated in commerce, the army and in clerical positions. However, their penetration into other sectors had been kept in check by a Northern led government. Now that an Igbo was head of state, there was nothing to stop them from perpetuating their success (so it was thought by other ethnic groups).

Another factor in the anti-Igbo hostility was the opportunism of the dispossessed politicians. With the military in power, the government would not change, and the disgruntled discredited former politicians could get their jobs back until Aguiyi-Ironsi voluntarily relinquished power, or if a different faction within the army overthrew Aguiyi-Ironsi. The politicians had grown used to the status, power and patronage of public office and suddenly found themselves out in the cold, as did their hangers on who now found that their meal tickets were unemployed. Attention should be given to an infrequently analyzed passage in Aguiyi-Ironsi's inaugural speech which emphasized that the handover to the military was intended as a brief interim measure to enable it to restore order. Aguiyi-Ironsi originally announced that:

> The Nigerian armed forces have been invited to form an *interim* military government.

The author does not believe that the use of the word "interim" was an oversight, but does believe that it was intended to convey that military rule by Aguiyi-Ironsi was originally envisaged by the ousted politicians as an extremely brief aberration, after which they would be allowed to return to business as usual. However, as constitutional review groups and corruption inquiries went to work, the SMC began to pass an ever increasing number of decrees, and Aguiyi-Ironsi announced a three year

---

1 Haruna was giving testimony at the Justice Chukwudifu Oputa chaired Human Rights Violations Investigations Commission in 2001.

term of office for the FMG, it became clear to the politicians that they were not going to get their jobs back any time soon.

The deposed NPC politicians were the primary losers after the January coup. In an effort to avoid further inflaming Northerners' sense of grievance, Aguiyi-Ironsi's regime naively did not arrest or detain NPC politicians, even though the politicians of other parties were detained. The FMG had the legal powers to detain NPC politicians under the State Security (Detention of Persons) Decree but declined to do so. Some of the NPC politicians used their freedom to great effect to whip Northerners into a frenzied and vengeful state of mind which was used for vicious group demonization of Igbos. Commenting on the May riots the US noted that:

> It is significant that the current disturbances are well organized and that they broke out in the north. I would attribute this to the fact that all of the northern politicians from the previous government got off scot-free. (After the coup, the military government did not arrest or detain any northerners for fear of arousing northern sentiment over the assassinations of the Federal Prime Minister and the Governor of Northern Nigeria, both Northerners.) These politicians have undoubtedly been involved in covert activities against the military government.[1]

Religion may also have played a part in the increasing hostility. Muslims had since independence controlled the government. The new SMC was now dominated by Christians. Aguiyi-Ironsi and three of the four military governors were Catholics (Fajuyi, Ejoor and Ojukwu). Lt-Colonel Katsina toured the Northern Region in an attempt to dampen wild speculation that Aguiyi-Ironsi had banned Muslims from pilgrimages to Mecca. The irony is that apart from Aguiyi-Ironsi, Lt-Colonel Ojukwu was the only Igbo member of the 11 member SMC. Even then Ojukwu's membership was automatic since he was a military governor. Aguiyi-Ironsi had four ADCs for the police, navy, air force and army (Assistant Superintendent of police Timothy Pam, Sub-Lieutenant D.E. Okujagu, Lieutenant Andrew Nwankwo and Lieutenant Sani Bello respectively). In reality the only Igbo that had easy access to Aguiyi-Ironsi was his air force ADC Lieutenant Andrew Nwankwo and he was merely an administrative assistant with no influence or involvement in governing policy. In an effort to prove that he was not heading an "Igbo regime," Aguiyi-Ironsi had with great, even daring courage entrusted his personal security to Northern soldiers. He posted the Principal Staff Officer Lt-Colonel Phillip Efiong[2] out of Supreme Headquarters in Lagos and replaced him with Major T.Y. Danjuma of the northern Jukun ethnic group. He even appointed relatives of the January victims to sensitive positions. On the civilian side he appointed a close relative of the Sardauna (Hamzat Ahmadu) to be his private secretary in replacement of Abdul Kareem Disu. His police ADC Timothy Pam was the younger brother of Lt-Colonel James Pam (who was murdered during the January coup), and most of his bodyguards were Northern. By surrounding himself with Northern soldiers, Aguiyi-Ironsi sealed his own fate.

---

1 Memorandum from Ulric Haynes of the National Security Council Staff to the president's special assistant: Foreign Relations of the United States 1964–68, Volume XXIV, Africa.

2 Efiong's name is also frequently spelled in its Anglicized form of "Effiong."

Chapter 7. The Army Implodes

"I knew there would be trouble when I heard that soldiers had been killing soldiers."

For the first few days of his regime, Aguiyi-Ironsi made the police headquarters his base. He conducted his first press conference flanked by a guard who kept his hand on a pistol half drawn from its holster, and he behaved as if he was genuinely concerned for his safety. His caution was justified. Just days after the January coup, Lt-Colonel Victor Banjo was arrested at the police headquarters by Lt-Colonel George Kurubo and Major Patrick Anwunah after he tried to take a gun into a room where Aguiyi-Ironsi was present. Banjo's deputy Major Ebenezer Aghanya was also arrested for allegedly supplying Banjo with the gun. Banjo was not Aguiyi-Ironsi's only problem. As the pattern of killings in the January coup emerged, Northern soldiers became increasingly enraged by the murder of their two most senior politicians (Prime Minister Tafawa Balewa, and Northern Region Premier, Ahmadu Bello), and four most senior soldiers (Brigadier Zakariya Maimalari, Colonel Kur Mohammed, Lt-Colonels Abogo Largema and James Pam)[1] by Igbo officers in January. As one Northern soldier put it: "I knew there would be trouble when I heard that soldiers had been killing soldiers."[2] It was not just the number of Northerners killed that rankled, but the caliber of those killed. Moreover the fact that three of the military victims were from the far north, and one (Pam) from the middle belt[3] united the entire Northern Region in grief and seemed to bring the murders home to every Northern soldier, regardless of whether they were of middle belt or far northern origin. The murders led to embellished rumors that the Majors had planned to murder of all Northern officers above the rank of major.

Despite the murders of the humble Balewa, and Bello — whom many Northerners regarded as a father figure, Northern soldiers were angrier at the death of their re-

---

1 Ironically, one of these men had an Igbo wife.

2 Gowon, *The Biography of a Soldier–Statesman*.

3 The "middle belt" refers to the geographic region straddling Nigeria's central region which lies between the mainly dry Muslim north and the mainly Christian south.

spected senior officers. The murder of Brigadier Maimalari in particular caused grief among Northern soldiers who revered him as "our model, our hero."[1] Major Murtala Muhammed named his newborn baby son "Zakari" in honor of Maimalari.

The public was totally disgusted with the venality of the politicians and generally had no sympathy for them. Politicians had been so thoroughly discredited that a majority of Nigerians would probably have voted for senior politicians to be publicly executed had a plebiscite been held on the issue. The Majors (and many members of the public) viewed the killing of politicians as the execution of criminals. However, Northern soldiers could not fathom why, even if the corrupt politicians had to be killed, army officers had to be killed too. While civilians looked largely at the political ramifications of the coup such as the overthrow of the Balewa government, and the murders of the Prime Minister and two regional Premiers, Northern soldiers were largely uninterested in the political debate and increasingly felt duty bound to restore their honor by avenging the death of their Northern colleagues murdered in January.

4ᵀᴴ Battalion — Ibadan, Western Region

Early warning signs of the trouble ahead appeared at the Ibadan based 4th battalion. Among the officers in that battalion who later rose to prominence were young Lieutenants named Jerry Useni, Babatunde Idiagbon, Mamman Vatsa, Ibrahim Bako, Mohammed Magoro, Mohammed Haladu, Abdullahi Shelleng, Garba Dada, and the intelligence NCO Yohanna Madaki.[2] The northern soldiers here were perhaps the most angry and hurt after the death of the battalion's current (Lt-Colonel Abogo Largema) and former (Colonel Kur Mohammed) commanding officers during the January coup. Largema was extremely popular among the Northern soldiers in his battalion and he had been in charge of it for three consecutive years. Northern fury in the battalion increased when the Igbo deputy commander (Major "Mac" Nzefili) took command of the battalion following Largema's death. Even though Nzefili was not at all involved in the January coup, Northern soldiers drove their Igbo colleagues out of the barracks and refused to take orders from Nzefili. Nzefili lasted only four weeks in the job before Aguiyi-Ironsi was forced to replace him with Major Joe Akahan (a Tiv officer from the Northern Region) due to Northern soldiers' refusal to cooperate with Nzefili. A Yoruba officer: Major Mobolaji Johnson was also brought in to be Akahan's second-in-command (Johnson was a former commander of the Federal Guards). In retrospect, being posted away from the notorious 4th battalion probably saved Nzefili's life. The same scenario was played out in the Kano based 5th battalion, where Mohammed Shuwa (a Shuwa Arab) was appointed to replace the Igbo Major David Okafor. Shuwa's Igbo second in command Captain Joseph Ihedigbo was also replaced by the Yoruba officer Major James Oluleye. Despite these attempts by Aguiyi-Ironsi to placate them, Northern soldiers remained in a near mutinous state and many openly voiced their intention to gain revenge for the murder of their Northern colleagues in January. The Northern soldiers that obeyed orders from Igbo officers did so without any respect for their martial abilities, and regarded Igbo officers as too articulate and erudite to be fighters.

The 4th battalion bitterly complained that no one explained to them what happened to their commanding officer Lt-Colonel Largema and that they were now serv-

---

1 Garba, *Revolution in Nigeria: Another View*, page 41.
2 All these men became leading figures in subsequent coups and military regimes.

ing under a new commanding officer and deputy whom they were unfamiliar with (Majors Akahan and Johnson). The furor in the barracks caused some soldiers to have unusually sensitive trigger fingers. On January 17 1966, the Deputy Assistant Adjutant and Quartermaster-General of 1 brigade Major Simeon Adegoke was shot dead by a twitchy Northern soldier at the 4th battalion who mistakenly believed that Adegoke was an accomplice to the January coup. Adegoke was on leave at the time of the coup but when he heard about it, he decided to visit the 4th battalion. He was arrested en route and detained, then shot when he tried to escape. Lt-Colonel Gowon was also a former member of the 4th battalion. Gowon's close friend James Pam was murdered during the January coup and he was also on good terms with some of the other men that were killed. Gowon tried to talk to, and pacify Northern soldiers who were becoming increasingly rebellious. He spent several hours trying to convince Northern soldiers in the Federal Guards to accept their new commanding officer Major Ochei (an Igbo). Even then, Northern soldiers in the Federal Guards acquiesced to Ochei's command on the condition that Captain Joe Garba (a Northerner) be appointed as Ochei's deputy. Gowon's pep talks and pleas for calm did not have the desired effect. Northern soldiers at the 4th battalion ostentatiously showed their displeasure at his involvement in Aguiyi-Ironsi's government. Some turned their backs on him and others sat down as he addressed them. Sensing that all was not well, Gowon was wisely moving around with a heavy security detail.

RESHUFFLING THE PACK

Command postings in the army *qualitatively* (not quantitatively) reinforced Igbo representation in the officer corps. Before the January coup Igbos held 7 of the 17 most senior positions in the army. That ratio increased slightly to 8 out of 17 by March 1966. However, Igbo officers in command positions were promoted to more senior posts. Although Igbo representation did not numerically increase by a significant margin, a number of Igbo officers were promoted to fill the void created by the officers murdered in January. After the drafting of commanding officers such as Lt-Colonels Ojukwu, Kurubo, Fajuyi, Katsina and Ejoor to the SMC, Aguiyi-Ironsi went with seniority and appointed the most senior officer then serving in the Northern Region (Lt-Colonel Bassey) to command 1 brigade in Kaduna, and the most senior officer serving in the south (Lt-Colonel Njoku) to command 2 brigade in Lagos. The second and third battalions of the army and the first Recce squadron were placed under the command of their deputy commanders (Majors Henry Igboba, Israel Okoro and Captain Ukpo Isong respectively). All three deputies were from the Eastern Region, and with the exception of Isong, were Igbo. With Lt-Colonels Hilary Njoku and Duke Bassey commanding the two brigades, Major Tony Eze commanding the Lagos Garrison Organization (LGO), Major John Obienu in charge of the second Recce squadron, Major Gabriel Okonweze commanding the Abeokuta garrison and Major Ogbugo Kalu commanding the NMTC, most of the army's prominent command postings were held by easterners.[1]

In fairness it should be pointed out that the surviving Northern officers were also elevated, with Lt-Colonel Gowon being appointed Chief of Staff at army headquarters, and Major Murtala Muhammed was appointed Inspector of Signals to replace Major Emmanuel Ifeajuna who before the coup had vacated the post to become the Brigade Major of 2 brigade. Majors Akahan and Shuwa were appointed commanders

---

1 See Table 4 of Appendix 1.

of the 4th and 5th battalions, respectively, and Major Ibrahim Haruna replaced Lt-Colonel Efiong as the Chief Ordnance Officer. These were substantial promotions for these Northern officers as there were many more experienced officers ahead of them. Additionally Captains Domkat Bali and Baba Usman succeeded into the posts vacated by the imprisoned January plotters Major Anuforo and Captain Nwobosi. Usman was appointed as the General Staff Officer (GSO) Grade II at army headquarters and Bali was appointed commander of the 2nd Field Battery, in succession to Anuforo and Nwobosi respectively. Aguiyi-Ironsi was clearly trying to placate Northern officers with these promotions. Some Igbo officers resented these Northern promotions and felt that Aguiyi-Ironsi was pandering to Northerners and over compensating them for the January coup. However, Igbo officers vastly outnumbered their Northern counterparts in both seniority and experience. Table 4 of Appendix 1 shows how the military high command rapidly changed after the coup.

TELLING TALES

In the absence of the vibrant and instant news media of today, an information chasm existed as the government (for fear of increasing tension in the country or further agitating the troops) made little or no comment about the events of January. Aguiyi-Ironsi did not help himself by not publicly explaining the circumstances of the January coup or the events that led to him assuming power. Most of the Nigerian public did not even know that some of the core January coup conspirators were not Igbo. The existence of plotters from other ethnic groups was not revealed for almost twenty years when some of the participants published inside accounts revealing the involvement of Yorubas and Northerners. The troops were already extremely restive and the government feared that releasing news regarding the dead senior officers would further incite them. Some of the units whose commanders were killed in January received no formal announcements about the fate of their former commanders. It seemed as if the dead officers had simply vanished into thin air and were replaced by new commanding officers without any explanations as to what happened to them. Thus rumors and wild conspiracy theories about victims' whereabouts, and miraculous manner of death/survival, thrived.

This did not stop news of the deaths (albeit embellished) from leaking through to some units. A Northern soldier (of the Idoma ethnic group) in the 4th battalion later remarked that "Our master who is our head here,[1] they have tricked him along to a hotel in Lagos and killed him. They have killed Brigadier Maimalari too. They did not tell us, but we know what they have done. They are soldiers! We are soldiers!"[2] The last six words of the foregoing quote were a cryptic warning that the Northern soldiers were very capable of emulating what their Igbo colleagues did in January.

Aside from not releasing an official account of the January events, the Aguiyi-Ironsi regime naively failed to issue propaganda to sell its own program. Perhaps this failure was because the regime had no program to speak of. It was a reactive government that adjusted hesitantly to events rather than set the agenda. Aguiyi-Ironsi was totally unprepared for, and oblivious to, the subtleties of politics. Unlike soldiers turned successful politicians such as Ariel Sharon or Muammar Ghaddafi, Aguiyi-Ironsi did not come to power with predetermined political, economic or social objec-

---

1 Lt-Colonel Largema.
2 Samson Amali, *The Ibos and their fellow Nigerians* (CMS Bookshop, Ibadan, 1967). Reproduced in NJ Miners: *The Nigerian Army 1956–66*, page 268.

tives. He had ended a working week in mid-January 1966 as a soldier and emerged at the beginning of the following week as head of state of the most populous black nation on earth, inheriting a poisoned chalice containing all the problems and mistakes of his predecessors. He also had no precedents to learn from and hence approved pivotal policy shifts without appreciating their dramatic effects, and incorrectly assuming that his good intentions would swing the public behind his point of view. Aguiyi-Ironsi showed little appetite for his political assignment. While still serving as GOC, he was questioned by the press on the proper role of the army, and replied "The army supports the government that is." Shortly after becoming head of state, he tersely replied "I hope not" when asked whether he envisaged a prolonged tenure as a military ruler. He also later admitted that he found governing Nigeria "more difficult than the Congo" (his command of the UN peacekeeping force in the Congo).

Since the government was not providing much news on the events of January 15, people (inside and outside the army) decided to make up the news themselves. This exacerbated the situation for the government by permitting subversive elements to spread dangerously inaccurate and inciting embellishments and rumors on January's events, and the creation of plain falsehood. A riot almost broke out when an attempt was made to remove Brigadier Maimalari's name from official notices at the 2 brigade headquarters in Lagos. Since no official announcement had been made regarding his death, many Northern soldiers believed that he was still alive. A heroic mythology grew around Maimalari. The common belief among Northern NCOs was that Maimalari made a miraculous escape from the January Majors. Even those who realized he was dead thought he had been strangled by Aguiyi-Ironsi (even though the January plotters admitted that they shot him). Fantastic tales also surrounded those reliably confirmed dead. Lurid tales of the manner in which the victims died were widespread. Several of these claimed that the Prime Minister and Finance Minister were mistreated before being killed. A popular account circulating among Northerners also claimed that the Prime Minister had palm wine poured over him in a mark of disrespect. The tales also added that the Prime Minister cursed the Igbo and claimed that they would not govern Nigeria for another 25 years.[1] Northern officer T.Y. Danjuma later claimed[2] that Lt-Colonel Largema's corpse was thrown through the 10-12th floor window of his hotel room and left lying in the driveway (even though the Majors admitted, and the Special Branch report clearly documented, that Major Ifeajuna and Second-Lieutenant Ezedigbo carried Largema's corpse down the hotel stairs and took it away in the boot of Ifeajuna's car). Such claims could easily be disseminated to, and believed by, the largely uneducated Northern public and Northern NCOs. In the mythology that grew around Igbos, some Northerners even suspected that Ojukwu had been one of the January plotters and that he was in Kaduna the morning the Sardauna was murdered. The fact that Ojukwu was at his base several miles in away in Kano, where he was seen by his men and by Northerners (including the Emir of Kano), did not dampen such stories.

Further rumors claimed that Igbo soldiers were planning a second coup to "finish" the job of January. *Agents provocateurs* circulated lists of Northern soldiers whom they claimed Igbos were going to execute. The story being peddled among Northerners was that during this second coup, Igbo soldiers would unleash an orgy of bloodlet-

---

1 Amazingly, the claim of this curse is still believed till today by many northerners, even those highly placed (including a former head of state) who have used it as a justification for opposing political leadership of Nigeria by an Igbo.

2 Momoh, *The Nigerian Civil War, 1967–1970: History and Reminiscences*, page 363.

ting that would dwarf the January coup in magnitude. At their lowest level, these rumors claimed that Igbos would murder every remaining Northern soldier. At their most incredible level, they claimed that Igbos would slaughter every Northern male whether civilian or military. As incredible as they seem, these stories were genuinely believed by Northerners. It is possible that some Igbo soldiers were planning another coup, but the target of the coup would most likely have Aguiyi-Ironsi, who was perceived by some left-wing Igbos as too hesitant to carry out sweeping reforms and of forestalling the "revolution" planned by the January 1966 coup leaders. The advocates of this view took the position that the Majors' planned revolution had been hijacked and derailed by undynamic senior officers who built their careers in servitude and loyalty to the deposed civilian government.

Northern officers were also subjected to incessant pressure to avenge the murders of Northerners in January, by the Northern politicians of the overthrown government, their families, and NCOs. Northern civilians accused their soldiers of cowardice, alleging that they stood idly by while Igbos murdered their military and civilian leaders. Joe Garba recalled being accosted by Clement Gomwalk,[1] who aggressively chastised him for not avenging the death of his colleagues. Gomwalk screamed at him, "There are no more men left in the army. You are all women."[2] The wives of Northern NCOs joined in and taunted their husbands, even questioning their masculinity for not avenging the death of their fellow Northerners. Relations were strained not just between Igbo and Northern soldiers, but also between their respective families. As far back as January the wives of Northern NCOs complained to Lt-Colonel Katsina of derogatory treatment by the wives of Igbo soldiers. In turn Northern NCOs stigmatized their officers, questioned their courage, and urged them to take the lead in avenging the murders of their Northern colleagues. There was no respite for Northern officers from pressure and taunting by their politicians, public, colleagues, families and spouses. Some Northern soldiers in retrospect now admit that they were being subtly and deliberately incited by their fellow Northerners, in a calculated process to get them to retaliate against Igbos.

Some Northern officers had personal stakes in the outcome of the January coup. Like the January Majors, Northern soldiers denied that their actions were influenced by civilians or politicians. However, there has been much hushed discussion and innuendo regarding the role of the former Defense Minister Inuwa Wada. Wada was also the NPC's treasurer and had access to large sums of money. He also had a cousin in the army (Murtala Muhammed). There were several concentric links between some Northern soldiers and the ousted NPC politicians, and some were children of, or were otherwise related to, leading NPC politicians. Apart from being a cousin of the former Defense Minister Inuwa Wada, Major Murtala Muhammed was also related to Aminu Kano (a leading Northern opposition politician), Nigeria's Permanent Representative to the United Nations Alhaji Aminu Wali, the Nigerian High Commissioner to Ghana Alhaji Isa Wali and to Wali's son — Lieutenant Abbas Wali. Abbas Wali later married the Sultan of Sokoto's daughter Zainab. Lieutenant Shehu Musa Yar'Adua's father Mallam Musa Yar'Adua was the former Minister for Lagos and the custodian of treasury of the Katsina Emirate Council (a position known as "Mutawallen Katsina"). Two brothers of the murdered Lt-Colonel James Pam were also serving in the security forces. Lt-Colonel Gowon and the senior defense civil servant Ahmadu Kurfi were schoolmates with the murdered Northern officers, and

---

1 Brother of Joseph Gomwalk.
2 Garba, *Revolution in Nigeria: Another View*, page 60.

the Northern Region's Governor Sir Kashim Ibrahim was Brigadier Maimalari's for-mer schoolteacher. Lt-Colonel Gowon was also close to the murdered Lt-Colonel Pam who was living in Gowon's former house, since succeeding him as the Adjutant-General. According to Lt-Colonel Njoku, Lt-Colonel Haruna's father was a police officer and narrowly escaped death at the Sardauna's lodge on January 15, but was ap-parently spared when Nzeogwu recognized him.[1] Haruna also had a younger brother serving as an NCO in the army. These personal connections may have amplified some Northern soldiers' sense of grievance and served as extra motivation for some deposed politicians to "tap" their Northern contacts in the army to avenge their misfortune.

It should be noted that anti-Igbo sentiment was not limited to the Northern Re-gion. There was resentment among NNDP Yoruba supporters too, although it did not reach the level of intensity present in the Northern Region (despite Yoruba casual-ties during the January coup).[2] This may have been due to any one or all of a number of reasons. Firstly, there were very few Yoruba soldiers, and they were mainly in non-combat roles from which they were not in a position to use force against Igbos even if they wanted to. Additionally, the coup actually caused a favorable outcome for some Yorubas by removing a government that had imprisoned their leader, Chief Awolowo, and perpetuated an intensely disliked regime in their region.

MAY 1966 ARMY PROMOTIONS

In May, a promotion exercise was carried out in the army. The promotions were most likely an attempt by Aguiyi-Ironsi to dilute discontent in the army. However, the attempt backfired and exacerbated disillusion amongst southern and Northern rank and file. Under normal circumstances these promotions would not have raised eyebrows. Moreover they could be justified on the basis of merit and correcting the anomaly of deserving officers that had been passed over for promotion in the past. However, in the ethnically charged environment where every move by Aguiyi-Ironsi was suspected as an Igbo plot, it proved to be a public relations disaster, and was once again, interpreted as favoring Igbos.

The pattern of the promotions gave Northern soldiers the impression that their superior officers were murdered in January with the deliberate intention to create vacancies for Igbo officers to fill. The rumor was that 21 majors had been promoted to lt-colonel, 18 of whom were "Igbo speaking." In fact two things happened: several majors were promoted to acting lt-colonel and some others were promoted substan-tive lt-colonels. The latter group included several officers who before the coup were already acting lt-colonels, and simply had their temporary/acting ranks confirmed. The true nature of the promotion exercise was submerged. Five of those promoted were Northerners, one was Yoruba and several were from the Mid-West. Those pro-moted from major to lt-colonel during Aguiyi-Ironsi's reign were:
- Northern Region: Joe Akahan, Ibrahim Haruna, Hassan Katsina, Murtala Muhammed, Mohammed Shuwa.
- Mid-West Region: Henry Igboba, Alphonsus Keshi, M.O. Morah, Sylvanus Nwajei, Macaulay Nzefili, Ben Ochei, David Okafor, Gabriel Okonweze, Mike Okwechime, Rudolph Trimnell.

---

1 Njoku, *A Tragedy Without Heroes*, page 33.
2 Brigadier Ademulegun, Colonel Shodeinde, Chief Akintola.

- Eastern Region: Festus Akagha, Patrick Anwunah, Emmanuel Ekpo, Anthony Eze, Mike Ivenso, Ogbugo Kalu, Alexander Madiebo, David Ogunewe, Israel Okoro, Christian Ude.[1]
- Western Region: Olufemi Olutoye.

Some of those promoted (such as Morah, Trimnell and Olutoye) were not even in combat units. Morah headed the pay and records department, and Olutoye headed the education unit. The promotion to lt-colonel of the Northerners Murtala, Shuwa and Haruna was particularly generous because at the time of the promotions, all three were only substantive captains (holding temporary ranks as majors) yet they were promoted to lt-colonel. If any group had been discriminated against, it was not Northerners but Yoruba soldiers like Majors Olusegun Obasanjo, Emmanuel Sotomi, Benjamin Adekunle and Oluwole Rotimi — who were not promoted. Several of those promoted had been passed over for promotion in the past. For example Majors Patrick Anwunah, Mike Okwechime, Tony Eze and Alex Madiebo were Gowon's course mates at Sandhurst. However, while Gowon had been promoted to lt-colonel in 1964, by mid 1966 the three men were still majors and were now junior to their former course mate Gowon, even though they were no less capable than him. A little discussed element of the promotion exercise was that not only Majors were promoted. Junior officers were promoted too. In the ethnic stratification of the officer corps, between 65–70% of the army's majors were Igbo. So if any promotion exercise was carried out in that rank, it logically followed that most of those promoted would be Igbo.

Conversely, most junior officers and NCOs were Northern and the primary beneficiaries of the promotion exercise in the junior ranks were logically also Northern. The promoted Northern soldiers included Theophilus Yakubu Danjuma, Muhammadu Buhari, Shehu Musa Yar'Adua, Abdullahi Shelleng, Ibrahim Bako, Muhammadu Jega,[2] Garba Dada ("Paiko") and Paul Tarfa. Strangely there were no complaints about the preponderance of Northern promotions in this category. All eyes remained focused on the Igbo majors promoted to lt-colonel. A group of Northern air force cadets were also dismissed due to their underwhelming educational achievements. The exercise seemed to be part of a broader leaning by Aguiyi-Ironsi away from quota towards a merit based system. Increased emphasis on academic achievement would indirectly discriminate against Northern soldiers.

Unlike some of his successors, Aguiyi-Ironsi did not promote himself, and none of the SMC members were promoted either (Hassan Katsina was promoted from major to lt-colonel when he was appointed military governor of the Northern Region back in January). Aguiyi-Ironsi and Muhammadu Buhari remain the only military heads of state in Nigeria's history who did not promote themselves while in office.

THE JANUARY DETAINEES

The fate of the January Majors was a dangerous and emotive issue. Unbeknown to most, not all of the Majors' accomplices were in detention. Some active plotters, participants and others who were not part of the original plot but obeyed the Majors' orders during the coup's execution had got off scot free. Majors Chude-Sokei and Obienu, and Lieutenant Waribor were in the first category, and Captains John Swanton, Agbogu and Lieutenants Kpera and Oguchi were in the latter category.

---

1 This is not the same "Ude" that took part in the Majors' coup.
2 Currently the Emir of Gwandu.

Rumors circulating among Northerners claimed that the Igbo soldiers imprisoned for their role in the January coup were being treated like royalty in prison, were still on full pay and had also been promoted. A letter from Major Nzeogwu to his former room-mate Major Obasanjo paints a starkly different picture of what life in prison was like:

> Troops under the influence of the Supreme Comd, edged [sic] on by certain tribalists, encouraged private soldiers and NCOs to cane and maltreat some of these officers and the men now in Kiri-Kiri whilst they were under detention in the Federal Guard and in 2 Bn. They were beaten with Kobokos [horsewhips] daily, starved, and forced to drink urine at gun point. Nwobosi[1] nearly had his eye poked out with a rifle muzzle and Oyewole who is still admitted to the military hospital had his forehead and nose smashed to bits with a rifle, in the presence of Ekanem, Captain Iwe, Maj Ally and a few other loyalist officers. If you see the men here in prison you will be sorry for them. Koboko and bayonet wounds all over the face and body! It is terrible. . . . One corporal was shot dead and one Sgt Nathaniel badly wounded by tribalist troops of the Federal Guard. . . . Northern officers and troops feel that the coup is aimed against the North. Everyone seems quite jittery at this end and they will fire at anything that moves.[2]

While it is true that the prisoners were still being paid (Aguiyi-Ironsi could not legally stop their salaries as they had not yet been tried and convicted), none of them had been promoted, and many of them were being beaten up and mistreated. During the May promotion exercise an officer called "D. Okafor" was promoted. Some may have wrongly assumed that this promoted soldier was Major Don Okafor (one of the January plotters). However, the promoted officer was *David* Okafor, who was commissioned into the army in the same year as *Don* Okafor, and whose army number (N/74) was only one digit different from Don Okafor's (N/73). There is also evidence that the detainees' pay was halved. In one of his letters from prison to his friend Olusegun Obasanjo, Major Nzeogwu wrote that he and his accomplices would have "to be a bit more cautious about money in view of the half pay action which is to be imposed on we rebels soon."[3]

Between a Rock and a Hard Place

A board of inquiry including Lt-Colonels Gowon and Nwawo, Captain Baba Usman and Alhaji M.D. Yusuf, was tasked with investigating the coup. Yusuf was formerly the Northern Region's Commissioner of Police but Aguiyi-Ironsi promoted him by appointing him to head the police's Special Branch. Captain Usman was the liaison officer tasked with the job of taking the detainees on a daily basis, from their prison cells to police headquarters where they were interrogated extensively and at length by an interrogation team including Special Branch police officers such as M.D. Yusuf, Assistant Commissioner of Police Isa Dejo, Lt-Colonel Gowon and British police officers. The detainees were monitored closely and Captain Usman screened their correspondence. The interrogations led to the production of an extraordinarily detailed Special Branch police report based on statements given by the suspects

---

1 Officer who led the group which killed Akintola at Ibadan after a gunfight.

2 Letter dated 4, 1966, reproduced in Obasanjo, *An Intimate Portrait of Chukwuma Kaduna Nzeogwu*, page 150.

3 Letter dated February 26, 1966, reproduced in Obasanjo, *An Intimate Portrait of Chukwuma Kaduna Nzeogwu*, page 156.

under interrogation. Back in February 1966, Ojukwu had sent a report on Dr. Michael Okpara to Aguiyi-Ironsi. The report alleged that

> On 15th January 1966 at approximately 2.15 hours ... two army officers, namely Major Emmanuel Ifeajuna and Major Okafor, were seen right at the ground floor corridor of the Premier's house. . . . Information gathered from one of the Premier's intimates was that the officers saw the Premier and had a conversation with him. Text is not known.

This report was seen by M.D. Yusuf and he included Ojukwu's text in the Special Branch report. The other Northerners on the investigation panel would have seen this text. It was unlikely to have reassured them that the January coup was not an Igbo plot. M.D. Yusuf was convinced of civilian involvement in the coup and he also included in the Special Branch Report a reference to unnamed civilians who assisted the Majors.

The report was originally submitted to and reviewed by the SMC, and was to be the basis for the production of a government white paper on the January coup. However, the white paper was never publicly published. Responsibility for the white paper's production and the government's intentions for it, have been the subject of much debate and controversy. According to the Eastern Region, Lt-Colonel Gowon was in charge of producing the white paper but procrastinated on it, and every time he was asked in SMC meetings to report on its progress, replied that he needed more time.[1] In a 2002 lecture at the National War College Lt-Colonel Efiong also claimed that "Aguiyi-Ironsi placed Lt-Colonel Gowon (as he then was) in charge of investigation of the coup and publication of a government white paper on the investigation and identification of the real culprits of the first coup d'état." Captain Baba Usman (who was closely involved in the investigation) subsequently claimed that the Special Branch report was ready at the end of March 1966.[2] According to the Eastern Region, the report was not ready till May 1966.[3] Lt-Colonel Efiong later recalled being present at an SMC meeting during which the report was discussed in June 1966 (Efiong was standing in for Brigadier Ogundipe, who was absent).[4] Although the report was secret, extracts from it were leaked in 1969 to the Emergency Information Service sponsored by the Coordinating Committee on Nigeria/Biafra (the author has read these extracts).

Despite the behind the scenes investigation the SMC made no public announcement regarding when the plotters would be tried. After being detained together at the Kirikiri maximum security prison in Lagos, the detainees were dispersed and sent to various prisons around the country. Northern soldiers were not impressed by Aguiyi-Ironsi's vague assurances that "justice will be done" and wanted the Majors to be immediately tried, while southerners viewed the Majors as heroes that had removed a hated regime. Putting the Majors on trial would not have met with universal public acclaim. A mini personality cult was developing around Nzeogwu in the south and he was being feted as an immortal hero. Given the contrasting forces pulling him in opposite directions it was difficult to see how Aguiyi-Ironsi could please anybody. From prison Major Nzeogwu wrote letters to his Northern friends such as Gowon,

---

1 *January 15: Before and After*, page 27.
2 Momoh, *The Nigerian Civil War, 1967–1970: History and Reminiscences*, page 859.
3 *January 15: Before and After*, page 27
4 Phillip Efiong, *Nigeria and Biafra: My Story*, page 90.

Katsina and Selem (often written in fluent Hausa)[1], and to his fellow plotters and former colleagues such as Second-Lieutenant Azubuogu. He amazingly sent a message to Aguiyi-Ironsi through the Director of Prisons Mr. Giwa-Osagie, requesting to be posted overseas to Kashmir, the UK, US or Germany. Aguiyi-Ironsi refused the request. Major Ifeajuna may have later regretted his actions. Lt-Colonel Banjo said of Ifeajuna: "I know about his involvement in the coup of January 1966. He was responsible for the death of a few people. He was with me in prison for quite some time. I have had the opportunity of discussing the details of that coup with him. I know he regrets the bloodshed that took place on that occasion."[2]

If Aguiyi-Ironsi bowed to northern pressure and immediately tried the Majors, he would face a backlash from southern officers, many of whom held sensitive military posts. If he went with southern opinion and released them, he might be faced with a mutiny by Northern soldiers who were still aggrieved at the murder of their Northern colleagues in January. Aguiyi-Ironsi was caught between the proverbial rock and a hard place and could not take a decision either way without further inflaming passions in the Northern Region and/or south. It proved impossible to keep both sides simultaneously content. Lt-Colonel Ejoor later admitted that he "did not envy" the daunting decision facing Aguiyi-Ironsi. The famous "Black Scorpion" Major Benjamin Adekunle felt the same way and admitted that "It was a difficult situation and I did not envy him one bit."[3] Opinion on the coup among Igbo officers was not unanimous either. The January coup had genuinely taken Lt-Colonel Patrick Anwunah by surprise. Anwunah disapproved of the Majors' coup even though his two immediate subordinates at army headquarters, Major Anuforo and Captain Oji, were among the key conspirators:

> To some the coup makers were heroes, to others, murderers. For me, my conscience told me it was wrong. I could not admire anybody who killed his colleagues at night in their homes or inside their bedrooms. . . . I do not accept that as heroism for whatever reasons.[4]

Due to the gravity of the offenses committed by the Majors (murder, mutiny, treason and kidnapping to name a few), a trial would certainly lead to their execution. Without a formal public announcement, the SMC decided to place the January Majors on public trial. The trial was originally scheduled to take place in August 1966 but was postponed to October.[5] This decision was recorded in the SMC's minutes and later confirmed by the military governor of the Northern Region Lt-Colonel Hassan Katsina, who said that "The minutes of the SMC recorded that the young Majors were to be court-martialled not later than October. The proceedings were to be in public."[6] The only two surviving military governors from that era, David Ejoor and C.O. Ojukwu, corroborated Katsina and confirmed that the SMC had decided to put the January coup plotters on trial. According to Ejoor, "Although, as was to be expected in the situation, there were conflicting views, there was a consensus that the coup leaders should be tried."[7] Ojukwu said that "I was there at the Supreme

---

1 Robert Melson and Howard Wolpe, *Nigeria, Modernization and the Politics of Communalism*, page 394.

2 Nelson Ottah, *Rebels Against Rebels*, pages 41-42.

3 Adekunle, *The Nigeria–Biafran War Letters: A Soldier's Story*.

4 Patrick Anwunah, *The Nigeria–Biafra War (1967–1970). My Memoirs*, page 100.

5 Melson and Howard Wolpe, *Nigeria, Modernization and the Politics of Communalism*, page 396.

6 Ruth First, *The Barrel of a Gun*, pages 307 and 488.

7 Ejoor, *Reminiscences*, page 39.

Military Council (SMC). General Ironsi said that those who were involved would be investigated and would, if found guilty, be charged accordingly. But who was in charge of investigating this matter, it was Gowon."[1]

Tragically this decision was not made public and Northern soldiers maintained the erroneous impression that Aguiyi-Ironsi approved of the Majors' actions and did not intend to punish them. The counter-coup which followed ironically prevented Nigeria from seeing its own "trial of the century." A show trial of the Majors would have given them a chance to publicly articulate their political grievances and *raison d'être* for the coup in the manner of defendants in other political trials such as Nelson Mandela or Marwan Barghouti. Additionally it may have assuaged the bitterness of Northern soldiers who felt that justice had not been done.

Other moves taken by Aguiyi-Ironsi further fuelled Northern discontent. He announced that the military governors would be rotated around the country. He also announced that the rowdy 4th battalion at Ibadan would rotate with the 1st battalion in Enugu. Northerners feared that the first measure was designed to transfer the Igbo military governor of the Eastern Region, Lt-Colonel Ojukwu, to the Northern Region as its new military governor, and that the second measure was a trap to ambush Northern soldiers during the switch. Both measures were in fact unremarkable as subsequent military regimes posted military governors to states other than their states of origin and rotated governors between different states. Being remarkably brave or oblivious to the seething rage in the unit, Aguiyi-Ironsi personally informed the 4th battalion of their rotation by appearing physically at the battalion's parade ground to deliver the news to the troops. Aguiyi-Ironsi also announced that "military prefects" would be posted around the country to ensure the full implementation of the government's policies. No one knew what a military prefect was, what they would do, when they would start work or who they would be. However, despite being oblivious to these facts, everyone was opposed to them and knew they could not possibly bring anything positive as they had been conceived by Aguiyi-Ironsi's regime.

The army which in January acclaimed itself as the only truly Nigerian institution capable of checking ethnic rivalry, became plagued by the very ill it came to cure. In the aftermath of Nigeria's first military coup in January, Hassan Katsina warned his troops that "Coups succeed coups. We will never be at peace again."[2]

---

1 *Vanguard*, 17 November 2003.
2 Karl Maier, *This House Has Fallen: Midnight in Nigeria*, page 52. Officers in Katsina's squadron at that time who later rose to prominence include Lieutenants Ibrahim Babangida, Garba Duba, Chris Ugokwe, Sunday Ifere and J.C. Ojukwu, and Sergeant Dantsoho Mohammed.

CHAPTER 8. THE JULY REMATCH

The suppressed rage of Northern NCOs had been a ticking time bomb since January. By mid 1966, there was an unwritten consensus among Northern soldiers that there would be a "July rematch" with their Igbo colleagues. This "rematch" is today referred to as the "counter-coup." With their overwhelming numerical presence in the infantry (approximately 70–80% of the army's infantrymen were Northerners), it was clear that a revenge coup by Northern soldiers would have drastic consequences. Northern soldiers decided to take the law into their own hands. Their long list of grievances was growing daily:

- The murder of their military and civilian leaders in January.
- The January Majors had still not been tried and were being paid while in detention.
- The Unification Decree.
- Rumors of a further Igbo coup to eliminate all remaining Northern soldiers.
- The promotion of several Igbo Majors to Lt-Colonel.
- Aguiyi-Ironsi allegedly surrounding himself with other Igbos.
- Aguiyi-Ironsi's plan to rotate the military governors.
- The planned swap of the 1st and 4th battalions.

A platoon commanders course in Kaduna brought several junior Northern officers together (including Lieutenants Sani Abacha, Abdullahi Shelleng, Haladu Hannaniya,[1] Muhammadu Jega, Yakubu Dambo and Wali). They typed and sent an anonymous letter to the most senior Northern officer Lt-Colonel Gowon. The letter warned that unless senior Northern officers took action to avenge the murders of January within a certain deadline, the junior Northern officers would take the law into their own hands. It is not known whether Gowon communicated the contents of this letter to his colleagues in the SMC.

---

[1] The first Northerner to join the army engineers corps. Later became Nigeria's High Commissioner to the UK.

Essentially there might have been a "race" between Igbo and Northern troops to carry out the second coup of 1966. Igbo soldiers sympathetic to the Majors' ideology were itching to overthrow Aguiyi-Ironsi, "finish the job" of January and replace him with a more politically vigorous leader. Northerners feared that they would again be targeted in this second Igbo led coup, and felt they had to act immediately in pre-emptive self defense.

The Eastern Region's account of the counter coup claims that there was a calculated and pre-planned Northern conspiracy to murder Aguiyi-Ironsi and replace him with Gowon.[1] The federal government's version[2] portrays the events as an accidental and uncoordinated mutiny. As is often the case in Nigeria, the truth lies somewhere in between. The eastern version accurately claims that an anti-Igbo revolt was planned. However, its intention was not to install Gowon in power. The federal government's account accurately portrays the events of July 28-29 as impromptu. Northern military anger had been simmering and growing since January 15. On July 28 that anger sought and found an outlet during a misunderstanding at the Abeokuta garrison. However, the events at Abeokuta were the catalyst for the premature execution of a pre-existing plan to mutiny. Although the primary motivation was revenge, some Northern soldiers felt emasculated by the combined effects of taunting from Igbos, their families and Northern civilians. This was an opportunity to re-affirm their masculinity. As with the January coup, what eventually occurred was another tragic case of good intentions and horrendous consequences.

PLOTTING THE COUNTER-COUP

The author was informed by an extremely reliable source that the restiveness of the Northern rank and file caused enough concern to justify review by a security council headed by Brigadier Ogundipe.[3] However, if the council had irrefutable evidence of a Northern military backlash, no aggressive pre-emptive action was taken. Although senior Northern officers were involved in the planning, most of the spade work for the revenge coup would be carried out by Northern NCOs and Lieutenants, many of whom had little interest in methodical planning or leniency, and were becoming impatient for an outlet for their grievances. Many Northern soldiers that participated in the January coup also played prominent roles in the July mutiny. Some of these Northern soldiers felt they had been duped in January into taking part in operations that led to the death of their military and civilian leaders. Some Northern NCOs and their wives consulted charms, herbalists and native doctors to assess the most auspicious time of retaliating. Pressure from their NCOs pushed many Northern officers into participation. They feared that NCOs would take over the situation (with disastrous consequences) unless officers took responsibility for planning and coordination.

Plotting by the Northern officers was carried out almost openly. Their bitterness and hostility toward their Igbo colleagues (whom they felt had betrayed them) was such that they made little effort to conceal their intentions. The de facto leader and co-coordinator of the revenge coup was the Inspector of Signals Lt-Colonel Murtala Muhammed, ably assisted by Majors Martin Adamu and Theophilus Danjuma. All three were under thirty years old. In a typically outspoken outburst in the presence

---

1 *January 15: Before and After.*
2 Nigeria 66.
3 Personal communication with the family of an SMC member.

of Igbo officers, Murtala referred to Aguiyi-Ironsi as a "fool" and made it clear that he would avenge the deaths of his Northern colleagues.[1] He also openly declared his intention to other officers including the senior police officer M.D. Yusuf. Murtala's conduct was not isolated. While addressing troops at 1 brigade headquarters in Kaduna, Hassan Katsina angrily declared that Northern troops would retaliate, and when they did, they would do so in broad daylight without sneaking around at night to kill officers and their wives inside their bedrooms as the January Majors had done. Again, this outburst was witnessed by Igbo soldiers including Alex Madiebo and Mike Okwechime.[2]

Lt-Colonel Madiebo claims that he warned Aguiyi-Ironsi that a coup was being planned against him by Northern soldiers. According to Madiebo, Aguiyi-Ironsi asked him to repeat the allegations in the presence of Lt-Colonel Gowon, the Inspector-General of Police Alhaji Kam Selem and the head of the police Special Branch Alhaji M.D. Yusuf (all three are Northerners). Major Mobolaji Johnson, the military governor of Lagos, was also present. In an effort to prove to doubters that he was not having clandestine meetings with his fellow Igbos, Aguiyi-Ironsi insisted that Mobolaji Johnson (a Yoruba) be present at all times when he spoke to others so that an impartial third party could listen in on his conversations. Gowon, Selem and Yusuf all denied Madiebo's allegations of a Northern coup and Madiebo was chastised for rumor mongering.[3]

Most of the initiators were based in the south at Lagos, Ibadan and Abeokuta. The planning and execution was not coordinated nationwide like the January coup and individual Northern soldiers were assembling their own plans for revenge. On the occasions when Northern officers felt the need to plan surreptitiously they adopted varied methods. Lt-Colonel Murtala Muhammed would often drive to Ibadan from Lagos, pick up Northern officers in Ibadan at a predetermined rendezvous point and then drive around Ibadan without stopping while brainstorming various options for the counter-coup. Captain Ahmadu Yakubu acted as a messenger by driving all the way from Lagos to Kaduna in order to update Northern soldiers in Kaduna.[4] The Lagos group would take advantage of athletic events by plotting during games on the football field at the LGO's Abalti barracks. They would often also meet at the 4 Lugard Avenue home of Captain Joe Garba in Ikoyi. According to Garba,[5] the prominent plotters stationed in the south included:

- In Lagos: Joe Garba, Murtala Muhammed, Yakubu Danjuma, Martin Adamu, Muhammadu Buhari, Paul Tarfa, William Walbe, John Longboem, Musa Usman, and Shittu Alao (the latter two — both of the air force).
- In Ibadan: Jerry Useni, Ibrahim Bako and Garba Dada.
- In Enugu: Lieutenant Shehu Musa Yar'Adua.
- In Abeokuta: Lieutenant Pam Mwadkon.

There were many other plotters. Garba admitted that "virtually all other northern officers serving in Ibadan, Abeokuta, Ikeja and Lagos became involved in the

---

1 See Madiebo, *The Nigerian Revolution and The Biafran War*, page 51.
2 Confirmed by Katsina during National Workshop on the Events, Issues and Sources of Nigerian History, 1960-1970, held at State House, Kawo, Kaduna, 7-9 June 1993, and corroborated by Patrick Anwunah, *The Nigeria-Biafra War (1967-1970). My Memoirs*, page 100.
3 Madiebo, *The Nigerian Revolution and The Biafran War*, pages 48-49.
4 See interview with Ibrahim Babangida in Momoh, *The Nigerian Civil War, 1967-1970: History and Reminiscences*, page 306.
5 Garba, *Revolution in Nigeria: Another View*, page 59.

coup in one way or another."[1] Plotters at the lieutenant level in Lagos also included Nuhu Nathan and Malami Nassarawa. Northern conspirators in Abeokuta included Lieutenant I.S. Umar. Lieutenant Abdullahi Shelleng and the Adjutant Garba Dada were among the prominent plotters stationed at the restive 4th battalion in Ibadan. Dada was a Northern soldier of Gwari ethnicity whose *nom de guerre* was "Paiko." The pseudonym was a useful cover for the conspirators. Even some of his colleagues in the army were unaware of his real surname and for several decades he has continually been referred to as "Paiko." Domkat Bali recalls being cryptically asked by Pam Mwadkon whether he was going to attend "Paiko's wedding" in Ibadan. Unaware that the phrase was a coded reference to the counter-coup, Bali innocently replied that he was unaware that Paiko was getting married.[2]

Crucially, the plotters also had "moles" in Aguiyi-Ironsi's entourage. Aguiyi-Ironsi had entrusted his security to Northern escorts and soldiers such as Major Danjuma and Lieutenant Walbe, who had now defected, and were among the core conspirators planning to kill him. Ojukwu also claimed that he confided to Aguiyi-Ironsi, his concerns about the large Northern contingent among Aguiyi-Ironsi's security team. Ojukwu claimed that Aguiyi-Ironsi nonchalantly brushed aside his concerns and simply told him that the Northerners in his security team were his "boys."[3] It is doubtful that Aguiyi-Ironsi was aware of the danger he was in.

There were at least three different plans to abduct or kill Aguiyi-Ironsi. According to then Lieutenant Abdullahi Shelleng, the original plan was scheduled for the planned rotation of the 1st and 4th battalions. The first battalion's Adjutant Lieutenant Yar'Adua was to create a commotion during the rotation, which would act as a signal for Northern soldiers to mutiny. Another idea was to abduct Aguiyi-Ironsi while he was on the northern lap of his national tour to explain the benefits of Decree 34, and then and fly him to a neighboring country.[4] During the northern lap of his nationwide tour, there was a security scare when gunshots were heard while Aguiyi-Ironsi was at an airport. Nothing further than this occurred on the northern lap of Aguiyi-Ironsi's tour, largely due to the personal intervention of the Emir of Kano (who was a personal acquaintance of Lt-Colonel Ojukwu and his millionaire father). Northern traditional rulers had cautioned against spilling Aguiyi-Ironsi's blood on Northern soil. The third plan was to abduct Aguiyi-Ironsi during the Western Region lap of his nationwide tour. The Western Region capital of Ibadan was an ideal location to neutralize Aguiyi-Ironsi. Ibadan had a large contingent of Northern soldiers and a "neutral" local population. However, the revenge coup was twice postponed partly because the coup leaders feared that the plot had leaked to Igbo officers who were ready and waiting.

After addressing an assembly of traditional rulers on July 28, Aguiyi-Ironsi decided to spend the night in the Ibadan State House with the members of his entourage. His tour entourage included the Principal Staff Officer at army headquarters Major T.Y. Danjuma, Lieutenant William Walbe, his ADCs Lieutenant Sani Bello and Lieutenant Andrew Nwankwo, Major Ignatius Obeya, Captain Tom Iweanya, the 1 brigade commander Lt-Colonel Hilary Njoku, Federal Guards commander Major Ben Ochei and Staff Sergeant Godwin Madu.

---

1 Ibid., page 59.
2 Momoh, *The Nigerian Civil War, 1967–1970: History and Reminiscences*, page 328.
3 *Vanguard*, 17 November 2003.
4 Momoh, *The Nigerian Civil War, 1967–1970: History and Reminiscences*, page 817.

Back in Lagos on the same day Lt-Colonel Murtala Muhammed unexpectedly showed up at the house of the Igbo GSO (Grade I) at army headquarters and head of military intelligence Lt-Colonel Patrick Anwunah. Anwunah confronted Murtala with the accusation that he (Murtala) was planning a Northern led coup and warned him that southern officers were aware of the plot and would be ready and waiting for him.[1] The two had an angry exchange of words. Anwunah hoped that the confrontation would convince Murtala to drop his coup plan. Murtala feared that the plot had leaked and would be countered so he again postponed the counter coup date and told his men to stand down. Given that this was not the first postponement, a group of Northern soldiers decided to ignore his orders and commence the counter- coup regardless.

ABEOKUTA: THE CATALYST

Abeokuta Garrison, Western Region —
Thursday Night, July 28, 1966 (Almost Midnight)

The commanding officer of the Abeokuta garrison was Lt-Colonel Gabriel Okon-weze. He had previously been the second in command of the 1st battalion in Enugu but was posted to Abeokuta following the January coup. Late on the night of July 28, Okonweze became concerned by reports he had received which indicated that another coup was imminent. Okonweze had received a tip from army headquarters warning him of a coup that night. To avoid a repeat of the killings that had occurred in January, Okonweze instructed Lieutenant Abdullahi Mamman to wake up the officers and called a meeting in the officers' mess. Contrary to popular myth which states that Okonweze invited only Igbo soldiers to the meeting, the officers who attended have vouched that all officers regardless of ethnic or regional origin were invited. Some of the attendees included Northern officers such as Lieutenants D.S. Abubakar, I.S. Umar and Gabriel Idoko. The two most senior Northern officers in Abeokuta, Captains Mohammed Remawa and Domkat Bali were absent from the meeting as they had gone out to the Abeokuta recreation club. Lieutenant Rowland Ogbonna had also gone out to celebrate his purchase of a new car. According to the officers attending the meeting, Okonweze informed them that Anwunah had alerted him of an impending coup. Okonweze urged any officer with information to come forward, and promised that he would not report anyone for doing so. Okonweze added that he did not want a repeat of the January shootings and that the best course of action would be to issue arms and ammunition to the soldiers in his unit so they could defend themselves if a coup began. In response to Okonweze's orders, an Igbo NCO went round waking up the other soldiers, with instructions for them to go and collect arms. The fact that the NCO was Igbo did not help to calm the fears of Northern soldiers.

In the highly tense and emotional atmosphere any unfounded rumor, minor mis-understanding or miscommunication was likely to spark violence. This was particu-larly so at Abeokuta which had several of the most embittered conspirators such as Lieutenants Pam Mwadkon and I.S. Umar. Rather than calm tempers and nerves, the meeting further agitated Northern NCOs who were not inside the mess. Some of the NCOs had already planned a mutiny and assumed that the meeting with Okonweze

---

1 Patrick Anwunah, *The Nigeria–Biafra War (1967–1970). My Memoirs*, page 122.

was discussing plans to eliminate them. A group of them decided that Okonweze's order was a chance to strike first against their Igbo colleagues. This group included Corporal John Shagaya and Lieutenant Pam Mwadkon of the Recce squadron. Mwadkon was the duty officer and Shagaya was an instructor in communications, gunnery, and driving and maintenance. They decided to pre-emptively get organized and armed. Two Bachama soldiers in the unit: Sergeant Sabo Kwale and Corporal Maisamari Maje, had a pivotal conversation in their native tongue. The Bachamas are an ethnic group renowned for their warrior tradition and fighting capabilities. Kwale told Maje (the unit's armorer) to ensure that weapons were issued to Northerners only. Another Northern soldier in the unit: Inuwa Sara procured other Northern soldiers to man the armory and to assist in the selective distribution of weapons to Northern soldiers only. While Okonweze continued to address the meeting in the officers' mess, Northern NCOs led by Sergeant Sabo Kwale and Corporal Maisamari Maje started advancing towards the mess. The officers in the mess initially thought the NCOs were coming in to receive instructions, and did not realize they were about to become eyewitnesses to a crime scene. Led by Kwale and Maje, the Northern soldiers stormed into the officers' mess, and shot dead Lt-Colonel Okonweze and the commander of the Recce Squadron in Abeokuta, Major John Obienu.[1] Obienu had been billed to appear in the January Majors' coup but lost his nerve on the D-Day and failed to show up. As will be shown later in this book, this was not the last prominent act of revolt by Sergeant Sabo Kwale. Kwale was never punished for shooting Okonweze and Obienu. Years later, even his fellow Northern soldiers would regret their failure to take punitive action against him.

After the shooting of Okonweze and Obienu all hell broke loose as soldiers started running for cover in all directions. Initially, no one was sure which side (Igbos or Northerners) was responsible for the shooting. Lieutenant Orok (an eastern officer of non-Igbo origin) was out when the shooting started. He returned to find the garrison in confusion. He was also shot dead after driving into the garrison and stumbling on the commotion occurring. Shortly afterwards, Captain Domkat Bali[2] returned from his outing with Captain Remawa and was shocked to discover the corpses of Okonweze, Obienu and Orok. Bali and Remawa stumbled upon Obienu's bullet riddled corpse still sitting in a chair inside the officers' mess. Remawa and Bali got changed into full battle attire and tried to restrain the NCOs.[3] However, not even the presence of Northern officers such as Remawa and Bali could restrain the rage of some of the NCOs. Second-Lieutenant Olaniyan was shot dead in the presence of Captain Bali who had promised him safe passage. As Bali was escorting him, Olaniyan was shot dead by other Northern troops, and died calling out Bali's name.[4]

Now in control of the Abeokuta garrison, Northern soldiers conducted a door to door search for Igbo soldiers. When found, Igbo soldiers were shot and their bodies dumped into a vehicle parked near one of the officers' quarters. They also mounted roadblocks on main roads to and from Abeokuta. Initial press reports were confused

---

1 The author's account of events at the Abeokuta garrison are corroborated in the interviews with Colonel D.S. Abubakar, Lt-General Domkat Bali and Lt-General T.Y. Danjuma in the Nigerian army's official history of the Nigerian civil war. See Momoh, *The Nigerian Civil War, 1967–1970: History and Reminiscences.*

2 Later General, Defense Secretary and Chairman of the Joint Chiefs of Staff in Babangida's regime.

3 Momoh, *The Nigerian Civil War, 1967–1970: History and Reminiscences,* page 328.

4 Femi Ahmed, *Domkat: A Biography of General Domkat Bali,* page 95.

and many news outlets reported the shootings as the beginning of another coup by Igbo soldiers against Aguiyi-Ironsi. The Northern officers at Abeokuta delegated their most senior member Captain Mohammed Remawa to telephone Lt-Colonel Gowon and inform him of what had happened. For the second time in six months, an army mutiny began in Abeokuta and spread to other cities, and also for the second time in six months Remawa found himself about to become an accomplice in a coup. During the January coup he had provided vehicles to Captain Nwobosi, unaware that Nwobosi would use those vehicles to drive to Ibadan and attack Chief Akintola. This time round he fully supported the coup. According to Lieutenant D.S. Abubakar the Abeokuta officers feared that they would be isolated, arrested and imprisoned. They resolved to fight on rather than let that happen. Now armed with the news of the Abeokuta mutiny, Lt-Colonel Gowon started phoning the various army formations around the country and warning them to be on alert. However, his calls to other army installations simply spurred Northern soldiers in those units into action.

Lagos, Overnight — Thursday July 28–Friday July 29, 1966

An Igbo member of the Abeokuta garrison, Lieutenant Rowland Ogbonna, had been out of the barracks when the trouble started but returned in time to stumble upon the mayhem. Ogbonna was the commander of A company. When he arrived he did not wait for clarification from the Northern soldiers but simply put two and two together, concluded another coup was in progress, and fled. Ogbonna was unaware that one of his old classmates from the Nigerian Military School (Inuwa Sara) was one of the ringleaders behind the mutiny. Panic stricken, Ogbonna managed to find his way to a police station from where he telephoned Lagos to inform the 2nd battalion of what he presumed was an isolated mutiny in the Abeokuta garrison. Lady luck smiled on the Northern plotters. Ogbonna's call was answered by Lieutenant Nuhu Nathan (who was in on the coup plot). Lieutenants Nathan and M.M. Nassarawa alerted their superiors, Lt-Colonel Murtala Muhammed and Major Martin Adamu. Murtala was initially reticent and unsure whether events at Abeokuta justified re-igniting the counter-coup plan. However, he decided that the Abeokuta mutiny created ideal conditions to re-start the original plan for revenge. He ordered two separate groups of the Abeokuta mutineers under Lieutenants D.S. Abubakar and Pam Mwadkon to head out from Abeokuta to provide reinforcements for their co-conspirators in Lagos and Ibadan respectively. Mwadkon was ferried to Ibadan by Corporal John Shagaya.

Federal Guard Barracks — Ikoyi, Lagos

After being alerted of the Abeokuta mutiny Lt-Colonel Murtala Muhammed woke up Captain Joe Garba of the Federal Guards, updated him and told him to adjust to the expedited situation created by events at Abeokuta. Murtala departed to rouse other Northern soldiers in Lagos while Garba in turn woke up his Federal Guards colleague Lieutenant Paul Tarfa. As Garba and Tarfa were getting changed and preparing to mobilize the Federal Guards, a call came in from Lt-Colonel Gowon confirming news of events at Abeokuta and urging them to be on alert.

2nd Battalion, Ikeja, Lagos

A group of the Abeokuta mutineers arrived at the 2nd battalion in Ikeja by early morning on July 29 to further ignite an already tense situation. The coup in Ikeja was initiated by Lieutenants Nathan and Nassarawa, who managed affairs until their superiors Lt-Colonel Murtala Muhammed, Majors Martin Adamu, Shittu Alao, and Musa Usman arrived. Other active participants in Lagos included Lieutenant Muhammadu Buhari of the 2 brigade transport company, Lieutenant John Longboem, Captains Ibrahim Taiwo and Alfred Gom, Lieutenant Tokkida of the LGO, and a notoriously violent Sergeant from the Idoma ethnic group named Paul Dickson.

Igbo soldiers were shot dead in their quarters, some as they rose in the morning, others as they reported for physical training. Northern soldiers had pre-selected Igbo soldiers for elimination. The casualties in Ikeja included Lieutenant Pius Onyeneho and the unit education officer Captain John Chukwueke, who was shot in the presence of his wife, children and mother-in-law. Lieutenant John Odigwe attempted to rescue Onyeneho but was unable to do so after he too came under heavy fire. Ironically, Onyeneho was a former classmate of one of the mutineers, Nuhu Nathan. Lieutenant Godson Mbabie and his wife were both shot, along with Mbabie's brother-in-law (a school boy). Mbabie's wife survived her wounds. Captain Kevin Megwa and his wife hid in their wardrobe while their young nanny went around the barracks weeping, carrying their two-month-old baby girl, pretending they had been killed.[1]

The Ikeja airport in Lagos also turned into an execution ground under the command of the fearsome Sergeant Paul Dickson. Captain Okoye (from Ojukwu's hometown of Nnewi) who was passing through Ikeja airport, was captured, tied to an iron cross, beaten, whipped and left to die an agonizing death in the guardroom in what bore the appearance of a ritual murder. Some of the Igbo survivors (military and civilian) at the airport where flogged on Dickson's orders. Dickson stayed on as head of security at the airport for several years and somehow bagged himself an automatic promotion to Captain in the process (and later again to Major). The air force officer that had been briefed to fly to Calabar to release Chief Awolowo from prison (Major Nzegwu) was also killed.

Ironically many of the Igbo officers attacked in Lagos were the same officers who played prominent roles in putting down the January coup. Two examples illustrate this. In January Captain Ugoala had actually interrogated the coup detainees. His anti-coup role in January was forgotten and he was killed by the Northern mutineers. The house of the 2nd battalion's commander Lt-Colonel Henry Igboba was also targeted even though he was one of the officers that were instrumental in putting down the January coup and had been accused of meting out brutal treatment to January detainees. Northern soldiers surrounded Igboba's house but Igboba managed to escape and shelter at the police college in Ikeja.

Ibadan, Western Region — 4 a.m., Friday July 29, 1966

In Ibadan, Aguiyi-Ironsi received a telephone call from Commissioner of Police Joseph Adeola in the early hours of Friday 29 July informing him of the mutiny at Abeokuta and the murder of Okonweze, Obienu and Orok. Aguiyi-Ironsi's host Fajuyi suggested that they should leave State House in Ibadan but Aguiyi-Ironsi would have none of it.

---

1 Hilary Njoku, *A Tragedy Without Heroes*, page 86.

From Abeokuta Lieutenant Ogbonna also made more panicky calls to other military units including the 4th battalion in Ibadan. His call was answered by the battalion's Adjutant Lieutenant Garba Dada who was also one of the core Northern conspirators. Dada recognized Ogbonna's voice as the two trained together as cadets. Ogbonna's distress calls merely served as the rallying alert for other Northern troops (who up till now were unaware that the coup had begun) to mobilize. Everything was going the Northerners' way. After the call from Ogbonna, Dada woke up Major Danjuma and updated him. Danjuma and Dada then phoned the Abeokuta garrison to get more information on what had happened.[1] This time Dada spoke to a Northern officer in Abeokuta: Lieutenant Pam Mwadkon who confirmed the murders at Abeokuta and urged Dada to commence the coup in Ibadan since they had liquidated the Igbo soldiers in Abeokuta and "liberated" the garrison. Emboldened by the outcome in Abeokuta, approximately two dozen Northern troops under the command of the lean, gangling Major T.Y. Danjuma (whom Aguiyi-Ironsi had recently promoted) turned up at the Ibadan State House. Danjuma was the Principal Staff Officer at army headquarters in Lagos and a member of Aguiyi-Ironsi's entourage during his tour. Danjuma asked all the guards on duty to line up. He disarmed, then ordered all the Igbo guards to leave, but picked out Northern guards to remain. After being briefed by Danjuma, the Northern guards switched sides and joined him and the troops he had brought along with him. The Northern guards, now reinforced by the other soldiers brought by Danjuma, surrounded State House. According to Danjuma, by sheer coincidence, Lt-Colonel Gowon placed a call to State House at that very moment. The call connected to a telephone immediately adjacent to Danjuma's location. Danjuma picked up the receiver, and after identifying himself to Gowon, informed Gowon of his plan to capture Aguiyi-Ironsi. The following is an account of the telephone conversation between Gowon and Danjuma as described by Danjuma:

> Gowon: "Hello. I want to speak to the brigade commander. I want to speak to Colonel Njoku."
>
> Danjuma: "May I know who is speaking?"
>
> Gowon: "My name is Gowon. Yakubu Gowon."
>
> Danjuma: "Ranka dede.[2] This is Yakubu Danjuma."
>
> Gowon: "Yakubu. What are you doing there? Where are you?"
>
> Danjuma: "I am in the State House here."
>
> Gowon: "Where is the brigade commander?"
>
> Danjuma: "He is not around."
>
> Gowon: "Have you heard what has happened?" [At Abeokuta]
>
> Danjuma: "Yes. I heard and that is why I am here. We are about to arrest the Supreme Commander. The alternative is that the Igbo boys who carried out the January coup will be released tit for tat since we killed their own officer."
>
> Gowon (after a long pause): "Can you do it?"
>
> Danjuma: "Yes. We have got the place surrounded."
>
> Gowon: "Alright but for goodness sake we have had enough of bloodshed. There must be no bloodshed."
>
> Danjuma: "No. We are only going to arrest him."[3]

1 Barrett, *Danjuma: The Making of a General*, page 49.

2 A Northern greeting.

3 Momoh, *The Nigerian Civil War, 1967–1970: History and Reminiscences*, page 372.

Danjuma's chance interception of a telephone call intended for Aguiyi-Ironsi was one of many coincidences and slices of good fortune that worked in the Northern soldiers' favor. Had that call been connected to Aguiyi-Ironsi, events may have taken a dramatically different turn. News of the Abeokuta killings had also reached Lt-Colonel Ojukwu. Around 4 a.m. he called Lt-Colonel Ejoor and passed on the news.

Ibadan, Western Region — 5 a.m.

Around 5 a.m. Aguiyi-Ironsi and his fellow occupants inside State House heard gunfire outside. This was actually an accidental discharge by Danjuma's men. The commander of 2 brigade Lt-Colonel Hilary Njoku was summoned from a guest house adjacent to the State House. When he arrived he found Aguiyi-Ironsi and Fajuyi alert and nervously pacing up and down the living room floor. Njoku was informed of the murder of Okonweze, Obienu and Orok, and was instructed to travel to Lagos and organize a suppression of the mutiny from there. Before Njoku departed he telephoned the commander of the 4th battalion in Ibadan, Lt-Colonel Joe Akahan. Akahan was already aware of events at Abeokuta but informed Njoku that nothing untoward was occurring in his unit, and that he was reluctant to alert his men as he felt it would be dangerous to get them further agitated. The military governor of the Mid-West Lt-Colonel David Ejoor also telephoned Akahan and asked him for an update on the situation in Ibadan and to check on Aguiyi-Ironsi's condition. Akahan again maintained that nothing unusual was happening and that his unit was quiet. In fact, men from Akahan's unit were neck deep in the plot and many of them were among the soldiers that had surrounded Aguiyi-Ironsi and Fajuyi at State House (including Lieutenants Abdullahi Shelleng, Garba Dada, Mohammed Haladu and James Onoja). According to Danjuma the other soldiers with him included an NCO that later retired as a Brigadier, and another soldier that was later killed during the Nigerian civil war.

As Njoku was leaving State House he was recognized by the Northern troops outside and they opened fire on him. Njoku was shot in the thigh but managed to escape. At this point the 4th battalion's duty officer Lieutenant James Onoja (one of the Northern soldiers with Danjuma) feared that the coup was going to fail and fled all the way to the Northern Region. Danjuma's men searched the grounds for Njoku but were unable to locate him. When Njoku's wife Rose rang State House to find out what was going on, her call was answered by Aguiyi-Ironsi who grimly informed her that her husband had departed a few minutes earlier, and that gunshots were heard not long after his departure. Njoku escaped for a second time when some Northern soldiers went looking for him at a hospital where he sought medical treatment for the gunshot wounds he sustained. Njoku managed to escape his pursuers again and was eventually smuggled to the Eastern Region.

8 a.m.– 9 a.m.

An increasingly isolated Aguiyi-Ironsi made a flurry of telephone calls to army formations around the country and spoke to many officers to advise them of his predicament. He telephoned 2 brigade headquarters in Lagos and spoke to the Deputy Assistant Adjutant and Quartermaster-General Major Frank Obioha, and unsuccessfully attempted to have a helicopter sent to rescue him. He also telephoned the 1 brigade headquarters in Kaduna and ominously informed the Brigade Major Samuel

Ogbemudia that "all is not well."[1] However, the 1 brigade was in Kaduna, hundreds of miles away from Ibadan and therefore unlikely to be of immediate assistance to Aguiyi-Ironsi. Aguiyi-Ironsi's panic stricken wife also spoke to her husband and to Lt-Colonel Njoku's wife Rose. The two wives wept as they realized the danger their husbands were in.

Back at State House Ibadan, aides were being quietly arrested by the now mutinous guards. The detainees included the Secretary to the National Military Government, Mr. S.O. Wey, Staff Sergeant Godwin Madu, Njoku's driver and Major Thomas of the medical corps. Having been in position outside State House for several hours, the NCOs under Danjuma grew increasingly nervous, impatient and were urging him to attack the building and destroy it with a high caliber weapon. They were concerned about the apocryphal stories about Aguiyi-Ironsi, and feared that he could use "Charlie" to make himself disappear from the building and appear at a different location from where he could neutralize them (the myths about Aguiyi-Ironsi's invincibility were reinforced by his suppression of the Majors' coup in January). Lieutenant Abdullahi Shelleng was on hand to urge the NCOs to continue to cooperate with Danjuma.

Danjuma had thus far resisted and contented himself with quietly arresting people that were seen coming out of State House. Aguiyi-Ironsi and Fajuyi sent out aides from the State House to appraise what was going on outside (not realizing that some of the men they were sending out and to whom they entrusted their safety were in league with the mutineers). Being privy to the coup plot, these men did not alert Fajuyi and Aguiyi-Ironsi of the danger they were in. Fajuyi's ADC, Lieutenant Umar was sent out to find out what was going on. He went outside and simply switched sides, joining Danjuma's troops. He returned to falsely inform the State House occupants that all was well.

9 a.m.

Aguiyi-Ironsi's air force ADC Lieutenant Andrew Nwankwo[2] also went outside to see what was going on. He was stalled by Major Danjuma who asked to see Aguiyi-Ironsi. Danjuma and Nwankwo knew each other personally. According to Nwankwo, Danjuma "pretended he didn't know what was happening.... While I was trying to go back, one Sergeant from Benue almost shot me, but Danjuma stopped him and spoke to him in Hausa. Danjuma later told me that he would like to see Ironsi, so that he could tell them what to do."[3]

Aguiyi-Ironsi and Fajuyi were becoming increasingly concerned. Some of the aides they sent to investigate had simply disappeared and not returned. After some time, Lt-Colonel Fajuyi also came outside to see what was taking Nwankwo so long. At this point Danjuma ordered the arrest of Fajuyi and Nwankwo. According to Danjuma, the following verbal exchange took place between he and Fajuyi:

> Danjuma: "Sir you are under arrest. Raise your hands."
>
> Fajuyi: "What do you want"?
>
> Danjuma: "I want the Supreme Commander"
>
> Fajuyi: "Promise me that no harm will come to him."[4]

1 Samuel Ogbemudia, *Years of Challenge*, page 44.

2 This officer had previously worked for Emperor Haile Selassie of Ethiopia.

3 *The Sun*, Monday, June 28, 2004.

4 Momoh, *The Nigerian Civil War, 1967–1970: History and Reminiscences*, page 371.

Fajuyi agreed to take Danjuma to see Aguiyi-Ironsi after eliciting an assurance from Danjuma that Aguiyi-Ironsi would come to no harm. According to Danjuma, he overruled a chorus of objections from the NCOs, who did not want Fajuyi to be allowed to go back inside. The NCOs agreed only after approximately half a dozen of them were allowed to enter with Fajuyi and Danjuma. While these conversations went on outside, upstairs inside State House, Aguiyi-Ironsi woke up his young son Thomas who was visiting him from England during his school holidays. Aguiyi-Ironsi gave Thomas instructions to find his way back to Lagos, embraced and bade farewell to him, then hid him inside a wardrobe. Fajuyi's younger brother was also hidden in the house as the mutineers entered.

Escorted by the now hostage Fajuyi, Danjuma and his troops entered State House. Danjuma walked behind Fajuyi with a grenade in his hand (with the pin removed). Danjuma originally brought the grenade as insurance in case the operation failed and he needed to kill himself.[1] They met two police guards on the staircase. The outgunned guards were told to drop their weapons and join the other detainees. They complied. Danjuma and his men went up to the first floor and entered the State House living room where Aguiyi-Ironsi was. Danjuma saluted Aguiyi-Ironsi, and Lieutenant Titus Numan snatched the ever-present crocodile mascot "Charlie" away from him (the stories of how the mascot rendered Aguiyi-Ironsi impervious to physical harm were obviously playing on their minds).

Over the years Danjuma has given two separate but broadly consistent accounts of the tense verbal exchange that ensued between him and Aguiyi-Ironsi:

> Ironsi: "Young man."
>
> Danjuma: "Sir, you are under arrest."
>
> Ironsi: "What is the matter?"
>
> Danjuma: "The matter is you, Sir. You told us in January when we supported you to quell the mutiny that all the dissident elements that took part in the mutiny will be court martialled. It is July now. You have done nothing. You kept these boys in prison and the rumours are now that they will be released because they are national heroes."
>
> Ironsi: "Look, what do you mean? It is not true."[2]
>
> Danjuma: "You are lying. You have been fooling us. . . . You told us that they would be tried. This is July and nothing has been done. You will answer for your actions."[3]

As Danjuma and Aguiyi-Ironsi argued, Aguiyi-Ironsi's air force ADC Lieutenant Nwankwo added a few choice words of his own, and Fajuyi repeatedly reminded Danjuma of the assurance of safety he had given. Nwankwo still had his pistol but did not use it as there were half a dozen Northern soldiers in the room, armed with automatic weapons, and one with a grenade. According to Nwankwo, "It was immediately (after) they arrested Ironsi that they turned violent."[4] Aguiyi-Ironsi's army ADC Lieutenant Sani Bello was also accosted. As a Northerner, he was suspected of being a traitor for serving as Aguiyi-Ironsi's army ADC. Aguiyi-Ironsi, Fajuyi, Nwankwo and Bello were led out with their hands tied behind their backs with telephone wire.

1Ibid., page 369.

2 Ibid., page 371.

3 Barrett, Danjuma, *The Making of a General*, page 55.

4 *The Sun*, Monday, June 28, 2004.

Aguiyi-Ironsi had first his major-general pips and then his shirt ripped off. This may have been a symbolic attempt to strip him of his authority.

At this point the protagonists' accounts diverge. The most detailed accounts of what happened at Ibadan emerge from Danjuma, Lieutenant Nwankwo and the Eastern Region publication *January 15: Before and After*. Danjuma claims that one of the NCOs tapped him on the shoulder with a rifle and together with the other NCOs and junior officers snatched Aguiyi-Ironsi and Fajuyi away from him. According to Danjuma, the NCOs lost patience with him for not ordering Aguiyi-Ironsi's summary elimination and were frightened that unless he was immediately neutralized, Aguiyi-Ironsi might use his "juju" to disappear before their very eyes. The captives were loaded into a Jeep and driven off in a convoy that included two other vehicles. The Eastern Region's account claims that Danjuma was in one of the convoy's vehicles, but at an intersection, waved the other vehicles on and drove off separately for the barracks.

The soldiers who remained in the convoy and took Aguiyi-Ironsi and Fajuyi to their final destination included Lieutenants William Walbe, Garba Dada, Titus Numan, Company Sergeant Major Useni Fegge, Warrant Officer I. Bako, and a soldier from Maiduguri called Sergeant Tijani.[1] Other Northern soldiers were present too. The captives were stripped down to their trousers, whipped and badly beaten. Aguiyi-Ironsi and Fajuyi took the brunt of the beatings. As the beatings continued, the captors "interrogated" Aguiyi-Ironsi about his knowledge of the January coup and the whereabouts of the men who had been killed in January. Some of the Northern soldiers accused Aguiyi-Ironsi of knowing the whereabouts of Brigadier Maimalari (whom they erroneously believed was still alive).

After denying any involvement in the January coup, Aguiyi-Ironsi switched off and endured the blows that were being rained down on him in silence and refused to admit complicity in the January coup or to answer further questions that were being fired at him by the junior officers. As an old school soldier, he showed immense courage in the circumstances and probably felt that would be dishonorable for him, as the head of the armed forces, to allow himself to be "interrogated" (even in order to save his own life) by subordinates like NCOs. Two of the "interrogators" began arguing amongst themselves about the fate of the captives. One argued that all captives were to be shot, and another maintained that they had not been instructed to kill all captives. The latter prevailed. However, Aguiyi-Ironsi and Fajuyi were so badly beaten and wounded that they could hardly stand. They were led out into the bush, where they were killed by machine gun fire. Aguiyi-Ironsi's air force ADC Lieutenant Nwankwo managed to escape as his captors' attention was focused on Aguiyi-Ironsi and Fajuyi. Lieutenant Nwankwo escaped due to a pre-existing gentleman's agreement he had with his fellow ADC Lieutenant Sani Bello. The two men had previously agreed that whomever of them came out on top during the counter-coup should save the life of the other. Despite the murders of Aguiyi-Ironsi and Fajuyi, Bello honored the gentleman's agreement. While the mutineers' attention was focused on Aguiyi-Ironsi and Fajuyi, Bello told Nwankwo to flee.[2] Bello himself also survived the ordeal and later became a military governor. There are different schools of thought regarding Danjuma's role:

Danjuma's account is true. Unfortunately most of the people who can corroborate or dispute it are dead.

---

1 Some accounts also implicate Abdullahi Shelleng but the author has been unable to corroborate them.

2 *The Sun*, Monday, June 28, 2004.

Is the account in *January 15: Before and After* reliable? Can it be believed, given that it was released during a propaganda war?

The common denominator in both accounts is that Danjuma was not present when Aguiyi-Ironsi and Fajuyi were killed.

Contrary to popular belief, Fajuyi was not taken captive and killed because he refused to be separated from his guest Aguiyi-Ironsi. A heroic legend has grown around Fajuyi for decades claiming that Fajuyi would have been spared but insisted on sharing Aguiyi-Ironsi's fate. This mythology originated in the Western Region's publication *Fajuyi The Great* and was later embellished in subsequent publications, one of the most poetic of which was *Fajuyi: The Martyred Soldier*, by Sanmi Ajiki. Ajiki claimed that Fajuyi told Aguiyi-Ironsi: "I make bold to declare to you that . . . I am with you soul, spirit and body. And mark my words, whatever happens to you today, happens to me. I am your true friend, dear J.U.T like the dove to the pigeon, and by the grace of our good God, so will I humbly yet proudly remain till the very end." According to Ajiki, Aguiyi-Ironsi replied "Yes! Francis, I retain my absolute confidence in you. I have never for once doubted your integrity." The soldiers that were present suggest that no such poetic dialogue took place and that Fajuyi was a target of the Northern soldiers all along. Many Northern soldiers suspected Fajuyi of at the very least being sympathetic to the Majors, and at worst to have assisted them in planning their coup. Major Ademoyega confirmed that the Majors did approach Fajuyi and that Fajuyi offered them advice on the coup's execution.[1] In September 1965, Fajuyi commanded an all arms battle group course in Abeokuta. Northern soldiers suspected that the course was nothing more than a recruiting and training exercise for the coup which eventually occurred in January 1966. Lieutenant Walbe was among the Northern soldiers that took Aguiyi-Ironsi and Fajuyi to their deaths in Ibadan. Walbe said of Fajuyi:

> It is a lie. We arrested him as we arrested Ironsi. We suspected him of being party to the January coup. You remember the battle group course which he held at Abeokuta. . . . He ran the course. All those who took part in the January coup were those who had taken part in that course. It gave us the impression that the battle course was arranged for the January coup, so he had to suffer it too. I am sorry about that but that it the nature of the life of the military man.[2]

Danjuma corroborated this view and maintained that Fajuyi was killed because the mutineers in Ibadan were convinced he was an accomplice of the January coup:

> They were dead sure that Fajuyi was part of the January coup because Nzeogwu then and others rehearsed the coup on Sardauna's place several times in Kachia during a training camp that was commanded by Fajuyi. Those boys were sure. One or two of them were mortar officers who were supporting the troops that were there. So they started to put two and two together. The chaps could not stomach Fajuyi such that if there was anybody who should die first, as far as they were concerned, it was Fajuyi not even Ironsi. I was not surprised that in the end he too was killed.[3]

The views of Danjuma and Walbe seem to surmise that Fajuyi's murder was premeditated and motivated by grievances tied to the January coup, rather than any refusal by Fajuyi to be separated from his guest Aguiyi-Ironsi. However, Danjuma's recollection of events contains a few mistakes that may have been caused by the pas-

---

1 Ademoyega, *Why We Struck*, page 59.
2 Elaigwu, *Gowon: The Biography of a Soldier-Statesman*, page 72.
3 Momoh, *The Nigerian Civil War, 1967–1970: History and Reminiscences*, page 373.

sage of time and fading of memory. Firstly he confused the battle group course commanded by Fajuyi in September 1965 with a training camp that took place in Kachia in mid April 1966. Fajuyi commanded the former and had no involvement in the latter, which occurred at a time when he was already military governor of the Western Region. Secondly, Danjuma claims that "Nzeogwu then and others rehearsed the coup on Sardauna's place several times in Kachia during a training camp." Major Nzeogwu was not a participant of the 1965 battle group course or the April 1966 Kachia training camp. During the former he was still an instructor at the NMTC in Kaduna, and he was imprisoned by the time the latter took place.

If the battle group course really was a surreptitious recruitment exercise for the January coup, then it failed miserably to achieve its objective. The course instructors were Lt-Colonel Fajuyi, Majors Wale Ademoyega, Simeon Adegoke, Iliya Bisalla, Mac Nzefili, Captain Abdul Wya and Second-Lieutenant Hammed. The course students were Captains Emmanuel Abisoye, Frank Aisida, Sule Apollo, David Bamigboye, Brown, Jonathan Egere, Pius Eremobor, Ben Gbulie, Tom Iweanya, Gibson Jalo, Bernard Nnamani, Frank Obioha, and Onifade.[1] Contrary to what Walbe said, of the twenty officers on that course, only Major Ademoyega and Captain Gbulie played any part in the January coup. Even then, Major Ademoyega was one of the course instructors so would have been on the course irrespective of his participation in the coup. Additionally several Northern soldiers such as Major Iliya Bisalla, Captains Sule Apollo and Gibson Jalo, and Second-Lieutenant Hammed were also present in the course. According to Major Ademoyega, Captain Emmanuel Abisoye was the outstanding course participant.[2] Abisoye later confirmed that the course was not organized in order to recruit for the January 1966 coup: "Army Headquarters decided that we had to start training. . . . It was not the intention of that course to build up people for a coup."[3]

Apart from their murderers, few knew or believed that Aguiyi-Ironsi and Fajuyi had been killed. The myths about Aguiyi-Ironsi's supposed invulnerability and crocodile cane "Charlie" made many disbelieve that he could possibly have been killed. However, even in death Aguiyi-Ironsi and Fajuyi did not immediately find peace. The next day Northern troops returned to bury their bodies in shallow graves near where they were killed. A search for Fajuyi and Aguiyi-Ironsi was conducted, leading to the discovery of their bodies adjacent to Iwo road just outside Ibadan. Their bodies were dug up and buried in the Ibadan cemetery. Until Aguiyi-Ironsi's funeral enabled them to internalize his death and release themselves from denial, many Igbo civilians did not believe he had been killed and kept mythological faith that somehow his crocodile swagger stick would have protected him from any would be assassins. These are the same sorts of beliefs that were popular among Northern soldiers earlier on in 1966, when they refused to believe that Brigadier Maimalari could have been killed. However, news of Aguiyi-Ironsi's death was not announced till early the following year (1967) when the bodies were once again exhumed and buried for a third time, this time with full military honors in their hometowns.

Incidentally Aguiyi-Ironsi's young son Thomas (who was less than 13 years old), was present at State House Ibadan when his father was snatched away to be killed on July 29, 1966. Thomas was rescued and smuggled out of Ibadan by the police. Thomas later became a diplomat and Nigeria's Defense Minister. Aguiyi-Ironsi's daughter

1 Gbulie, Nigeria's Five Majors, page 159.
2 Ademoyega: Why We Struck, page 64.
3 Momoh, The Nigerian Civil War, 1967–1970: History and Reminiscences, page 225.

Louisa is a journalist and his grandson Uchenna Ejike is a musician. Aguiyi-Ironsi's widow Victoria refused all entreaties for any of her children to follow in their father's footsteps and join the army. Aguiyi-Ironsi paid for the Majors' adventurism with his life. All of the Northern anger, malice and mistrust caused by the Majors' coup was directed at Aguiyi-Ironsi and Igbos in general. He had some extraordinarily bad luck too. Not long before his murder, he had ordered the release of the opposition leader Chief Awolowo. A few days after Aguiyi-Ironsi was murdered, his successor released Awolowo and got all the credit and goodwill for the move.

Back to Letmauck Barracks: 4ᵗʰ Battalion Headquarters, Ibadan — Western Region

Back at Letmauck barracks, the commanding officer Lt-Colonel Akahan lost control. The soldiers that murdered Aguiyi-Ironsi and Fajuyi returned to the barracks and joined their colleagues to round up Igbo soldiers and lock them up in the guardroom. They were now reinforced by the group of mutineers from Abeokuta that arrived earlier in the day with Lieutenant Pam Mwadkon. A Northern soldier "from Maiduguri" was allegedly seen triumphantly striding around the barracks with Aguiyi-Ironsi's "Charlie" crocodile mascot. Some southern members of Aguiyi-Ironsi's entourage that had been arrested outside State House in Ibadan were also taken to the battalion for detention. In the mayhem and atmosphere of jungle justice the Cameroonian Major Hans Anogho was bundled in with the Igbo detainees. Anogho was released when one of the Northern soldiers recognized that he was not Igbo. The other Igbo army detainees were killed when grenades were tossed into their guardroom by Northern soldiers. The Igbo casualties in Ibadan included the unit's former Adjutant Captain Tom Iweanya and Lieutenant Eleazar Achebe. The victims' bodies were then hauled onto jeeps. The battalion's Motor Transport Officer was Lieutenant Jerry Useni. Other coup participants in Ibadan included Lieutenant Ibrahim Bako who was to play a prominent role many years later in the coup in which President Shagari was overthrown.

Lt-Colonel Gowon rang the battalion commander Lt-Colonel Akahan during the late afternoon to request Aguiyi-Ironsi's whereabouts. Akahan relayed Gowon's inquiry to Danjuma who replied that he arrested Aguiyi-Ironsi but lost him to soldiers from Akahan's unit. Danjuma gave Akahan the culprits' names, and Akahan passed the names on to Gowon.[1]

Back to Lagos — July 29, 1966

In less than twenty four hours, Northern soldiers had managed to seize control of all military units in Lagos. The Federal Guards were now in the control of Captain Joe Garba and his troops, the airport was in the control of Northern soldiers and a larger concentration of Northern troops were also in control at the 2ⁿᵈ battalion's Ikeja cantonment. Two of the three Igbo commanding officers in Lagos (Ochei and Igboba) had been dislodged from their command, and the new Quartermaster-General Lt-Colonel Keshi was out of the country with Lt-Colonel Haruna and Major Sule Apollo on a procurement trip.

Brigadier Ogundipe could not rely on or trust the regular troops. Of the three army units in Lagos, the Federal Guards and 2ⁿᵈ battalion were already controlled

---

1 Ibid., pages 372-373.

by the mutineers and the LGO was the only unit not already totally in the muti-neers' control. Ogundipe therefore sent a platoon of troops under the command of Captain Ephraim Opara[1] of the LGO to recapture the airport. Most of these troops were non-combat soldiers such as clerks, marching band members and drivers that were not used to handling firearms on a regular basis. They stood no chance against heavily armed and mutinous Northern infantrymen who knew they were coming and laid in wait for them. They were ambushed on Ikorodu road, routed and took heavy casualties at the hands of Northern soldiers who had been expecting them. Some civilians were killed in the crossfire, including Mr. I.O. Wood, a British national who worked as the manager of a shoe factory in Ikeja, and a German national. The survi-vors, such as Corporal Adah, tore off their uniforms and fled back to base, chastened. Further attempts by Ogundipe to send reinforcements failed as firstly both Captain Garba (who was among the mutineers) and Lt-Colonel Ruddy Trimnell refused to go. The ill-prepared troops he eventually managed to muster up simply drove around Lagos and returned to base without firing a shot. Lt-Colonel Murtala Muhammed sent Lieutenant D.S. Abubakar's group of Abeokuta mutineers to the LGO's Abalti barracks to suppress further counter-attacks by the LGO. When they got to the LGO, they liquidated several Igbo NCOs.

KADUNA, NORTHERN REGION

The theory that the counter-coup was prematurely triggered by events in Abeo-kuta is lent credence by the fact that nothing happened in the Northern Region until 24 hours after the murders of Okonweze, Obienu, and Orok at Abeokuta. It seems that Northern troops stationed in the Northern Region were not willing to make their move until they were certain of the outcome of the revolt in the south. They may have been mindful of what happened in January when Aguiyi-Ironsi managed to escape, put down the Majors' coup, and have them locked up. It took some time for news from the south to filter through to the north, as unlike the January coup, the July mutiny was not a simultaneous coup or assault on strategic locations around the country. The July counter-coup was conducted with much improvisation via a series of separate but connected sequential mutinies. After each army unit had been "liberated" by Northern soldiers, the soldiers would inform their colleagues in other units and urge them to do the same. Northern soldiers in other units would then act in reaction to the news, even if they were not within the original circle of plotters. At first, reports from Abeokuta were confused and it was unclear who (Igbos or North-erners) was responsible for the violence. Northern soldiers in other locations had the confidence to move in their respective units only when it became apparent that their Northern colleagues in Abeokuta had prevailed.

Although the Northern Region was quiet, it was also tense. As with the Janu-ary coup, key unit commanders were conveniently absent. The 1 brigade commander Lt-Colonel Bassey and his deputy Lt-Colonel Phillip Efiong were both away, and the Deputy Commandant of the NDA Lt-Colonel Imo was also away in Jos. In their absence artillery commander Lt-Colonel Alex Madiebo advised the Brigade Major in Kaduna Major Samuel Ogbemudia (an Edo from the Mid-West Region) to order all units to surrender their weapons. Some soldiers refused to disarm for the osten-sible reason that they feared for their safety and needed their guns for self defense. A few days earlier Ogbemudia had detained and interrogated Lieutenant Bukar Suka

---

1 Opara was a classmate of Joe Garba and Bukar Suka Dimka at the Nigerian Military School.

Dimka for violating an order forbidding all troop movements not authorized by brigade headquarters. Dimka and other Northern soldiers were arrested after they had been spotted suspiciously moving around strategic Kaduna locations at night without the prior authorization of brigade headquarters or the battalion commander. The unauthorized troop movement was observed at various locations including the Hamdala Hotel, broadcasting facilities and the police headquarters, where the troops met with some police officers including Dimka's older brother Assistant Superintendent of Police S.K. Dimka.[1] Under interrogation by Ogbemudia, Dimka complained that he was being victimized because he was Northern.[2] He was released by Ogbemudia in what subsequently proved to be an inauspicious decision.

The Igbo commander of the 3rd battalion Lt-Colonel Okoro was dissuaded from disarming his men by his RSM, a man ironically also named Ahmadu Bello. With tension and mutual suspicion at its highest point, Lt-Colonel Alex Madiebo claims that the last time he saw one of his Northern artillery officers Major Abba Kyari, Kyari ominously wished him and other Igbo officers "good luck."[3] Madiebo was in a difficult position because two of his southern officers: Lieutenants Bob Egbikor and Festus Olafimihan had participated in the January coup in Kaduna. Second- Lieutenants Abdul Wya and Gado Nasko were also a member of Madiebo's artillery unit.[4]

1 p.m.

Lt-Colonel Okoro believed he could defuse the situation through dialogue. He addressed his troops during the afternoon of July 29. His men assured him of their loyalty and Okoro naively dropped his guard. He was no longer commanding a battalion under conditions of normal honesty and military discipline. His plea for loyalty unwittingly served as a springboard for the extension of the mutiny to the Northern Region.

Late Night, Friday July 29 1966 — 3rd Battalion,
Kawo–Kaduna, Northern Region

Late in the day, Okoro's RSM Ahmadu Bello (a Northerner) informed him that he was required in the guardroom. When Okoro arrived for the non-existent assignment, he was questioned and then shot dead by two of his Northern troops. The Eastern Region's report of the coup claims that the soldiers who shot Okoro dead were Lieutenants Yakubu Dambo[5] and B.S. Dimka.[6] Dimka also led an attack on Major Ogbemudia, who had earlier detained and interrogated him. Ogbemudia was lucky to escape.

After Okoro's death, Northern soldiers rounded up and arrested their Igbo colleagues and held private "trials" during which the Igbo soldiers were sentenced to death and killed. Among the officers in Okoro's battalion was a young Kano born

---

1 Phillip Efiong, *Nigeria and Biafra: My Story*, page 100.
2 Madiebo, *The Nigerian Revolution and The Biafran War*, page 63.
3 Ibid., page 65.
4 Both Wya and Nasko later succeeded Madiebo as commanders of the Nigerian army's artillery corps.
5 Dambo was of Bajju ethnicity and was said to have also participated in the January coup. The Bajju are also referred to as the "Kaje" by other ethnicities.
6 *January 15: Before and After*, page 55. Nine years later, Dimka went on to play a prominent role in another coup.

Lieutenant of Kanuri ethnicity named Sani Abacha. After Okoro was shot his body was dumped at the military hospital in Kaduna. Sometime after Okoro's murder an alarm was sounded for a battalion muster parade. When soldiers showed up for the parade, Igbo soldiers were separated and herded into trucks. There were driven out onto the Kaduna-Jos road and shot dead. Deception played a large part in the murders of Igbo soldiers. A consistent pattern emerged whereby Northern soldiers would sound an alarm, disarm, and then segregate and murder Igbo soldiers when they came to answer the alarm.

The commander of the 2nd Recce Squadron; Major Ukpo Isong (an eastern officer of non-Igbo origin) was also killed. Isong had succeeded Hassan Katsina as the squadron's commander only six months earlier. Among the officers stationed in Isong's squadron in Kaduna were two young Lieutenants named Ibrahim Babangida and Garba Duba. Two non-Igbo eastern officers (Second-Lieutenants Patrick Ibik and Dag Waribor) that took part in the January coup were also killed. As direct participants in the January coup their names would have been at the top of the death list. Ibik had occupied the P & T telephone exchange on Captain Gbulie's orders and Waribor was involved in the attack on the Sardauna's lodge and the attempt to arrest the Northern Region's Finance Minister the Makanam Bida. The circumstances in which they were killed are not clear. Despite their participation in the coup, their names do not appear on the list of detainees compiled by the federal government, Eastern Region, Major Nzeogwu or Captain Gbulie. Lieutenants Sani Abacha and Bukar Suka Dimka were accused by eastern publications of being members of death squads that murdered Igbo soldiers.[1]

KANO, 5TH BATTALION — NORTHERN REGION

There was no immediate bloodshed at 5th battalion in Kano for two reasons. First-ly the battalion was commanded by a Northerner: the disciplined and non-confron-tational Lt-Colonel Mohammed Shuwa. Thus Northern soldiers did not have to forc-ibly take control there. Secondly when Lt-Colonel Gowon telephoned the battalion early on the morning of July 29 to break news of the Abeokuta mutiny, Lt-Colonel Shuwa had not yet arrived in his office so the call was received by the battalion's second in command, the Yoruba Major James Oluleye. Oluleye immediately called his company commanders, told them to lock the armory and to hand their armory keys to him. He locked all the armory keys in his combination safe.[2] By the time news of events at Abeokuta filtered through to the rest of the battalion, it was too late for them to do anything as the armory was sealed, thus denying them access to weapons. The troops were ordered to remain in the barracks.

ENUGU — 1ST BATTALION, EASTERN REGION

A coup in the Eastern Region and the elimination of its military governor Lt-Colonel Emeka Ojukwu was also planned. Captain Baba Usman of military intel-ligence had been tasked with coordinating the mutiny with the 1st battalion. He was in the eastern market town of Aba when the news and timing of the Abeokuta mu-tiny caught him by surprise. However, the planned mutiny in Enugu was forestalled firstly by one of Lieutenant Ogbonna's distress calls from Abeokuta, and secondly by the outstanding leadership of the veteran commander of the Enugu based 1st bat-

---

1 Ibid., page 55.
2 Oluleye, *Military Leadership in Nigeria*, page 36.

talion, Lt-Colonel David "Baba" Ogunewe. Ogbonna's call to the battalion came early enough to alert Ogunewe of what was going on. By the time Northern officers called their colleagues in Enugu to swing into action there, Ogunewe had already been fore-warned. Ogunewe had been posted to the battalion during the redeployments that followed the January coup. His second in command was Major Benjamin Adekunle. Although Ogunewe was a former commander of the Federal Guards, this was to be an acid test of his leadership in his new unit. Ogunewe found Northern soldiers in his battalion (including Captain Gibson Jalo[1] and Lieutenants Shehu Musa Yar'Adua, M.D. Jega and A.A. Abubakar) dressed in combat fatigues and readying themselves to commence an assault in Enugu. Using all his persuasive powers, he managed to convince them to hand over the armory keys and negotiated a tense but effective truce with the Northern soldiers. He also locked his battalion's armory, placed it under the joint guard of unarmed Northern and southern officers, and encouraged Northern and southern soldiers to live together in the mess and grounds of the bat-talion. Ogunewe was the only officer authorized to carry a weapon. This way neither group could make a surreptitious move against the other. Surrounded by a hostile population, the Northern officers were content with the truce in order to avoid risk-ing their families' lives, but were resolute in their determination to defend themselves should the need arise. Lt-Colonel Ogunewe's crisis management skills under such extraordinarily extenuating circumstances are all the more remarkable when it is considered that over 75% of the soldiers under his command were Northern and he was Igbo. He could easily have fled for his safety but chose to remain at his post even though he was surrounded by hundreds of Northern soldiers, any of whom could have killed him at any time. His role in limiting the bloodshed that occurred in 1966 has been understated.

However, Lt-Colonel Ojukwu, the military governor of the Eastern Region, was not taking chances with his safety. He correctly suspected that he was marked for elimination by the Northern soldiers in Enugu and left State House to take refuge at the regional police headquarters. As in January, the coup did not take off in the Eastern Region or Mid-West (where no troops were stationed). Ojukwu feared that the Northern troops at Enugu could mutiny at any time and demanded that they should be moved away from Enugu. Ojukwu's caution was wise. Lt-Colonel Murtala Muhammed repeatedly sent signals for Northern soldiers in Enugu to extend the mutiny to the Eastern Region. Some Northern soldiers attempted to break into the Enugu armory but were overpowered. The failure of the coup in the Eastern Region created a stalemate similar to the one that existed in January 1966 when Nzeogwu was in control of the Northern Region, while Aguiyi-Ironsi had the south. This time, the counter-coup had succeeded in every region other than the Eastern Region.

Benin — Mid-West Region

As in January, there was no shooting in the Mid-West Region as it had no per-manent military base. The Northern soldiers in the region were members of the secu-rity detail of Lt-Colonel Ejoor, the region's military governor. Nonetheless, Ejoor was sufficiently concerned that he called out and addressed his men, urging them not to shed any blood. Ejoor claimed that he pleaded with his Northern soldiers that if they wanted to kill anyone, they should kill him alone and leave all the others unharmed.[2]

---

1 Later became Chief of Defense Staff under President Shagari.
2 Ejoor, *Reminiscences*.

Chapter 9. Mutineers in Power

Ogundipe in Distress

Aguiyi-Ironsi's deputy Brigadier Babafemi Ogundipe (a mild mannered Yoruba officer with no political ambition) was now the most senior surviving officer in the army. Before the UK handed over command of the Nigerian army to indigenous soldiers in 1965, the outgoing GOC, Major-General Welby-Everard had recommended Ogundipe as his replacement without success. In a confidential report written in 1964, Welby-Everard gave Ogundipe a glowing reference:

> Brigadier Ogundipe has proved himself to be a splendid commander and has been an excellent influence both on 2 brigade and on the army as a whole. His quiet but firm manner is very impressive and his marked leadership qualities produce first class results. He is greatly respected and held in high esteem by his subordinates of all ranks and by his brother officers. His military knowledge and judgment are very sound and his ideas are always constructive. I have a very high opinion of his character and his outlook is invariably absolutely fair and impartial. He sets the highest standards and will accept nothing less. He has been absolutely loyal to me at all times.... He is fully equipped to be GOC and would make a very good one.[1]

However, this was a situation beyond Ogundipe's military capabilities and he could not assert his authority over the Northern troops. On Friday afternoon July 29 Ogundipe made a broadcast to the nation on Radio Nigeria. The message (which was repeated from 2:30 p.m. onwards for the rest of the day) stated that:

> As a result of some trouble by dissidents in the army, mainly in Ibadan, Abeokuta and Ikeja, the National Military Government has declared a state of emergency in the affected areas. Consequently, the following areas have been declared military areas under the Suppression of Disorder Decree of 1966: Ibadan, Ikeja and Abeokuta. Military tribunals have been considered and accordingly set up. Curfew has been declared in the affected areas from 6:30 p.m. The Na-

---

1 Confidential report dated November 25, 1964.

tional Military Government wishes to state that the situation is under control and hopes to restore peace and tranquility very soon. The government appeals to the public for cooperation in its effort to restore law and order in the affected areas.

However, the situation was anything but tranquil, and was deteriorating rapidly out of control. The Ikeja cantonment became the undeclared headquarters of the mutineers, and the exasperated Ogundipe sent the Chief of Staff (Army), Lt-Colonel Yakubu Gowon there to talk to them. When Gowon arrived, it appears that he was not a free agent and was placed under guard. There he found that the leading figures were Northern officers stationed in Lagos such as Lt-Colonel Murtala Muhammed, Majors Martin Adamu, Shittu Alao and Musa Usman, and Captain Joe Garba.

Northern Secession: Araba

The military governor of the Eastern Region Lt-Colonel Ojukwu was not initially contacted but when he managed to reach Ogundipe by telephone, Ogundipe informed him that Northern troops had given their conditions for a "ceasefire": (i) the repatriation of Northerners and southerners to their respective regions of origin, and (ii) the secession of the Northern Region from Nigeria. Ojukwu replied: "If that is what they want, I agree. Let them go!" and replaced the receiver.[1] At this stage Ojukwu was willing to accept either the Northern Region's secession or a continuation of the federation, but the latter choice on the condition that political leadership of Nigeria should follow army seniority.

The Northern soldiers were uninterested in a continuation of the status quo and wanted the Northern Region to secede from Nigeria. To aid this objective they hijacked a British VC10 plane which was supposed to fly to London. The plane's captain, Alan Kerr, flew 96 of the mutineers' family members and their property back to Kano in the north. The mutineers also gave Northern civilians and civil servants a forty hour deadline to evacuate Lagos,[2] after which they would destroy all symbols of central authority in the south, and then pull northward leaving chaos and a government vacuum in the south. Ilorin (a town in the Northern Region close to its border with the Western Region) was put on alert to be ready to accommodate large numbers of northward bound soldiers. Secessionist sentiment among the Northern troops may have been strengthened by the fear that staying in Nigeria would give Igbos an opportunity to gain revenge for the murder of Aguiyi-Ironsi and other Igbos, or might increase the prospect of them being tried and punished.

A THREE DAY DEBATE IN LAGOS, JULY 29–31, 1966

The Eastern Region's account claims that "Gowon hoisted and flew in front of the 2nd battalion headquarters at Ikeja the secessionist red, yellow, black, green and khaki flag of the "Republic of the North."[3] Eyewitnesses did not see such a flag. Although there was tremendous secessionist sentiment among Northern soldiers, Gowon was among the more conciliatory of them. Gowon was pressed by his junior colleagues to join their rebellion. When Gowon became aware of the gravity of the situation and the uncompromising mood of his Northern colleagues, he called the

---

1 See N.U. Akpan, *The Struggle for Secession*, page 33.
2 Confirmed by M.D. Yusuf during National Workshop on the Events, Issues and Sources of Nigerian History, 1960–1970, held at State House, Kawo, Kaduna, 7-9 June 1993.
3 *January 15: Before and After*, pages 49-50.

head of the police Special Branch Alhaji M.D. Yusuf and informed Yusuf that the mutineers had drafted a speech declaring the secession of the Northern Region (Lt-Colonel Murtala Muhammed and Major Martin Adamu were instrumental in producing the speech).[1] Gowon asked for a lawyer to review the draft speech. He may have been trying to buy time. Fortuitously, a Northern judge, Mr. Justice Bello[2] (who was also M.D. Yusuf's cousin) was in Lagos at the time, heading the government inquiry into the Electricity Corporation of Nigeria. After speaking to Gowon, Yusuf refused to come to Ikeja cantonment but was willing to organize a meeting at the Federal Guard barracks between Justice Bello, Murtala Muhammed and Martin Adamu. Yusuf and Bello tried to dissuade Muhammed and Adamu. However, the two army officers were adamant on seceding and Murtala (leader of the Northern hardliners in the army) continued to press for Northern troops to destroy Lagos, pull out to the Northern Region and secede. As M.D. Yusuf later noted: "Argument with Murtala was always an impossible task."[3] Bello reminded the soldiers that all the nation's money was in the Central Bank of Nigeria in Lagos. He hypothetically asked the soldiers how they would pay their troops' salaries after secession without access to the Central Bank (this prompted them to throw a cordon around the Central Bank). He also reminded them that Brigadier Ogundipe was the next most senior officer after Aguiyi-Ironsi and after the Northern Region's secession might rally the support of friendly countries to attack the Northern Region.

THE ROLE OF CIVIL SERVANTS

As with the January coup, the police headquarters at Lion Building became centre stage. The Chairman of the Federal Public Service Commission Alhaji Sule Katagum rallied the civil servants. On July 30 Brigadier Ogundipe was visited at Lion Building by a group of federal permanent secretaries who looked to him for guidance on how they should react to the revolt. Ogundipe informed them that the mutineers were refusing to accept governmental responsibility, and that he was not prepared to assume power himself to replace Aguiyi-Ironsi unless and until: (a) he was made aware of Aguiyi-Ironsi's fate; (b) he had the full support of the armed forces; and (c) he received legal advice confirming that he could replace Aguiyi-Ironsi. The Attorney-General Gabriel Onyuike advised Ogundipe that the Constitution (Suspension and Modification) Decree (Decree 1) made no provision for the armed forces Chief of Staff to temporarily act as the Supreme Commander. This was a grave lacuna by the federal legal officers who drafted the decree, who should have learnt from the similar leadership vacuum that ensued after the January coup when the Prime Minister was missing. For the second time in six months, Nigeria's leader was missing, presumed dead. With Aguiyi-Ironsi's whereabouts unknown and both Ogundipe and the mutineers unwilling to form a new government, the balance of influence shifted to the Ikeja cantonment. The civil servants' delegation heeded Ogundipe's pleas for them to go to Ikeja cantonment to try to broker a compromise with the mutineers. When they arrived they were met by heavily armed Northern soldiers who were dug in deeply in defensive firing positions. The civil servants were asked in Hausa to identify their ethnic origin. The secretaries' escort replied, on their behalf, "They are civil servants,"

1 National Workshop on the Events, Issues and Sources of Nigerian History, 1960–1970, held at State House, Kawo, Kaduna, 7-9 June 1993.
2 Later became Chief Justice.
3 National Workshop on the Events, Issues and Sources of Nigerian History, 1960–1970, held at State House, Kawo, Kaduna, 7-9 June 1993.

and the secretaries were allowed to enter (including the one Igbo permanent secretary among them, although it is not clear whether the Northern soldiers realized he was Igbo). Their escort was Captain Joe Garba.

!There were three broad camps at Ikeja: the junior Northern soldiers who favored secession, the more senior Northern officers who advocated revenge against Igbos but did not favor secession, and thirdly the civil servants and diplomats who opposed dissolution of the federation. The civilian camp included the Chairman of the Federal Public Service Commission Alhaji Sule Katagum, the head of the Northern Region's civil service Alhaji Ali Akilu, Mukhtar Tahir (a relative of Lt-Colonel Murtala Muhammed), the Chief Justice Sir Adetokunbo Ademola and several civil servants and permanent secretaries including Alhaji Musa Daggash (Defense), Abdul Aziz Atta (Finance), B.N. Okagbue (Health), M.A. Tokunbo, Eneli (both Establishments), Allison Ayida (Economic Planning), S.O. Williams (Works), Solicitor-General Booyamin Oladiran Kazeem,[1] Philip Asiodu, Ibrahim Damcida, H.A. Ejueyitchie, Yusuf Gobir, Anirejuoritse, Ahmed Joda and Buba Ardo.[2] All of the above were Northern (except Chief Justice Ademola and the permanent secretaries Ejueyitchie, Tokunbo, Okagbue, Ayida and Asiodu). Okagbue was the only Igbo among them. Police participants included the Inspector-General of police Alhaji Kam Selem, Commissioner of Police Theophilus Fagbola, and the head of the police Special Branch Alhaji M.D. Yusuf. Some others not physically present participated by telephone (including the military governor of the Mid-West Lt-Colonel Ejoor and Northern Region Governor Sir Kashim Ibrahim). Other Northern officers (including from other locations) filtered in and out after the debate began. The military participants present included Lt-Colonel Murtala Muhammed, Majors Martin Adamu, Shittu Alao and Musa Usman, Captain Joe Garba. Lieutenants Malami Nassarawa, D.S. Abubakar and Nuhu Nathan, and the fearsome Sergeant Paul Dickson of Ikeja airport infamy. Gowon like other senior Northern officers Lt-Colonels Hassan Katsina and Mohammed Shuwa, was not personally involved in the mutiny. However, the senior Northern officers gave their assent to the fait accompli and were brought in to participate in the Ikeja debate. Although Gowon knew that Aguiyi-Ironsi was dead, the news was not revealed and the public were simply told that Aguiyi-Ironsi was "missing" (a repetition of what happened in January when Prime Minister Balewa was presumed "missing" for several days after he had been murdered).

Over the weekend of July 30 and 31, the Northern soldiers engaged the civilians in an apocalyptic and emotionally explosive debate. The debate raged in a dangerous power vacuum as the nation drifted precariously without a head of state. The most vociferous and uncompromising advocate of the Northern Region's secession was 28-year-old Lt-Colonel Murtala Muhammed. He dominated the debate, verbally harangued the civilians in a forceful manner and became the official spokesman for the mutineers. The military governor of the Eastern Region, Lt-Colonel Emeka Ojukwu was continually excluded from the debate and took it upon himself to contact Gowon by telephone. However, Murtala Muhammed continued to be the mutineers' spokesman until he suddenly and unexpectedly acknowledged Gowon's seniority over him. According to Captain Garba, Murtala suddenly turned to Gowon and told him, "You are the senior, go ahead."[3] However, Murtala repeatedly interrupted

---

1 Later became a Supreme Court Judge.
2 Shagari, *Beckoned to Serve*, page 118 and Jane Ejueyitchie, *H.A. Ejueyitchie — Portrait of a Civil Servant*, pages 173–174.
3 Garba, *Revolution in Nigeria: Another View*, page 69.

Gowon as the debate continued, leading Gowon to become so exasperated that at one point he threatened to step down unless the hard-line Northern soldiers agreed to listen to his views. The British and American ambassadors, Sir Francis Cumming-Bruce and Elbert Matthews, respectively, also joined the parley. Matthews made it clear that the US would not give aid to the Northern Region if it seceded, and he and Cumming-Bruce relayed the US and British position which was strongly opposed to a break-up of the federation:

> Both US Ambassador Mathews and UKHICOM Cumming-Bruce have made strong representations in opposition to secession of any area of Nigeria. We consider such development would be major political and economic disaster for Nigerian people and severe setback to independent Africa.[1]

The more pragmatic civilian participants articulated with reason that Northerners would have the most to lose by seceding and explained the stark future that would face Northerners if they left the federation: they would be trapped, landlocked, cut off from the sea, and deprived of economic benefits from the south. The advocates of secession finally acknowledged how incoherent their strategy was. Sanity prevailed as the Northern hawks in the army were grudgingly won over and the civilians managed to persuade the majority of the Northern officers that secession would be injurious to their interests. Northern officers from minority ethnic groups were the first to be convinced of the futility of secession. They feared Hausa–Fulani domination in a future northern state. Several years later Domkat Bali articulated the fears of Northern minority ethnicities:

> "I come from a small tribe — the Tarok tribe in Langtang. It is a small tribe within a small group. If the north secures independence from the rest of the country, the Hausa/Fulani will be so dominant that they will lord it over us whether we like it or not. A bigger Nigeria will check such excesses. So the bigger Nigeria is, the freer my tribe and myself will be."[2]

With secession finally off the agenda, the discussion turned to the fraught question of how the country could possibly remain united given the scale of killing that had occurred, and was continuing to occur. Additionally the extent of distrust between Northern and Igbo soldiers meant that both sides were no longer willing to share barracks with each other. As the debate continued in Ikeja, Northern soldiers elsewhere continued to round up and kill their Igbo colleagues. The mood of the Northern soldiers meant that the country could not be kept together without massively disrupting or eliminating the military command hierarchy. Prominent Northern politicians such as Sir Kashim Ibrahim added their view via telephone. Kashim felt that it would be foolhardy for Northern soldiers to hand power back to another southerner on a platter.[3] Allowing a southern soldier to succeed Aguiyi-Ironsi also carried the risk that the mutinous Northern soldiers would be prosecuted and punished by the new southern leader.

Ojukwu continued to argue that as Aguiyi-Ironsi's whereabouts were unknown, Brigadier Ogundipe should succeed him since he was the next most senior army officer. Ojukwu urged Ogundipe to take over with the promise that if Ogundipe made a broadcast to the nation announcing himself as the new leader, he would make a follow up broadcast in support within thirty minutes. However, Northern officers were uninterested in a return to a southern led military government and refused to

---

1 Circular Telegram from the Department of State to all African posts, August 2, 1966.
2 *The News*, May 13, 2006.
3 Akinjide Osuntokun, *Power Broker: A Biography of Sir Kashim Ibrahim*.

co-operate with, or accept the leadership of Brigadier Ogundipe or any southern officer.[1] The mutineers' opposition to Ogundipe hardened when they discovered that it was he who sent troops from the LGO to attack them on Friday July 29. In a much publicized incident, the "limit" came for the Brigadier when a Northern sergeant quipped to him: "I do not take orders from you until my (Northern) captain comes." The captain to whom the sergeant was referring was Captain Joe Garba. To a seasoned professional soldier like Ogundipe (accustomed to unquestioning obedience of his orders during a military career spanning over twenty years), such insubordination was beyond comprehension. A Northern private similarly refused to obey orders from Major Mobolaji Johnson, the Lagos military governor. Three junior Northern soldiers working under the Igbo GSO (Grade I) at army headquarters Lt-Colonel Patrick Anwunah refused to carry out instructions given to them by Anwunah. Anwunah walked out from his office in disgust and never returned. In Anwunah's career, that was the first time his orders had been disobeyed, and it turned out to be the last order that Anwunah ever gave as a Nigerian army officer. After lying low in a Lagos safe house for a few weeks, Anwunah escaped to the Eastern Region. Anwunah was an apolitical and professional Sandhurst-trained officer that was in the same Sandhurst intake as Alex Madiebo, Arthur Unegbe, Mike Okwechime and his good friend Yakubu Gowon. After graduating from Sandhurst, Anwunah, Gowon and Unegbe opted to join the army's infantry, Madiebo joined the artillery and Okwechime went to the engineers unit. The five former classmates never reunited.

After Ogundipe was sidelined, Ojukwu argued that the next most senior officer, Colonel Adebayo should be the new leader. The head of the navy Commodore Wey was not considered. As he was not an army officer Wey did not feel he could press his own, or Brigadier Ogundipe's case very forcefully. He later admitted that,

> If they [northern soldiers] cannot take orders from an army officer like themselves they will not take [sic] from a naval officer. I retired and called Brigadier Ogundipe. He went out and [said] if an ordinary Sergeant can tell a Brigadier 'I do not take orders from you, until my Captain comes,' I think this was the limit and this is the truth about it.[2]

Ogundipe's own apolitical outlook also meant that he was unwilling to risk bloodshed for the sake of attaining power. He later confessed that "It is not in the nature of officers with my upbringing to want to interfere in politics. We are taught to be good soldiers, not politicians."[3] Even if he had taken a firmer stand, Ogundipe did not have a "critical support network" in the army as there were very few Yoruba soldiers due to Yorubas' famed reluctance to enlist in the army. Additionally Yoruba representation in the army had been reduced as Yoruba soldiers were casualties during the two coups (Ademulegun, Shodeinde, Fajuyi, Adegoke), and some others were imprisoned for their role in the January coup (Ademoyega, Adeleke, Olafimihan, Oyewole). Many of those Yoruba officers that remained were from the Northern Region (such as Benjamin Adekunle, Emmanuel Abisoye, and David Jemibewon), whilst Ogundipe was an Ijebu Yoruba. Ogundipe had no means of enforcing his seniority over an army purged of most non-Northerners. For the second time in eighteen months, Brigadier Ogun-

---

1 One of the Northern officers who refused to co-operate with Ogundipe was Captain Alfred Gom, who in 1979 (as a Lt-Colonel) was convicted by Israel of smuggling explosives to terrorists. At the time Gom was serving as a member of the United Nations Interim Force in Lebanon (UNIFIL).
2 Meeting of Nigeria's military leaders at Aburi in Ghana in January 1967.
3 Ralph Uwechue, *Reflections On The Nigerian Civil War: Facing the Future*, page 35

dipe was passed over for a position he probably merited (after having been passed over for GOC in February 1965). One wonders how different history might have been, had he secured either or both of those appointments. Brigadier Ogundipe's son (who was a schoolboy during the crisis) is currently a lawyer.

To Northerners the only way that the federation could continue without dissolution was on the basis of a Northern soldier replacing Aguiyi-Ironsi. If Nigeria was led by a Northerner, the rationale for secession (Aguiyi-Ironsi's distribution of power in a manner disadvantageous to them) would no longer exist. Major Martin Adamu recommended Lt-Colonel Gowon. After three days of marathon talks, the Northern soldiers agreed to drop their plan to secede, but on the condition that their most senior member Lt-Colonel Gowon was appointed head of state. Another flurry of telephone calls followed to the military governors of the North, Mid-West and Lagos. They were briefed regarding, and accepted the inevitability of Gowon's assumption of power. Commodore Wey had little choice but to accept. The Northern soldiers were emboldened that by sheer force of their numerical representation in the infantry, they could sustain a government led by a Northern officer, even if there were more senior southern officers around. At this point, traditional concepts of military seniority were not concerns for them. Lt-Colonel Ojukwu was not initially contacted nor were his views sought. Tellingly, Ojukwu did not at any point recognize Gowon's leadership. His greatest concession was to vaguely promise to co-operate with Gowon to restore some semblance of order and stop the murders being carried out by Northern soldiers. The SMC tacitly acknowledged Ojukwu's non-recognition of Gowon by stating that Gowon had been chosen to be the new Supreme Commander by a "majority" of the SMC. It was initially envisaged that Gowon would rule for a brief period of time only, and his position was precarious due to some Northern hardliners (led by Lt-Colonel Murtala Muhammed) who felt that Gowon would be too conciliatory to Igbos.

August 1, 1966 — Good Old Jack

So far the counter coup was a purely military affair and the public were unaware of what had occurred in the barracks (although before long, civilians would get a taste of the brutal violence that soldiers had been meting out to each other). Only army personnel knew the bitter ethnic conflict taking place in the barracks. Most Nigerians do not know how perilously close their country came to disintegration over that weekend. On Monday August 1, 1966, Lt-Colonel Gowon who had been inside Ikeja barracks incommunicado with the outside world over the weekend, finally broke his silence to a mystified population. As a bachelor of 32 years old, Lt-Colonel Yakubu Gowon became the youngest head of state in Africa, despite the presence of several more senior officers in the chain of command (all from the south) such as Brigadier Ogundipe, Commodore Wey and Colonel Robert Adebayo. There were also several other Lt-Colonels who were either commissioned before Gowon or who were his cohorts (Lt-Colonels Nwawo, Imo, Kurubo, Efiong, Njoku, Ojukwu and Ejoor). The January coup changed the rules of the game and military seniority no longer mattered. Political power rested not with the titular leader or with cabinet ministers. It now lay with those who had first access to, and use of instruments of violence. Northern soldiers had an immense advantage in this regard. With their overwhelming numerical advantage in the infantry, their Igbo colleagues did not stand a chance. It was easy for Northern infantry soldiers to get access to weapons and take over their units as they had ready access to armories. The mismatch was compounded by the *laissez-faire* attitude of Igbo soldiers who retreated into a comfortable complacency in the expectation that Aguiyi-Ironsi would somehow save the situation as he did in January (they were unaware that he had already been murdered). Within three days every Igbo soldier was either dead, wounded or fleeing for their life. For the second time in six months, the political leadership was deposed, but in an unintentional manner.

Although a Northerner, Gowon was a Christian (his father was a minister) from a Northern minority ethnic group called the Angas and was engaged to an Igbo woman named Edith Ike.[1] Unlike his predecessor Aguiyi-Ironsi, Gowon did not have an ethnically hostile army against him. Many of the infantrymen in the army were like Gowon, from Northern minority ethnic groups in Nigeria's middle belt. Although many southerners ignorantly claim that the counter-coup was the work of "Hausa" soldiers, it was mainly middle belt soldiers from varied ethnicities that did most of the damage. There was substantial cohesion among Northerners, and the desire for revenge united them despite their diverse ethnicities and religions. For example Walbe[2] and Dimka were Angas, Danjuma (Jukun), Garba (Tarok), Mwadkon (Birom), Dickson (Idoma) and all the foregoing were Christians. Whereas others such as Murtala (Hausa) and Abacha (Kanuri) were Muslims from the far north. The dichotomy between soldiers from the middle belt and the far north did however resurface in bloody fashion a decade later. A non-smoker and a teetotaller, the dashing Gowon, with his beaming smile and boyish good looks, radiated a telegenic "good old Jack" bonhomie that endeared him to the Northern soldiers. He also appeared unthreatening to non-Igbo southerners due to his Christianity and personal charm. In retrospect more blood would have been shed had one of the more volatile hotheads that staged the counter-coup become head of state instead of Gowon. Gowon was the fifth of eleven children. His parents were Mallam Yohanna Gowon and Mama Saraya Kuryan Gowon. He attended St. Bartholomew Christian Missionary School in Zaria, and thereafter went on to the famous Government College (now Barewa College) in Zaria. Upon enlistment in the Nigeria army he trained firstly at the RWAFF's Regular Officers Special Training School at Teshie in Ghana (1954), after which he went on to attend the Royal Military Academy at Sandhurst in the UK between 1955 and 1956. His Nigerian course mates at Sandhurst were Alex Madiebo, Arthur Unegbe, Patrick Anwunah and Mike Okwechime. He also served twice as part of the Nigerian contingent of the UN peacekeeping mission in the Congo (now Zaire). He first went to the Congo mission in 1960 and returned again in 1963. In between he attended staff college at Camberley in the UK in 1962. After returning to Nigeria form his second Congo mission, he was appointed as the first indigenous Adjutant-General in the history of the Nigeria army. This was his last posting before the Majors' coup. He had just returned from attending another staff college course at the Joint Services Staff College in the UK when the Majors struck in January 1966. Unlike Aguiyi-Ironsi before him who moved into the State House formerly occupied by ex-President Azikiwe, Gowon modestly made the Federal Guard officers' mess at Dodan Barracks his new home. Dodan Barracks at number 1 Ribadu Road was the former residence of ex-Minister of Defense Muhammadu Ribadu, and it remained the official residence of the Nigerian head of state for the next quarter of a century.[3]

---

1 The relationship did not survive the crisis of the late 1960s.

2 Later became Gowon's ADC.

3 It was briefly renamed "State House, Ribadu Road" between 1979–1983, during the civilian government of Shehu Shagari.

Contrary to popular opinion which states that Brigadier Ogundipe simply fled, he did try to take over but stood down when he realized that his position was untenable and that pushing his case too assertively might lead to his physical elimination. Convinced that he was to be the next target of the Northern soldiers, Brigadier Ogundipe departed to emerge in London as Nigeria's High Commissioner in the United Kingdom. He had been due to attend the Commonwealth Prime Ministers' Conference in London in September, 1966. As a way of quietly easing him out of the scene, he would be permitted to attend the conference, but would remain in the UK to replace Alhaji Abdulmaliki as the High Commissioner (Abdulmaliki had been reassigned by Aguiyi-Ironsi to Paris). Ogundipe was also transferred from the army to the civil service. This neatly placed Ogundipe outside local politics and the military chain of command, thereby sidestepping issues about his rank and seniority to Gowon. His family left Nigeria separately from him on board the MV Auriol. They reunited with the Brigadier two weeks later in Liverpool in the UK. Ogundipe felt betrayed by Gowon. In his view he sent Gowon to negotiate with the mutineers, only for Gowon to emerge as leader of the mutineers he was supposed to negotiate with. The subsequent bloodshed that occurred may have been avoided if Ogundipe had been allowed to become head of state as the most senior surviving officer in the chain of command. Having a Yoruba at the helm at that time may have acted as a neutral buffer between Northern and Igbo soldiers. The choice of Gowon made the crisis seem like a straightforward confrontation between Igbos and Northerners.

Coup or Mutiny?

In contrast to the events of January, the July counter-"coup" was not actually a coup at all. It was a mutiny. The revolt lacked the common characteristics of a coup such as the seizure of broadcasting facilities, public announcement of a change of regime and denunciation of the previous regime. Unlike the Majors' attempted political revolution, the rebellion was a matter of internal army discipline for Northern soldiers, and vengeance against colleagues that had behaved dishonorably by violating their sacred military traditions. This aspect of the revolt was greatly underestimated by the civilian population. The term *coup d'état* translated from French means "a blow to the state." The term refers to the sudden overthrow, often violent, of an existing government by a group of conspirators.[1] The phrase originated in France after Louis Napoleon Bonaparte dissolved the *Assemblée Nationale* (French national assembly) in 1851. In the author's opinion a coup conceptually connotes that its executors *intend* to seize the apparatus of governance. The July plotters did not originally intend to replace the Aguiyi-Ironsi regime, although that is what their actions inadvertently achieved. They originally had no political objective or pre-defined parameters for their mutiny. Their intent was purely vengeance, but having achieved their primary objective they suddenly found themselves in a position to determine the nation's political destiny and leadership. It was at this point that an army mutiny evolved into a coup. Lt-Colonel David Ejoor later observed that "There is one valid point which must be considered and that is the coup we have had so far. The January 15 one was a failure and the army came in to correct it; the one of the 29th I personally believe was a mutiny to start with but it has now turned out to be a coup."[2]

---

1 Also see Appendix 1.
2 Meeting of Nigeria's military leaders at Aburi in Ghana in January 1967.

Chapter 10. The Killing Continues

In his early days Gowon moved very tactfully, slowly and with great caution, anxious not to further fan the flames of violence sweeping across the country. This was entirely prudent given the fate of his two predecessors Balewa and Aguiyi-Ironsi. Additionally Gowon's position was not assured. He was engaged in a power struggle with Murtala Muhammed who remained independent and had considerable influence in the army. Gowon was also unsure of his position as he was surrounded by men who were senior to him militarily, and in age, and experience, such as Commodore Wey of the navy and even Colonel Adebayo of the army, military governor of the Western Region — both of whom outranked him. Despite Gowon becoming head of state, Lt-Colonel Murtala Muhammed remained the power behind the throne. As Gowon tried to consolidate his political leadership of the country, Murtala lurked in the background at the army's *de facto* strongman. He also made a nuisance of himself by turning up uninvited at SMC meetings. Tension between the two was never far beneath the surface, and it simmered between them for a decade. Murtala was convinced that war with Ojukwu's Eastern Region was inevitable and that steps should immediately be taken to prepare for that eventuality. He felt that Gowon was treating the belligerent Ojukwu with kid gloves. On one occasion, Murtala gave Gowon a dose of his famed volcanic anger and banged his first down on his table — threatening to march into, and overrun, the Eastern Region if Gowon did not stop being so soft with Ojukwu. This threat was also sporadically repeated by other Northern officers who were restrained by the ever conciliatory Gowon.

As Gowon struggled to stabilize himself in power, random murders of Eastern Region soldiers continued to occur. On August 12, several NCOs from the Eastern Region were rounded up and killed by Northern soldiers in Apapa, Lagos. Less than two weeks before that, the army's Provost Marshal, Major Ibanga Ekanem (an Eastern officer of the Annang ethnic group) and his driver were shot dead at a checkpoint on Carter Bridge by Sergeant Lapdam while *en route* to an errand for Gowon. Ironically Ekanem was identified by Major Nzeogwu as an officer that was not in support of the January coup[1]. As the Provost Marshal, Ekanem was in charge of the military police. The military police is the army branch responsible for the investigation, arrest and detention of soldiers charged with offenses. Ekanem's investigatory position may have been a motivating factor in his murder, as the men at the checkpoint were neck deep in the revolt and may have feared investigation and prosecution by Ekanem if he remained alive. One author observed that after Ekanem's murder, Lapdam for some reason maintained a pretence that he had succeeded to Ekanem's position and referred to himself as "Provost Marshal" for almost a week, until he was reminded that he was not really the provost marshal.[2] Lapdam's strange behavior was not isolated. Other Northern NCOs became prone to strange superstitious behavior bordering on mysticism. Such acts included mutilating the bodies of murdered Igbo soldiers and addressing themselves by the rank and names of the men they had killed. It is likely that some of the NCOs were psychologically affected by the murders they had carried out. Such an outcome would not be surprising. After murdering the Sardauna of Sokoto in January, the normally fluent Major Nzeogwu became uncomfortable when a journalist asked him about the night he killed the Sardauna: "No, no no. Don't ask me anything about that. I don't want to remember."[3]

The nature of the rebellion became less about avenging the January coup and more about acting on the exhilaration of power and unfettered access to weapons. Attacks on Igbo soldiers continued. The commander of the LGO, Lt-Colonel Tony Eze, had a lucky escape.[4] Eze had emerged from hiding and returned to work after being assured by Gowon that things had calmed down. On his first day back at work, he was alerted just in time to jump out of a window as a group of armed Northern soldiers were making their way to his office to kill him. Dodging machine gun fire, Eze escaped by tearing his way through a barbed wire fence, which severely lacerated his flesh. One of his staff officers was not so lucky. Angered by their failure to capture Eze, the soldiers directed their aggression at Captain Iloputaife. Iloputaife was tied up, picked up and repeatedly thrown down onto the floor, and then tied to a Land Rover and dragged around on the concrete in front of his office.[5] Eze's RSM Warrant Officer (I) Elijah Anosike was also killed. Anosike had been awarded a gold medal for his service during the UN peacekeeping mission in Congo.

After these incidents southern soldiers at the LGO decided it would not be prudent to return to work (including Captains E.E. Nkana, Babalola and Joseph Adeboyejo Olubobokun — the Nigerian army's director of music and first indigenous Nigerian to be commissioned into the Nigerian army band corps). Northerners Captain Ibrahim Taiwo and Lieutenant Tokkida were brought in as reinforcements. Warrant Officer (II) Shuaibu Bobe[6] replaced Anosike as RSM. In several units the property of murdered Igbo soldiers and of absent Northern soldiers was looted. With no predetermined objective for the mutiny and its uncoordinated manner, every Northern soldier involved did what he felt most expedient, unhindered by any pre-ordained parameters. Eliminating Aguiyi-Ironsi and having a Northerner as head of state did not mollify some Northern soldiers. It intensified the scale of killings instead. Killing

1 See Obasanjo, *An Intimate Portrait of Chukwuma Kaduna Nzeogwu.*
2 Robert Melson and Howard Wolpe, *Nigeria: Modernization and the Politics of Communalism,* page 388.
3 Ejindu, interview with Major Nzeogwu, *Africa and the World,* May 1967.
4 Eze had a northern orderly named Corporal Adamu Kablai.
5 See Madiebo, *The Biafran Revolution and the Nigerian Civil War,* page 85.
6 Bobe received a gold medal for his service during the UN operation in the Congo.

was often preceded by beatings, flogging, torture, and other unprintable degradations and was most widespread and indiscriminate in Ibadan and Lagos. Ironically many Igbo officers knew in advance that a Northern counter-coup was being planned, but in a fatally lackadaisical attitude, assumed that the affair would be a straight shoot-out between soldiers that were for and against the January coup. Unfortunately for Igbo officers, Northern officers had become so paranoid about Igbos that they did not compartmentalize Igbos into those who said "yea" or "nay" to the January coup. Even Lt-Colonel Gowon admitted that the anti-Igbo feeling made him doubt whether he could trust his Igbo girlfriend Edith Ike.[1] Among the early Igbo victims were what Northern soldiers termed "jubilators" (those who either did not react with sufficient sympathy to the death of Northerners in January or those who welcomed the January coup). Later on, Northern soldiers became decreasingly selective about their victims and simply being Igbo was reason enough to be killed. The exercise turned into a wildly misdirected act of revenge. The killing became so indiscriminate that it even included many that neither supported, nor had any foreknowledge of the January coup, such as clerks, and soldiers in administrative non-combat positions who were killed based on guilt by association.

COLLAPSE OF DISCIPLINE: THE INMATES TAKE OVER THE ASYLUM

Northern NCOs and Lieutenants were more likely to mercilessly dispatch Igbos than senior Northern officers. Igbo officers were largely strangers to Northern NCOs and junior ranks, whereas senior Northern officers had trained with, and were personally acquainted with Igbo officers. Even Ojukwu later admitted that most of the killing was perpetrated by junior ranks and NCOs:

> I will swear on anything that is brought before me today, and I know in my heart that Hassan [Katsina] never ordered anybody to do anything to an east-erner. I can swear to that here, anywhere. If somebody tells me that, I know it is not true. That is not the problem. It is what the people underneath did.[2]

NCOs became so undisciplined and unpredictable that some Northern officers decided they had seen enough killing and tried to intervene to save Igbo soldiers. On occasions they would lock up Igbo soldiers for their own safety. These officers were usually overruled or ignored by their NCOs who would simply release the Igbo soldiers from detention and kill them. If they tried to intervene too forcefully, Northern officers were on occasion told by their NCOs to put their hands up and reminded that they were not immune. Relations between Northern officers and NCOs became strained as the NCOs felt their officers were not as eager as they should have been to squeeze the trigger, and officers feared that they would be targeted by their NCOs for not being ruthless enough when it came to killing Igbos. Discipline among Northern troops got so bad that Northern officers became cautious around their own NCOs. Lt-Colonel Hassan Katsina at great risk to himself tried to put down an army mutiny by Northern soldiers in Kano (to be discussed later in this Chapter). Even respected Northern figures such as he felt threatened by the behavior of their Northern subordinates.

---

1 Gowon's relationship with Edith did not survive the crisis and Gowon eventually married another lady named Victoria Zakari. As an aside, Edith later filed a paternity suit against Gowon, alleging that Gowon is the father of her son.
2 Meeting of Nigeria's military leaders at Aburi in Ghana in January 1967.

THE 4ᵀᴴ BATTALION AGAIN

The Ibadan based 4th battalion proved to be the most undisciplined and violent unit in the history of the Nigerian army (quite an achievement in a country as unruly as Nigeria). The battalion seemed to be the epicenter of Northern military anger as it had a large concentration of Northern soldiers and many of its former members were also prominent in the revolt that overthrew Aguiyi-Ironsi (Danjuma, Joe Garba, Gowon, Walbe, Longboem). The battalion had also not endeared itself to the local population in Ibadan due its allegedly partisan and heavy handed tactics during the state of emergency in the Western Region that preceded the January coup. Most of the key January plotters such as Majors Ifeajuna, Nzeogwu, Ademoyega and On-wuatuegwu were unscathed as they were incarcerated and inaccessible to North-ern soldiers. However, a few of them were not so lucky and were unfortunate to be detained in prisons that were accessible to Northern soldiers. Such detainees were subjected to grisly treatment by Northern soldiers.

The most prominent of these incidents occurred on August 19th and once again involved the notorious 4th battalion who managed to take their exploits as far afield as Benin in the Mid-West Region. Soldiers from the 4th battalion came to Benin for a funeral. Mindful of the 4th battalion's reputation, the police kept a cautious eye on their activities. After the funeral the soldiers learned that some of the January detainees were held at the nearby Benin prison. Rather than heading home after the funeral the soldiers took a detour to the Benin prison, broke into and raided it, then released Northern troops who were detained there for their part in the January coup. Igbo officers also held for the same offense were not spared. Five of them were tor-tured to death.[1] These five included two soldiers that had taken part in the arrest of Okotie-Eboh and the shooting of Chief Akintola. According to the Special Branch report Warrant Officer James Ogbu was involved in the arrest of Okotie-Eboh and Sergeant Ambrose Chukwu was one of those that engaged Akintola in a shootout in Ibadan. Major Anuforo was shot dead at Ilesha, and Major Okafor was buried alive after being abducted from Abeokuta prison.[2] Njoku claimed that the soldier who led the attack on Okafor was a Federal Guard soldier that formerly served under, and clashed with Okafor.[3] The 4th battalion's raid on Benin prison led to a vehement but ultimately fruitless protest to Gowon by the military governor of the Mid-West Re-gion, Lt-Colonel David Ejoor. The 4th battalion also raided the Agodi prison in the Western Region and released former ministers and officials of the Akintola regime that were detained there by Lt-Colonel Fajuyi.

Some remaining Yoruba officers at the 4th battalion were wisely taking precau-tionary measures. Major James Oluleye noted in a rather understated way that "Ma-jors Ayo-Ariyo and Sotomi were not sleeping in the barracks for fear of their lives as the behavior of the northern troops at Ibadan was not too conducive to person-al security."[4] The behavior of the unit in Ibadan got so out of control that some of them were posted to the Northern Region in the forlorn hope that this would calm them down. When they eventually moved northwards they were dispersed to vari-

---

1 Warrant Officers James Ogbu and B.Okuge and Sergeants Ambrose Chukwu, A Ogbuhara and Ndukife.
2 See Ruth First, *The Barrel of a Gun*, page 293, and Alex Madiebo, *The Nigerian Revolution and the Biafran War*, page 85.
3 Njoku, *A Tragedy Without Heroes*, page 61.
4 Oluleye, *Military Leadership in Nigeria*, page 46.

ous Northern towns including Kaduna, Gboko, Makurdi and Jos, with the intent to free the more violent members of the unit from each other's malignant influence. The move made matters worse as it enabled the battalion to export their mayhem over a wider geographic area. When they arrived in the Northern Region, they continued their murderous operations there. When the troops ran out of Igbo colleagues to kill, they acted as *agent provocateurs* and joined Northern civilian mobs in doggedly pursuing, murdering and terrorizing Igbo civilians. The battalion's infamy continued into 1967 when a decision was made to return all soldiers to their regions of origin. Even then it took two attempts to get them to leave. When ordered to move to the Northern Region, they initially refused to budge and only agreed to move when Lt-Colonels Akahan and Katsina visited them to ask them in person to move, and Katsina gave them broad license to defend themselves on their way. Katsina ordered them to take all their weapons and ammunition with them, instructing them not to leave even a rifle sling behind. They rendered heavy artillery guns inoperable by removing their firing pins as the guns themselves were too large to be taken with them. Katsina also informed them that if they received any reports that a Northerner had been mistreated or attacked, they should return and advance southward shooting everything they saw until they reached Nigeria's southern coast.[1] Some elements of the 3rd battalion in Kaduna (including Lieutenant Sani Abacha) were also rotated with the 4th battalion in Ibadan. The officer at Ibadan who received Abacha and other members of the 3rd battalion was Lieutenant Jerry Useni. From there a decades' long coup plotting fraternization between Abacha and Useni was born.

Tied in to the furious violence of the coup were strange attempts by junior Northern officers to militarily legitimize their actions by asking their superior officers for "orders" to kill Igbo soldiers or to turn a blind eye when they did so. This pattern of behavior was repeated in 1975 when the officers who were planning to overthrow the head of state General Gowon (Babangida, Yar'Adua, Buhari, Ibrahim Taiwo, Abdullahi Mohammed) asked their superior officers (Danjuma, Murtala Muhammed, Martin Adamu) to turn a blind eye while they got on with the job of removing Gowon. Bizarrely, some Northern troops would "report" their murder of Igbo colleagues to their Northern superior officers by claiming that Igbos had been killed due to an "accidental discharge, sir." The inmates had taken over the asylum.

THE ROLE OF SOUTHERN SOLDIERS

The counter-coup was carried out almost exclusively by Northern soldiers. However, consternation at Igbos was so great that a few Yoruba officers also participated. Most of them were Yorubas from the Yoruba speaking areas in the Northern Region. Among them Ibrahim Taiwo was to later play a leading role in a subsequent coup in 1975. Some Yoruba soldiers from Ogbomosho were aggrieved at the murder of their kinsman Chief Akintola during the January coup and also joined in. It was time for everyone to extract their pound of flesh. Among the Ogbomosho officers participating, Major Shittu Alao (whose father was a Yoruba from Ogbomosho and his mother a Northerner from Shendam) later commanded the air force. Southern officers of non-eastern origin were largely left alone during the early stages of the mutiny unless they obstructed the work of the mutineers. In the early stages of the mutiny, some Yoruba soldiers were detained, but then later released. With their distinctive facial mark-

---

1 See interviews with Lt-Generals Domkat Bali Garba Duba in Momoh, *The Nigerian Civil War 1967–1970: History and Reminiscences*, pages 329 and 448.

ings, Yorubas were more easily distinguishable from Igbos. However, several Yoruba soldiers were still killed (including Major Ogunro of the NMTC and Second-Lieutenants Olaniyan and Kasaba at Abeokuta). It was not so easy to distinguish Mid-Westerners and non-Igbo easterners, and some of them were killed as a result. These included Lieutenant Zacchareus Idowu (a Mid-Westerner) of the 2nd battalion.

Yoruba Soldiers

Yoruba officers were also afraid that after Northerners finished off Igbo officers, they would be next. Concerned for their safety Yoruba soldiers sent a delegation consisting of Lt-Colonel Obasanjo, Major Oluleye and Captains Akinfenwa and Timothy B. Ogundeko to the Northern Region's military governor Lt-Colonel Katsina, to report their fears. Katsina arranged for Major Obasanjo to be smuggled away for his own protection. Some Yoruba officers wanted to desert the army either individually or *en masse* as part of a self protective Yoruba withdrawal. Colonel Adebayo was out of the country when the July 29 revolt commenced. He returned a few days later and succeeded Fajuyi as the Western Region's military governor. Adebayo later articulated Yoruba fears as follows: "The Yorubas are afraid of moving around with the northern troops because they feel 'Well, they have done something to the easterners; maybe it is our turn next."[1] Adebayo also felt personally threatened on two fronts. He was reportedly reluctant to allow Yoruba officers to return to the Western Region as he felt threatened that one of them could stage a coup to remove him from his new post. Additionally he felt his freedom of action was limited as his bodyguards were Northerners. The fate of Aguiyi-Ironsi and Fajuyi at the hands of their Northern bodyguards may have played on Adebayo's mind.

After some time killing Igbos became a status symbol for some Northern soldiers. Two incidents involving the 1st and 5th battalions illustrate this. These two battalions were the only two of the five army battalions not to have participated in the overthrow of Aguiyi-Ironsi and other senior Igbo officers. Both battalions had been restrained from joining the mutiny by the precipitate action of their commanders. This created a perception within the Northern troops in both battalions that their prestige had been degraded in comparison with their mutinous colleagues elsewhere in the 2nd, 3rd and 4th battalions, which had all been active participants in overthrowing Aguiyi-Ironsi. The 1st and 5th battalion's lack of involvement meant that Northern soldiers in both units were eager for an opportunity to prove to their Northern colleagues elsewhere that they too had played their part. Both units were urged by their colleagues in other units to contribute their own "quota" to the Igbo death toll.

The first illustrative example involved the 1st battalion. Then Major Benjamin Adekunle (the famed "Black Scorpion") was the deputy commander of the 1st battalion in Enugu. When a decision was made to repatriate army officers to their regions of origin, Adekunle and Northern soldiers in his unit were to leave Enugu and head firstly to Kaduna, and then to Lagos. Simultaneously a group of surviving Igbo soldiers that had been detained in Kaduna prison for their own safety were to be repatriated to Enugu via Lagos. When they were released for transportation by train to Enugu, Adekunle promised them safe passage to Lagos from where they could then proceed to Enugu. The Northern soldiers in Adekunle's battalion and the Igbo soldiers were placed on the same train. Some Northern soldiers having long been frustrated at their inability to kill Igbos thus far, finally got their opportunity. They

---

1 Meeting of Nigeria's military leaders at Aburi in Ghana in January 1967.

descended upon the Igbo soldiers, killed them and threw their bodies off the train. For promising safe passage to the Igbo soldiers, Adekunle too was attacked, but was saved by the intervention of Captain Gibson Jalo.[1] Although his father was a Yoruba from Ogbomosho, Adekunle's mother was like Jalo, from the Bachama ethnic group of the Northern Region. In the mayhem of the time, such tenuous links could determine life and death. Nigerians often speak of "detribalized" Nigerians. Adekunle must be a top candidate for that title. His father is from the Western Region, his mother from the Northern Region and his first wife was from the Eastern Region.

On September 27, a radio broadcast by Radio Cotonou in the neighboring Francophone country of Benin falsely claimed that Igbos had been attacked and murdered in the Eastern. A series of measures gave serious indications that this story was planted by highly placed individuals in Nigeria. The Radio Cotonou report was re-broadcast several times by the government owned Radio Kaduna. As has been pointed out elsewhere, it required considerable effort to translate the original Radio Cotonou report from French into English and Hausa for re-broadcast in Nigeria (without bothering to verify the original report).[2] The following day the Northern Region government-owned *New Nigerian* newspaper carried the report as its lead story. The *New Nigerian* was founded by the Sardauna and was regarded as the voice of the Northern Region's government. The Northern Region Ministry of Information also issued a press release repeating the Radio Cotonou broadcast. According to one author, the redistribution of the report via government owned media was authorized by senior government personnel including the head of the Northern Region civil service, Alhaji Ali Akilu, and Lt-Colonel Katsina, military governor of the Northern Region.[3]

These measures gave the impression of the deliberate placing of an incendiary report in order to provoke further attacks on Igbos. What had actually happened in the Eastern Region was that when Igbo corpses and severely injured Igbo refugees arrived back from the Northern Region with terrible tales of their suffering, a number of Northerners in the Eastern Region were attacked in misplaced retaliation. This occurred *after* the Radio Cotonou broadcast. The New Nigerian later retracted its redistribution of the Radio Cotonou report and announced that after investigation, it discovered that the Radio Cotonou report was false. Despite this the Radio Cotonou report was wildly exaggerated and within hours reports circulating in the Northern Region were claiming that tens of thousands of Northerners had been massacred in the Eastern Region. This was the ultimate spark to ignite Northern soldiers who so far had been prevented from participating in the mutiny.

Back to Kano — Northern Region

The 5th battalion in Kano had been prevented from taking immediate action on July 29 due to the precipitate action of the second-in command Major Oluleye in locking the armory and confining the soldiers to the barracks. However, as the weeks passed tension continued to grow between Igbo and Northern soldiers in the battalion, and Hausa mobs hunting for Igbos surrounded the barracks, armed with bows and arrows. The battalion's RSM Dauda Mumuni spoke to the mob and convinced them to disperse. Although Mumuni had won a medal for his service during

---

1 Jalo later became a Lt-General and served as the Chief of Army Staff, and Chief of Defense Staff under President Shehu Shagari.
2 De St Jorre, *The Brothers' War*, page 85.
3 Ruth First, *The Barrel of a Gun*, page 333.

the UN peacekeeping operation in the Congo, his pacification of the mob may not have made him popular among his Northern colleagues, and was not the end of the matter. Northern soldiers in the unit still felt that respect was withheld from them as they did not participate in the overthrow of Aguiyi-Ironsi. Other factors may have amplified their psychological isolation from their colleagues elsewhere. They had been deployed by their commander Lt-Colonel Shuwa to stop attacks on Igbos in May during the anti-Unification Decree riots, and their former commander was after all Lt-Colonel Ojukwu (who had now replaced Aguiyi-Ironsi as the ultimate symbol of Igbo hegemony). All these factors had them seething and they desperately sought an opportunity to revalidate their martial credentials. Shuwa decided to separate the Igbo soldiers in the battalion for their own safety by moving them to Wudil camp along Katsina road. On their way there, the Igbo soldiers Major Joseph Ihedigbo (the former second in command that Oluleye replaced), Captains Egbuna, Maduabam, Lieutenant Ovueziri and six NCOs were condemned to death and shot by the Northern escorts that were supposed to lead them to safety. The six NCOs were Warrant Officer Mbeisike Sylvanus, Corporals Lawrence Okoro and Patrick Osegi, Staff Sergeant Benjamin Akhideno, and Privates Michael Abam and Benedict Anuforo.

SEPTEMBER–OCTOBER 1966 — THINGS FALL APART

When the January 1966 coup took place, the 5th battalion's second in command Major Oluleye was out of the country serving as a member of the United Nations Military Observer Mission in India/Pakistan. For the second time in 1966 fate was once again about to take him out of the danger zone. In late September 1966 Shuwa and Oluleye were posted away from the 5th battalion and replaced by Major Abba Kyari and Captain Auna respectively. Shuwa and Oluleye's redeployment was a blessing in disguise for them. A relatively benign incident gave the Northern soldiers in the battalion an un-missable opportunity to show their mettle, prove to their Northern colleagues elsewhere that they were not cowards, and that they had contributed their own "quota" to the Igbo death toll. A District Officer in the nearby village of Nguru was reported missing during a civil disturbance. When the police refused to go to Nguru without an army escort, they were given a platoon escort consisting of soldiers from the 5th battalion. Crucially, the escort soldiers were issued with live ammunition prior to their departure.[1] On the afternoon of Saturday October 1, 1966, the 5th battalion's troops mutinied and opened fire as their commander Major Kyari addressed them on the battalion parade ground. The rampaging soldiers were so out of control that even Northerners who tried to restrain them were murdered. They murdered their fellow Northern officers, including the second in command Captain Auna and the RSM Dauda Mumuni. Their commanding officer Major Abba Kyari, the Adjutant Lieutenant Abubakar Gora and other officers had to flee for their lives and hid off base.[2] Second-Lieutenant Ike Nwachukwu was among the officers fortunate to escape being killed. The troops raided the battalion armory, broke out of the barracks and headed into town to pick up local civilian *yan daba*[3] whom they asked to

---

1 Douglas A. Anthony, *Poison and Medicine: Ethnicity and Power in a Nigerian City, 1966 to 1986*, page 97.

2 Kyari later resurfaced as the military governor of North-Central State. Although eastern publications claimed he was killed in the mutiny, the 5th battalion's Adjutant Lieutenant Gora survived.

3 Local thugs. Usually disenfranchised young men without educational or employment prospects.

take them to locations where they could find Igbos (including the Sabon Gari, hotels, and the Electricity Corporation of Nigeria). Igbos trying to escape were not spared. At Kano Airport, the soldiers set upon a crowd of Igbo refugees boarding a south-bound flight and killed them. Some were dragged out of the plane cabin and shot. Igbo workers at the airport were also hunted down and killed, sometimes inside the terminal.[1] The soldiers also made their presence felt at the railway station where Igbo civilians were waiting to board trains to escape. Many of the Igbo would-be passengers and railway staff were shot dead. One of the victims was the uncle of Professor Humphrey Nwosu (former head of the National Electoral Commission), who was a railway station master in Kano. This massacre on October 1, 1966 (the sixth anniversary of Nigeria's independence) was possibly the worst of the whole mutiny. The participation of soldiers with firearms greatly increased the kill rate. Several thousand Igbos were killed that day alone in Kano due to the combined efforts of the 5th battalion and civilian mobs. The situation was beyond police control. The military governor of the Northern Region, Lt-Colonel Katsina, travelled to Kano to bravely confront the mutineers. He later narrated the frightening scene that confronted him:

> I have seen an army mutiny in Kano and if you see me trembling you will know what a mutiny is. . . . [F]or two good days I saw a real mutiny when a C.O. of northern origin[2] commanding soldiers of northern origin had to run away. . . . I feel it is my responsibility. This was what made me face the mutiny in Kano. Soldiers were ready to shoot me but all the same it is my responsibility to save lives and I did it.[3]

Katsina called Lt-Colonel Shuwa, Major Martin Adamu and Lieutenant Garba Duba to assist him in suppressing the mutiny but they were overwhelmed and feared being shot themselves. Katsina eventually managed to put down the mutiny by heading out from the airport and driving street to street for several hours in a Jeep accompanied by the Emir of Kano. The sight and authority of the Emir shamed the looters into fleeing, and the soldiers into returning to their barracks. Katsina, Shuwa and the Emir followed the soldiers into the barracks and addressed them there. The 5th battalion was the only army unit to be reprimanded for its role in the mutiny (they went too far by killing their fellow Northerners). Lt-Colonel Katsina later announced that the battalion would be dissolved as a result of the mutiny.

POGROM

However, the mutiny was not confined to the army, nor were the victims Igbo soldiers alone. The mutiny became indiscriminate in nature and every Igbo whether military or civilian, became a target. The acclaimed Igbo author Chinua Achebe had shortly before the January coup, published a book entitled *A Man of the People*, which told the fictional story of a country ravaged by political crises, that culminates in a military coup. To some Northern soldiers, the book was evidence of Achebe's foreknowledge or complicity in the January "Igbo coup." He too was hunted by Northern soldiers, and he had to hide at a safe house in Lagos for weeks before he was able to escape to the Eastern Region with his family. Mobs (assisted in many cases by Northern soldiers) massacred tens of thousands of Igbos resident in the Northern Region. The resentment of Igbos that had simmered beneath the surface for years

---

1 The events at Kano airport are chronicled in an article in the October 14, 1966 edition of *Time Magazine* entitled *"Massacre in Kano."*
2 Major Abba Kyari.
3 Meeting of Nigeria's military leaders at Aburi in Ghana.

was released in a violent burst of volcanic rage and extreme bloodlust. The massacres were too widespread and intense to have been spontaneous. Some civilian *agent
provocateurs* were active, assisted by some of the less disciplined Northern soldiers. A
Northern corporal gave a plausibly simple rationale for the pogroms: "Igbos killed our
leaders in January; they were taking all the top jobs; we had to get rid of them. Now
we have only got northerners in this barracks; all the southerners have run away."[1]
The following report encapsulates the horror of the massacres.

> For fear of promoting an even greater tragedy, the Nigerians have been shel-
> tered from knowing the full magnitude of the disaster that has overtaken the
> Igbos in the northern region. The danger is that the truth will not be believed
> and so proper lessons learnt, once the horror is over. While the Hausas in each
> town and village in the north know what happened in their own localities, only
> the Igbos know the whole story, from the 600,000 or so refugees who have fled
> to the safety of the eastern region — hacked, slashed, mangled, stripped naked
> and robbed of all their possessions, the orphans, the widows, the traumatized.
> A woman, mute and dazed, arrived back in her village after travelling for five
> days with only a bowl in her lap. She held her child's head which was severed
> before her eyes. Another stepped off a refugee lorry, her face battered. By her
> side was a little boy, one of whose eyes had been gouged out, and her little girl
> who had severe scalp wounds. "What," she kept on repeating, "has happened
> to my baby?" It had been tied to her back before she was knocked to the ground.
> Men, women and children arrived with arms and legs broken, hands hacked off,
> mouths split open. Pregnant women were cut open and the unborn children
> killed. . . . After a fortnight, the scene in the eastern region continues to be remi-
> niscent of the ingathering of exiles into Israel after the end of the last war. The
> parallel is not fanciful.[2]

A favored tactic was to halt southern bound trains (which were on occasion
stoned as they were departing) and order all Igbos on board to disembark, after
which they would be shot. This occurred frequently at the river Benue crossing at
Makurdi. In one incident reported to the author by an eyewitness, Igbo males who
were suspected to be soldiers or of fighting age were hauled off a train and tossed off
the side of the bridge into the river. Several innocent people were murdered based on
mere suspicion or based on the regional/ethnic "profiling" of suspect's names, physical features and accents. The wearing of Western attire and frequently speaking
English publicly became perceived Igbo identifiers. During the initial mutiny at the
Abeokuta garrison on the night of July 28, Lieutenant Gabriel Idoko was shot at by
his fellow Northern soldiers when they mistakenly presumed he was Igbo because
he was "wearing a western type suit." Idoko had a lucky escape. The bullet passed
through his jacket and did not hurt him. The soldiers who shot at him apologized
when they realized he was Northern.[3] Killing was sometimes confused by the fact
that many Igbos were fluent Hausa speakers. Where ethnicity was in doubt, suspects would be asked to pronounce difficult Hausa words in an attempt to elicit an
"Igbo" pronunciation of such words. Some impatient Northern NCOs did not bother
with such niceties and simply enlarged the scope of killing, with the result that some
members of eastern minority ethnic groups were also killed. This led to official appeals against the molestation or killing of non-Igbo southerners. In Bauchi (hometown of murdered Prime Minister Balewa) a Ministry of Information sound truck

---

1 Miners, *The Nigerian Army 1956–66*, page 215.
2 Colin Legum, *Observer*, October 16, 1966.
3 Momoh, *The Nigerian Civil War, 1967–1970: History and Reminiscences*, page 242.

drove around appealing for Northerners not to attack non-Igbos. The cynical subtext of this message was that it remained acceptable to attack Igbos.

There were a few isolated acts of clemency by Northern officers. Lt-Colonel Katsina arranged for his Igbo ADC Lieutenant Chris Ugokwe to be hidden, then safely repatriated to the Eastern Region. Ugokwe would return to prominence a decade later during another coup, and subsequently became Chairman of the National Population Commission. In Kaduna Captain Mamudu[1] of the first brigade signals troops advised his eastern soldiers to stop showing up to work for their own safety. The surviving eastern soldiers took his advice to heart and fled to the Eastern Region. Also in Kaduna the same RSM Ahmadu Bello that lured Lt-Colonel Okoro into being murdered in the 3rd battalion guardroom, and Captain John Swanton[2] saved some southern soldiers from being killed after they had been assembled on a hockey pitch surrounded by Northern troops. Major Abba Kyari also helped Igbo soldiers to escape. Lieutenant D.S. Abubakar saved two junior air force officers from being murdered at Sergeant Lapdam's notorious checkpoint on Carter bridge. The wife of former UMBC leader Joe Tarka also sheltered Igbos inside her home as Northern troops gathered outside baying for their blood. Ojukwu's sister was saved by a Yoruba named Dr. Oshodi who hid her under one of the beds in his house.

Amidst the murders, tension, and mutual suspicion, there was a remarkable display of military camaraderie at Lt-Colonel David Ogunewe's 1st battalion at Enugu. Northern and Igbo officers toasted each other with drinks, and posed together for a final photograph before Northern soldiers departed the battalion following the agreement to return all soldiers to their respective regions of origin. Such comradeship in the midst of bitterness was isolated, but was shown again the following year, when members of the Supreme Military Council met and deliberated at Aburi, Ghana, in the most cordial manner despite months of mutual suspicion, accusations, and murder.

The Eastern Region authorities made great efforts to collect testimony from survivors. Lt-Colonel Ojukwu later said that "Gentlemen, Officers and men of eastern Nigeria origin who had moved from other parts of the country know the names, the faces of individuals who perpetrated these atrocities. Mention a name, we know who killed him, mention somebody we know who at least hounded him out of his barracks."[3] Ojukwu felt a burden of responsibility and personal guilt for those Igbos killed in the pogroms. He later reminisced that after the May 1966 riots he went on the air and told Igbos that it was safe for them to return to the Northern Region. Not long after, many of those that heeded his call to return to the Northern Region were murdered in the September and October 1966 pogroms. Ojukwu revealed the depth of his personal feelings of guilt:

> I am only a human being. It is a thing on my conscience and will always remain there. I get letters, at least 150 daily; out of those, at least 60% are from wives without husbands, children without fathers, families without their bread winners, that you Ojukwu told our bread-winner to go, now that he is dead what can you do?. . . So many people hold me personally responsible for the death of

---

1 Years later Mamudu became the Military Administrator of Gongola State and also commanded the signals corps.

2 Gbulie claims Swanton was one of the officers that backed Nzeogwu during the January coup.

3 Meeting of Nigeria's military leaders at Aburi in Ghana in January 1967.

their people who went back. For that reason I cannot go up again and say "go back.[1]

There was little sympathy for the Igbos and the attitude of many was that they "deserved" their fate or "had it coming." Ojukwu eventually ordered all non-easterners to leave the Eastern Region for their own safety. Contrary to popular opinion, this measure was not a retaliatory measure against Northerners resident in the Eastern Region (who were few in number). This measure was taken in order to prevent conflict between Igbos and Yorubas resident in the Eastern Region. Igbo survivors of the pogroms felt that some of their Yoruba neighbors had not done enough to protect them. Ojukwu later explained that:

> When the easterners came back from the north, they knew there were not many northerners in the east. Really what sparked off trouble was that there were attempts to start molesting the westerners. The reason for that was, I can understand it although I was not there, when this started in the north, the easterner ran from his house, usually in Sabon Gari and houses are mixed, to the westerner. The westerners got together and just sat tight and.... The poor Igbo man rushed into the Yoruba man's house to say, "Afolabi, I have come to your house to take refuge," and his western friend said, "No, no, don't bring your problems to me." And this is precisely what incensed the easterner.[2]

In the words of one author, the consequences of the January 1966 coup "hung like a curse over Nigeria for three years"[3].

---

1 Ibid.
2 Ibid.
3 Elizabeth Isichei, *A History of the Igbo People*, page 243.

CHAPTER 11. LEGACY OF THE 1966 COUPS

There are probably only three living people who know the full truth behind what happened during those horrendous days of 1966: Yakubu Gowon, Chukwuemeka Ojukwu and the former head of the police Special Branch M.D. Yusuf. Two of the January 1966 coup participants have given their own inside accounts of the coup,[1] and some Northerners have written about their own perspectives on the coup.[2] None of these accounts by the protagonists is balanced. Two of the driving forces behind the coup, Majors Nzeogwu and Ifeajuna, also wrote notes on it. Neither man's account has ever been published. Ifeajuna's manuscript was given to the acclaimed author Chinua Achebe. However, Achebe refused to publish the manuscript as he felt it contained factual inconsistencies and a great deal of self-embellishment by Ifeajuna. Brigadier Ogundipe also began to write a book on the 1966 crisis, but the manuscript was not completed before his death, and was subsequently lost. Obtaining accurate corroborated information on what transpired during the Northern soldiers' mutiny has been made difficult by the fact that the participants originally agreed at the behest of Murtala Muhammed, to never publicly discuss what they did. Some of the participants who rigidly adhered to this code of silence took their memories with them to their graves (such as Murtala Muhammed, Martin Adamu, Paul Dickson, Sani Abacha and Ibrahim Bako). Others have been more forthcoming.

In early 1967 both the federal government and the Eastern Region produced (mainly for propaganda purposes) booklets on the two coups of 1966. The federal government's booklet was entitled *Nigeria 1966* and portrayed the January 1966 coup as an Igbo plot (which it covered in great detail) while the Northern led revenge coup that followed it six months later was an unplanned chain of isolated mutinies. The Eastern Region retaliated shortly afterward with a publication entitled *January 15: Before and After* which was diametrically opposed to *Nigeria 1966* and glossed over the January 1966 coup but portrayed the Northern revenge coup as a systematically planned slaughter of Igbos. As historical accounts, the polarized political climate of

---

1 Ademoyega, *Why We Struck*, and Gbulie, *Nigeria's Five Majors*.
2 D.J.M. Muffet. *Let Truth Be Told* and Mainasara, *The Five Majors: Why They Struck*.

that era should be borne in mind when assessing the reliability of some of the claims in those documents.

THE "FIVE MAJORS"?

One enduring myth is that Nigeria's first military coup was carried out by "five Igbo Majors." The source of this myth is the "we were five in number" comment, which the coup's most visible participant Major Nzeogwu, made in an interview with Dennis Ejindu after the coup.[1] The "Five Majors" myth was later further perpetuated by Captain Ben Gbulie's book on the coup, *Nigeria's Five Majors*, the title of which he later admitted borrowing from a play of the same name. When Nzeogwu made his infamous "we were five in number" comment, he made no reference to the *rank* of the "five." He was merely referring to the five designated strategic regional commanders of the coup. In fact, no less than nine Majors were originally billed to take part in the coup. These nine were Majors Nzeogwu, Ifeajuna, Ademoyega, Okafor, Anuforo, Chukwuka, Obienu, Onwuatuegwu and Chude-Sokei. Shortly before the coup, Chude-Sokei was posted overseas. On the coup day itself, Obienu failed to appear, leaving seven Majors as participants. When it came to execution, the Majors designated five officers as regional commanders. Of Nzeogwu's "five," there were "the two of us in the North" (Nzeogwu and Major Tim Onwuatuegwu), and three more in the south.

The head of the Lagos operations was Major Emmanuel Ifeajuna. That makes *three* Majors so far. The squad which killed Chief Samuel Akintola in Ibadan was led by *Captain* Nwobosi. That makes four (three Majors and one Captain). There was no coup in the Mid-West as no military formation was based in that Region. However, Lieutenant Jerome Oguchi was to arrest the Premier of the Eastern Region Dr. Michael Okpara. The identity of the fifth member is the most problematic. Majors Don Okafor and Adewale Ademoyega were given much responsibility for the Lagos branch of the coup, and it is likely that one of these two men was the fifth commander.

Additionally, an overlooked issue regarding Nzeogwu's now near legendary "interview" with Ejindu is that it was not a formal "interview" at all. The only surviving military officer that was present when Nzeogwu spoke to Ejindu is Lieutenant Fola Oyewole (who also took part in the Majors' coup). According to Oyewole the background to the "interview" was in fact a social gathering at Major Nzeogwu's residence shortly before the Nigerian civil war. The gathering was attended by approximately a dozen people including Major Onwuatuegwu (another of the coup Majors), Oyewole and several civilians including the journalist Ejindu. This gathering took place after Major Nzeogwu had been released in March 1967 by Lt-Colonel Ojukwu. As drinks were served to the guests and the atmosphere relaxed, the conversation turned to politics and Nzeogwu gave his view on a number of issues. According to Oyewole, Ejindu later cleverly reconstructed Nzeogwu's conversational responses into a question-and-answer style exclusive "interview" session.[2] Ejindu did so even though he did not take contemporaneous notes or tape record Nzeogwu's responses. Strangely, Oyewole did not at any point in his book chronicle his role in the coup of January 1966.

---

1 Ejindu, interview with Major Nzeogwu, *Africa and the World*, May 1967. *Daily Telegraph*, 22 January 1966
2 Fola Oyewole, *Reluctant Rebel*.

WHO WAS THE LEADER?

Major Nzeogwu has since 1966, been touted as the leader of the January 1966 coup. This has been widely presumed due to the visible role which Nzeogwu played during and after the coup. Nzeogwu was the only Major to successfully execute the coup in his designated target region. He then followed up his coup success with his infamous "our enemies are the. . . . " speech. Thus the (false) assumption that he was the coup leader spread. The truth may be somewhat different. It was not until the coup plot reached its logistical stage that Nzeogwu was brought in to the conspiratorial group. The ideological inspiration behind the coup was Major Emmanuel Ifeajuna, not Nzeogwu. However, Ifeajuna was chased out of Nigeria's then capital city of Lagos by Major-General Aguiyi-Ironsi. Realizing that Aguiyi-Ironsi was rounding up those that took part in the coup, Ifeajuna fled to Ghana, leaving Nzeogwu behind as the coup's spokesman and giving the impression that he was its leader.

THE MAJORS' COUP: AN "IGBO COUP"?

The ethnic composition of the officers that carried out the coup is incompatible with a grand Igbo design. Several of the soldiers executing the coup were Yoruba (including Major Ademoyega, Captain Adeleke and Lieutenants Fola Oyewole, Olafimihan). The role of Northern soldiers has not been sufficiently chronicled. Several officers of Northern origin took part in Nigeria's first military coup. The "Igbo coup" tag attached to the Majors' assault ignores the fact that scores of Northern soldiers took part in the Lagos operations, and even assisted Nzeogwu when he stormed the Sardauna's residence. Nzeogwu pointed out that

> . . . any man had the chance to drop out. More than that, they had bullets. They had been issued with bullets but I was unarmed. If they disagreed they could have shot me. . . . Most of the other ranks were northerners but they followed.[1]

He described the detachment of troops accompanying him to Sardauna's house as "a truly Nigerian gathering. . . . Only in the army do you get true Nigerianism." Among the prominent Northern soldiers that accompanied Nzeogwu was John Atom Kpera. Kpera later became the military governor of Benue State. Witnesses present when Nzeogwu' troops stormed the Sardauna's residence have testified that many of the soldiers accompanying him spoke to each other in Hausa. Many of the soldiers that accompanied Major Ifeajuna when he abducted the Prime Minister were also Northerners. Appendix 1 shows a sample of Northern soldiers who were named as active participants in the Special Branch report.

It is unlikely that Yoruba (many of whom are antagonistic towards Igbos) and Northern soldiers would risk their lives to stage a coup whose stated aim was to release the Yoruba leader of the opposition and install him as the country's President, all in the name of establishing "Igbo domination" of Nigeria. Aside from the multi-ethnic participants of the January coup, Yoruba soldiers such as Major Adegoke and Lt-Colonel Fajuyi were later gunned down by Northern soldiers who suspected them of being sympathizers of the Majors. The "Igbo coup" analysis is further blurred when even Northern soldiers acknowledge that the plotters had accomplices from other ethnic groups. In an interview published in the January 8, 1990 edition of

---

1 *New Nigerian*, January 18, 1966.

Newswatch, Nigeria's most prolific coup plotter Ibrahim Babangida admitted that the Majors' coup was:

> not an Igbo based thing as far as I could imagine but the execution of the coup was poorly done and made people to think that it was one sided. I could recall Nzeogwu saying that some chaps in the south let him down because they had not been able to carry out the instruction the way he wanted them.[1]

The personality and background of Major Nzeogwu is also instructive in this regard. Nzeogwu was an Igbo in name only. He was born and raised in the Northern Region, had visited his ancestral home of Okpanam only a few times in his entire life, and did not know his way around it. He had Hausa neighbors, friends and was very popular among Hausa soldiers. In the days immediately following the coup, Nzeogwu was so distrustful of those around him that he would accept medical treatment[2] only from a Northern doctor (Dr. Rimi),[3] and refused to eat any food not prepared by his Hausa cook. Till this day, even Northern soldiers refuse to believe that Nzeogwu could have planned or executed an "Igbo coup." The worst they are willing to say about him is that he was "misled" by the other Igbo soldiers in the plot. Several decades later, the Northern Colonel Yohana Madaki said that had he been approached by Nzeogwu to participate in the January 1966 coup, he would have taken part gladly. Major Nzeogwu's close friend Olusegun Obasanjo later wrote that:

> Chukwuma was by nature and upbringing, incapable of planning, let alone executing a coup d'état designed to deliberately suppress one tribe politically and elevate another. . . . There was no intention on Chukwuma's part to collude or conspire with Igbo officers in the army and with Igbo politicians and academics, to lead a coup for the purpose of ensuring the political leadership of Nigeria by Igbos.[4]

The reason for the ethnic concentration of southerners in the coup is that at this stage, the southern officer corps was more perturbed by the deteriorating political events in the country than their Northern counterparts. It was southerners (both military and civilian) that were aggrieved by the government's handling of various crises. Northern soldiers had no reason to overthrow a government headed by their region's party and whose policies were favorable to them.

A UPGA Coup?

If the coup has to be characterized in a partisan manner, it would be a UPGA coup since most of the victims, and those that were dispossessed of political power came from the ruling NNA coalition created by the NPC and NNDP. The soldiers who were killed by the Majors were also those who were supportive of NPC/NNDP politicians. For example Brigadier Ademulegun was on good terms with the Sardauna and Largema's 4th battalion had been used to suppress opposition protests against Chief Akintola's NNDP regime. Okotie-Eboh was the only UPGA minister killed, and even then, he was a good friend of the NPC Prime Minister. It is surprising that this line of thought has not been explored in greater detail over the years. Although there is no incontrovertible evidence to link UPGA politicians with the Majors' plot, some of the Majors were certainly sympathetic to UPGA ideology, and wanted to release

---

1 *Newswatch*, January 8, 1990.
2 Nzeogwu had injured himself with a grenade he threw during his assault on the Sardauna's lodge.
3 Later became a Major-General and the head of the army's medical corps.
4 See Obasanjo, *An Intimate Portrait of Chukwuma Kaduna Nzeogwu*, page 107.

the leader of the opposition (Chief Awolowo) from prison and install him as the President to replace the NPC leadership. The January 1966 coup was not *ethnically* partisan, but it was *politically* partisan — in favor of the UPGA. Since political affiliations and loyalties in Nigeria tended to follow ethnic and regional patterns, violence by a political faction against an opposing faction would similarly be ethnically and/or regionally lopsided.

Nigeria's former High Commissioner in Ghana Isa Sulaiman Wali later claimed that the Majors were in contact with the AG's former General-Secretary Samuel Ikoku who had been granted political refuge in Ghana and became an adviser to Ghanaian President Kwame Nkrumah after fleeing from Nigeria to evade trial in the Awolowo treason trial in 1962. When he escaped to Ghana, Major Ifeajuna was housed with Ikoku. Awolowo's secretary Odia Ofeimun later confirmed the pro Awolowo leanings of the coup's executors, their plan to release Awolowo from prison and make him Nigeria's leader (see discussion in Chapter 3). The UPGA leaders had tried everything (both constitutional and extra-constitutional) to remove the NPC from power and failed. There was the attempt by Awolowo to overthrow the government, Dr. Michael Okpara's disputing of census results, and the UPGA's election boycott. All these methods had failed miserably, and the UPGA's aims were by accident or design, carried out for them by a group of army officers that were sympathetic to UPGA ideology.

The Majors' Objectives

Whilst it is clear that the Majors were disgusted with the government's creation of endless crises, were their aims purely political? Other factors may have been at play. Several of the Majors expressed dissatisfaction at political interference with the military and had professional tensions with some of the officers that were killed in the January coup. For example Captain Ben Gbulie savagely critiqued the army's high command and had no good words to say about any of them. He had the following to say about his superior officers:

- Major-General Aguiyi-Ironsi: "inept and inefficient — hardly the caliber of officer to command an army. In fact, the coup planners considered him unfit to command even a funeral detail."
- Brigadier Ademulegun: accused him of being a "tribalist," of trying to curry favor with politicians, and of illegally storing weapons for the Sardauna.
- Brigadier Maimalari: Major Okafor was unhappy when Brigadier Maimalari revoked a punishment that Okafor had imposed on a Northern soldier.
- Colonel Kur Mohammed: accused him of being frequently in a drunken state and of receiving money from Northern politicians.
- Colonel Shodeinde: was also accused of being a tribalist and of being "dull, indolent and inefficient."
- Lt-Colonel Largema: accused of complicity in the rigging of Western Region elections.
- Lt-Colonel Pam: claimed that his house was a gift from the NPC.[1]
- Lt-Colonel Unegbe: claims he was corrupt and "associated with graft."

---

1 This accusation in Gbulie's book irked Pam's family sufficiently for Pam's son to demand an apology from Gbulie in 2001.

It may not be pure coincidence that all but one of the above officers were murdered in the January coup. The manner in which some of the victims were murdered suggests personal animosity towards them. Even if it is accepted that, somehow, neutralizing the senior officers was a tactical necessity in the coup's execution, the murder of staff officers like Colonel Mohammed and Lt-Colonels Pam and Unegbe did not seem necessary since these men held staff appointments at army headquarters and were not in command of any troops. The manner in which Lt-Colonel Largema was hunted down to his Ikoyi hotel appeared particularly vindictive and unnecessary given that he was several miles away from his battalion in Ibadan. It is not implausible that in the heat of the moment, some of the plotters used the coup as an opportunity to settle old scores and grievances they had with their senior officers.

THE "CLASSMATE SYNDROME"

As has been demonstrated in subsequent coups, military coups are clannish affairs usually executed by soldiers tied by bonds of kinship, common rank, regional origin or ethnicity. That the January 1966 coup was carried out mostly by officers in the rank of Major is therefore unremarkable. The sensitive nature of a coup and the need to maintain secrecy and trust prior to executing it requires strong bonds of trust to exist between the members of the coup plot. Many of the Majors were of a similar age, had trained together and risen up through the ranks together. They also shared the same political objectives and disgust with the politicians. Hence bonds had formed between them for years prior to the coup. The leading personalities in Nigerian coups have always been dominated by a "classmate syndrome" featuring officers who attended school or defense academy together. For example alumni of the St John's school in Kaduna such as Majors Nzeogwu, Anuforo and Captain Nwobosi were prominent members of the January 1966 Majors' coup. Among Northern officers, several overlapping circles of fraternity were, and are in existence. Joe Garba, Jerry Useni, Domkat Bali and John Shagaya were among the first group of soldiers that were dubbed "The Langtang Mafia" by the Nigerian press and public. "The Langtang Mafia" is a euphemism used to refer to a group of soldiers of Tarok ethnicity from the middle belt town of Langtang, all of whom rose to prominence and powerful positions in military governments over several decades. Apart from Garba, Useni, Bali and Shagaya, other powerful members of the Langtang "Mafia" who later rose to prominence include Lt-General Joshua Dogonyaro, Air Marshal Jonah Wuyep, Brigadiers Yakubu Domven Rimdan and John Temlong, and Air Commodore Bernard Banfa. The Langtang Mafia is the most prominent, but is not the only Northern geo-ethnic military clique in Nigeria. Mohammed Magoro was the first prominent officer to emerge from the minority Zuru ethnic group in the far north-west of Nigeria in what is now modern day Kebbi State. Former Chief of Army Staff Lt-General Ishaya Bamaiyi and his brother Major-General Musa Bamaiyi, Major-Generals S.O.G. Ango, Sani Sami and Tanko Ayuba are also members of the Zuru group. Musa was the former head of the Nigerian Drug Law Enforcement Agency. Additionally an Angas clique followed in Gowon's footsteps. Although a small ethnic group, the Angas were heavily represented in the army in proportion to their numerical strength in the general population.

Alumni of the Government College in Bida featured in the July 1966 Northern soldiers' counter-coup. Many of the Bida alumni such as Ibrahim Babangida, Mamman Vatsa, Ibrahim Taiwo, G.A. Dada ("Paiko"), Mohammed Magoro, Garba Duba, M.I. Wushishi, Sani Bello and Gado Nasko also played prominent roles in subsequent coups and military governments.[1] The July 1966 coup also included a massive concentration of former Nigerian Military School students (J.N. Garba, B.S. Dimka, Musa Usman, John Shagaya, Isa Bukar, Inuwa Sara, Nuhu Nathan, Pam Mwadkon, Clement Dabang, Tijani Aliyu).

Every single one of Nigeria's coups has been executed by soldiers sharing the same political outlook, of similar rank, and from a specific region:

- January 1966 (mainly southern left-wing majors)
- July 1966 (junior northern officers and NCOs)
- July 1975 (northern Colonels)
- February 1976 (junior and middle ranking officers from northern Christian minority ethnic groups)
- December 1983 (mainly Muslim senior northern Brigadiers and Major-Generals)
- August 1985 (mainly northern Brigadiers and Major-Generals)
- April 1990 (minority ethnic groups)

Military coups in Nigeria become violent only when one group of soldiers is attempting to take power from another group of soldiers from a different ethnic, geographic or religious grouping. For example the southern Majors' coup was bloody when they tried to overthrow a Northern led government. An even bloodier coup followed when seven months later, Northern soldiers sought to remove a military government led by an Igbo. In 1975, 1983 and 1985, northern soldiers managed to stage coups without resorting to killing, because those they overthrew were either from the same region or religion. Witness the bloodshed that followed in 1976 and 1990 when soldiers from different ethnic groups and religions tried to depose incumbent Northern led regimes.

Aguiyi-Ironsi once referred to the army as "a brotherhood," and Gowon later described it as an institution "built up as a family over one hundred years."[2] Many soldiers had been friendly and familiar with each other down to family level. Most soldiers were familiar with each other's families and several had served as the Best Man at their colleagues' weddings. Many had known each other since childhood, even attending the same schools. For example Lt-Colonel David Ejoor attended Government College Ughelli with Lt-Colonels Nwajei, Okwechime, Nzefili and Major John Obienu. The two 1966 coups shattered the bonds of brotherhood that had hitherto existed between Nigerian soldiers and planted seeds of distrust between them that germinated into a deadly toxin in the army. The coup of January 1966 was the first to break a military taboo by introducing the specter of Nigerian soldiers turning their guns on each other and killing their own colleagues. This opened the window for another military tradition to be shattered during the July coup when junior officers disobeyed their superiors' orders, this time destroying the military tradition of reflexive and unquestioning obedience to superiors' orders.

Attrition also contributed to the breakdown of order. Of the Nigerian army's ten most senior officers as at January 14, 1966, eight were murdered within the next seven months, and the two survivors were displaced from their posts. Discipline and professionalism was further degraded by the drafting of capable and experienced officers into political or non-military positions. Of the surviving senior officers, Lt-Colonel Gowon was head of state and Brigadier Ogundipe and Lt-Colonels Kurubo

---

1 The Bida alumni subsequently formed an old boys association including NDA course one graduate Ndakotsu and S.Gamba.

2 Meeting of Nigeria's military leaders at Aburi in Ghana in January 1967.

and Bassey were posted to ambassadorial positions. This left army command in the hands of junior inexperienced officers. It proved impossible for the military to maintain standards with such attrition and political distractions. Table 5 in Appendix 1 shows the decimation of the army's high command between January and July 1966.[1]

The absence of the experienced senior officers made it difficult for their less experienced replacements to maintain prior standards of discipline and reduced the gap in age, experience, and seniority between officers and their men thus making it more likely that orders would be challenged or disobeyed. Orders which had been routinely obeyed in the past now became simply a "basis for discussion." A far cry from the stern discipline of the days of Brigadier Maimalari. The commanding officers for their part, held postings which were totally disproportionate to their rank, experience and capability. This was one of the reasons why the Nigerian army made so much hard work of winning the civil war. For example the commanding officers of the Nigerian army's three divisions at the start of the Nigerian civil war, had prior to the war only had experience of commanding battalions consisting of a few hundred soldiers. By the war's start and due to accelerated promotions caused by the death of senior officers, they were suddenly commanding entire divisions with tens of thousands of men and millions of pounds worth of military equipment at their disposal. The greatest command position hitherto held by the new Chief of Army Staff, Lt-Colonel Joe Akahan was his brief command of the rowdy 4th battalion for a few months. When Akahan died in a helicopter crash, Hassan Katsina whose greatest command post to date was a small reconnaissance squadron, found himself as Chief of Staff of the entire army. Men whose biggest career decisions had related to matters of internal army discipline, supplies and training, suddenly found themselves in control of thousands of men, and making complex decisions affecting a nation of several million people. In business terms this would be the equivalent of appointing a recent school leaver or graduate with no managerial experience to the board of, or as CEO of a large multi-national corporation.

In retrospect the caution of British soldiers to the pace at which command of the Nigerian army was being transitioned to Nigerian soldiers was probably justified. It took only eleven months after the departure of the last British GOC before the Nigerian army turned its guns on itself and started to tear itself apart. It is inconceivable that the events described in this book would have occurred had the British senior officers still been present. At the very least, the fear of causing a major diplomatic incident by harming an expatriate officer may have restrained some of the coup plotters. It is also inconceivable that the British officers, with their culture of military subordination to civilian authority, would have staged a military coup against the government of their host country. The professional manner in which Major-General Welby-Everard handled the 1964 election crisis is also illuminating. Welby-Everard remained apolitical, refused to allow the army to become partisan in the crisis, and took his fellow security chiefs to explain his position to the President. If Nigerian soldiers had acted in the same manner during times of political crisis, an entire generation of dead officers such as Aguiyi-Ironsi, Muhammed, Fajuyi, Bako, Taiwo, and Vatsa may still be alive today.

---

1 Amazingly, though, the Indian expatriate officer in charge of the NDA (Brigadier Varma) managed to physically and professionally survive the two coups and remained in his job until 1969.

A CULTURE OF BETRAYAL

Among the most disturbing elements of the January and July 1966 coups is the shockingly cold blooded manner in which soldiers turned on, and murdered colleagues they had known for years. On the night of Friday January 14, 1966, some of the Majors attended a party at Brigadier Maimalari's house on the night before the coup. A few hours later they hunted down and killed some of the men they had been drinking and socializing with not long before. Major Ifeajuna shot his own commanding officer Brigadier Maimalari. Major Anuforo shot Lt-Colonel James Pam whom he had served with during the Tiv operation, as well as Colonel Mohammed and Lt-Colonel Unegbe, both of whom he worked with at army headquarters. Major Don Okafor was an accomplice in the murder of the Prime Minister even though he commanded the Federal Guards: the unit of the army that was supposed to protect the Prime Minister. Captain Oji was a former intelligence officer in the 4th battalion under Kur Mohammed, and went to work with Kur again in Lagos when Kur was appointed Chief of Staff at army headquarters. Yet he still participated in a coup that led to Kur's murder.

In July this pattern of betrayal was repeated as Major-General Aguiyi-Ironsi and Lt-Colonel Fajuyi were abducted by soldiers in their own entourage such as Major Danjuma and Lieutenant Walbe, and then tortured and killed. Fajuyi's own ADC Lieutenant Umar switched sides and joined their murderers. Lt-Colonel Okoro was lured to his death by his own Regimental Sergeant Major, and Lt-Colonel Okonweze and Major Obienu knew the men who shot them in the officers' mess at Abeokuta. These are illuminating insights into the extent to which seemingly rational men in possession of instruments of violence can revert to barbarism when confronted with adversity or grief.

The executors of the 1966 coups were never tried. After the end of the Nigerian civil war in 1970, the surviving officers who executed the January 1966 coup were imprisoned (without trial). They were also dismissed from the army. All were subsequently released. None of the executors of the July 1966 coup was ever tried or punished. Most of them went on to have long and fruitful careers in the military, and government. All military and political victims of the January 1966 coup have been honored by having monuments or streets named after them. Prime Minister Balewa has a square named after him in Lagos. Additionally, the Federal University of Technology, Bauchi was renamed the "Abubakar Tafawa Balewa University." His tomb in Bauchi is now a national monument and tourist attraction. The University at Zaria was renamed the "Ahmadu Bello University" in honor of the Sardauna. Major-General Aguiyi-Ironsi belatedly had a street and army barracks named after him in Abuja. The seven army officers killed during the Majors' coup of January 1966 also have streets, barracks and monuments named after them. Brigadier Ademulegun has streets named after him in Abuja and at the Ikeja Cantonment. A statue of him was erected in Ondo town, Ondo State. The children of many of those killed in the 1966 coups were given scholarships or financial assistance by the federal government.

Most of the January Majors are not alive today to tell their stories. Of the original conspirators Humphrey Chukwuka is the only one of the Majors that is still alive. Table 1 of Appendix 4 shows the fate of the January 1966 coup participants.

LONG LASTING EFFECTS OF THE JULY COUNTER-COUP

As a purely revenge coup, the July counter-coup was a spectacular success and there was not a single Northern casualty at the hands of Igbo soldiers. The federal government's *Nigeria 1966* publication ridiculously claimed that just over a dozen Igbo soldiers were killed in the counter-coup. This was a gross underestimate and the real death toll was around twenty times that number. A list of the casualties is in Appendix 3. An incomplete list of approximately 200 casualties was published by the Eastern Region, but even this publication admitted its incompleteness and that it was hard to track the whereabouts of single or newly admitted soldiers that were unaccounted for.[1] A death toll in the region of 200–300 is the closest approximation. The Eastern Region also published a list of over 300 additional eastern soldiers who were missing or imprisoned. Some of these later returned safely to the Eastern Region, or otherwise survived (such as Lt-Colonels Bassey and Ekpo). Although most NCOs were Northerners, Igbo soldiers formed two thirds of the army's officer corps. The July counter-coup permanently reversed the ethnic composition of the army. Virtually all of the Igbo soldiers were killed, permanently incapacitated or forced out of their positions. After eliminating Igbos from the army, Northern soldiers consolidated their supremacy at all levels:

- Lt-Colonel Akahan moved into the Chief of Staff (Army) position vacated by Gowon when the latter became head of state.
- Lt-Colonel Shuwa succeeded Lt-Colonel Bassey as commander of 1 brigade.
- Major Adamu took command of the 2nd battalion after Lt-Colonel Igboba was forced out of his post by the mutiny.
- Major Danjuma took command of the 4th battalion.
- Major Kyari took command of the 5th battalion.
- Captain Abbas Wali succeeded Lt-Colonel Akagha as commander of the depot in Zaria
- Captain Mohammed Remawa succeeded the murdered Major Anuforo as commander of the 2 Recce squadron in Abeokuta
- Captain Joe Garba succeeded Major Ochei as Federal Guards commander.

Superior Northern numerical representation in the military effectively created a Northern military dynasty for the next three decades. During the 33 year period of time starting from the counter-coup in July 1966 until the second return to civilian democratic rule in 1999, 15 officers occupied the post of Chief of Army Staff. Of these 15, 14 were Northerners. The only southerner to occupy the post during that time (Lt-General Alani Akinrinade) was appointed by then head of state General Obasanjo in 1979. After Obasanjo left office, his successor President Shehu Shagari created a new post of Chief of Defense Staff for Akinrinade, which removed Akinrinade from operational control of the army only six months after being appointed to the job. Akinrinade retired soon afterwards. One of Akinrinade's colleagues later revealed that Akinrinade retired in frustration as he regarded the position of Chief of Defense Staff as a sinecure position, lacking the day to day involvement and command of troops enjoyed by the Chief of Army Staff.[2] When Obasanjo returned for his second stint as Nigeria's head of state, two more southerners occupied the position: General Alexan-

---

1 Names, ranks, units and numbers are listed in Hilary Njoku's: *A Tragedy Without Heroes* and the Eastern Ministry of Information's *January 15th: Before and After*.
2 Akin Aduwo. Interviewed in *The Sun*, January 13, 2007.

der Ogomudia (Isoko) and Lt-General Owoye Andrew Azazi (Ijaw), both of whom ironically come from the much maligned Niger Delta which is the source of Nigeria's wealth, and volatile conflict regarding oil and resource control, Appendix 5 lists the officers that occupied the post of Chief of Army Staff from August 1966 to the present day.

The January 1966 coup caused many Northern soldiers to distrust military command by southerners. Major-General David Ejoor claimed that Northern soldiers were unhappy with Gowon's choice of him (a southerner) as Chief of Staff (Army).[1] They instead preferred a Northern soldier to occupy the post. The Northern coup's success strangely replaced Nigerians' fear of domination by Igbos, with the fear of domination by Northerners. Of the soldiers who took part in the counter-coup, four (Murtala, Buhari, Babangida, Abacha) became head of state. Several of them held prominent government and security positions throughout the following three decades. Table 2 of Appendix 4 shows the subsequent career progression of some of the prominent soldiers behind the counter-coup.

Igbo soldiers for their part have paid a steep price for the January counter-coup. Despite forming the majority of the army's officer corps in January 1966, those Igbo soldiers that survived the civil war were either dismissed from the army, demoted or had their career progression stunted. Igbo soldiers were distrusted and it took over two decades for an Igbo soldier to be appointed GOC, when in 1990, Major-General Ike Nwachukwu (Igbo father, Northern mother) was appointed the GOC of the elite 1 mechanized infantry division in Kaduna. He also became only the second Igbo Major-General in the army's history — following in the footsteps of Major-General Aguiyi-Ironsi. After the death of Aguiyi-Ironsi it took another 27 years for an Igbo service Chief to be appointed when Rear-Admiral Allison Madueke was appointed Chief of Naval Staff in 1993. The current Chief of Defense Staff, Air Chief Marshal Paul Dike is Igbo and is the highest ranking Igbo officer in the history of the Nigerian armed forces. His rank is equal to that of a four star General in the army.

The failure to bring any of the mutineers and murderers of 1966 to book gave a platform for the numerous military coups of the following years. The 1966 coups established that a "successful" coup plotter would never be called to account for his actions. Nigeria paid a heavy price for its failure to enforce justice on the perpetrators. The Majors' coup proved to be the catalyst for several military regimes — each one progressively more authoritarian than the one that preceded it. The Nigerian army, and society, have never recovered from the wild days of 1966.

---

1 Ejoor, *Reminiscences*, page 149.

CHAPTER 12. ABURI: THE "SOVEREIGN NATIONAL CONFERENCE" THAT GOT AWAY

After Nigeria was dragged to the brink of the abyss by two military coups in 1966, its military leaders met to try to bring the country back from the brink. The meeting evolved into perhaps the best documented constitutional debate of all time which discussed fundamental concepts regarding the balance of power between the central and regional governments in a federation. It also revealed soldiers' conceptual evaluation of military coups and seniority. It was a potential breakthrough occasion. On January 4th and 5th 1967, all members of the SMC met for the first time in six months at Aburi in Ghana under the auspices of the Ghanaian head of state Lt-General Joseph Ankrah. Ankrah was no stranger to coup plots as he became Ghana's first military head of state after Ghana's first President Kwame Nkrumah was deposed in a coup while Nkrumah was abroad visiting China. Ankrah served in the Congo during the UN peace-keeping mission there in the early 1960s and he personally knew some of the Nigerian soldiers who served in the same mission. Ankrah was later forced to resign in April 1969 after admitting his role in a bribery scandal.

The Road to Secession

Following a second bloody army coup in July 1966, Lt-Colonel 'Emeka' Ojukwu, the military governor of the Eastern Region, had refused to attend any SMC meeting outside the Eastern Region due to concerns over his safety. The massacre of tens of thousands of Igbos in the Northern Region heightened Ojukwu's sense of isolation and insecurity. In turn, Ojukwu's public belligerence towards the SMC (whom he suspected of tacitly supporting, or having a hand in the massacres) served to antagonize the SMC, who began to suspect that Ojukwu was planning the secession of the Eastern Region from the rest of Nigeria.

The fashionable political theory being bandied about in Nigeria today is that a "Sovereign National Conference" (SNC) should be held to resolve the country's constitutional problems. Many do not realize that Nigeria has already had half a dozen constitutional debates — none of which has ever resolved the constitutional issues which have dogged Nigeria from independence till today. Ironically the best recorded of these constitutional debates was never implemented. To plan for the future Nigeria might do well to go back into its archives and learn from the "SNC" which it has already had. Virtually everything discussed at that Aburi conference is relevant till today. So much so that a reader would be tempted to believe that the discussion was on Nigeria's current problems, rather than over forty years earlier, in 1967.

BETWEEN ONE AMBITIOUS MAN AND THE REST OF THE COUNTRY

In the months preceding Aburi, the FMG and Ojukwu engaged in a war of words with the two sides trading multiple accusations and blaming each other for causing or exacerbating the crisis. Lt-Colonel Hassan Usman Katsina, the military governor of the Northern Region, dismissed Ojukwu's confident and eloquent public statements on the crisis as attempts by Ojukwu "to show how much English he knows." As far as Katsina was concerned, Nigeria's problem was a stand-off "between one ambitious man and the rest of the country." Throughout the six months following the coup which began on July 29, 1966, Ojukwu repeated his mantra that "I, as the Military Governor of the east cannot meet anywhere in Nigeria where there are northern troops." That virtually ruled out an SMC meeting inside Nigeria's borders. Ojukwu even turned down offers to attend an SMC meeting on board a British (whom Ojukwu, and Igbos in general did not entirely trust) naval ship, and at Benin, but was finally convinced to attend in the neutral territory of Aburi in Ghana.

Ojukwu's aides were cynical. Some warned him that the Aburi meeting could be a trap set by anti-Igbo members of the FMG to arrest or kill him. Ojukwu brushed aside their concerns by pointing out that he had received a guarantee of safe passage from Lt-Colonel Gowon and that he had to trust Gowon's word as an officer and a gentleman. In attendance on the FMG side were:

Name	Position
Lt-Colonel Yakubu Gowon	Chairman of the SMC*
Commodore Joseph Edet Akinwale Wey	Commander of the Nigerian Navy
Colonel Robert Adeyinka Adebayo	Military Governor of the Western Region
Lt-Colonel Hassan Usman Katsina	Military Governor of the Northern Region
Lt-Colonel David Akpode Ejoor	Governor of the Mid-West Region
Major Mobolaji Johnson	Military Governor of Lagos
Alhaji Kam Selem	Inspector-General of Police
Timothy Omo-Bare	Deputy Inspector-General of Police

*Chairman of the SMC, as Ironsi's whereabouts were "unknown."

Lt-General Joseph Ankrah — Chairman of the Ghana National Liberation Council.

Secretaries:
- Solomon Akenzua — Permanent Under-Secretary, Federal Cabinet Office
- Peter Odumosu — Secretary to the Military Government of the Western Region
- Ntieyong Udo Akpan — Secretary to the Military Government of the Eastern Region
- D.P. Lawani — Under-Secretary, Military Governor's Office, Mid-West Region
- Alhaji Ali Akilu — Secretary to the Military Government of the Northern Region

Ojukwu was in attendance as the Eastern Region's military governor. Security was tight and the federal and eastern delegations arrived separately. Ankrah sent a Ghanaian air force plane to fly the eastern delegation from Enugu to Ghana. The FMG delegation arrived "wreathed in smiles"[1] and anxious to mollify their former colleague Ojukwu. Colonels Adebayo and Gowon even offered to embrace Ojukwu. However, Ojukwu was still stung by the terrible massacres of his Igbo kinsmen in the Northern Region the previous year and was in no mood to embrace his former colleagues. The contrast in the demeanor of the participants was in itself a microcosm of what took place over the course of the next two days. While the federal delegation behaved as if the Aburi conference was a social gathering to reunite former friends who had fallen out in a social tiff, Ojukwu saw the conference for what it really was: a historic constitutional debate that would determine Nigeria's future social and political structure.

Typically, Western perspective was focused on image rather than on the genuine problems of the protagonists. Secret diplomatic dispatches later declassified by the United States State Department depicted the FMG-Eastern Region stand-off as a personality clash between Ojukwu and Gowon. The American perspective was that:

> Many Americans admire Ojukwu. We like romantic leaders, and Ojukwu has panache, quick intelligence and an actor's voice and fluency. The contrast with Gowon — troubled by the enormity of his task, painfully earnest and slow to react, hesitant and repetitive in speech — led some Americans to view the Nigerian-Biafran conflict as a personal duel between two mismatched individuals.[2]

As they were busy fighting in Vietnam and fighting a "cold war" against the USSR, the Americans did not become militarily or politically involved in the dispute. Instead, they treated the conflict as one falling within the UK's sphere of influence.

THE REUNION

Aware that something momentous was occurring, the Ghanaians had the conference tape recorded. The tape of the discussions was later released by Ojukwu as a series of long-playing gramophone records. The Ghanaian host Lt-General Ankrah made a few introductory remarks and reminded his guests that "the whole world is looking up to you as military men and if there is any failure to reunify or even bring perfect understanding to Nigeria as a whole, you will find that the blame will rest with us through the centuries." Ankrah added that although he understood that the

---

1 Akpan: *The Struggle for Secession*, page 51.
2 Airgram from US Embassy in Nigeria to the Department of State: Lagos A-419, February 11, 1968.

crisis was an internal matter for Nigerians, they should not hesitate to ask him for help should they feel the need. He concluded by urging his guests to conduct the meeting in good spirit. Ankrah's opening remarks were met with applause by the Nigerians.

Gowon spoke first and proposed that the meeting should not have a chairman as each of them was a joint chairman, in his opinion. His proposal was unanimously accepted. Although Commodore Wey played an avuncular role, the discussion revolved around the younger Colonels: Adebayo, Ejoor, Katsina, Ojukwu and Gowon. Ojukwu showed from the beginning that he was prepared for serious business. He arrived at the conference armed with notes and secretaries. He gave the other debaters copies of documents which enunciated his ideas. Given his preparedness, the other debaters should have realized that some serious bargaining was going to occur.

Despite the grave nature of the issues at hand, the last vestiges of the officers' brotherly Sandhurst code of honor, with emphasis on orderly comportment, was still evident. The jocular back slapping mess camaraderie of the pre-coup days briefly returned. After the hostility and bitterness that preceded the Aburi meeting, the civilian observers were stunned. The debaters threw off formality and addressed each other by their first names: "Emeka," "Bolaji," "Jack" (nickname of Lt-Colonel Gowon) were thrown around as if addressing each other in at a social gathering. Mixed in with the good natured banter and humor were solemn requests by the FMG delegation for Ojukwu to attend future SMC meetings. Ojukwu was repeatedly assured of his safety by Gowon, Wey, Katsina and Selem. At one point Wey emotionally declared to Ojukwu, "I am going to offer my life to you so that if you lose yours, you can take mine." Gowon turned to Wey and comically told him, "Your life is older than his!" (a comment which was met with laughter by the other officers). With Ojukwu continuing to insist that he would not attend SMC meetings in any place where Northern soldiers were present, Selem and Katsina offered to host SMC meetings in their hometowns (Gombe and Katsina respectively) as there were no army units there. Ojukwu upped the humor ante by inviting them to his own hometown of Nnewi, since there were no army units there either. Again, the soldiers descended into hearty laughter. One of Ojukwu's secretaries was amazed to observe that:

> the meeting went on in a most friendly and cordial atmosphere which made us, the non-military advisers, develop a genuine respect and admiration for the military men and their sense of comradeship. The meeting continued so smoothly and ended so successfully . . . that I, for one, was convinced that among themselves, the military had their own methods.[1]

Ojukwu decided to show his good faith, and to test the good faith of the others, by asking all present to renounce the use of force to settle the crisis. Ojukwu's motion was accepted without objection. While this request by Ojukwu may sound very noble, he was in fact a cunning soldier-politician. Ojukwu (despite his boasts of the Eastern Region's military prowess) realized that he could not succeed in a military conflict against the far more heavily armed FMG. By getting them to renounce the use of force, Ojukwu was trying to negate the FMG's military advantage. For he knew that if the political situation eventually got out of control, the FMG would find it difficult to resort to a military campaign having already given an assurance that they would not use force. This may have been an influential factor in Gowon's subsequent reluctance to engage the Eastern Region in a fully fledged war.

---

1 Akpan, *The Struggle For Secession, 1966–1970: A Personal Account of the Nigerian Civil War*, page 52.

COUP PLOTTERS: OJUKWU'S PROPHECY

Despite Aguiyi-Ironsi's murder six months earlier, no public announcement regarding his death had been made and his whereabouts were still presumed unknown, although most of the SMC knew he was dead. Gowon's regime repeated the mistake made by his predecessor Aguiyi-Ironsi: failing to publicly acknowledge the army officers killed in a *coup d'état*. By not announcing Aguiyi-Ironsi's death, Gowon also made his own position tenuous and gave Ojukwu the opportunity to reason that since the Supreme Commander Aguiyi-Ironsi was "missing," only the officer directly behind Aguiyi-Ironsi in army seniority could replace him as Supreme Commander. Despite agreeing to attend the conference, Ojukwu was still refusing to recognize Lt-Colonel Gowon as Supreme Commander. Ojukwu had defiantly continued to address Gowon as "the Chief of Army Staff" (the post which Gowon occupied before the July mutiny) in his public statements. Ojukwu almost prophetically warned that allowing a middle ranking officer backed by coup plotters to become the head of state irrespective of seniority, would create a dangerous precedent which Nigeria would find difficult to emerge from. He told Gowon:

> [A]ny break at this time from our normal line would write in something into the Nigerian army which is bigger than all of us and that thing is indiscipline... .How can you ride above people's heads purely because you are at the head of a group who have their fingers poised on the trigger? If you do it you remain forever a living example of that indiscipline which we want to get rid of because tomorrow a Corporal will think.... He could just take over the company from the Major commanding the company....

Ojukwu's warning was of course not heeded and his prediction that junior officers would in future overthrow their superior officers was entirely accurate. Ojukwu's impassioned monologue at Aburi could serve as an anti coup plotter thesis. He continued to Gowon:

> "[Y]ou announced yourself as Supreme Commander. Now, Supreme Commander by virtue of the fact that you head or that you are acceptable to people who had mutinied against their commander, kidnapped him and taken him away? By virtue of the support of officers and men who had in the dead of night murdered their brother officers, by virtue of the fact that you stood at the head of a group who had turned their brother officers from the eastern region out of the barracks they shared?."

Major Mobolaji Johnson summarized Ojukwu's position:

> The main problem now is that as far as the east is concerned, there is no central government. Why? This is what we must find out.... For all the east knows the former Supreme Commander [Aguiyi-Ironsi] is only missing and until such a time that they know his whereabouts they do not know any other Supreme Commander. These are the points that have been brought out by the east.

Ojukwu demanded that Gowon make a categorical public statement on the fate of Aguiyi-Ironsi and in the months leading up to Aburi, repeatedly asked Gowon, "Where is the Supreme Commander?" Katsina bluntly replied, "They were kidnapped, they were dead, finished," before Gowon mildly rebuked him, saying it was not for him to say so. Despite Ojukwu's request for an announcement, most if not all the participants already knew that Aguiyi-Ironsi had been murdered. Gowon was informed of the death of Aguiyi-Ironsi and Fajuyi not long after they had been killed. Gowon's ADC Lieutenant William Walbe was one of the junior Northern soldiers who had led Aguiyi-Ironsi and Fajuyi into a bush alongside Iwo road outside Ibadan and murdered them there. Colonel Adebayo had ordered a search for their bodies, which were eventually discovered by the police. The Inspector-General of Police Kam Selem would have been informed when his men discovered the bodies. Although Ojukwu was several hundred miles away in the Eastern Region when Aguiyi-Ironsi and Fajuyi were murdered, the story of their death likely would have been relayed to him by Aguiyi-Ironsi's air force ADC Lieutenant Andrew Nwankwo who was captured along with Aguiyi-Ironsi and Fajuyi but managed to escape moments before they were shot. Commodore Wey admitted that all the debaters already knew what happened to Aguiyi-Ironsi. Ojukwu simply wanted Gowon to publicly acknowledge what the SMC members already knew: that Aguiyi-Ironsi was dead. Ojukwu later confirmed that "I heard the rumor that he [Ironsi] had been assassinated, so I began making contacts because I wanted to force them out in the open so that we could start dealing with the real situation."[1] Gowon agreed to make a public announcement, and Kam Selem concurred, although he counseled that "the statement should be made in Nigeria so that the necessary honor can be given."

After the soldiers agreed to make a public statement formally announcing Aguiyi-Ironsi's death, the microphones were switched off and the civilians were asked to leave the room. Ankrah left the Nigerian officers alone in the inner chamber to discuss Aguiyi-Ironsi's fate. Gowon then narrated the grisly tale of how Aguiyi-Ironsi and Fajuyi were abducted from State House in Ibadan by junior Northern soldiers (including Gowon's ADC Lieutenant Walbe), driven out to an isolated bush outside Ibadan and shot there. The corpses of Aguiyi-Ironsi and Fajuyi were exhumed twice. Firstly the bodies were recovered from the shallow graves they were buried in along Iwo road just outside Ibadan. Then they were reburied in the Ibadan military cemetery where they remained for six months before being exhumed again, this time for fitting burials with full military honors. Aguiyi-Ironsi was finally laid to rest in Umuahia and Fajuyi in Ado-Ekiti. The head of the navy, Commodore Wey, represented the federal government at Aguiyi-Ironsi's funeral along with Lt-Colonel David Ejoor, the military governor of the Mid-West Region. They were the only SMC members to attend the funeral. Wey and Ejoor, along with Kam Selem, the Inspector-General of Police; Major Mobolaji Johnson, the military governor of Lagos; and Fajuyi's successor, Colonel Robert Adebayo, also attended Fajuyi's funeral at Liberty Stadium Ibadan, where the funeral service was conducted by the army's chaplain, Reverend Father Pedro Martins. Fajuyi's widow Eunice is still alive. His son Dayo was the chairman of Ado-Ekiti Local Government Area and was also given the traditional title *Ezigbo Enyi Ndigbo*[2] by the Igbo National Council.

When Ojukwu expressed his disgust over the murder of Igbo army officers by their Northern colleagues in July 1966, Lt-Colonel Katsina interjected by asking Ojukwu why he had not reacted with the same revulsion when senior Northern military officers were murdered by Igbo soldiers seven months earlier. Ojukwu reasoned that, in January 1966, soldiers from every region of the federation (Nzeogwu: Mid-West, Ifeajuna: Eastern, Ademoyega: Western, Kpera: Northern) had staged a coup in which soldiers and politicians from every region of the federation (Akintola: Western, Balewa: Northern, Unegbe: Eastern, Okotie-Eboh: Mid-Western) were also killed. When Northern soldiers staged a revenge coup in July, soldiers from one region only (North: Danjuma, Murtala, Martin Adamu et al) singled out soldiers from one other region in the federation as their targets (Eastern: Okoro, Aguiyi-Ironsi,

---

1 *Vanguard*, 17 November 2003.
2 Loose translates to "Great friend of the Igbo people."

etc.). Katsina took this opportunity to remind Ojukwu of the effort he had made to prevent the murder of Igbos. Katsina said to Ojukwu, "If you know how much ... we have tried to counsel the people to stop all these movements and mass killings, you will give me and others a medal tonight."

The Star of the Show

The stage of Aburi was tailor made for Ojukwu, who is a born orator. It was his finest hour. As has been pointed out elsewhere, "Ojukwu is a born talker. He loves words, their sound, articulation and infinite subtleties of meaning."[1] It was obvious to the non military observers of the Aburi conference that Ojukwu "was clearly the star performer. Everyone wanted to please and concede to him."[2] On the federal side, only the military governor of the Northern Region, Lt-Colonel Katsina, seemed to realize the significance of what was going on. Anxious not to allow Ojukwu's domination of the proceedings to continue for too long, he at one point dared Ojukwu to "secede, and let the three of us (West, North, Mid-West) join together." Alarmed by talk of a possible break-up of Nigeria, Ankrah quickly interjected and told his guests that "There is no question of secession when you come here [to Ghana]." Although the FMG delegation were keen to mollify and make concessions to Ojukwu, Lt-Colonel Katsina was more blunt than his colleagues. He declared matter-of-factly to Ojukwu: "You command the east; if you want to come into Nigeria, come into Nigeria and that is that."

The Constitutional Debate

The debate regarding Nigeria's future constitutional structure also exposed the cynicism of Nigeria's geo-political groups. At the Aburi conference, the Northern led FMG advocated a strong central government, while the Eastern Region advocated a weaker central government with devolution of power to each regional government. This was an almost comical reversal of each side's position a few months earlier. Northerners had been so opposed to a strong federal government only a few months earlier that they carried out mass pogroms against Igbos in revolt against a decree passed by an Igbo head of state that sought to fortify the powers of the federal government. Now that a Northerner was head of state, the Northern Region suddenly found the concept of a strong central government attractive. Conversely, the mainly Igbo Eastern Region had long advocated concentrating stronger powers in the central government. Now that the central government was no longer headed by an Igbo, the Eastern Region was arguing for the dilution of the central government's powers. Each side's *volte face* is an instructive lesson in how seemingly ideological political positions in Nigeria are often guided by geographic and ethnic sentiment.

Using his "skilful histrionics and superior intellectual adroitness,"[3] Ojukwu managed to get the other Colonels to understand, and share his reasoning that in order to keep Nigeria together as one nation, its constituent regions first had to move a little further apart from each other. Ojukwu used a metaphor to explain his reasoning: "It is better that we move slightly apart and survive, it is much worse that we move closer and perish in the collision." This may have been a paradox, but the Colonels accepted the logic of Ojukwu's argument. Amazingly Gowon accepted Ojukwu's thesis

---

1 St Jorre, *The Brothers War*, page 131.
2 Akpan, *The Struggle for Secession*, page 52.
3 Kirk-Greene, *Crisis and Conflict*, page 75.

without really understanding the constitutional implications of what he was agree- ing to. Gowon was effectively sanctioning measures that would paralyze his own powers. Lt-Colonel Katsina and Colonel Adebayo also agreed and were attracted to the concept of regional autonomy. Adebayo agreed so enthusiastically that he advo- cated a "repeal [of] those Decrees that were passed after 15th January, 1966 but I think we should revert to what the country was as at 14th January, 1966, that is regional autonomy."

Ojukwu envisaged a titular head of state that would act only with the concur- rence of the various regional governments: "What I envisage is that whoever is at the top is a constitutional chap — constitutional within the context of the military gov- ernment. That is, he is a titular head, but he would only act where, say when we have met and taken a decision." Having got what he wanted, Ojukwu was not content with the agreement to be an oral one (even though it had been taped). He insisted that "we must write it down in our decisions quite categorically that the legislative and ex- ecutive authority of the Federal Military Government shall be vested in the Supreme Military Council because previously it had been vested in the Supreme Commander." By vesting official authority in the SMC (of which Ojukwu was a member) rather than the Supreme Commander Gowon, Ojukwu could ensure that no meaningful governmental decisions would be taken without his consent. To signify the limited powers that would be exercised by the head of state envisaged, Ojukwu proposed that the diluted phrase "Commander-in-Chief" should be used to address the head of state as opposed to "Supreme Commander." The title "Commander-in-Chief" has been employed by every Nigerian head of state subsequent to Aburi. Although this suited Ojukwu's objectives and protected his vulnerable position, from the FMG's perspective it came with the hidden danger that its decisions could be held hostage by one rogue region or military governor.

While the other delegates arrived at Aburi with a simple, but unformulated idea that somehow, Nigeria must stay together, Ojukwu arrived with a well prepared vision of his desired outcome and convinced his colleagues in the SMC to accept resolutions that if implemented, would have turned Nigeria into a glorified tax and currency union. Ojukwu managed to get virtually everything he wanted, and was so pleased by his success that he even declared that he would serve under Gowon if he (Gowon) kept to the agreements reached. At that point, Gowon arose from his table position and embraced Ojukwu. Ankrah drove Ojukwu and Gowon back to the air- port in his car, with Gowon and Ojukwu either side of him.

The fulcrum of the agreement at Aburi was that each region would be respon- sible for its own affairs, and that the FMG would be responsible for matters that affected the entire country. Afterwards the officers toasted their reconciliation and agreement with champagne. The federal delegation's jubilation was such that on his plane flight home, Ojukwu asked one of his secretaries whether the federal delega- tion had fully understood the implications of what had been agreed. Hindsight tells us that no one at Aburi (other than Ojukwu) really understood the constitutional implications of what was agreed. Ojukwu was obviously delighted with this — that is why he was in such a hurry to implement the decisions taken, and why the FMG had to renege on them.

The Aburi accords were never implemented for a number of reasons. When Gowon returned to Lagos, his civil servants were aghast at the depth of his conces- sions to Ojukwu. They regarded the accords as unworkable. Although many parts of the accords were impractical to implement, the all or nothing approach to them taken by the protagonists was myopic. There were many positives in the accords, the best perhaps being the implicit concept of regional autonomy skillfully negotiated by Ojukwu. Under this proposal no significant decisions affecting a region could be taken without its consent. The failure to implement this part of the accord has enabled the FMG to time and time again, impose its will on the regions, even when the federal will is opposed by that region.

The Aburi failure was the beginning of the end of the concept of regional autonomy and self sufficiency in Nigeria. The clash, and ill defined relationship between Nigeria's central and regional governments, has been the greatest source of political bloodletting in the country's history. It is the source of the current armed conflict in the Niger Delta.

The discovery of large deposits of lucrative crude oil in Ojukwu's Eastern Region reinforced federal desire to maintain a united Nigeria, and to strengthen the powers of the central government in order to obtain and maintain control of earnings from crude oil exports. Permitting regional autonomy and control over natural resources would have led to a spectacular wealth disparity between the Eastern Region and the other regions. The presence of massive deposits of crude oil in the southern minority areas subsequently encouraged the increasing concentration of economic and executive power in the FMG rather than in state governments. This was not due to unitary idealism, but to the desire of Nigeria's non-oil producing regions to gain access to the revenues derived from oil exportation. The only way this could be effected was by ensuring that the federal government became the controlling repository for oil earnings. The FMG became the custodian of all oil proceeds, subject to paying a token "derivation formula" royalty[1] to the individual state that the oil was obtained from. After collating all oil proceeds, the FMG then shared it among all regions in the federation regardless of whether or not they produced oil. While this ostensibly seemed equitable, it caused great bitterness among the communities of the oil producing states, who felt that wealth derived from their communities was being used to develop distant states that did not produce any oil or contribute anything material to "the national cake."

Federal control of oil proceeds subsequently weakened and discouraged the economic prowess and financial autonomy of each region, turning them into little more than beggar subsidiaries of the federal government, totally beholden to, and dependant on remittances from the FMG. Federal control of oil revenues thus led to continuous agitation for new states to be created. Whereas new states were previously demanded on the basis of self determination and in order to prevent minority ethnic groups from being dominated by the large ethnicities, state creation became a way of creating new economic entities that could demand their own share of revenue from the FMG.

It is a sad commentary on the lack of progress that Nigeria has made since Aburi that these issues discussed then (over forty years ago years ago) are still being debated today.

---

1 The derivation started at 50% but was decreased several times until it fell to a miserly 2% by the 1980s. It was eventually raised to 13% by the time civilian democratic rule returned in 1999.

Chapter 13. Murtala Muhammed — Human Tempest

Very few of Nigeria's former military leaders are spoken of with any great affection. The one notable exception is General Murtala Muhammed. He is recalled with nostalgia by many Nigerians (both civilian and military), and his time is regarded as a golden age. Whereas today, military rule and military rulers have been demonized, Murtala is one of the few Nigerian military leaders still held in high regard. Here, the author analyzes the most popular soldier in Nigeria's history.

The Early Days

Murtala Ramat Muhammed was born in the Kurawa quarter of the ancient city of Kano on November 8, 1938. His parents were Risqua Muhammed and Uwani Rahamat, and he was one of eleven children. The former Defense Minister Inuwa Wada was his cousin. Murtala's father was a brother of Wada's mother. Their grandfather the Al-kalin Kano, Malam Sulaiman, was the Chief Qhadi of Kano. Murtala was educated at Cikin Gida and Gidan Makama primary schools in Kano. As a school student he went by the name "Murtala Kurawa" and changed his name to "Murtala Muhammed" later. After his primary school education he followed in the footsteps of many of his Northern colleagues in the army such as Brigadier Maimalari, Colonel Kur Mohammed, and Lt-Colonels Pam, Gowon and Largema, by attending the famous Government College (now Barewa College) in Zaria, and obtained his school certificate from there in 1957. One of his classmates at Barewa College was Mohammed Shuwa. He began his military training in 1959 and trained at the Regular Officers Special Training School in Teshie, Ghana. At Teshie Murtala was taught military law and tactics by an eloquent, erudite and intelligent Oxford University educated Nigerian officer that had been seconded to the school as a lecturer. The name of Murtala's teacher was Chukwuemeka Ojukwu. Little did teacher and student realize that, one day, they would end up as protagonists on opposing sides of the battlefield. Like many Nigerian army officers of his generation including future head of state Yakubu Gowon, after leaving Teshie, Murtala trained at the Royal Military Academy at Sandhurst in England. His fellow Nigerian colleagues at Sandhurst included Ibrahim Haruna, Emmanuel Ikwue, and Mohammed Shuwa. Another young man named Iliyasu Bisalla was his colleague at Teshie and Sandhurst. Murtala was commissioned into the Nigerian army as a Second Lieutenant in 1961, and he joined the army's signal corps. He also attended the Catterick School of Signals in England, and in 1962 served as a member of the Nigerian led UN peacekeeping force in the Congo. When he returned from the UN mission in Congo, Murtala was appointed ADC to the Administrator of the Western Region of Nigeria Koyejo Majekodunmi. Majekodunmi was appointed Administra- tor after the Western Region's government had been suspended and a state of emer- gency declared due to a massive political crisis. In 1963, he was appointed officer in chief of the first brigade signal troops in Kaduna. He returned to Catterick School of Signals later in 1963 for a further advanced signals course in telecommunications. In 1964, he was promoted to (temporary) Major and appointed the officer commanding one signal squadron in Apapa, Lagos.

Murtala's talismanic role in the mutiny that overthrew Major-General Aguiyi- Ironsi has been chronicled in Chapter eight and does not require further elaboration here. It suffices to say that Murtala was the motivational inspiration behind the mu- tiny, and commanded almost mythical loyalty from Northern soldiers. He succeeded Brigadier Maimalari as the role model Northern officer. He was from an influential northern family with close links to the NPC, and his cousin Inuwa Wada was the for- mer Defense Minister. If anyone was going to rebel against a perceived anti-Northern regime — it was Murtala. If the young Majors that carried out the January coup were UPGA sympathizers, then Murtala was the NPC's enforcer in the barracks.

CONFRONTATION IN THE MID-WEST

When it became clear that the problems between the Northern Region and the Eastern Region were not going to be resolved by negotiations, the Eastern Region seceded from Nigeria in May 1967 and declared itself the independent republic of Biafra. Gowon countered by ordering his troops to retake the Eastern Region in a "police action." The police action turned into a full blown war when the Biafrans made a lightning invasion of the Mid-West Region which caught the federal army off guard and shook it out of its complacency. The Mid-West invasion was a disastrous political miscalculation by Biafra which dissipated sympathy for it in the Western and Mid-West Regions. It also gave some non-Eastern Nigerians the impression that Biafra's objectives were not limited to self defense, but that it also had ambitions for territorial expansion.

Murtala through his own civilian contacts independently took steps to procure weapons for the impending war. In rumor-rife Nigeria, this led to unfounded rumors that the weapons were to be used by Murtala to overthrow Gowon. Murtala was ap- pointed GOC of the hastily formed 2 division of the army, and had the task of evicting the Biafrans from the Mid-West. Murtala literally built 2 division from scratch. He commandeered all available vehicles (including those supposed to be used for other divisions and for other purposes) and men he could lay his hands on to form his new division. Among the men drafted into Murtala's division was an up and coming Lt-Colonel named Alani Akinrinade. Murtala's forceful persona also allowed him to poach men from other divisions such as Captain Remawa and Lieutenant Moham- med Mayaki of the 1 division who had been sent to Lagos to collect vehicles for their own division but were instead drafted by Murtala, along with the vehicles they had procured for the 1 division. Lieutenant Shehu Musa Yar'Adua of the 3 division was also commandeered by Murtala when he travelled to Lagos on an errand for his divisional commander Colonel Benjamin Adekunle. Other officers in Murtala's division that would later rise to prominence included Sani Abacha, and Lieutenants Chris Alli and Ola Ogunmekan (both of the 7ᵗʰ infantry brigade).

Murtala's newly assembled 2 division drove the Biafrans out of the Mid-West Region in a blistering counter offensive. For the sake of historical accuracy, it should be pointed out that the speed and success of the counter-attack was due as much to Murtala's purposeful energy as it was to the disorganization of the enemy. Once the Biafran forces in the Mid-West had been overrun, members of the 2 division carried out a terrible massacre of civilians so grotesque that Gowon had to apologize for it decades after the end of the Nigerian civil war. As punishment for their sympathy for the Biafrans, hundreds of Igbo civilians in the Mid-West were summarily executed by soldiers belonging to the 2 division. One of the officers who served under him, then Lieutenant Ishola Williams, alleged that Murtala ordered the summary execution of Biafran prisoners of war.[1] In an episode typical of his unpredictable nature, although his troops had killed hundreds of innocent civilians, Murtala personally saw to it that the mother of Major Nzeogwu was protected and not harmed. After recapturing the Mid-West, Murtala installed Major Samuel Ogbemudia as its new military governor without seeking or obtaining Gowon's approval for the appointment.[2] Nonetheless Ogbemudia remained in that post for a further eight years until he was removed by Murtala in events that will be chronicled later in this book.

THE CIVIL WAR YEARS

Buoyed by his Mid-West success, Murtala's next target was the strategically important Biafran city of Onitsha. Murtala's attack plan for Onitsha changed dramatically when Biafran troops blew up the Niger bridge (which linked the Mid-West and Eastern Region) as Murtala was at the bridge's entrance, considering driving across it. The 2 division could now either attack Onitsha via: (a) a dangerous and direct assault via a river crossing, or (b) by crossing the Niger river unopposed via territory held by the neighboring 1 division, then proceeding overland to Onitsha. Realizing the dangers and complexities of a direct river based assault on Onitsha, army headquarters advised Murtala to choose option (b). However Murtala was unwilling to advance through territory held by 1 division as he did not want to cooperate with his former classmate at Barewa College and Sandhurst Lt-Colonel Shuwa. Shuwa was the commander of 1 division and although he and Murtala had known each other since childhood, and enlisted in the army on the same day, they frequently clashed.

Murtala decided to proceed with the dangerous river crossing, disregarding the advice of army headquarters, and instructions not to proceed from his Sandhurst course mate Iliya Bisalla, and Hassan Katsina. Lt-Colonel Frank Aisida (one of Murtala's brigade commanders) urged him to reconsider. Aisida considered a river crossing to be suicidal, and was so convinced that it was doomed to fail, that he requested time to write a final letter to his wife.[3] Aisida eventually refused to take part in the crossing. Murtala was unmoved and insisted that he would have his way. So controversial was Murtala's plan that even the commander of the neighboring 1 division Colonel Mohammed Shuwa tried to intervene. The difference in the two men's person-

---

1 Momoh, *The Nigerian Civil War 1967–1970: History and Reminiscences*, page 880.

2 The previous Governor Lt-Colonel Ejoor had fled after Biafran troops attempted to capture him.

3 Interview with Major-General Mohammed Shuwa in Momoh, *The Nigerian Civil War 1967–1970: History and Reminiscences*, page 844.

alities was reflected in the manner in which they commanded their respective army divisions. While Murtala's 2 division embarked on daring gung-ho assaults against the enemy (often against orders from army headquarters), Shuwa's 1 division was methodical and quietly efficient. While Shuwa was conventional to the point of caution, Murtala was impulsive, fearless, and unorthodox to the point of chaos. He paid little or no regard to orthodox combat doctrine, and did not bother to issue written operational orders, instead preferring verbal orders. He did not believe in surprising the enemy either and would announce assaults in advance by instructing his men to sound a bugle before advancing. This was part of his psychological warfare, and was intended to demonstrate to the enemy that he did not fear, or have respect for their ability to resist an attack, even if notified to the enemy in advance. According to his colleague James Oluleye, Murtala also disregarded logic when it came to planning his battles and would rely on the advice of religious soothsayers to determine the most auspicious dates for executing battlefield offensives.[1]

At a meeting between Shuwa and Murtala to review operational aspects for the attack on Onitsha,[2] Shuwa urged Murtala to drop his dangerous river assault plan for Onitsha, but Murtala refused and ignored the objections by army headquarters, his brigade commander Lt-Colonel Aisida and fellow divisional commander Colonel Shuwa. His exchange of views with Shuwa became so heated that Captain Baba Usman had to stand between Murtala and Shuwa as he feared that they would come to blows.

Murtala proceeded to attack Onitsha via a river crossing even though his navigational instruments were not working, the water level was high, he had no reconnaissance, and most of his troops were not soldiers with combatant commissions. These problems were compounded by the fact that many of them could not even swim; they certainly had no expertise or experience of complex amphibious assaults. Were he a citizen of any country other than Nigeria, Murtala would almost certainly have been court-martialled for disobeying orders. Murtala personally led his men during the crossing. Biafran troops led by the tough Colonel Joe "Hannibal" Achuzia repelled and routed Murtala's one-thousand strong troops and inflicted many casualties on them, some by drowning under fierce Biafran fire. Among those federal soldiers lucky enough to survive the Biafran onslaught were Lieutenants Shehu Musa Yar'Adua, Oladipo Diya and Ishola Williams. Diya and Williams had just been commissioned into the army from the NDA's first regular combatant course, and this baptism of fire was their first experience of combat.

Undeterred by this setback and displaying his characteristic never say die attitude, Murtala again tried the amphibious capture of Onitsha. Federal troops were again routed by the Biafrans who shot and wounded one of Murtala's ferry captains. Water flooded into the pilotless ferry and several soldiers drowned. Others dived into the water in a panic and also drowned. Still determined to get his way, and displaying great mental strength and determination after such heavy losses, Murtala tried the ambitious river crossing for a third time, and failed again. His stubborn persistence with the river crossing was reinforced by the advice of his religious sooth-

---

1 Interview with Major-General James Oluleye in Momoh, *The Nigerian Civil War 1967–1970: History and Reminiscences*, page 775.
2 Also attended by Martin Adamu, Baba Usman, Muhammadu Buhari and Shehu Musa Yar'Adua.

sayers who had assured him that it would succeed.[1] Having sustained heavy losses, the fragile discipline in 2 division broke down as some troops started looting, and refused to contemplate any more amphibious based attacks on Onitsha. After this third failure, Murtala swallowed his pride and agreed to execute the plan initially approved by army headquarters and finally captured Onitsha. Even then he grudgingly agreed to advance through territory held by the neighboring 1 division without bothering to coordinate with, or inform 1 division's commander Lt-Colonel Shuwa, and risking an inadvertent confrontation between friendly forces. But victory came at a great price, as by this time, 2 division were dispirited, undisciplined and battered after suffering heavy losses against the Biafrans including the destruction of an entire convoy of vehicles near Abagana. This occurred on March 31 1968 after an opportunistic Biafran soldier disobeyed orders and fired the single last mortar in the possession of the Biafrans at Murtala's convoy. The plucky soldier scored a direct hit on a vehicle in the convoy carrying ammunition, which ignited. The resulting fire set the convoy of almost one hundred vehicles ablaze and proved to be one of the most spectacular Biafran successes of the Nigerian civil war. The disaster was possible because Murtala authorized the mass movement of a large logistics and supply convoy along a narrow route on which the bulky vehicles could not turn around or reverse, and on which they were susceptible to ambush. Murtala was recalled from the front and replaced by Colonel Haruna. However, 2 division was so dispirited that Haruna himself was later replaced by Colonel Gibson Jalo. The discipline in 2 division deteriorated further with some of its soldiers looting occupied towns, harassing the wives of civilians and fraudulently drawing the pay of dead or missing soldiers. Lt-Colonel Adeniran was court martialled for the latter practice. Murtala's successor Colonel Haruna had some members of 2 division executed by a firing squad after they carried out an armed robbery on a bank in the Mid-West town of Asaba.[2]

The Onitsha episode was instructive *vis-à-vis* Murtala's positive and negative personality traits. Murtala had seemingly limitless courage, led his troops by example and would often accompany his men into battle. His willingness to share the physical danger of battle endeared him to, and emboldened, his men. He was a natural leader although his leadership often relied on coercion and intimidation of subordinates rather than persuasion. He was very much from the Brigadier Maimalari school of discipline. While he was a strict disciplinarian who would not accept insubordination from others, he was often disobedient and contemptuous toward his own superiors. His colleague James Oluleye noted that Murtala "was kind hearted even as a bully. He did not tolerate opposition except he realized you outwitted him. . . . To him every human organization was a military machine that can be worked to death without question. . . . He had very little respect for authority, while he would not tolerate disrespect from subordinates."[3] Once he decided on a course of action, there would be no going back on his decision. He also demonstrated tremendous tenacity by picking himself up and refusing to be deterred after each defeat. After leaving the 2 division Murtala returned to Lagos and resumed his pre-war post of Inspector of Signals. He was promoted to Colonel in April 1968. After the war, Murtala was promoted to Brigadier in October 1971, after a taking a staff college course at the Joint Services Staff College in England.

1 Interview with Major-General Ibrahim Haruna in Momoh, *The Nigerian Civil War 1967–1970: History and Reminiscences*, page 583.

2 Ibid., page 584.

3 Oluleye, *Military Leadership in Nigeria*, page 74.

CHAPTER 14. THE POST WAR YEARS: CIVIL AND MILITARY DISCONTENT

BEYOND BIAFRA: FORGIVENESS AND RECONCILIATION — THE AFRICAN LINCOLN

Nigeria's victory in the civil war against Biafra made Gowon a hero and a symbol of Nigerian national unity. His success in uniting a fractured and volatile country behind the war effort gained him immense prestige locally and internationally, and his surname was used as a slogan calling for the continued unity of Nigeria: "Go On With One Nigeria." He gained a Lincolnesque aura as a statesman for his unprecedented policy of reconciliation and magnanimity to the defeated Biafrans.

Most Biafrans and some federal officers believed that Biafra's defeat would be followed by massive reprisals against, and executions of Igbos. Brigade of Guards commander Colonel Joe Garba advocated taking a tough line with the former Biafran soldiers. According to Garba "We needed to demonstrate to our country people that it doesn't pay to pick up arms against one's brothers."[1] Brigadier Ogbemudia also recalled that some officers were unhappy that the Biafrans were not tried by Nuremberg-style tribunals.[2] Resisting urgings for reprisals by some of his officers, Gowon declared a general amnesty for all Biafran fighters and for Igbo soldiers and civilians that defected from official posts in Nigeria to Biafra.[3] None of the Biafran soldiers were tried or executed for fighting against the federal army, and some Igbo soldiers who served in the Nigerian army before the civil war were reabsorbed (with a loss of seniority). Some Igbo civilians who fled to Biafra were also reinstated to the jobs they had held before the civil war. Under his "no victor, no vanquished" policy, Gowon also refused to award medals to his own soldiers who fought in the civil war as there could be no victory in a war between brothers.

---

1 Douglas Johnston, Cynthia Sampson, *Religion, The Missing Dimension of Statecraft*, page 117.
2 Ogbemudia, *Years of Challenge*, page 241.
3 A notable exception was Ojukwu. Additionally the surviving officers that executed the January 1966 coup were jailed (without trial).

Biafra was not asked to pay compensation to the FMG. Gowon's conciliatory stance even earned him grudging admiration from the Igbos, who knew that their fate would have been very different under a less magnanimous leader. Gowon had urged, during and after the civil war, that the war against Biafra should be fought with restraint as it was a war between brothers and that Nigerians would one day have to welcome the Igbos back.

When he accepted the formal Biafran surrender at Dodan Barracks on January 15, 1970, he warmly shook hands and greeted his former colleague and adversary Lt-Colonel Efiong with the words, "How are you, my friend?" On the remarkably rapid reconciliation, one observer commented that:

> When one considers the brutality, the proscription, the carefully maintained immensely durable hatred that have so often followed the wars in the "civilised" West....it may be that when history takes a longer view of Nigeria's war it will be shown that while the black man has little to teach us about making war he has a real contribution to offer in making peace.[1]

THE CURSE OF OIL

Gowon' reconstructive efforts fortuitously coincided with spiraling and unprecedented high oil prices which brought an influx of revenue to the federal government beyond the country's wildest dreams. Crude oil was first discovered in Nigeria in 1956 by Shell, at Oloibiri, in present day Bayelsa State of Nigeria. Further exploration led to the discovery of massive onshore and offshore deposits of crude oil which made Nigeria one of the world's largest oil producers. Oil exploration and exportation increased rapidly after the civil war and Nigeria joined the Organization of Petroleum Exporting Countries (OPEC) in 1971. Its membership of the petroleum price fixing cartel enabled it to benefit from massive OPEC induced spikes in oil prices of the 1970s. Between 1970 and 1974, Nigeria's earnings from crude oil exports increased by over 500%. Nigeria also became strategically important during the Arab oil embargo on the United States, as it did not join the embargo and thus became the second largest supplier of petroleum to the United States.

Although the oil boom increased the spending power of the federal government, it caused more problems than it solved. The FMG was able to monopolize control of the oil industry because oil was located entirely either within the former Eastern Region of Biafra which it conquered during the civil war, or in other Christian minority areas close to Nigeria's southern coast. The massive funds generated by the oil boom encouraged the FMG to embark upon a series of unprecedented and grandiose developmental construction projects to rapidly modernize Nigeria. City topography was transformed with the construction of new multi-lane highways and flyovers, bridges, hospitals, schools, universities, dams, factories, hotels, army barracks and office complexes. The FMG imported several million tons of cement from abroad for the execution of these projects. This wasteful extravagance meant that at one point, half of the world's cement orders were headed for Nigeria. Nigeria somehow managed to order over twenty million tons[2] of cement without considering how such a massive order could be unloaded, and that this was about ten times the total amount that the Lagos ports could handle in a year — even if they had no other cargo to unload. This caused a massive backlog at Lagos ports as over four hundred ships battled

---

1 St Jorre, *The Brothers War*, page 407.
2 Some 16 million tons were ordered by the Ministry of Defense alone.

for dock space and waited to offload in what was termed a "cement armada." Some ships remained docked for a year, waiting to offload, and collecting demurrage fees. Other ships carrying inferior goods took advantage of the situation, and worsened the congestion by also docking at the port, so that they too could collect demurrage fees from a government that was seemingly determined to find elaborate ways to squander its new found wealth. Some of the cement either sank or was rendered unusable by the time it could be unloaded. A subsequent inquiry revealed that both the cost and quantity of the cement orders had been massively inflated in a scam aimed at squeezing as much money as possible out of the cash rich FMG. The cement backlog took on a tragi-comic air when fifty large cranes were imported from the UK to assist with unloading. However, as no one knew how to operate the cranes, they too were left to rust in the port. Gowon's successor regime inherited the cement fiasco and was forced to suspend all shipping of cargo to its ports and appointed army officers to ease the ports' congestion. Amazingly, the cement scandal was not the zenith of federal corrupt incompetence. A 1973 census ended in farce after being tainted by the same allegations of count inflation that marred the census exercise of the previous decade. This time the census results were even more flagrantly inflated and implausible.

As funds at federal level increased by spectacular ratios, corruption at federal level was also amplified from small time bribery to large scale racketeering and looting of state funds by government ministers and officials. The military proved that it was not immune to corruption and matched or exceeded the scale of corruption practiced by the civilian government it deposed in 1966. The corruption got so serious that a private citizen (Godwin Daboh) went to court to swear to allegations of corruption against the Commissioner for Communications Joseph Tarka. Despite the press furor, Gowon did not sack Tarka, who instead later resigned under intense criticism. Brigadier Murtala Muhammed replaced Tarka as Commissioner for Communications in August 1974. Murtala combined his new political responsibilities with his military duties, and continued to serve as Inspector of Signals. A civil servant named Chief Aper Aku also accused the military governor of Benue-Plateau State, Joseph Gomwalk, of corrupt enrichment. Gomwalk had created a company called "Voteninski" whose board of directors included many people close to Gomwalk, including his sister-in-law Helen Gomwalk. Voteninski was alleged to have been used to siphon state funds. A police investigation exonerated Gomwalk and the complainant Aku was arrested. Gowon also publicly backed Gomwalk. Both Tarka and Gomwalk were from Gowon's home state of Benue-Plateau, and Gowon's failure to take immediate punitive action against Tarka or Gomwalk degraded his moral authority. The fact that Gomwalk was his cousin also made Gomwalk's exoneration seem contrived.

WANT IN THE MIDST OF PLENTY

The influx of petrodollars into government coffers also amplified both the Nigerian government and people's developmental ambitions. However the oil boom came too soon and too quickly. The FMG proved ineffective at managing the wealth, and was unable to use it to significantly increase Nigerians' living standards. Although the oil boom created a tiny coterie of powerful economic oligarchs and patronage system amongst senior military officers, their families and their civilian associates, living conditions for the rest of the population either remained stagnant or deteriorated. This created the paradox of a rich country with poor people. Gowon described the problem as "want in the midst of plenty" and observed that Nigeria's problem was not lack of money, but how to effectively spend its sudden new found wealth. Civil perceptions that Nigeria was "rich" also made the population impatient for the oil boom wealth to trickle down to the society at large. In an attempt to distribute federal wealth to workers, the FMG in January 1975 decided to award public sector employees massive pay rises exceeding 100%. The pay increases were backdated to April 1974 and half of them were tax free. The Public Service Review Commission (headed by Jerome Udoji) which evaluated the pay rises had recommended only a staggered 60% pay rise, with no payment of arrears. Nonetheless a more grandiose pay increase was implemented by the FMG. The increased spending power of public sector workers led traders to increase their prices, fuelling inflation and wiping out the economic benefits the pay rises were intended to create. Private sector workers then went on strike to demand pay rises for themselves.

Gowon's charm ensured his personal popularity. Therefore criticism from outside the regime tended to be directed not at him personally, but at his administrators. Within the military though some officers expected Gowon to reenergize his regime by replacing the military governors, many of whom had been in office for nearly a decade. Brigadier Danjuma was among their critics and declared two of them to be "completely useless and giving the army a bad name."[1] However, some of the military governors refused to stand down and pointed out to Gowon that some of them had been in their positions throughout his leadership. Their logic was that if they were stale, then Gowon must be stale also, since he had been in office as long as, or longer than them. The military governors had gone from junior officers to senior officers, and gained several promotions in rank even though none of them had seen active military service for nearly a decade. Gowon was sensitive to the military governors' increasing unpopularity, but kept postponing decisive action on the issue. He announced in October 1974 that he would change the military governors, but by July 1975 was telling a conference of RSMs that the military governors would be changed by the end of the year, but not before a royal visit scheduled for October 1975 (in order to give them the honor of shaking hands with Queen Elizabeth II of the United Kingdom). The corruption issue segued into the issue of replacing the military governors. A former Director of Works in North-Western State claimed that more contracts had been executed in the past year than in the previous six years. Some of the military governors had apparently reconciled themselves to being replaced and decided to engage in a free for all bazaar to award contracts before their replacement.[2]

The Military and Civil Society

The upper echelons of the officer corps became extremely politicized and many senior officers were *de facto* politicians. Increasing numbers of officers were brought into the political decision making process. The FEC contained the following officers:

---

1 Lindsay Barrett, Danjuma: *The Making of a General*, page 77.
2 Panter-Brick, *Soldiers and Oil: The Political Transformation of Nigeria*, page 97.

Name	FEC Post
Vice-Admiral Joseph Wey	Chief of Staff, Supreme Headquarters
Major-General Hassan Katsina	Commissioner for Establishments
Major-General Emmanuel Eyo Ekpo	Commissioner for Agriculture and Natural Resources
Brigadier Olusegun Obasanjo	Commissioner for Works and Housing
Brigadier Murtala Muhammed	Commissioner for Communications
Brigadier Emmanuel Abisoye	Commissioner for Health
Brigadier Henry Adefope	Commissioner for Labor
Colonel Mohammed Inuwa Wushishi	Commissioner for Industries
Colonel Dan Suleiman	Commissioner for Special Duties
Lt-Colonel A.A. Ali	Commissioner for Education
Captain Olufemi Olumide	Commissioner for Transport

These were in addition to several other military officers serving in the SMC, which acted as the FMG's legislature and which ratified FEC decisions. By the 1970s, many junior officers had never served under a civilian government and were not familiar with concepts of military subordination to civilian authority. Some of them doctrinally believed that civilians were subordinate to soldiers and were contemptuous of civilian conduct such as tardiness and imprecision. The phrase "bloody civilian!" entered every-day discourse. Within the military there was concern that cadets enrolling at the NDA did so not merely for the love of soldiering, or for the ambition of becoming a battalion or brigade commander, but in order to give themselves the best chance of one day being appointed to a lucrative political position. There was always the risk that one day one of these recruits would get tired of waiting for a political post, and decide to take such a post by force. Some senior officers were genuinely concerned that military rule had a corrosive effect on military professionalism and efficiency, and made it more difficult for them to maintain standards of discipline in their units. They were also apprehensive about an emerging cadre of politically ambitious junior officers behind them whose ambitions could not be satisfied by military postings alone and who desired political postings or patronage. Professionally oriented senior officers feared that this cadre was a ticking time bomb and were keen for the military to disengage from politics. Some NCOs and junior officers forcefully extracted "entitlements" from cowed civilians. A favored "perk" was refusing to pay for taxi and bus rides. Senior officers were also not immune to arrogating themselves above civilians, and would sometimes ride over pothole ridden streets with sirens blaring and gun toting soldiers in their motorcade knocking civilian vehicles out of the way. Motorists and pedestrians who did not move out of the way quickly enough were often whipped and assaulted.

Civilian perceptions of the military also began to change and a common civilian complaint was that certain military officers were behaving as if military rule was the status quo, and forgot that military rule was an aberration. Some officers foresaw an era of entrenched military rule. Gowon himself remarked that "by the time I leave office, I will be too old to return to the barracks." On a visit to the Mid-West Region (governed by one of Gowon's loyalists Brigadier Ogbemudia), the government of the Region welcomed Gowon with a banner inscribed "Gowon Forever." The FMG also paid for an 80,000 pounds (sterling) advertisement in a London newspaper which described Gowon as "The Lincoln of Nigeria." These measures gave outsiders the impression that the military intended to remain in office for an extended period of time.

When the civil war ended in 1970, Gowon promised that Nigeria would return to civilian democratic rule in 1976. However a few years later the military seriously considered whether the country's fragile unity could survive the cut and thrust of partisan party politics. Opinion within the military was not unanimous. Some officers canvassed an indefinite extension of military rule on the basis that as the only truly national institution, the military was the only organization that could ensure political stability. Unsurprisingly this view was more prevalent among military members of the regime who had nothing to gain, and lots of power, wealth and perks to lose from the military leaving office. The massive concentration of wealth at federal level made political activity a tremendous opportunity for amassing wealth, and disincentivized the incumbent regime from relinquishing control of governance and its ancillary control of the lucrative petroleum industry. It also made political participation more attractive for politicians and tempted some military officers outside the FMG to emulate their superiors in the FMG. These factors aggravated concerns within the military leadership that returning the country to civilian rule would permit corrupt politicians back into the government and give them a free reign to loot the much enlarged treasury. Other officers favored a return to democracy as a matter of principle, but only when political conditions permitted it, and the military government had completed its program. By 1974 there was a body of military opinion that favored Gowon's transformation from military head of state to executive President in a future dispensation. The proposal had the support of some senior officers such as Emmanuel Ekpo and Olu Bajowa.[1] The former president Nnamdi Azikiwe seemed to have accepted the inevitability of military entrenchment in politics and proposed a diarchy under which the military could share power with civilians. Some members of the military held similar views. Brigadier Bisalla stated, "If the country's constitution allowed an army *cum* civilian regime, the members of the armed forces would participate in the future government."[2] A minister later remarked that there were two political parties in Nigeria: the military and the civilians.[3]

The issue was officially considered during a conference of senior army officers in September 1974. Although admitting that some officers wanted a return to democracy, Gowon claimed that the majority of officers advocated a continuation of military rule. On a rain soaked Independence Day parade on October 1, 1974, Gowon indefinitely postponed the return to democracy:

> Four years ago when I gave 1976 as the target date for returning the country to normal constitutional government, both myself and the military hierarchy believed that by that date, especially after a bloody civil war for which there had been a great deal of human and material sacrifice and from which we had

1 Ibid., page 66.
2 Ibid., page 68.
3 Comment by Shehu Shagari.

expected that every Nigerian would have learnt a lesson, there would have developed an atmosphere of sufficient stability. We had thought that genuine demonstration of moderation and self control in pursuing sectional ends in the overall interest of the country would have become the second nature of all Nigerians. Regrettably, from all the information at our disposal, from the general attitude, utterances and maneuvers of some individual groups and from some publications during the past few months, it is clear that those who aspire to lead the nation on the return to civilian rule have not learnt any lesson from our past experiences. In spite of the existence of a state of emergency which has so far precluded political activity there has already emerged a high degree of sectional politicking, intemperate utterances and writings which were deliberately designed to whip up ill feelings within the country to the benefit of the political aspirations of a few. There is no doubt that it would not take them long to return to the old cut-throat politics that once led this nation into a serious crisis. We are convinced that this is not what the honest people of this country want.

The postponement was out of synch with the yearnings of a significant section of civil and military opinion. Some officers genuinely believed that the postponement of civil rule blemished the military's reputation as honorable men of their word.

When there is no credible democratic alternative, Nigerian military regimes are inherently unstable and ironically more susceptible to a coup as they can only be replaced by an intra-military revolt. The corruption scandals, unpopularity of the military governors and civil discontent about another delay of the return to democracy created an opportunity for disaffected officers to consider deposing Gowon. Ostensibly reformist motivations, a desire to tackle corruption and frustration at Gowon's delay at returning the country to civilian democratic rule were the reasons for discontent within the military. However, there were other less altruistic reasons. Soldiers had initially been reluctant to govern and involve themselves in politics. Some of the army's officers had evolved from the apolitical and unassuming soldiers of the 1950s and 1960s, into immensely confident and powerful men with a large "following" of loyal soldiers in the army that made them *de facto* private warlords. Having brought Gowon to power, and fought in the civil war which made him a hero, some of them felt disenfranchised at their exclusion from the political decision making process, and their decreasing influence over Gowon. There was also a perception that the "Good Old Jack" of the pre-war years had become "His Excellency, the head of state and Commander-in-Chief of the Nigerian Armed Forces General Yakubu Gowon." The personal ambition of some officers outside the regime, and jealousy of the incumbent military governors were other sources of discontent. The military governors did not help matters with their ostentatious displays of wealth which were damaging to the morale of officers in purely military postings and dented military *esprit de corps*. The spectacular wealth differential between the military governors and their colleagues in non-political posts reinforced discontent among some non-regime officers who felt they had risked their lives in the mutiny that brought Gowon to power, and again to fight a civil war that enhanced Gowon's reputation, but had not been adequately "compensated" for their efforts with the spoils of office.

Brigadier Murtala Muhammed felt he was Gowon's maker, and frequently directed insubordinate criticism at Gowon and other senior officers. On one occasion Murtala, in the presence of a cabinet minister, said of Gowon: "We shall soon change him. We put him there, and we can remove him anytime."[1] Murtala and Gowon had

---

1 Shehu Shagari, *Beckoned to Serve*, page 178.

frequent verbal altercations. Domkat Bali revealed that these verbal confrontations took place "in Dodan Barracks, meetings, just anywhere. You know Murtala could be so rude."[1] While Gowon was a great wartime leader, Murtala accused him of procrastination and indecision in peacetime. Gowon's methodical style was apt for the explosive environment in 1966, but appeared undynamic in an era of spiraling oil revenues and civil desire for rapid reform and development. As far back as the civil war, Murtala had at the least tried to undermine Gowon, or at most tried to sabotage his rule, by asking then Colonel Obasanjo (the commander of the 3 Marine Commando division) to slow down his advance and the progress of the war so that Gowon's wartime field commanders could use the pace of war progress to issue an ultimatum to Gowon. Murtala's idea was to pressure Gowon into stepping down and being replaced by a three man presidential commission. Murtala was a thorn in the side of not only Gowon but other senior officers too. Major-General David Ejoor later conceded that during his time as Chief of Staff, Army "Brigadier Murtala Muhammed was particularly difficult to handle."[2] Gowon found it difficult to act against Murtala's insubordination as it was Murtala who had led the revolt that catapulted Gowon to office. Additionally, Murtala had a large loyal following of Northern officers in the army who idolized him. Punitive action against Murtala would have provoked a backlash from these officers. Murtala also felt that as the kingmaker whose revolt brought Gowon to power, he had a privileged status enabling him to criticize Gowon.

---

1 Ahmed, Femi, *Domkat, A Biography of General Domkat Bali*, page 114.
2 Ejoor, *Reminiscences*, page 149.

CHAPTER 15. ANOTHER ARMY PLOT: ANOTHER MILITARY GOVERNMENT

In July 1975, the head of the police Special Branch M.D. Yusuf informed Brigadier Obasanjo that for the second time in his life, someone had told him to his face that a coup was being planned. The first time was in 1966 when Murtala told him that a coup was being planned and dared him (Yusuf) to go and tell anyone he liked. Even before the latest incident Yusuf had been suspicious since some middle ranking army officers had started frequently visiting his cousin Major-General Hassan Katsina. Yusuf informed Gowon of intelligence reports regarding coup plotting by middle ranking officers. The names that featured prominently on these reports were the same officers that brought Gowon to power, and surprisingly included the commander of the elite Brigade of Guards[1] (the unit responsible for Gowon's personal security) Colonel Joe Garba. The Provost Marshal Colonel Anthony Ochefu was also mentioned in these reports. Gowon tried to contact Ochefu repeatedly without success, as Ochefu either made himself scarce or somehow missed Gowon's attempts to reach him. An incredulous Gowon doubted these security reports and found it difficult to believe that his trusted security chief could plot a coup against him. He doubted that the same officers who brought him to power could plot to overthrow him, and wondered if he was being fed false intelligence in order to goad him into eliminating his trusted aides.

M.D. Yusuf pressed Gowon on the seriousness of the intelligence reports and offered to personally confront Garba with the allegations in the hope that it would "put the frighteners" on the plotters and give them the impression that their plot had been detected. This had a historical parallel with the manner in which Lt-Colonel Patrick Anwunah confronted Murtala Muhammed nine years earlier on the eve of the "Araba" counter-coup. Gowon restrained Yusuf and said that he would speak to Garba himself when he returned from an OAU conference in Uganda. Gowon may have placed great faith in the personal security apparatus around him and his security conscious ADC Colonel William Walbe (from the same Angas ethnic group as

---

1 The Federal Guards was renamed the "Brigade of Guards" in 1968.

Gowon) who was so effective at isolating Gowon that Gowon did not even know the numbers of his own internal telephones. Unbeknown to Gowon the all star cast from the July 1966 coup that brought him to power was being quietly reassembled for a sequel nine years later. However, this time, the lead role was to be given to someone other than Gowon.

As Gowon prepared for the OAU summit, a coup plot against him had crystallized. According to Joe Garba the coup plot began around April 1975. At the centre of the plot were a group of Colonels who had two things in common: (i) they took part in the July 1966 counter-coup that brought Gowon to power (ii) they fought in the civil war and felt excluded from the corridors of power. The senior figures in Gowon's regime were officers such as Hassan Katsina, David Ejoor, Commodore Wey, and Brigadier Ikwue who were not coup plotters and who did not fight in the civil war.

Then Lt-Colonel Ibrahim Babangida recalled that while en route to a football match with Lt-Colonel Shehu Musa Yar'Adua, Yar'Adua asked him whether the country's political condition would remain the same. Babangida understood that this was obviously a leading question to elicit support from Babangida for a military coup.[1] Yar'Adua's conversation with Babangida was reminiscent of the manner in which a decade earlier, Majors Nzeogwu and Ifeajuna would casually drop leading political questions into conversation with their colleagues as a way of ascertaining which officers they could recruit for a coup.

Although northern soldiers were united in vengeance against Igbos in 1966, in the following decade northern soldiers in the mid and upper echelons of the army had become factionalized into pro-Gowon and pro-Murtala camps. With a few exceptions these factions ran along broadly geographic lines. In the pro-Gowon camp were minority ethnicity middle belt soldiers such as Colonel Walbe and Brigadier Martin Adamu, and in the latter category were Muslim soldiers from the far north such as Lt-Colonels Muhammadu Buhari, Shehu Musa Yar'Adua and Ibrahim Babangida. The key plotters against Gowon came from within the pro-Murtala camp and included men such as Colonels Shehu Musa Yar'Adua, Ibrahim Taiwo, Abdullahi Mohammed (later Chief of Staff at the Presidency), Ibrahim Babangida, the director of supply and transport Muhammadu Buhari, and the Provost Marshal Anthony Ochefu. The involvement of Abdullahi Mohammed and Ochefu significantly reduced the risk of detection and prevention. Mohammed was the head of army intelligence and Ochefu headed the military police, which would be expected to arrest coup plotters.

In early 1975, Colonel Garba's Brigade of Guards conducted a major ten day field exercise named "Exercise Sunstroke." The exercise was essentially a 'war games' rehearsal and featured cross country foot marching and vehicular movement from Lagos to Lanlate in the Western State. Although the commanding officer of the LGO Brigadier Godwin Ally presided over the post exercise analysis, the exercise's umpires included Colonel Abubakar Waziri and Lt-Colonels Babangida and Yar'Adua. The involvement of these Colonels in "Exercise Sunstroke" and in the coup plot against Gowon led one of the other exercise participants to suspect that "Exercise Sunstroke" was a dress rehearsal for a coup against Gowon.[2]

Shortly before his departure for the OAU summit in Uganda, Gowon finally decided to speak to the commander of the Brigade of Guards Colonel Joe Garba regarding the coup rumors. Garba denied all knowledge of, or involvement in, any coup

---

1 Karl Maier, *This House Has Fallen: Midnight in Nigeria*, page 55.
2 Chris Alli, *The Federal Republic of Nigeria Army*, page 63.

plot. Gowon told Garba that if he indeed was part of a coup plot, then, "Let it be on your own conscience and let it be without bloodshed. I must go to Kampala anyway."[1] Gowon departed for Uganda to attend the OAU summit in July 1975. He was far too trusting.

ANOTHER COUP PLOT

Although the Colonels had resolved to replace Gowon they were not independently powerful enough to drive through their ideas and depose Gowon without the support of senior officers. To attempt Gowon's removal without senior officer support would lead to bloodshed. To succeed the plot required the support senior officers directly below the Generals in the SMC. This intermediate level of officers (mostly Brigadiers) were the men who could turn the Colonels' ideas into reality and included Brigadiers Danjuma, Martin Adamu, Iliya Bisalla, Gibson Jalo and Ibrahim Haruna. The passivity of the Brigadiers during the operation would be essential to removing Gowon. Colonel Joe Garba and Lt-Colonel Shehu Yar'Adua operated as the link between the Colonels and the senior officer echelon.

THE BRIGADIERS APPROACHED

Brigadier Murtala Muhammed was the most charismatic northern officer in the Nigerian army then. It would be impossible to stage a coup and to govern without his consent given the loyal following he had in the army. Garba and Yar'Adua went to Murtala's Lagos house at number 6 Second Avenue in Ikoyi, to ask for his co-operation. When they arrived they found Murtala characteristically sitting under the almond tree in his compound. He was listening to an audio cassette tape of Koranic verses while reciting the verses contemporaneously. According to Garba, Murtala barely acknowledged their presence and continued reciting Koranic verses without interruption. Garba and Yar'Adua waited sheepishly in silence for over half an hour until the tape finished. When the tape finished Yar'Adua finally spoke. As he was closer to Murtala than Garba was, Yar'Adua did most of the talking. He laid out their case against Gowon by accusing him of misrule, and explaining that Gowon's regime was tarnishing the military's prestige. Therefore the Colonels had decided to depose Gowon and replace him with Murtala. Garba said he added a few words for amplification. After pondering over what he just heard, Murtala reiterated his usual contempt for Gowon, and agreed that Gowon's overthrow was long overdue. However, after witnessing two bloody military coups, and taking part in an even bloodier civil war, he was not prepared to take up arms for Nigeria again. Although he agreed with the Colonels' aims, Murtala refused to physically take part in the coup, and limited himself to giving a moral blessing to it, and promising to do everything to defend them and save their lives should the planned coup fail. Murtala then re-inserted the tape, and went back to his Koranic recitation. Garba and Yar'Adua departed, with Yar'Adua telling Garba not to worry as he would find a way to talk Murtala round.[2]

Colonel Anthony Ochefu approached the GOC of the 3rd division Brigadier T.Y. Danjuma, and elicited a pledge of passive assistance from him. While Ochefu was at Danjuma's house, Colonel Garba called and told Danjuma, "Sir we do not need your help. All that we need is for you to do nothing."[3] Assurances of passive assistance

---

1 *The Times*, July 30 1975.

2 Joe Garba , *Diplomatic Soldiering*, prologue.

3 Ibid., page 79.

or friendly neutrality were also obtained from Brigadiers Bisalla and Jalo and from the other GOCs.[1] On the eve of the coup Colonel Abdullahi Mohammed separately informed Brigadier Obasanjo and Colonel Bali that a coup would occur overnight. Obasanjo asked Mohammed to avoid bloodshed. After his conversation with Mohammed, Obasanjo travelled to the home of M.D. Yusuf to alert him. Yusuf appeared unsurprised and simply informed Obasanjo that his men would conduct extra surveillance that night. The plot also leaked to S.K. Dimka — a senior police officer that was the older brother of Lt-Colonel Dimka of the army's physical training corps.[2] Overnight Colonel Ochefu and Lt-Colonel Yar'Adua also approached Brigadier Martin Adamu at his house and asked him to read their coup speech announcing Gowon's overthrow. However, Adamu was less cooperative than the other Brigadiers. Nine years earlier he had nominated Gowon to become head of state and remained loyal to him. He refused to read the speech. Still in his pyjamas, Adamu pleaded that Gowon should be given another chance and bloodshed avoided. He was reminded that his refusal to play ball might lead to bloodshed.

Although Gowon's absence from Nigeria saved Garba the embarrassment of having to arrest or harm him, there was a last minute scare for the plotters when Gowon's ADC Colonel William Walbe unexpectedly returned to Nigeria from Uganda, ostensibly to collect a file that Gowon had inadvertently left behind. News of Walbe's return spooked the plotters and they feared their plot had been uncovered. Walbe was asked to come to Garba's house. When Walbe arrived he was astonished to see Colonel Anthony Ochefu. He knew that Garba and Ochefu usually could not stand the sight of each other. Garba and Ochefu did not believe Walbe's innocuous explanation and thought he had been sent back by Gowon to keep tabs on them.[3] Ochefu informed Walbe that it would be unwise for him to return to Uganda, and that his colleagues were unhappy with him for being overly loyal to Gowon. Walbe became suspicious and told them to count him out of whatever they were up to.

July 28, 1975

Colonel Walbe's House

Close to midnight on July 28, Garba dramatically showed up at the house of Gowon's ADC Colonel Walbe. Garba was dressed in full combat fatigues, accompanied by other troops and armed, "looking fierce with a pistol here and a grenade there."[4] Garba told Walbe to wake up his wife so she could listen in on their conversation. Garba explained to Mrs. Walbe that he did not want her to hold him responsible if her husband came to any harm. In the presence of Walbe's wife, Garba demanded to know if Walbe was still loyal to Gowon or whether he would join the plotters. During the tense exchange Garba at one point drew his pistol. When Walbe did not unequivocally commit to the plot, Garba told Walbe that Brigadiers Adamu and Danjuma and Colonel Ochefu wanted to see him. Garba departed after warning Walbe not to attempt anything heroic as his house was surrounded by armed troops. Walbe now thought the coup was army wide. Walbe claimed he was later approached by a Brigade of Guards soldier from Pankshin in Benue-Plateau State, who offered to

---

1 Elaigwu, Gowon: *The Biography of a Soldier–Statesman*, page 226.
2 Ibid., page 226.
3 Ibid., page 230.
4 Ihonde, *First Call — An Account of the Gowon Years*, page 19.

ambush the plotters with his colleagues and fight to prevent Gowon's overthrow. Walbe dissuaded the soldier and explained that, as most of the senior officers supported the coup, it would be suicidal to resist.[1]

In the early hours of July 29, 1975, the core officers in the coup such as Lt-Colonels Yar'Adua, Abdullahi Mohammed, Ibrahim Taiwo, Babangida, Buhari, Muktar Mohammed, Alfred Aduloju, Paul Tarfa and Sani Bello met at the headquarters of the Lagos Garrison Organization to confirm each officer's operational orders for the coup. Walbe joined them in the mess to discover that, of those he expected to see, only Ochefu was present. He had simply been taken to the mess in order to isolate and keep tabs on him so that he would not cause any problems for the plotters. When Walbe arrived he was greeted with sarcastic salutations of "Welcome, Your Excellency!," "Welcome, Deputy Head of State!" "Welcome, Acting Head of State!"[2] Exactly nine years to the day after Walbe and other junior northern soldiers led Major-General Aguiyi-Ironsi and Lt-Colonel Fajuyi into a bush alongside Iwo road outside Ibadan and murdered them, Walbe discovered that coup plotting can be a double edged sword.

By 2 a.m. soldiers surrounded the Lagos airport, sealed off all approach roads to it and suspended all Nigeria Airways flights. External communications were also severed. While Gowon was still in Uganda, he was overthrown in a military coup announced by Colonel Joseph Garba. Speaking with a tense and emotional voice, Garba announced in a dawn broadcast that Gowon had been overthrown in a bloodless coup without any physical casualties:

> Fellow countrymen and women, I, Colonel Joseph Nanven Garba, in consultation with my colleagues, do hereby declare that in view of what has been happening in our country in the past few months, the Nigerian armed forces decided to effect a change of the leadership of the Federal Military Government. As from now, General Yakubu Gowon ceases to be head of the Federal Military Government and Commander-in-Chief of the armed forces of Nigeria. The general public is advised to be calm and to go about their lawful duties. However, in view of the traffic situation in Lagos area, all workers other than those on essential services like NEPA, medical services, water works, NPA, the P & T, all workers and all tanker drivers will observe today, 29th of July, 1975, as a work free day. A dusk to dawn curfew is hereby imposed until further notice. Nigeria Airways operations are suspended and all airports and borders are closed till further notice. Fellow countrymen, this has been a bloodless operation and we do not want anyone to lose his or her life. You are therefore warned in your own interest to be law abiding. Anyone caught disturbing the public order will be summarily dealt with. We appeal to everyone to co-operate in the task ahead. Further announcements will be made in due course. Long live the Federal Republic of Nigeria.

MILITARY COUPS: BACKING THE RIGHT HORSE

Joseph Gomwalk, military governor of Benue-Plateau State, called Brigadier Danjuma to ask him what he would do about Garba's announcement. Danjuma replied that he would not do anything to resist the coup, and advised Gomwalk to go to a safe house if he was worried for his safety. The period of time during which a military coup is active is among the most tense and dangerous professional moments of a military officer's life. This is especially the case for officers not involved in, or who are

1 Ibid., page 19.
2 Ibid., page 21.

ambivalent to the coup. If an officer goes "by the book" and attempts to stop the coup, he could be killed in the process of doing so, or even if he survives, may be unceremoniously dismissed by the new regime if the coup succeeds. Conversely, if the officer cooperates with the coup plotters but the coup fails, he could later be dismissed or executed for supporting a mutiny. Military coups subject bystander officers to gut wrenching life and death decisions in which they must ensure that they back the right horse. Backing the wrong horse could result in death. One officer faced with such a dilemma was Colonel Domkat Bali who was temporarily commanding the 2 division in Ibadan, in the absence of its substantive commander Brigadier James Oluleye. Bali and his officers resolved to avoid bloodshed by assenting to the coup, rather than risk an escalation by fighting against it. After receiving a telephone call from Colonel Garba to ascertain his disposition to the coup, Bali ordered broadcasting facilities in Ibadan to interrupt normal programming and play martial music. He also briefed, then ordered, that Brigadier Rotimi, military governor of the Western State, be placed under house arrest. Bali's cooperation may have been influenced by the fact that he is of Tarok ethnicity like Garba and also hails from Garba's hometown of Langtang. In July 1975 most officers in the upper echelons of the Nigerian army backed the right horse. There seems to have been an unconscious consensus among key unit commanders to avoid bloodshed by declining to resist the coup. Several officers decided that it was better to let the coup succeed rather than risk mass bloodshed by resisting it. Only one prominent commander attempted to resist the coup, but his action came too late. He was severely reprimanded by the plotters but was spared.

Garba was recruited into the plot and chosen to read the coup speech for strategic reasons. As the commander of Gowon's personal security unit the Brigade of Guards, the sound of his voice as the coup announcer would have a placating effect on Gowon's other security officers who would be unlikely to resist the coup, and would assume it was an "inside" job if their commander was part of the plot. Major John Shagaya was a member of the Brigade of Guards in command of 2 Guards battalion.[1] Resistance by the Brigade of Guards could be dangerous as Garba had personally trained and recruited a company of Gowon's Angas kinsmen into the Brigade of Guards to protect Gowon. This special company of Angas guards was led by McDonald Gotip.[2] Garba's command of the Brigade of Guards and intimate knowledge of Gowon's routine and security apparatus can be seen as parallel to the way the January 1966 Majors used Garba's predecessor Major Don Okafor, as Okafor was familiar with Prime Minister Balewa's routine and domestic security arrangements. Garba was commissioned into the army at the age of 19, making him at that time the youngest infantry officer in the Nigerian army. His role in the coup was a shocking betrayal of Gowon. He was, like Gowon, a Christian from a northern minority ethnic group, and may even have been a distant relative of Gowon. Although Garba was of Tarok ethnicity, his maternal grandfather was an Angas from Kabwir, only two miles away from Gowon's ancestral village of Lur. Garba's involvement in the coup was crucial for avoiding the ethnic overtones of the two coups of 1966. The core conspirators in the coup against Gowon were Muslim officers from the far north, thus Garba's participation was essential to avoid antagonizing officers from middle belt ethnic groups who might interpret the coup as an attempt by officers from the far

---

1 Almost 200 members of the 2 Guards Battalion later staged a mass desertion in mid 1976 which resulted in them being dismissed by the Chief of Army Staff.
2 Gotip was subsequently implicated in Nigeria's next coup plot.

north to wrest power away from Christian middle belt officers. As will be shown in a subsequent Chapter, this was the exact interpretation given to the coup by some middle belt soldiers. Garba may also have had other motivations for participating in the coup. His relationship with Gowon's wife Victoria had become increasingly frosty over time and the other plotters may have exploited this in order to recruit Garba. The reader may be incredulous that officers would risk their careers and lives, and those of their colleagues and families, to overthrow a government for personal disputes and professional rivalries. However, this demonstrates how politicized the army had become after nearly a decade of military rule.

July 29 was the ninth anniversary of the bloody revenge coup that had brought Gowon to power and was chosen as the date for the latest coup precisely for that reason. The plotters reasoned that it was the last day that anyone would expect a coup. Once again, proving that coup plotting in Nigeria is addictive, many of the same officers that participated in the coup that brought Gowon to power were also instrumental in the coup that removed him, and in subsequent coups.

News of the coup filtered back to the OAU conference in Uganda. Uganda's eccentric leader Idi Amin broke the news to Gowon. After brushing Amin off, Gowon took a seat in the conference hall and listened to a speech by the Director-General of UNESCO, Dr. Amadou-Mahtar M'Bow. During M'bow's speech, Gowon turned to Usman Faruk, the military governor of the North-Western State, and whispered in Hausa, "What we have always feared has happened."[1] When M'Bow concluded his speech President Ahmadou Ahidjo of Cameroon approached Gowon and offered his sympathy. Gowon reconciled himself to the new reality and was his typically conciliatory self. The bloodless nature of the coup was partly due to his refusal to resist it. He wished the new leaders well and said that:

> From all indications a new government has been established in Nigeria. I wish to state that I on my part have also accepted the change and pledged my full loyalty to my nation, my country and the new government. Therefore, in the overall interest of the nation and our beloved country, I appeal to all concerned to cooperate fully with the new government and ensure the preservation of the peace, unity and stability of our dear motherland. As a Nigerian, I am prepared to serve my country in any capacity which my country may consider appropriate. I am a professional soldier and I can do any duty that I am called upon to do. May I take this opportunity to thank all the people of Nigeria and friends of Nigeria for the support and cooperation that you all gave me during my tenure of office and call upon all of you to give the new government of our nation the same support and cooperation in the interest of our beloved country. Love live one united, happy and prosperous Nigeria. Long live the Organization of African Unity. May God bless you all.

Gowon declined to answer questions from the press but joked, "We will next meet as private citizen Gowon." He also quoted a few lines from William Shakespeare's "As You Like It":

> All the world is a stage, and all the men and women merely players. They have their exits and their entrances and one man in his time plays many parts.

Gowon travelled to England and enrolled for a course in political science at Warwick University. The lack of bitterness between the new and past leaders even led some to suspect that Gowon's overthrow was a cleverly orchestrated transfer of power from senior to middle grade officers. Such perceptions were given credence by

---

1 Ihonde, *First Call: An Account of the Gowon Years*, page 23.

the fact that Gowon's wife and children, and Chief of Staff (Army) Major-General David Ejoor, all left for London just before the coup and were conveniently overseas while it was executed. Ejoor was quick to pledge his loyalty to the new regime. Gowon's brother Captain Isaiah Gowon was also in London, having just completed an artillery course.

THE NEW LEADERS

Brigadier Murtala Muhammed had been informed of the details and timing of the coup, and he too, was in London when events took their course. The plane carrying him back was the only plane that was permitted to land in Nigeria that day. However, the drama was not over. Colonel M.I. Wushishi called a meeting of senior officers, GOCs and brigade commanders at Dodan Barracks on the evening of July 29. The Colonels had already decided that three of their superior officers, Brigadiers Murtala Muhammed, Olusegun Obasanjo and Theophilus Danjuma, would form a troika at the head of the new regime, with Murtala replacing Gowon as head of state. Murtala, Danjuma and Obasanjo were called into a separate room by Lt-Colonels Garba, Yar'Adua and Abdullahi Mohammed. The three Brigadiers were informed that decisions of the new SMC would only be taken with the concurrence of a majority of its members, and that any decision that was opposed by two thirds of the SMC could not be implemented. Murtala angrily objected and insisted that, as head of state, he should be given a free hand to govern unrestricted by his colleagues. The Colonels warned him that they could easily nominate someone else if he did not agree, but Murtala continued to argue and remonstrate with them, and screamed, "To hell with all of you." According to Garba, "Twenty minutes later he was still arguing."[1] At this point Garba became frustrated. He had been awake for 48 straight hours in a state of anxiety, heightened tension and mental preparedness. The commander of the LGO, Brigadier Godwin Ally,[2] came in to ask if everything was alright. He noted that the other officers waiting outside in an adjacent room were becoming restless and might leave in frustration. The normally taciturn intelligence officer Colonel Abdullahi Mohammed also tried to persuade Murtala and pointed out that Murtala had a large army following who might wonder why he had been passed over. If they offered the position of head of state to someone else, they would leak the outcome of their discussions with Murtala and let the public know the conditions he had refused. Murtala exploded again and began screaming, "This is blackmail! I am not going to have you blackmailing me!"[3] Despite his ostensible anger and reluctance, the Colonels could tell that they had got their man and that his resistance was softening, even if Murtala had to have a further theatrical outburst to show he would not go down without a fight. After some calming words from Danjuma and Obasanjo, Murtala agreed to the Colonels' proposal. However, in typically forthright manner, Murtala told the Colonels that once he assumed power, he would not allow himself to be a stooge of, or be dictated to by, the officers who had got him there. Murtala made it clear that he would be independent and would govern as he saw fit. The meeting at Dodan Barracks did not end till 4 a.m.

---

1 Joseph Garba, *Diplomatic Soldiering*, prologue page xiv.
2 Ally's ADC was future coup plotter Lawan Gwadabe.
3 Joseph Garba, *Diplomatic Soldiering*, prologue page xv. Also see interview with Danjuma in Guardian, February 17, 2008.

A No Nonsense Leader

The new head of state, 37-year-old Brigadier Murtala Ramat Muhammed, broadcast to the nation on July 30, 1975 (full text of speech reproduced at Appendix 2). Murtala dismantled the apparatus of Gowon's governing regime and removed his key men. Gowon's deputy, Vice-Admiral Wey, was retired and was replaced as Chief of Staff, Supreme Headquarters, by Commissioner for Works and Housing Brigadier Obasanjo. Obasanjo's appointment owed as much to his ethnicity as it did to his capabilities. Obasanjo was the most senior surviving southern officer after the retirement of Admiral Wey and Major-General Adebayo. In the delicate ethnic balancing act that dominates Nigerian politics, the plotters needed a southern deputy. Obasanjo was given the unenviable task of politely informing the former military governors, ministers and SMC members that their services were no longer required. Both Obasanjo and Murtala were specialists outside the army's core infantry, artillery and armored corps. Prior to the coup, Murtala headed the signal corps, and Obasanjo was the head of the army engineers.

The commandant of the NDA Brigadier Iliya Bisalla became the new Commissioner for Defense. Gowon previously kept responsibility for the defense portfolio in conjunction with his duties as head of state and Commander-in-Chief of the armed forces. Bisalla was the only member of Gowon's SMC retained by the new regime. Bisalla had prior administrative experience, having served as the Military Secretary before being moved to Enugu to become a divisional GOC during the civil war. Brigadier Danjuma replaced Major-General David Ejoor as the Chief of Staff (Army). On Danjuma's assumption of this post, its title was changed to "Chief of Army Staff" — the designation which has been used till today. The heads of the air force, navy, Inspector-General of Police Kam Selem and his deputy T.A. Fagbola were also compulsorily retired along with all officers of the rank of Major-General and above (i.e. anyone that was senior to any member of the new regime). These mass retirements caused the first wave of what Nigerians refer to as "baby Generals." Many of the retired officers such as Major-Generals Ejoor, Katsina and Ekpo were only in their early 40s. The pension and benefits of the retired "baby generals" were, and still remain a massive expenditure as vast sums of federal revenue is required to fund their lengthy retirements. The veteran navy officer Vice-Admiral Wey and Major-General Adebayo were the only retired officers from the older generation. Wey was the first Nigerian to command the Nigerian navy and Adebayo was the eighth officer to be commissioned into the Nigerian army. Overnight, experience (Wey and Adebayo) and excellent professional training and competence that could not be quantified (Ejoor, Katsina, Ikwue) was lost.

Murtala initially opposed the appointment of M.D. Yusuf as Inspector-General of police. This may have been because Yusuf had mentioned Murtala as a coup plotting suspect in his intelligence reports to Gowon. This may have ignited some latent hostility that Murtala had held dating back to the civil war days when the police searched the house of Murtala's cousin Inuwa Wada in connection with allegations that funds in the Central Bank branch in Benin City had been looted. Murtala regarded the search as a personal slight. Colonel Garba was elevated after the coup by being appointed as Nigeria's new Commissioner for External Affairs. Now serving in a diplomatic role, Garba relinquished command of the Brigade of Guards which he had held for most of the previous decade. Garba claimed he accepted his new role after being persuaded to do so from his kinsmen from the town of Langtang Lt-Colonel Jerry Useni and Major John Shagaya (Shagaya is Garba's cousin).

Eventually, the following senior redeployments were made:

Position	Holder Under Gowon	Holder Under Murtala Muhammed
Chief of Staff, Supreme Headquarters	Vice-Admiral Joseph Wey	Brigadier Olusegun Obasanjo
Deputy Chief of Staff, Supreme Headquarters	Major-General Hassan Katsina	N/A
Chief of Staff (Army)	Major-General David Ejoor	Brigadier Theophilus Danjuma
Chief of Air Staff	Brigadier Emmanuel Ikwue	Colonel John Yisa Doko
Chief of Naval Staff	Rear Admiral Nelson Soroh	Commodore Michael Adelanwa
Inspector-General of Police	Alhaji Kam Selem	Alhaji Mohammed Dikko Yusuf

A new SMC consisting of the following members was formed.

Supreme Military Council

Name	Position
Brigadier Murtala Ramat Muhammed	Head of State, Commander-in-Chief of the Nigerian Armed Forces, Chairman of the Supreme Military Council and Chairman of the Federal Executive Council
Brigadier Olusegun Obasanjo	Chief of Staff, Supreme Headquarters
Brigadier Iliya Bisalla	Commissioner for Defense
Brigadier Theophilus Yakubu Danjuma	Chief of Army Staff
Commodore Michael Adelanwa	Chief of Naval Staff
Colonel John Yisa Doko	Chief of Air Staff
Alhaji Mohammed Dikko Yusuf	Inspector-General of Police
Brigadier Julius Ipoola Alani Akinrinade[1]	GOC, 1 Division — Kaduna
Brigadier Martin Adamu	GOC, 2 Division — Ibadan
Brigadier Emmanuel Abisoye	GOC, 3 Division — Jos
Brigadier John Obada	GOC, Lagos Garrison Organization
Brigadier James Oluleye	Commissioner for Establishments

Colonel Joseph Nanven Garba	Commissioner for External Affairs
Colonel Dan Suleiman	Commissioner for Health
Lt-Colonel Ibrahim Badamasi Babangida[2]	Commander, Nigerian Army Armored Corps
Lt-Colonel Shehu Musa Yar'Adua	Commissioner for Transport
Lt-Colonel Alfred Aduloju	Commander, Nigerian Army Signal Corps
Navy Captain Olufemi Olumide	Commissioner for Works and Housing
Lt-Commander Godwin Ndubuisi Kanu (Navy)[3]	Navy
Lt-Colonel Muktar Mohammed	Army

[1] Later became Nigeria's first Chief of Defense Staff.
[2] Later became head of state.
[3] Later became Military Governor of Imo State.

The July 1975 coup was a watershed in that it was the first time in Nigeria's history that the executors of a coup apportioned political appointments between themselves. The two coups of 1966 were carried out by officers with real and perceived political and military grievances. Despite their murderous intent, they had no interest in personally participating in political activity, and most of the key figures in the 1966 coups did not participate in the new governments established by their revolts. While most perpetrators of the two 1966 coups were not appointed to political positions, the inner circle of the 1975 coup plotters were appointed military governors and SMC members irrespective of seniority. Insiders such as Ibrahim Taiwo, Shehu Yar'Adua, Muhammadu Buhari and Joe Garba all took political appointments. While the plotters could not reasonably be expected to risk their lives for the benefit of other officers, the July 1975 coup seem to have made coup plotting "fashionable." Prior to then, staging coups had been considered dishonorable conduct. The two 1966 coups were regarded as isolated cataclysmic events, but the clean, precise and surgical success of the 1975 coup carried the hidden danger that one day, a different faction of the army would try to emulate it. The plotters became famous household names, moved into plush government offices and became wealthy; thus motivating other officers to try to emulate them. It also demonstrated how simple it was for an army faction to overthrow the government if they were dissatisfied with the government's performance.

MURTALA AS HEAD OF STATE

It was as head of state that Murtala etched his name into Nigerian folklore. Although he was no longer the bellicose firebrand from the July 1966 mutiny, it was clear from the outset that Murtala's character and governing style would be a stark contrast to that of Gowon. While Gowon was diplomatic, conciliatory and cautious, Murtala was brisk, volatile and displayed decisiveness with major issues that bordered on impulse. Gone was the methodical pace of Gowon's administration. All of Murtala's decisions were "with immediate effect." In his almost legendary book *"The Trouble With Nigeria,"* Chinua Achebe tells the story of how on the first morning of Murtala's regime, the notoriously tardy Lagos employees managed to find a way to get to work on time, beating the stifling traffic and transport problems which had always formed part of their standard excuse for being late for work. The new helmsman's ferocious reputation was such that Lagosians dared not cross him on his first day in office. Despite the fact that there were just as many vehicles on the road, Lagosians got to work on time for fear of offending the military strongman from Kano.

As soon as Murtala became the head of state, all of the twelve military governors that served under Gowon were immediately retired. Murtala also ordered a probe into their conduct in office. Ten of the twelve were found to have illegally enriched themselves while in office. Murtala said they had "betrayed the trust and confidence reposed in them by the nation . . . [and] betrayed the ethics of their professions and they are a disgrace to those professions. They are, therefore, all dismissed with ignominy." The retirement of the military governors found guilty of corrupt enrichment was converted to dismissal. Among the dismissed military governors was Brigadier Samuel Ogbemudia of the Mid-West who was appointed to his position by Murtala eight years earlier after Murtala had recaptured the Mid-West Region during the Nigerian civil war. Only Brigadiers Oluwole Rotimi and Mobolaji Johnson were found innocent of corruption.

Military rule had badly distorted the principle of separation of powers between the executive and legislature. Under Gowon, many members of the military government were members of the executive *and* the legislature since the military governors were members of the SMC too. Under Murtala the new military governors were excluded from the SMC as a way of curbing the power of the military governors who under Gowon, ran their states like personal fiefdoms and were difficult to control. This achieved greater separation of powers (although that was the not the reason for excluding them from the SMC). The four GOCs were also included in the SMC. New military governors were appointed as follows:

MILITARY GOVERNORS

State	Governor Under Gowon	Governor Under Murtala
Benue-Plateau	Chief Superintendent of Police Joseph Gomwalk	Colonel Abdullahi Mohammed[1]
East-Central	Ukpabi Asika	Colonel Anthony Ochefu[2]
Kano	Deputy Police Commissioner Audu Bako	Lt-Colonel Sani Bello[3]
Kwara	Brigadier David Bamigboye	Colonel Ibrahim Taiwo
Lagos	Brigadier Mobolaji Johnson	Navy Captain Adekunle Lawal
Mid-West	Brigadier Samuel Ogbemudia	Colonel George Agbazika Innih
North-Central	Brigadier Abba Kyari	Lt-Colonel Usman Jibril
North-East	Brigadier Musa Usman (Air Force)	Lt-Colonel Muhammadu Buhari[4]
North-West	Police Superintendent Usman Faruk	Lt-Colonel Umaru Mohammed
Rivers	Lieutenant Alfred Diete-Spiff (Navy)	Lt-Colonel Zamani Lekwot
South-East	Brigadier Uduokaha Jacob Esuene (Air Force)	Lt-Colonel Paul Omu

West	Brigadier Christopher Oluwole Rotimi	Navy Captain Akintunde Aduwo[5]

[1] Later Chief of Staff at the Presidency.
[2] Ochefu was murdered in 2000.
[3] Ironsi's former ADC who was with him when he was killed in Ibadan in 1966.
[4] Later became head of state.
[5] Later became the Chief of Naval Staff under President Shagari.

A note of interest is that some of the military governors were posted to govern states other than their states of origin. For example the northern officers Colonels Anthony Ochefu and Zamani Lekwot were posted to govern East-Central and Rivers states respectively, even though there were officers from those states available (such as Ebitu Ukiwe). When Major-General Aguiyi-Ironsi proposed the same measure nine years earlier, it was hotly opposed by many northerners and he was killed in a mutiny in which Murtala played the leading part. Nine years on, Murtala was now enacting the same measure he had so bitterly opposed.

Exemplifying the dynamism of the new regime, Akin Aduwo was removed from his post as military governor of the Western Region after only a few weeks in office. Aduwo was replaced by Colonel David Jemibewon. Colonel Ochefu, the military governor of the East Central State, was also removed from his post and retired even though he was one of the primary movers behind the coup that brought Murtala to power. Ochefu's retirement was not on account of his political performance, but because of misconduct in his prior military duties.[1] The move was intended to demonstrate that the new regime would not tolerate underperformance and that no one was untouchable. In another delicate ethnic balancing act, Ochefu was replaced by Colonel John Atom Kpera who was from the same state as Ochefu. Kpera was a surviving executor of the "Exercise Damisa" Nzeogwu coup in January 1966.

Apart from the Commissioner of Finance Shehu Shagari and the Commissioner for Mines and Power Ali Monguno, all of Gowon's civilian ministers were also found guilty of corrupt enrichment and were stripped of illegally obtained assets. Among those found to have corruptly enriched himself was the veteran nationalist politician Anthony Enahoro, who several years later would become a staunch opponent of military rule. Of the military governors, Ogbemudia forfeited 11 properties in the Mid-West Region, Bako forfeited 23 properties across Nigeria, Asika 5 properties, Gomwalk 6 developed plots, Diete-Spiff 18 developed plots in Port Harcourt, Faruk 14 buildings, Johnson forfeited plot 9, W.N.H.C. Estate in Ikeja, and Bamigboye, Usman and Kyari forfeited 4 properties each. Esuene had to reimburse N25, 672 and Edwin Clark (a federal commissioner) lost 16 properties including eight cinema houses, an undeveloped plot at Ijora, a supermarket and other developed plots in Warri, Benin and Lagos. Other public officials made to forfeit properties and assets included J.E. Adetoro, Philip Asiodu, J.H. Bassey, V.I. Bello, I.M. Damcida, O. Ahmadu-Suka, and F.A. Ijewere. Bello and Ijewere had to refund N59,776 and N186,641 respectively.[2] Much of the ill-gotten assets seized by Murtala were returned several years later by the regime of General Ibrahim Babangida for reasons that have never been fully explained. This decision by Babangida was all the more baffling, given that he was a member of the regime that stripped the assets in the first place. The Babangida regime issued the Forfeiture of Assets (Release of Certain Forfeited Properties etc) Decree

---

1 Colonel Domkat Bali was chairman of the panel that recommended Ochefu's retirement.
2 *Newswatch*, February 7, 1994.

Number 24 of 1993 which returned some of the forfeited properties to Faruk and his wife Asika, Gomwalk, Kam Selem, Adetoro, Asiodu, Bako, Johnson and Usman. The decree was silent on Ogbemudia, Bamigboye, Diette-Spiff, Clark, Kyari and Esuene.

THE MASS PURGE

Repeating the mantra of military governments all the way back to Major-General Aguiyi-Ironsi's regime, Murtala declared his government a "corrective" regime. After dismantling the inner core of Gowon's regime, Murtala turned his gaze to the civil service. A massive onslaught was instituted against public sector corruption and in-efficiency on a scale never seen before in Africa. This led to a wave of dismissals and retirements of over 10,000 public officials who were summarily dismissed or retired on the grounds of inefficiency, corruption or old age. Long serving officials considered "part of the furniture" were not spared. The esteemed long serving Chairman of the Federal Public Service Commission Alhaji Sule Katagum was dismissed and replaced by Professor Okoronkwo Kesandu Ogan. The army and police were not exempt from the gale of retirements. Over two hundred army officers were retired or dismissed including the director of the armed forces' medical corps Brigadier Austen-Peters and the Ambassador to Iran and Turkey Brigadier George Kurubo. Clara Ogbemudia was among the prominent police officers retired (she is the wife of Brigadier Ogbemudia, the former military governor of the Mid-West Region). The campaign was launched not just at senior personnel. Public sector janitors, gardeners and cleaners also found themselves retired. The dismissed officials were not permitted to challenge their ter-minations or claim unfair dismissal. Such rights were suspended as part of the purge, which was eventually halted in November 1975.

The remaining officers detained for their role in the civil war and the January 1966 coup were also released (Lt-Colonel Ochei, Major Chukwuka, and Captains Oji, Adeleke, and Ude). However, Igbo soldiers were still sufficiently distrusted after the January 1966 coup that none of them was appointed a military governor, and only one (navy officer Ndubuisi Kanu) was in the SMC. In another act typical of his contradictory nature, Murtala restored benefits to the family of Major-General Aguiyi-Ironsi, his former GOC and head of state whom he had led a rebellion against almost a decade earlier.

In response to national debate on the military's continual hold on governance, Murtala announced plans for the military to disengage from politics, and that Nigeria would be returned to civilian democratic rule on October 1ˢᵗ 1979. A Constitution Drafting Committee (CDC) would debate and prepare a new constitution. Anxious to avoid the blatant ethnic based party politics of the 1960s, Murtala told the CDC that the SMC would prefer it if they came up with a system of government without political parties. In the end several "new" political parties emerged as clones of the parties of the 1960s. One of the justifications for the coup that removed Gowon was that Gowon had postponed the return to civilian rule. If that was a genuine motivat-ing factor for deposing Gowon, it is perplexing that on taking power, the officers who overthrew Gowon then announced a *four year* transition to civil rule program.

CREATION OF STATES

The number of states was increased from twelve to nineteen with the creation of seven new states, which were carved out of existing states. Firstly the Yoruba domi-nated Western State (which had since the creation of Nigeria been the only ethnically homogenous state) was split into three separate states to be known as Ogun, Ondo and Oyo states. The Igbo South-Eastern State was split into Anambra and Imo states, the North-Western state was split into Niger and Sokoto states, Benue-Plateau state was split into Benue and Plateau states and the North-Eastern state was split into three new states of Bauchi, Borno and Gongola. Seven states remained unchanged (except for minor boundary adjustments): Kano, Kwara, Lagos, Mid-West, North-Central, Rivers and South-Eastern. All nineteen states were given new names without geographical links in order to erase memories of past political ties and emotional or regional attachments.

New military governors were appointed to the new states as follows:
- Anambra — Colonel John Atom Kpera
- Bauchi — Lt-Colonel Bello Kaliel[1]
- Benue — Lt-Colonel Abdullahi Shelleng
- Gongola — Lt-Colonel M.D. Jega
- Imo — Lt-Commander Godwin Ndubuisi Kanu
- Niger — Navy Commander Murtala Nyako[2]
- Ogun — Lt-Colonel Saidu Ayodele Balogun
- Ondo — Squadron Leader Ita David Ikpeme
- Oyo — Colonel David Jemibewon

Foreign Affairs

Gowon's regime had maintained a policy of "non alignment," preferring to stay neutral in the simmering "cold war" between the world's then two super powers: the United States and the Soviet Union. Gowon's regime bought weapons from the Soviets while remaining on cordial terms with Western nations. However, Murtala's regime embarked on a more assertive foreign policy. Contrary to the wishes of the USA, it unilaterally recognized the Marxist Movimento Popular de Libertação de Angola (Popular Movement for the Liberation of Angola, or MPLA) as the legitimate government of Angola. Murtala then rallied other African countries to follow suit, and backed his diplomatic action with massive financial aid to the MPLA. Western powers became concerned that the new regime in Africa's richest country was galvanizing African countries to recognize a government with communist ideology. The United States, the Central Intelligence Agency (CIA) and apartheid South Africa gave financial and military assistance to the rival Frente Nacional de Libertação de Angola (National Front for the Liberation of Angola, or FNLA), and União Nacional para a Independência Total de Angola (National Union for the Total Independence of Angola, or UNITA) movements. This, from the Nigerian vantage point, placed the United States on the same side as the Apartheid regime in South Africa. Relations between Nigeria and the United States became further strained when the administration of President Gerald Ford urged other African countries not to follow Nigeria's lead in recognizing the MPLA. This enraged the FMG which refused to entertain a visit by United States Secretary of State Henry Kissinger, and Murtala declared, "Gone are the days when Africa will ever bow to the threat of any so called superpower."

---

1 Kaliel later became the commander of the Brigade of Guards under President Shagari.
2 Nyako later became the Chief of Naval Staff under the regime of Ibrahim Babangida, and later the democratically elected Governor of Adamawa state. His wife Justice Binta Murtala-Nyako is a Federal High Court judge.

ABUJA: A NEW CAPITAL

Another ambitious plan saw the FMG announce the relocation of the country's federal capital away from the crowded, teeming, dirty, polluted and crime-ridden Lagos. With its exploding population and miles of traffic jams which slowed down commerce, Lagos was thought to be an unsuitable city to serve as capital for the world's first anticipated black superpower. Little did Murtala know that he would one day become a victim of the Lagos traffic. His regime decided to move the capital to a location near Abuja in the centre of Nigeria. Although heralded at the time, construction work in Abuja proved to be a massive strain on the federal budget and a source of massive corruption.

Justice Akinola Aguda was the head of the panel that recommended Abuja to the FMG as the site of the new capital. Aguda remarked decades later that, "Those of us who are still alive will continue to take the blame for recommending the relocation of the federal capital from Lagos to virgin land which we thought would be a blessing but has now turned to be the tragedy of Abuja."[1]

BUDGET STRAINS

During the civil war, the Nigerian army grew from a light colonial army of approximately 10,000 into a bloated and heavily armed force of 250,000. An army of that size was viewed as superfluous in peacetime, an internal security risk and a potential source of future instability. Some elements of the army were perceived as little more than armed political parties that could threaten the existence of a future civilian government. Defense became, and remained, the largest budget item. In the year prior to military rule (1965–66), defense accounted for less than ten percent of the federal government's expenditure. A decade later defense constituted over forty five percent of federal government expenditure. Brigadier Danjuma explained that ninety percent of defense spending was on soldiers' salaries and complained that "since the civil war, the Nigerian army has been run as a social service, maintaining and paying an exceedingly large body of men that we do not really need and whom we cannot properly equip....We are about the only army in the world where serving soldiers die of old age."[2] Several leading figures in the FMG therefore proposed a reduction of the army's manpower in order to lessen defense expenditure's strain on the federal budget. The Commissioner for Defense Brigadier Bisalla proposed reducing the size of the army. Brigadier Danjuma added detail to the proposal by articulating a demobilization program to reduce the army's numerical strength below 100,000. Colonel Isa Bukar also advocated demobilization. However, demobilization was a potentially explosive issue and many were skeptical that it could be carried out without accusations of ethnic bias or discrimination. Demobilization was also fraught with danger and Gowon had trod very carefully around the issue of throwing thousands of men with no career prospects or skills onto the job market. The most notable expertise of some of the field commissioned soldiers from the civil war was their proficiency in the use of firearms. While he was untouchable in the eyes of the civilian population, Murtala's demobilization plan (although justified on economic grounds) upset some in his primary constituency: the army. Some officers were also not overjoyed at the prospect of being removed from the army and thrown into an uncertain life on the employment market.

1 *New African*, November 1997.
2 *The Times*, July 22, 1976.

THE BEGINNING OF THE END

By his swashbuckling decisiveness, Murtala became the darling of the Nigerian public and he gave the country a dynamic sense of direction and purpose. As stories of his no-nonsense reputation began to spread, Nigerians began to feel at last that they had the dynamic leader they so craved. While riding the crest of the wave of popular opinion, Murtala made the first of two mistakes that may have cost him his life. Murtala was Nigeria's first military strongman. Both Gowon and Aguiyi-Ironsi governed benevolently by consensus. Gowon was always careful to seek out opposing viewpoints in an effort not to alienate any faction (although this attribute made him ultra-cautious and reluctant to carry out reforms). Murtala was the first Nigerian military leader to rule by force of will. His uncomplicated black and white approach to issues carried the danger that he would alienate a military or civilian faction somewhere along the line. When then Lt-Colonel Yakubu Gowon became the head of state in 1966, he waited till the days preceding the outbreak of the Nigerian civil war in 1967 before promoting himself to Major-General. After the war finished, Gowon promoted himself again and became Nigeria's first four star General. These promotions were necessary at first, in order to stabilize Gowon's position as head of state despite the presence of officers having superior rank in his regime (Commodore Joseph Wey and Colonel Robert Adebayo). For several months, Murtala's government functioned with four Brigadiers at its apex (Murtala, Olusegun Obasanjo, T.Y. Danjuma and Iliya Bisalla). However, in January 1976, Murtala's regime embarked on a bizarre promotion exercise which served no purpose other than to create tensions within the regime. Murtala was promoted to a four star General, his deputy Olusegun Obasanjo and the Chief of Army Staff Theophilus Danjuma, were both promoted to Lt-General. The promotions of Murtala and Obasanjo had retroactive effect and were backdated to July 29, 1975 (the date that Gowon was overthrown). The other promotions took effect from January 1, 1976. The other officers promoted from brigadier to major-general were:

Emmanuel Abisoye
Martin Adamu
Henry Adefope
Alani Akinrinade
Iliya Bisalla
Ibrahim Haruna
Gibson Jalo
John Obada
James Oluleye
Olufemi Olutoye
Mohammed Shuwa
Michael Adelanwa* (navy officer — promoted to Rear Admiral)
John Yisa Doko* (air force officer — promoted to Air Commodore)

According to the Commissioner for Information Major-General Ibrahim Haruna, these promotions had been in the pipeline for several years but were kept in suspense as Gowon was reluctant to authorize them. The affected officers were therefore simply paid their salary at a higher rank while they kept their gazetted rank, and a decision on whether to confirm the promotions remained pending.[1]

---

1 Panter-Brick, *Soldiers and Oil: The Political Transformation of Nigeria*, page 86.

However, the promotions caused discontent and were extremely controversial within the army. The most controversial promotion may have been that of the Commissioner for Defense Iliya Bisalla, who was promoted to Major-General only. This limited promotion for Bisalla discombobulated the army and Ministry of Defense chain of command as it made Bisalla subordinate in rank to the Chief of Army Staff Lt-General Danjuma. Bisalla understandably felt slighted and humiliated that a former subordinate of his was now his superior. Moreover, the limited promotion for Bisalla had little logic as Danjuma's post as Chief of Army Staff was within, and under, Bisalla's Ministry of Defense. This meant that Bisalla was now outranked by an officer that was supposed to be working under him. The promotions created bad blood between Danjuma and Bisalla, and gave the impression that a favored clique was developing within the SMC. Bisalla complained vehemently about his treatment. Murtala and Obasanjo met with him and explained rather unconvincingly that his rank was without prejudice to his position as Commissioner of Defense. However, they refused to budge and Bisalla remained in his rank of Major-General. Bisalla's complaints did not go unnoticed, and would come back to haunt him. Bisalla had unwittingly begun to dig his own grave.

The haphazard promotions placed many officers in positions of subordination to their former juniors. Danjuma was also promoted over the head of his other seniors such as Mohammed Shuwa, Ibrahim Haruna, Gibson Jalo, James Oluleye, Godwin Ally and Olufemi Olutoye. Senior officers who were not on good terms with the junta and/or with Murtala were also controversially excluded from the SMC. These included officers such as Olufemi Olutoye and Mohammed Shuwa who were senior to the leading figures in the regime but found themselves leapfrogged by their juniors and excluded from the FMG's most important decision making body.

There was no need for the promotion exercise, as at that time there were no officers in the army above the rank of brigadier. The promotions also created new spheres of discontent and professional insecurity amongst middle ranks that were excluded from the exercise. Subjectively dispossessed officers from Gowon's home state posed a threat to the regime in the same way that dispossessed politicians engaged in subversive activities which eventually brought down Major-General Aguiyi-Ironsi's regime in 1966. It was claimed that prior discontent amongst middle ranks led to a Christmas Eve coup plot that was detected and defused.[1] If there really was such a plot, it was managed with an uncharacteristic lack of fanfare and severity.

Murtala's second fatal mistake was his failure to take his personal security more seriously. Perhaps due to his popularity, Murtala never bothered with the massive security detail characteristic of heads of state. He continued to live at his house at number 6 Second Avenue in Ikoyi, Lagos, a house he had lived in for over a decade. Murtala mingled with the masses in the teeming streets of Lagos and drove around town without a motorcade. He would startle others by arriving unannounced at various locations without security. In early 1976 Murtala's deputy, Lt-General Obasanjo, urged him to take his personal security more seriously. Murtala refused replied that if anyone was planning to overthrow him, then "if they succeed in killing all of us, good luck to them" in running the affairs of Nigeria. He perhaps sealed his own fate with those words.

---

1 Ibid., page 130.

CHAPTER 16. FRIDAY THE 13TH: THE WATERSHED COUP OF 1976

Security and routine do not go together. Having dispensed with sizeable personal security and a motorcade, on Friday 13th February 1976, Murtala departed for work along his usual route on George Street. Shortly after 8 a.m. his car crawled in the infamous Lagos traffic near the Federal Secretariat at Ikoyi in Lagos, and a group of soldiers emerged from an adjacent petrol station, rushed over to the car and unleashed a volley of gunshots which killed Murtala, his ADC Lieutenant Akintunde Akinsehinwa and his driver Sergeant Adamu Minchika. His orderly Staff Sergeant Michael Otuwe was badly wounded but later recovered. The gunmen were so ruthless that one of them exhausted an entire magazine of ammunition while firing at Murtala's car, walked away to fit a new magazine, and emptied that one too into the car and its occupants.

Unbeknown to Murtala, as he made his way to work that day, a group of assassins including Lt-Colonel Dimka, Major Ibrahim Rabo, Captain Malaki Parwang and Lieutenant William Seri were lying in wait for him. Each man had a different task. Captain Parwang was the "lookout" and his job was to signal the others when Murtala's car approached. Seri aimed his shots at Murtala, while Dimka instructed Rabo to aim his shots at Murtala's ADC Lieutenant Akintunde Akinsehinwa.

After only six months in office, General Murtala Muhammed was assassinated in yet another military coup. Lagos traffic was almost brought to a standstill and chaos reigned as panic-stricken civilians frantically rushed home. Shortly after Murtala was murdered, Lt-Colonel Bukar Suka Dimka (the head of the army's physical training corps) rushed up the road to the nearby Nigerian Broadcasting Corporation (NBC) from where he made the following nationwide broadcast that was repeated intermittently and interspersed with martial music:

> Good morning fellow Nigerians, this is Lt-Colonel B.S. Dimka of the Nigerian army calling. I bring you good tidings. Murtala Muhammed's hypocrisy has been detected. His government is now overthrown by the young revolutionaries. All the military governors have no powers over the states they now govern. The state affairs will be run by the military brigade commanders until further

notice. All commissioners are sacked, except for the armed forces and police commissioners who will be redeployed. All senior military officers should remain calm in their respective spots. No divisional commanders will issue orders to his formations until further notice. Any attempt to foil this plan from any quarter will be met with death. You are warned, it is all over the 19 states. All acts of resistance will be met with death. Everyone should be calm. Please stay by your radio for further announcements. All borders, airports and sea ports are closed until further notice. Curfew is imposed from 6 a.m. to 6 p.m. Thank you. We are all together.

The clumsy syntax and inadvertent imposition of a "6 a.m. to 6 p.m." curfew in the above speech is an appropriate barometer of this coup (Dimka obviously meant 6 p.m. to 6 a.m., but got the hours the wrong way round).

Colonel Ibrahim Taiwo, military governor of Kwara State, was murdered three miles outside Offa after being abducted by Lieutenant Zagni and some NCOs including Sergeants Rege and Bala Javan. His body was discovered in a shallow grave outside Ilorin. Troops led by Major Gagara mutinied and took over the 26th infantry battalion in Ibadan, the 2 division training school at Offa, and deployed at strategic locations including radio stations. However, they failed to capture or kill Colonel David Jemibewon, the Oyo State military governor. Other government members had lucky escapes. In a case of mistaken identity, the mutineers ambushed and shot up the car of Colonel Ray Dumuje on Awolowo Road, thinking that Lt-General Obasanjo was inside. Obasanjo hid at the home of his civilian friend Chief S.B. Bakare and monitored the situation via phone calls to M.D. Yusuf and Lt-General Danjuma. Obasanjo later claimed that Danjuma escaped his would-be assassins due to his routine as an early riser, by passing through the designated murder point before the selected gunman was in place. However, in subsequent statements, Dimka stated that he had ordered Lieutenant Lawrence Garba (the officer detailed to ambush Lt-General Danjuma) to shoot only if Danjuma was unaccompanied. Garba later reported to Dimka that Danjuma was travelling with Colonels Gordon Alabi Isama and Domkat Bali, and the Chief of Naval Staff Rear-Admiral Adelanwa (the accounts of Danjuma and Bali also corroborated that they travelled with Isama and Adelanwa on that fateful morning).

Defense Headquarters and Bonny Camp

Lt-General Danjuma and Major-General Bisalla were both working in the defense headquarters. Danjuma left his office at the vulnerable and insecure defense headquarters to set up a temporary base in the office of Major John Shagaya at Bonny Camp to plan a counter-attack against the mutineers. The mutineers amateurishly did not disrupt or sever communication networks. Danjuma was in continuous telephone contact with senior officers and the military governors; and he was able to rally loyal officers without having to step outside Bonny Camp.

Bonny Camp became the unofficial temporary operating headquarters of surviving members of the government. Several senior officers congregated there — including Colonel Ibrahim Babangida, Colonel Domkat Bali, Joe Garba, John Shagaya, Paul Tarfa (Provost Marshal), Olu Bajowa (Quartermaster-General), John Yisa Doko, Gordon Alabi-Isama, Tunde Togun, and Joe Kasai. As Danjuma addressed the officers and gave operational orders, he was unaware that soldiers within the plot were among those he was addressing (these included Majors Joe Kasai and Ola Ogunmekan).

In response to Dimka's broadcast claiming that all military governors had been dismissed, Colonel Isa Bukar unwisely placed Brigadier George Innih, the military governor of Bendel State under house arrest (under troops led by Lieutenant Peter Temlong). Bukar would later pay dearly for that decision. When Lt-General Danjuma called Bukar to ask him why he had Innih arrested, Bukar replied that he did so in response to Dimka's broadcast. Danjuma asked Bukar, "Do you take orders from broadcasts?"[1] and told him to rescind Innih's arrest.

Then came several gestures which, although small in isolation, demonstrated Murtala's popularity across Nigeria. All the army's GOCs were in Lagos attending a conference. From Lagos the GOC of the elite 1 division in Kaduna: Major-General Alani Akinrinade, sent a message to his division in Kaduna proclaiming his loyalty to Murtala and disassociating himself from the coup. Akinrinade's message was relayed by Lt-Colonel Ibrahim Bako. Messages of support also came in from other locations. Lt-Colonel E.K. Fakunle re-affirmed his loyalty to Murtala from Kano. Lt-Colonels Usman Jubrin and Umaru Mohammed, military governors of Kaduna and Sokoto states also did the same, as did John Atom Kpera, the military governor of Anambra State, who was ordered to do so by Danjuma, and to relay the order to neighboring states. Affirmations of support for Murtala were not confined to the army. Students at the University of Benin marched into the streets and staged an angry demonstration against the soldiers that killed their hero. They also burned effigies of Dimka.

Loyal troops moved into position to seal off the Ministry of Defense and communications buildings. Yohanna Madaki and Sabo Aliyu travelled round Lagos (dressed in mufti) to carry out reconnaissance on the rebels. Some soldiers in the Brigade of Guards under Captains Abdullahi Sarki Mukhtar[2] and Mohammed Abdullahi Wase[3] also mobilized to resist the coup. Two officers and boyhood friends whose lives would later cross paths in deadly fashion, Colonels Babangida and Vatsa, each made separate contributions against the coup. From Calabar, Vatsa pledged his continuing loyalty to the government and disassociated himself from the coup.

THE CONTRIBUTION OF BABANGIDA

Colonel Ibrahim Babangida was dispatched by Lt-General Danjuma to dislodge Dimka from the radio station. To avoid detection, Danjuma ordered Babangida to travel on a motorcycle. This was going to be a dangerous mission for Babangida as he had been marked for death by the plotters (he was to have been ambushed by a team of soldiers under Lieutenant Peter Cigari). It was also deeply personal as Dimka was a good friend and colleague of his. Dimka even attended Babangida's wedding several years earlier. According to Babangida he missed the hit squad assigned to kill him due to an impromptu change of route on February 13:

> I was living at No. 19 Ikoyi Crescent and in setting out to Defense Headquarters, my driver could either take the right and go on to Osborne or take the left and go on to Kingsway Road. On this morning, as I saw him indicating a right turn, by sheer I don't know what, I said, no, go left. And that was how we just avoided the path of danger.[4]

En route to the radio station Babangida decided to check the situation at Ikeja cantonment. During the July 1966 coup, the Ikeja cantonment was used as an unofficial base by the coup plotters (several of whom were now involved in this current coup). Babangida entered the cantonment via a quiet rear entrance and proceeded to

1 Lindsay Barrett, *Danjuma: The Making of a General*, page 85.
2 Later Major-General and National Security Adviser.
3 Later Colonel, and Military Administrator of Kano State.
4 Gabriel E Umoden, *The Babangida Years*, page 29.

the residence of his friend and air force officer Hamza Abdullahi.[1] From Abdullahi's residence Babangida rang other officers to confirm their disposition and that the cantonment was not in rebel hands. He dispensed with the motorcycle, borrowed Abdullahi's car and contacted Lt-Colonel Chris Ugokwe. With the assistance of Lt-Colonel Joshua Dogonyaro, Babangida and Ugokwe mobilized vehicles, troops and weapons to head back to the NBC radio station. Before departing for the NBC, Babangida telephoned his concerned wife to reassure her that he was unharmed.

BABANGIDA AND DIMKA AT THE RADIO STATION

When Babangida walked into the radio station he was stopped by Dimka's sentry. Dimka overruled his sentry and instructed him to let Babangida enter. Dimka had a rifle in his hand. Babangida was unarmed and at this stage was unaware that Murtala had already been assassinated. The famous Nigerian journalist Bisi Lawrence was at the radio station and he and some of his colleagues were locked in an office on Dimka's orders to allow Dimka and Babangida to speak privately.[2] Babangida's first observation was that, "When I got in there, those boys were terribly drunk. Only God knows what they took. The slightest thing would have provoked unnecessary blood-letting."[3] After assuring Dimka that he was unarmed and did not come to harm him, Babangida spoke to Dimka in Hausa and tried to talk Dimka down, playing on Dimka's knowledge of Babangida's family and the fact that he had a wife. Babangida told Dimka that if Dimka wanted to kill him, he would be pleased to die at the hands of a friend who would surely look after his wife and children. Dimka sarcastically asked Babangida if he had come to play "Chukwuma and Nwawo" with him. This was an ironic reference by Dimka to the way in which a decade earlier, Lt-Colonel Conrad Nwawo came to Kaduna to negotiate with, and convince Major Chukwuma Nzeogwu to give himself up. Babangida might have been reassured of his personal safety by his long standing knowledge of Dimka. Dimka then boastfully informed Babangida that Babangida had been marked for death by the other plotters but that he (Dimka) did not want Babangida killed. He also added for good measure that if he wanted Babangida dead, he could have killed him the moment he walked into the radio station. Babangida fell into the plotters' bad books by (in their opinion) his undeserved elevation to the SMC. The *tête à tête* continued until Dimka asked Babangida to relay a message to the Chief of Army Staff Lt-General Danjuma. Dimka realized by now that the coup lacked support, and he asked Babangida to request from Danjuma a written amnesty for the coup plotters. Babangida departed but informed Dimka that he would return at 3 p.m. Babangida reported back to Danjuma and was ordered to return to the NBC station, storm it with armored corps troops, and flush out the rebels.

Meanwhile Dimka left the radio station and went to see his accomplice Lt-Colonel Tense. At Tense's house, Tense urged Dimka to contact Colonel Garba and Major-Generals Oluleye and Shuwa, to see whether they were willing to act as intermediaries to Lt-General Danjuma. When Dimka returned to the NBC he was reminded that his earlier broadcast (including his imposition of a daytime curfew) was still playing. Dimka was preparing to make another recording to correct the curfew time when

---

1 Ten years later Abdullahi's friendship with Babangida was rewarded when Babangida appointed him Minister of the Federal Capital Territory.

2 *Sunday Vanguard*, July 16, 1995.

3 *Pointblanknews.com*, Friday, 25 January 2008.

---

armored vehicles showed up again. Dimka and Lieutenant Lawrence Garba (who was inside the radio station with him) initially thought that it might be Babangida returning with a message from Lt-General Danjuma. The armored vehicles were not carrying messengers, nor did they bring "good tidings," to use Dimka's phraseology.

FIREFIGHT AT THE RADIO STATION

Babangida had returned with armed troops including Chris Ugokwe, John Shagaya, Mike Otuwa, Jack Ikentubosin and James Ojokojo. The loyalist troops re-captured and cordoned off the radio station after engaging Dimka's men in a fierce but brief ten minute gun battle. Major Ibrahim Rabo clumsily walked into the hands of loyal troops at the NBC and was arrested by Captain Yomi Williams. He was taken to Bonny Camp and under interrogation, revealed the identities of his accom-plices. There were civilian casualties during the gun battle. As the firefight continued, Lieutenant Lawrence Garba urged Dimka to go into an inner room for shelter, or to escape. Dimka initially refused and agreed only when Garba threatened to abandon him. In circumstances that have never been fully explained, Dimka somehow man-aged to drive away from the radio station unscathed and fled. From the radio station, Dimka went home. Someone must have been aware of his location, because press men arrived at his house on Macpherson Road to request an interview. He left his home before long and randomly drove round Lagos — first going to the airport, and then to Flight Lieutenant Akinfenwa's house. However, many of his co-conspirators were arrested.

Babangida later realized that, besides Dimka, many of the other plotters were also his close friends and colleagues (including Joe Kasai, Alfa Aliyu, Kola Afolabi and Ola Ogunmekan). The sense of betrayal he felt at being pencilled for elimination by his own friends shaped the prism through which he viewed future military coups. He was especially hurt that his friend Clement Dabang had urged the other plotters to kill him.[1] Babangida's encounter with Dimka at the radio station nevertheless thrust him into the public spotlight, greatly raised his profile and marked him out as a rising star in the army.

At 5 p.m. the FMG announced that it had suppressed a coup attempt. All borders were closed and a dusk-to-dawn curfew imposed. The coup attempt was doomed from the beginning, even if it had not been so incoherently planned and clumsily executed. The SMC had many veteran coup "specialists" who could not be dislodged without a gargantuan effort.

A second speech had been drafted for Dimka but he never got to read it. Ac-cording to Dimka, it was to be a replica (with minor variations) of Colonel Ignatius Acheampong's coup speech after he deposed Kofi Busia in Ghana in 1972.

SUCCESSION

Murtala was buried in Kano. Senior SMC members such as Lt-Generals Obasan-jo and Danjuma and Major-General Obada saluted his coffin in a military farewell prior to its departure from Lagos. Thousands thronged the streets of Murtala's home-town Kano as he was buried on February 14 in a funeral attended by SMC dignitaries including Major-General Bisalla and M.D. Yusuf, and former SMC member Major-General (retired) Hassan Katsina. Mindful of the dangerous power vacuum that oc-curred after the assassination of Major-General Aguiyi-Ironsi in July 1966, the SMC

---

1 Gabriel Umoden, *The Babangida Years*, page 33.

promptly met to choose a new head of state. The leading candidates were the Chief of Staff (Supreme Headquarters) Lt-General Obasanjo and the Chief of Army Staff Lt-General Danjuma. Obasanjo was the more senior and experienced of the two. A sizeable faction of SMC members and senior officers including the Chief of Air Staff John Yisa Doko and Colonel Domkat Bali nonetheless favored Danjuma. Doko argued that having put down the coup, Danjuma enjoyed the loyalty and confidence of the army. He considered Obasanjo an outsider that would not command the same loyalty as Danjuma. Obasanjo himself endorsed Danjuma's candidacy. Danjuma insisted that the SMC should follow seniority by permitting Murtala's deputy Lt-General Obasanjo to succeed Murtala as head of state. The disillusioned Obasanjo refused and said that he no longer had faith in the loyalty of the Nigerian army. He offered to retire and let Danjuma become head of state. Danjuma wisely declined. The coup plotters were like Danjuma, Christians from northern minority ethnic groups. Danjuma doubtless remembered what happened to Major-General Aguiyi-Ironsi when ten years earlier, Aguiyi-Ironsi agreed to become head of state after officers from the far north were killed in a military coup executed by officers mostly from his region. Some northern Muslims were already speculating that the coup was a premeditated assault by middle belt Christians against a Muslim head of state. Despite Obasanjo's reluctance, Danjuma was unmoved and insisted that he should succeed Murtala.

Although he was visibly shaken and apprehensive, Lt-General (later General) Olusegun Obasanjo relented and succeeded Murtala as head of state. However, before accepting he sought an assurance from Danjuma that Danjuma would rally the army behind Obasanjo. He pledged to continue with the policies of his predecessor. The emotional strain got to Obasanjo and he burst into tears upon his appointment. Obasanjo made a broadcast to the nation eulogizing Murtala:

> We are once again passing through a critical period in the history of this country. For me personally, this has been one of the saddest moments of my life. The Supreme Military Council has already announced the assassination of His Excellency General Murtala Muhammed. We all mourn the passing away of one of the greatest sons of Nigeria. I had the privilege of serving as the Chief of Staff, Supreme Headquarters under him, and I have no doubt in my mind that the late General Muhammed gave this country a unique sense of direction and purpose. We are now obliged to continue with this policy laid down by the Supreme Military Council under the dynamic leadership of the late General Muhammed.

Now that Obasanjo was head of state, the post of Chief of Staff (Supreme Headquarters) was vacant. The SMC was keen to assuage Hausa–Fulani feelings after Murtala's assassination and wanted to place another Hausa–Fulani soldier in a prominent position. However, there were no Hausa–Fulani officers senior enough to fill in the strata between the new head of state Obasanjo and the Chief of Army Staff Danjuma. The two leading Hausa–Fulani officers in contention were Colonels Buhari and Yar'Adua (Yar'Adua was out of the country when the coup took place). Contrary to popular perception, Buhari and Yar'Adua were not the most senior Hausa–Fulani officers at the time. Colonels Mohammed Remawa (from Katsina) and Abbas Wali (from Kano) were still in active service but none of them was a serious contender as they were not part of the junta that overthrew Gowon. The situation required not just a pacification of volatile Hausa–Fulani civil opinion, but the placation and inclusion of Murtala Muhammed's military constituency in the highest levels of the SMC. Buhari and Yar'Adua were the logical candidates as both were instrumental participants in the coup that brought Murtala to power, both were loyal to Murtala, and closely identified with his ideology. Both Buhari and Yar'Adua were Fulani officers from the same geographic region in north-western Nigeria. Buhari was from Daura and was the military governor of Borno State, while the Sandhurst trained Yar'Adua was from Katsina and was then the federal Commissioner for Transport. Although acknowledged as hard working and principled, Buhari was edged out by Yar'Adua for a number of reasons. Firstly Buhari was thought too inflexible for the post. According to Danjuma:

> [Buhari] is one of the most upright army officers that the Nigerian army has produced — very clean, a very strict officer. Unfortunately for him, he served under me for a short time in Port Harcourt and I observed that he was a very inflexible person. I reasoned that Buhari any day could be a first class Chief of Army Staff. Why waste him in a political post? Why shorten his career because if he became Chief of Staff, he would have to leave at the end of the tenure. Why waste him there? Besides, I observed that he was too rigid, he was too inflexible to hold a political post. If you are in politics, you must be flexible; you must compromise from time to time. In politics, they call it pragmatism. But in the military, if you are pragmatic, it is regarded as a weakness. I said no, not Buhari. Shehu, I didn't know him well except that I knew that, of all the officers of his rank, he was the most politicized. So, sending a politicized army officer to a political post, I thought, was a good thing. That was how I named Shehu the next Chief of Staff [Supreme Headquarters].[1]

Yar'Adua was the son of the former Minister for Lagos and prominent NPC politician Alhaji Musa Yar'Adua, and he was a nephew of former Chief of Staff (Army) Major-General Hassan Usman Katsina. As such, Yar'Adua's name was the more recognizable and acceptable among Hausa–Fulani ruling circles. Proving that no lessons had been learnt from the previous promotion exercise that partly served as a motivating factor for the coup, Lt-Colonel Shehu Musa Yar'Adua,[2] a Fulani officer from an aristocratic northern family, was catapulted over the heads of over a dozen non Hausa–Fulani officers, promoted to brigadier (and later again to major-general) and appointed to fill the position of Chief of Staff, Supreme Headquarters which had been vacated by Obasanjo. So embarrassed were some of the senior officers he leap-frogged that they reported directly to Obasanjo as a way of avoiding the humiliation of reporting to their former subordinate Yar'Adua. Buhari's time would come later. Yar'Adua's ADC Mustapha Jokolo would come to prominence in subsequent coups. Lt-Colonel Mohammed Magoro succeeded Yar'Adua as federal Commissioner for Transport.

DIPLOMATIC RIFTS: CONFRONTATION WITH THE UK AND THE UNITED STATES

Seven days of national mourning were declared in Murtala's honor. At the end of these seven days, grief stricken Nigerians were given a public holiday. Investigations after the coup caused a public furor when it was disclosed that Dimka (with gun toting soldiers in tow) visited the British High Commission while the coup was in progress. Dimka informed the British High Commissioner Sir Martin Le Quesne that there had been a change of government and asked him to relay a message to General Gowon, asking Gowon to travel from London to Togo. Although Le Quesne refused to relay the message and declared that he would not be Dimka's messenger, Dimka's visit severely compromised his position and would later cost him his job. The FMG

---

1 *Guardian*, February 17, 2008.
2 His younger brother is the current president.

later claimed that Dimka visited Le Quesne at the High Commission at 9:15 a.m. but that Le Quesne did not report the visit to the Nigerian authorities until 1 p.m. (nearly four hours later). Le Quesne claimed he reported Dimka's visit without undue delay. However, the time lag was believed by senior regime figures, who were angered that Le Quesne allowed Dimka into the British High Commission premises at all.

News of Dimka's visit was published by the news agency Reuters, who might have obtained the story because they were located in the same Campbell Street office building as the British High Commission. The High Commission affair allied to suspected CIA foreknowledge of the coup caused anti-British and anti-American sentiment. Matters came to a head when at the height of the national mourning for the slain head of state, Le Quesne insensitively reminded Nigerians that he expected them to pay for the damage caused to the British High Commission's windows by Nigerian demonstrators. Although correct in principle, Sir Martin's reminder was poorly timed and insensitive to the mourning of his hosts. This proved to be the last straw for the government and Sir Martin was declared *persona non grata* and told to leave the country. The diplomatic rift caused by these affairs lingered and in the case of the United States, was not fully normalized until Jimmy Carter visited Nigeria in 1978 and became the first United States President in history to visit sub-Saharan Africa.

The FMG seemed to be lashing out in all directions. Reuters' Lagos bureau was also closed after it falsely reported that sectional murders were taking place in Kano in response to the coup. The Reuters Lagos bureau chief Colin Fox was also deported. Despite the FMG's reaction, there was genuine fear that soldiers from the far north would interpret the coup as being a sectionally motivated political revolt against them by Christian middle belt minorities, and that officers from the far north may retaliate as they did in 1966. There were reports of southern officers and civilians making plans to return to their regions of origin in anticipation of further inter-ethnic conflict and instability.

FUGITIVE

The police issued a warrant for Dimka's arrest. They warned that "he is dangerous and believed to be armed" and that "he drinks and is fond of pub houses." A nationwide manhunt was launched. According to the government Dimka checked into a hotel in the eastern town of Afikpo under the fictitious name of "Mr. C. Godwin" of the Federal Ministry of Agriculture. At Dimka's request the hotel manager procured a lady of the night named Beatrice Agboli for him. When the authorities were alerted to his whereabouts, Dimka escaped through a window in the hotel and abandoned his car with a fake license plate. He was captured on March 5, 1976, at a joint military and police checkpoint near Abakaliki in Anambra State by an alert police constable named PC Jika Iyah. Dimka was the officer who a decade earlier had been accused of murdering his commanding officer Lt-Colonel Okoro in Kaduna and of participating in death squads that summarily executed Igbo soldiers during the northern soldiers' mutiny of July 1966. During his time in the army he had acquired a reputation for instability, womanizing and plentiful alcoholic consumption. Yet somehow he had been allowed to remain in, and rise up the army.

The assassination of Murtala was the third coup by a faction of the northern soldiers that mutinied in 1966. It was not the last. Dimka graduated from the Australian army officer cadet school in Portsea on December 13 1963 along with Boniface Ikejiofor, an officer who took part in the Majors' coup of January 1966. The two men were the first Nigerian army officers to train in Australia and successfully complete the course. Cadets from Australia, New Zealand, Malaysia, the Philippines and the Pacific Islands also trained with them. Both young men ruined promising lives and careers by choosing to join different coup plots. Ironically Arthur Unegbe (then a Major) who was murdered during the January 1966 coup, in which Ikejiofor took part, attended Dimka and Ikejiofor's passing out (graduation) parade in 1963.

Chapter 17. Crime and Punishment

Anatomy of a Plot

Dimka's arrest and subsequent confessions turned into a media circus. He was presented to the press strangely wearing a fixed grin. A tape recording from Dimka's confession was played after which Dimka confirmed that the voice on the tape was his, and he told the press that he confessed without duress. Just like the plotters of January 1966, the February 1976 conspirators attended a party the night before their coup. The genesis of the plot seems to have been a conversion exercise in Kaduna to re-assess officers' intellectual and professional military aptitude via a series of tests and exams. The aggressive professional re-orientation favored by the exercise, combined with latent resentment at Gowon's overthrow, and opposition to the government's policies regarding promotions and demobilization, was enough to spur three Majors (the most prominent of whom was Major Clement Dabang) on the conversion course into an incoherent coup plot. The army was so bloated and politicized at this stage that a military coup was viewed by some disgruntled elements as a legitimate response to professional grievances such as these. An officer who trained with Dabang at the Nigerian Defense Academy (NDA) described him as "a most forceful personality, intensely regimental, efficient and upright junior leader."[1] Dabang was a classmate of John Shagaya at the Nigerian Military School and trained in the NDA's course 2 with other officers that would later rise to prominence including "triple A" Alhaji Abdulsalami Abubakar (later head of state), Chris Alli (later Chief of Army Staff), and Ola Ogunmekan who himself was an alleged accomplice to this coup. Embarrassingly Dabang was the commanding officer of 1 Guards Battalion in the Brigade of Guards — the unit that was responsible for Murtala's security. The involvement of the Brigade of Guards was not without precedent. In Nigerian governments, it is those to whom the leader entrusts his safety that need to be most feared. In January 1966, Prime Minister Balewa was abducted by soldiers from the Brigade of Guards,

---

1 Chris Alli, *The Federal Republic of Nigeria Army: The Siege of a Nation*, page 37.

and murdered. Only seven months later, Balewa's successor Major-General Aguiyi-Ironsi was abducted, tortured and shot dead by soldiers in his own entourage. Aguiyi-Ironsi's successor General Gowon was overthrown in July 1975, again with the connivance of officers from the Brigade of Guards – which as in Balewa's case in 1966, was supposed to protect him. This was the fourth successive coup in which the head of state's own bodyguards tried to overthrow him.

The coup seems to have been motivated as much by the actions of the SMC, as it was by a host of real and imagined grievances and personal animosity towards leading figures in the government. It can be simplified as an attempt by a faction of middle belt officers to regain privileges and prestige which they felt had been taken from them by the new regime. The mutineers' antipathy can be grouped into the following categories:

- they were unnerved by the conversion exercise which was interpreted by the plotters as carrying attendant risks for their career prospects, and was mentally associated with rumors that the government planned to reduce the size of the army via mass layoffs. The fact that some of the plotters were short service commissioned officers that were commissioned in the emergency of the Nigerian civil war, created professional insecurity in them and a presumption that they would be the first to lose their jobs in a demobilization program;
- they felt that the SMC was increasingly pursuing communist policies (perhaps an oblique reference to the SMC's support of a Marxist movement in Angola);
- the coup that deposed Gowon removed middle belt minority officers from prominence;
- the recent army promotions were unmerited (especially that of Lt-General Danjuma).

The FMG also added that in the plotters' view, Gowon was not given sufficient opportunity to change his governing style, the plotters opposed the dismissal of the former military governors, and they wanted to return Gowon and all his military governors back to office.

Initially, the plotters were more concerned with eliminating government figures than they were with political reform. They intended violence of much greater magnitude than they eventually managed to achieve. According to Dimka, some of the hard-line plotters initially proposed a full scale assault on, and elimination of all SMC members. Dimka claimed that the plotters argued that the coup "should be bloody and wild." They projected a shoot-fest and killing spree along similar lines to the July 1966 coup (in which many of them were participants). Dimka pointed out the folly and senseless nature of trying to kill so many senior figures. The plot he argued, would never succeed if they pre-occupied themselves with trying to eliminate so many people. The plotters even had plans for some senior police officers including the Inspector-General of police M.D. Yusuf and his deputy. According to Dimka, Major Dabang felt that Yusuf and his deputy were "traitors" who should at least be retired because they had cracked down on petty trade around army barracks. Dimka argued that he knew both police officers and that they should be left alone as he had no quarrel with them. By the time of the coup's execution Dabang was in hospital, but the other plotters decided to go ahead without him. Dimka claimed he was relieved that Dabang was hospitalized at the time of the coup as Dabang was one of the most enthusiastic advocates of eliminating key figures in the government. In Major

Dabang's absence, Major Rabo was allegedly in charge of distributing tasks among the plotters as follows:

- Major Rabo was to target General Murtala Muhammed.
- Lieutenant Dauda Usman was to target Lt-General Obasanjo.
- Lieutenant Lawrence Garba was to target Lt-General Danjuma.
- Major Gagara was to lead the coup in Ilorin.

Their other targets for elimination were the four GOCs Major-Generals Abisoye, Obada, Akinrinade, and Adamu. For less strategic reasons Colonels Babangida, Ibrahim Taiwo, Olu Bajowa, Abdullahi Mohammed, Umaru Mohammed and David Jemibewon were also on the hit list. Yar'Adua and Taiwo were targeted presumably because of the primary role they played in the coup that deposed Gowon. The plotters' stated reason for placing Jemibewon on the elimination list was that he was a member of the conversion exercise board and one of the plotters (T.K. Adamu) did not get along with him. Babangida was targeted as the plotters felt his prominence in the regime was unmerited and that he was too junior to be a member of the SMC.

THE PLOT — THE GOVERNMENT'S CASE

The official case was that apart from Major Dabang's group, another group of disaffected soldiers in Lagos had similar grievances and were preparing their own plot under the guidance of Major-General Bisalla. Although Dimka has been cast in the role of the villainous mastermind behind the plot, he was no more than a willing conduit in a plot that was already active by the time he was recruited. Dimka's role was to act as the link man or "coordinator" between the Kaduna and Lagos groups. Although the coup is referred to nowadays as the "Dimka coup" and Dimka is erroneously referred to as its mastermind, Dimka seems to have been selected by the plotters to be their coordinator and political face due partly to his frequent travelling and access to key figures.

Dimka claimed he met and briefed General Gowon in London on the coup plot of the Kaduna Majors, and that Gowon made him aware of a separate group of plotters in Lagos headed by Major-General Bisalla. He alleged that Gowon told him to report to Bisalla for further instructions when he returned to Nigeria in order to coordinate the efforts of the Kaduna and Lagos plotters. Dimka's testimony was that Gowon advised, "You boys make sure you take time and make no mistakes." According to the FMG, after returning to Nigeria, Dimka met with Bisalla on three occasions. The first occasion was at Bisalla's house in Lagos, during which Bisalla allegedly informed Dimka that he wanted the government to be overthrown. Bisalla was allegedly aggrieved by (i) the government's planned army demobilizations (ii) Lt-General Danjuma's promotion over his head, and (iii) the government seemingly "going communist." Bisalla allegedly told Dimka to plan the coup's operational aspects with Dabang and named other officers in Lagos, Kaduna, Jos, Onitsha, Benin and other locations who were to be briefed. The second meeting allegedly took place at Bisalla's house in Kaduna in the presence of Lt-Colonel A.B. Umaru. At this second meeting Bisalla allegedly informed Dimka and Umaru of the SMC's decision to create new states, and to convert the retirement of former military governors found guilty of corruption, to dismissal. Bisalla apparently urged Dimka and Umaru to delay the coup till after the public announcement of these decisions, as then would be a more favorable climate for a coup. At the alleged third meeting, Bisalla directed that the coup should be staged on February 13, and gave operational orders for the tasks to be carried out by the plotters. However, as will be shown later in this Chapter, the FMG's case is inconsistent with Dimka's confessions and known facts in many places.

TREASON AND OTHER OFFENSES (SPECIAL MILITARY TRIBUNAL) DECREE 1976

Since the executors of the two 1966 coups were never tried there was no law in Nigeria prescribing punishment for coup plotting against a military regime. The existing treason laws in Nigeria's statute books did not contemplate the existence of a military regime. As one of the army's most experienced officers in military law and procedure, Lt-General Danjuma dictated the creation of a board of inquiry to investigate the coup, and a military court marshal to try the culprits. He dictated these measures to the Attorney-General Dan Ibekwe, leading to the speedy enactment in late February 1976 of the Treason and Other Offenses (Special Military Tribunal) Decree (Decree 8 of 1976). It was the first decree signed into law by the new head of state Lt-General Obasanjo and it empowered the FMG to create a Special Military Tribunal (composed of military officers) to try the coup plotters (including civilian accomplices) for treason, murder or any other offense committed before the decree came into effect. Retroactive criminal legislation is extremely unusual and is unconstitutional in many countries (it would almost certainly have been unconstitutional in Nigeria too had it been passed in any circumstance other than under military rule). The decree stated that the tribunal was to have the following composition: a tribunal president who had to be an army officer of the rank of Colonel or above (or a navy or air force officer of corresponding rank or above), and at least four other members, each of whom had to be an army or police officer holding a commission of not less than five years. The tribunal members would be appointed by the SMC. The Special Military Tribunal was also empowered to impose the death penalty by firing squad. The first use of a firing squad in Nigeria had ironically been in the breakaway Eastern Region of Biafra when Lt-Colonel Banjo, Major Ifeajuna and Philip Alale were sentenced to death and executed by firing squad in 1967.

A military board of inquiry headed by Major-General Emmanuel Abisoye investigated the coup.[1] The board subpoenaed witnesses, conducted investigations and compiled evidence upon which a trial would be based. The other board members were Deputy Inspector-General of Police Adamu Suleiman, Navy Captain Olufemi Olumide, and Lt-Colonels Muktar Mohammed, Joshua Dogonyaro and Mamman Vatsa (Vatsa was the board's secretary)[2]. The board's findings were submitted to Brigadier Yar'Adua. The coup investigation took on witch hunting proportions as almost 220 people were arrested. Of those, 130 were recommended for trial, and 66 were discharged. The investigators were ruthless. The hospitalized Major Dabang was forcefully discharged from hospital, arrested and taken to face the Special Military Tribunal. As he was being discharged from hospital, Dabang bitterly criticized Dimka for rushing the coup's timing and executing it before Dabang could recover from his illness and participate. Eyewitnesses at a hospital reported to the author that other military patients were forcefully discharged from treatment and taken to interrogation. Soldiers were being hunted as far away as London.

---

1 General Obasanjo's biography *Not My Will* claims that Major-General Akinrinade headed the board of inquiry. This is probably a typographical error. Brigadier Yar'Adua's broadcast shortly after the coup made it clear that Abisoye chaired the board of inquiry.

2 Ironically Dogonyaro and Vatsa themselves became coup plotters in the 1980s. Dogonyaro participated in coups in 1983 and 1985, and Vatsa was tried and executed in 1986 for his alleged role in a coup.

Danjuma was the only SMC member with significant experience of military coup tribunals. In 1971, he headed a Commonwealth military tribunal that tried suspects after an attempted military coup in Trinidad and Tobago against Prime Minister Eric Williams. That coup was led by Lieutenants Raffique Shah and Rex Lassalle. The Commonwealth military tribunal headed by Danjuma also included a Ghanaian Colonel named Ignatius Acheampong. Less than a year later Acheampong overthrew Ghana's Prime Minister Kofi Busia in a military coup. The cynic may be tempted to deduce that the experiences of officers serving on that tribunal were useful lessons for them in how not to stage a coup. Any lessons learned by Acheampong did not prevent his execution in 1979 after yet another military rebellion, this time led by a young Flight Lieutenant named Jerry Rawlings.

THE SPECIAL MILITARY TRIBUNAL

Surprisingly, the SMC did not appoint officers with military coup tribunal experience to the Special Military Tribunal. Lt-Colonel Paul Omu and Major Inyang served on the Commonwealth military tribunal with Danjuma but both were overlooked. The coup investigation and trial was shrouded in such secrecy that even today, the identity of the Special Military Tribunal's chairman is not widely known. The confusion was compounded by a typographical error in General Obasanjo's biography, *Not My Will*, which stated that the Special Military Tribunal was chaired by Major-General Abisoye. However, Obasanjo's writer may have got this confused with the preliminary board of inquiry that investigated the coup prior to trial (which is what Abisoye chaired). According to Gowon's biographer Jonah Isawa Elaigwu, the Special Military Tribunal was chaired by Major-General John Obada (an Urhobo officer from Bendel State in the south). One of the other tribunal members was Colonel Domkat Yah Bali and he later confirmed that Obada was the tribunal's chairman.[1] As a junior officer Obada once served as ADC to former President Nnamdi Azikiwe. Obada's tribunal was unprecedented and was Nigeria's first trial for coup plotting.

The irony of the tribunal was that the defendants were on trial for offenses that had also been committed in the past by their accusers in the government. Many of the government's leading figures such as Lt-General Danjuma, Major-General Adamu, and Colonels Babangida, Buhari, Garba and Yar'Adua had prior coup plotting experience. The government applied a double standard to differentiate the defendants' offenses from those of its own leading personalities. Lt-General Danjuma enunciated the double standard as follows: "If you carry out a coup you must jolly well succeed. If you don't, you are a traitor and must be prepared to take the consequences."[2] This created a decades-long bifurcation between successful and unsuccessful coup plotters. The former are never investigated, tried or punished, are deemed to be "revolutionaries" and can look forward to wealth and rewarding government careers. Death awaits the latter. In modern Nigerian parlance, a "coup" never succeeds. The term "coup" is not used to refer to successful military assumptions of power. Words such as "revolution," "takeover" or "change of government" are often employed.

Some of the accused junior officers argued in their defense that they had simply been obeying orders. This was the same argument used by many junior officers that took part in the January 1966 Majors' coup. The authorities were unconvinced and

---

1 *This Day*, Sunday June 20, 2008.
2 Lindsay Barrett, *Danjuma: The Making of a General*, page 70.

refused to allow defenses based on obeying illegal orders. In the grief and atmosphere of vengeance following the coup, no one questioned:

- why the plotters were being tried by a secret tribunal;
- that the decree under which the plotters were being tried had retroactive effect;
- the fact that two members of the investigation board of inquiry (Muktar Mohammed and Olufemi Olumide), and the Special Military Tribunal chairman were all members of the SMC, and thus could hardly be deemed impartial;
- that suspects could be sentenced to death based on evidence that would not be made public;
- not only was the Treason and Other Offenses (Special Military Tribunal) Decree empowered to try civilians, but it extended the jurisdiction of military law (normally applicable to armed forces personnel only) to civilians.
- the Special Military Tribunal could adopt whatever procedure it thought fit, without reference to ordinary civil or military court marshal procedure. In effect, the Special Military Tribunal was free to make up the rules as it went along;
- the decree contained no provisions regarding what burden of proof had to be established in order to secure a conviction, nor was there a right of appeal from its verdicts (which were subject to confirmation by the SMC).

The SMC was effectively acting as investigator, judge, jury and executioner. This was a dangerous precedent that would come back to haunt some of the SMC members several years later, when two of them (Obasanjo and Yar'Adua) fell victim to the mechanism they created. The fact that the Special Military Tribunal could try *any* offense was also later abused in subsequent tribunals. Most of the defendants were middle belt officers from minority ethnic groups in Gowon's home state of Plateau. Since officers from this area had murdered a Muslim Hausa leader from the far north, the tension between middle belt officers and those from the far north resurfaced as minority middle belt officers replaced Igbos as the new treacherous scapegoats of the day. Only two of the suspects were southern (Majors Afolabi and Ogunmekan), and only a few were *not* from middle belt minority ethnic groups. Colonel Isa Bukar was from Borno state and Colonel Wya, Lt-Colonel Umaru, Major Rabo, Captain Aliyu, Lieutenant Wayah and Sergeant Rege were all from southern Zaria. The rest were overwhelmingly from Plateau state. Both Major-General Bisalla and Major Gagara were from the town of Gindiri in Mangu Local Government Area of Plateau State.

DIMKA'S CONFESSIONS

Dimka's confessional statements were crucial to the prosecution's case. They took on a life of their own as he implicated an ever increasing circle of officers. At one stage Dimka claimed that esteemed retired officers from Gowon's regime such as Brigadier Ikwue and Major-General Hassan Katsina (former Chief of Staff (Army)) had foreknowledge of the plot. The intervention of Katsina's fellow blue blood Fulani, Brigadier Yar'Adua, saved Katsina from prosecution and possible death.[1] Colonel Remawa was also interrogated for several days due to Dimka's over-inclusive testi-

---

1 Katsina's former ADC Lieutenant Abubakar Umar would later become a prominent coup plotter.

mony. Brigadier Yar'Adua remarked to his colleagues that the scale and hysteria of the investigations might give unscrupulous elements an opportunity to frame and eliminate their enemies. Relations between Murtala's regime and Gowon had been cordial. Before his death Murtala was embarrassed to see pictures of Gowon queuing for food with other students at the Warwick University student canteen. He therefore sent Brigadier Danjuma to meet with, and try to persuade Gowon to discontinue his course and return home. The meeting took place in the presence of Murtala's relative Colonel Abbas Wali, who was then serving as Nigeria's military adviser in the UK. Gowon refused and insisted on continuing his studies. The new regime therefore started to pay him his full pension and a monthly stipend via the Nigerian High Commission in London. However, Dimka's confessions badly soured relations with Gowon as Dimka implicated Gowon by claiming that he visited Gowon in the UK to discuss the coup plot. There were some other disturbing links between Gowon and the suspects which alarmed the FMG sufficiently to declare Gowon a suspect and ask for his extradition from the UK (a request that was denied). Dimka was an in-law of Gowon and like Gowon, was also a member of the Angas ethnic group. Dimka's older brother (the Kwara State Commissioner of Police S.K. Dimka) was married to Gowon's older sister. Although he admitted that Dimka visited him in the UK, Gowon denied the allegations against him and claimed that his only recollection of meeting Dimka was Dimka's incoherent and drunken statements. Gowon swore:

> "as an officer and as a gentleman and by the God who made me that I had nothing whatsoever to do with it . . . If it was their plan to carry out the coup and then ask me to go back, well, that is their own look out."

The manner in which the investigation was sometimes conducted based on concepts of guilt by association meant that any officer who visited Gowon in England was a suspect. When Dimka told investigators that the Chief of Army Staff Lt-General Danjuma visited Gowon, Danjuma had to explain to the board of inquiry that he visited Gowon with the prior approval of former head of state General Muhammed. Gowon wisely declined the FMG's invitation to come to Nigeria for interrogation. His refusal led to him being declared a wanted person, being stripped of his rank and having his benefits revoked.[1] Unable to get their hands on Gowon, the FMG took some actions against those close to Gowon that bore the appearance of a vendetta. Gowon's younger brothers Isaiah and Moses were arrested and their Angas kinsmen suffered heavily. Joseph Gomwalk (Gowon's cousin), the former military governor of Benue-Plateau State, was also roped into the plot. Gomwalk was also Angas and was a university graduate, unlike the other military governors.[2] He had a BSC degree in Zoology from the University of Ibadan (in which he graduated with first class honors). Dimka alleged that Gomwalk gave him input on his second coup broadcast (which never aired). Gomwalk's sister-in-law Mrs. Helen Gomwalk was also arrested after Dimka's confessions cast her in the role of the plotters' messenger. Helen Gomwalk was married to Joseph Gomwalk's brother Clement Gomwalk, who was a former permanent secretary in Benue-Plateau state. Additionally a civilian broadcaster (Abdulkarim Zakari) was also arrested and tried. Zakari was the older brother of Gowon's wife Victoria, and he allegedly provided Dimka with the martial music that he played with his coup broadcast. He allegedly showed Dimka into the broadcasting section of the radio station on the day before the coup, and was on duty the

---

1 His rank and benefits were subsequently restored in 1986.
2 The only civilian governor Ukpabi Asika was also a graduate.

day of the coup even though it was supposed to be his day off. Some Angas soldiers in the Brigade of Guards that were naively inherited from Gowon were also implicated. These included Captain McDonald Gotip, who led the special Angas company of guards that Joe Garba personally recruited to protect Gowon during his rule.

BISALLA'S CASE

The Commissioner for Defense Major-General Iliya Bisalla was suspected by members of the FMG. Bisalla was first implicated by Lt-Colonel T.K. Adamu who claimed that he reported the coup plot to Bisalla. Adamu's allegation led to Bisalla being arrested and interrogated. However, when he appeared before the board of inquiry, Bisalla denied that Adamu ever reported the plot to him. Stalemate ensued as it was Bisalla's word against Adamu's. Bisalla's release was therefore authorized. Nonetheless Lt-General Obasanjo was pressurized by other senior officers to put Bisalla on trial and many of them shunned Bisalla, refusing to attend FEC meetings if he was invited. Bisalla was on the verge of being cleared when Dimka's shocking revelations also implicated him. Dimka alleged that he executed the coup at the behest of Bisalla. Bisalla was re-arrested and placed on trial. When Dimka saw Bisalla at the Special Military Tribunal, he cursed and spat at him, accusing him of being the mastermind behind the whole plot. Bisalla had been a close friend of Murtala, trained with him at Teshie and Sandhurst and even attended Murtala's funeral. Murtala affectionately referred to him as "Giwa." However, in the minds of investigators and his detractors, Bisalla's earlier complaints about Danjuma being promoted over his head, coupled with Dimka's implication of him, could now be used to attribute dangerous intentions to Bisalla. Simply put, Bisalla had a motive. In another twist to the familial connections which seemed to shape implication in the plot, Mrs. Helen Gomwalk was also the older sister of Major-General Bisalla's wife Mildred.[1]

THE VERDICT

Despite protesting his innocence throughout, Bisalla was convicted of treason and sentenced to death by a firing squad, less than one week after Dimka's capture. Thirty-nine other officers were also convicted. All but four of the convicts were Christians. Bisalla blamed Dimka for his fate, claiming that "I was to be set free yesterday, but for this boy Dimka who implicated me. God knows I didn't know anything about it."

In the intensely vengeful atmosphere there was little prospect that the SMC would show clemency. The government claimed that:

> Standing military and civil legal processes were adopted to adduce evidence. Witnesses were freely called upon and each defendant was given ample opportunity to call in any witnesses or refute any evidence against him. In cases where guilt had been established, charges were framed by legal personnel and passed up to the tribunal for trial. Each of those bodies has worked intensively since the tragic Friday, most of the time working 18 hours a day in order to arrive at some conclusions.

The Special Military Tribunal acquitted 56 of the suspects. Among the acquitted were Gowon's brother Moses who was a Squadron Leader in the air force, and Brigadier Samuel Ogbemudia, the former military governor of the Mid-West Region. However, some of those acquitted were retried by a second Special Military Tribu-

---

1 Mrs Helen Gomwalk and Mrs Bisalla's maiden name was "Kwashi."

nal chaired by another officer from Bendel State Brigadier Pius Eremobor (an Esan). Some of those retried were sentenced to death by the second tribunal. Joseph Gomwalk, Lt-Colonel Adamu, Major J.K. Abang, Warrant Officer (II) Pankshin, and Gowon's younger brother Isaiah were among those tried twice. Gomwalk was originally convicted of concealment of treason by the Obada tribunal for having foreknowledge of, but not reporting it to the authorities. He was originally sentenced to life imprisonment and dismissed from the police force. Lt-Colonel Adamu was also sentenced to life imprisonment by the Obada tribunal. However, when Gomwalk, Abang and Adamu's sentences were sent to the SMC for confirmation, the SMC ordered that they should be retried for the same offense (despite the fact that legally, the "double jeopardy" rule states that a defendant cannot be tried twice for the same offense). Several SMC members including Joe Garba considered the original verdicts to be lenient. Gomwalk, Abang and Adamu were subsequently sentenced to death at the retrial by the Eremobor tribunal. Isaiah Gowon was originally acquitted by the Obada tribunal but then retried under Eremobor and sentenced to 15 years imprisonment. Many of the convicts were not members of the plot's inner circle, nor were they even consciously involved in it. At times the plotters had expressed their nebulous political and professional grievances with the FMG in the presence of unsuspecting officers. These bystander officers were later convicted as accessories, and for concealment of treason (failing to report the plot despite prior knowledge of it). Among them was Colonel Wya who admitted that he was informed of the plot by Lt-Colonel Tense.[1] For failing to report the plot to the authorities, Wya was convicted of concealment of treason and sentenced to death.

EXECUTIONS

As expected the SMC showed no mercy and confirmed the death sentences. The SMC and Special Military Tribunal Members had to harden their hearts and send their close colleagues to their graves. Some of the condemned men's last words were somber as they recalled their loved ones. Major Gagara asked "pardon from my wife because she has been good to me. She should be free to remarry." Lt-Colonel Adamu said, "Please tell my wife to remember her God. I ask for forgiveness of anybody I have offended. My wife, please check with my bankers about my house in Kaduna. Clear all debts even if by selling my things so that my wife who is carrying a pregnancy of eight months can at last live in peace." Major Joe Kasai was however unrepentant and maintained that he had "no regrets whatsoever. We thought of changing the social order; we have failed, so we must pay the price."

The convicts were executed in two batches. 32 of the condemned men were executed on March 11, 1976. Bisalla continued to protest his innocence even as he was being led to the execution ground at the famous Bar Beach in Lagos. The *New Nigerian* newspaper reported that Bisalla said "I am going to heaven, I need no prayers any longer." Dimka, Gomwalk, Colonel Isa Bukar, Major J.K. Afolabi, Lieutenant Sabo Kwale, Warrant Officer (II) Edward Bawa and the police officer H. Shaiyen were executed on May 15, 1976. Just before the firing squad went to work, Dimka grinned as a priest administered a final prayer for him while he was tied to a stake. Colonel Isa Bukar was the officer that had placed Brigadier George Innih, the military governor of Bendel State, under house arrest. The attentive reader will note that Lieutenant Sabo Kwale was the soldier who triggered a bloodbath almost a decade earlier,

---

1 Tense was a mechanical engineer and was a schoolmate of Haladu Hannaniya.

when late at night on July 28, 1966 he strode into the officers' mess at the Abeokuta garrison and along with others, shot to death the garrison's commander Lt-Colonel Okonweze and Major John Obienu in the presence of several other officers. It seemed that time and ageing had not diminished his bloodlust. Not only had be not been punished or dismissed for murdering his commanding officer in 1966, not only had he been allowed to remain in the army, but he was double rewarded by being given a full commission as an officer of the Nigerian army. According to Dimka, during one of his conversations with Kwale regarding the plot, Kwale had proudly recalled his exploits at the Abeokuta garrison in 1966. His superiors may have rued not punishing him back then.

The executions took place at Lagos' famous Bar Beach and at the Kirikiri maximum security prison. Some of the executions were carried out in front of thousands of spectators, and were nationally televised. Macabre photographs of the bullet shattered bodies of the executed men got into public circulation (including Bisalla). Newspapers carried photos of the firing squad lining up. Gowon's brother-in-law Zakari was the only civilian executed. The executions sent a chilling message from the SMC to the rest of the army. Death would be the penalty for a failed coup plot, and for disloyalty. For Nigerian soldiers, a fence became a very dangerous place to sit. Uncorroborated "beer parlor" talk also claimed that extra-judicial executions took place — excluding the "official" list of convicts.

A Tiv officer named Major Victor Malu was then the chief instructor of the Nigerian Military School in Zaria. Major Malu was a guest of his friend Major Mshelia on the eve of the coup. On Friday February 13, 1976, Malu and Mshelia were having breakfast when Mshelia brought a radio to the breakfast table. When he heard martial music, Malu jokingly asked if the head of state was dead. Malu thought that the radio station had made put martial music on the airwaves accidentally. Then he eventually heard Dimka's coup speech, and wondered out loud how any sane person could try to overthrow Murtala at the height of his popularity. Mshelia disagreed with Malu's characterization of Murtala as popular and the two men got into a verbal altercation over the issue.[1] When Malu tried to leave Lagos to return to Zaria, he was prevented from doing so due to security restrictions and coup investigations which barred army officers from travelling without authorization. Malu was called in and interrogated for two weeks as he was acquainted with many of the suspects, such as Major Ogunmekan. He had also visited Major Dabang in hospital. Malu was exonerated but was shocked to subsequently discover that his host and friend Major Mshelia was one of those implicated. Malu discovered that his friend Major Mshelia had been sentenced to death when he switched on his television and saw Mshelia being tied to a stake in readiness for the firing squad. Two decades later, Malu himself chaired a coup tribunal and later became the Chief of Army Staff. He claimed that his experience of being a coup suspect allowed him to treat defendants fairly at the tribunal. A full list of those executed and imprisoned for the coup against Murtala Muhammed is at Table 2 of Appendix 4.

Two of the coup suspects: Sergeant Clement Yildar and Corporal Dauda Usman[2] were dismissed from the army, and never apprehended despite photos of them being released to the public. They remain at large (if still alive) till today.

---

1 See interview with Malu in *Onlinenigeria.com*, March 7, 2006

2 At the Nigerian Military School Usman was a classmate of one of the January 1966 coup plotter Ganiyu Adeleke, and of Yohanna Madaki. Usman fought with bravery during the Nigerian civil war as a member of the 23rd battalion commanded by John Nenge.

- It is not certain how reliable some of the convictions were, given the haste with which the defendants were tried and convicted.
- While the guilt of direct participants such as Dimka, Seri, Parwang and Rabo is not in doubt, the guilt of some of those convicted of conspiracy and concealment of treason is not certain since much of the evidence against them was based on Dimka's uncorroborated testimony. The cases of Bisalla, Joseph Gomwalk and his sister-in-law Mrs. Gomwalk fall into this category. By convicting defendants based on Dimka's testimony, the Special Military Tribunal ignored the fundamental legal principle that a defendant's confession is evidence against that defendant only, and is not admissible evidence of other co-accused/defendants' guilt.
- Some of the suspects were tried twice for the same offense, in violation of constitutional protections and laws protecting a defendant from being tried more than once for the same crime. Some of those tried twice were originally acquitted, but then had their sentences elongated, or were sentenced to death at their retrial. Tribunal member Colonel Domkat Bali later criticized the process that led to Joseph Gomwalk being tried twice, and claimed that the SMC deliberately ordered his retrial as a premeditated way of ensuring his death. Bali went so far as to say that, "Gomwalk, for instance, ought not to have been killed."[1]
- Some of Dimka's inarticulate confessions were inconsistent. For example he alleges that the core conspirators did not want any officer of the rank of Lt-Colonel and above to be involved in the plot. A pertinent question then, is why and how Dimka himself (a Lt-Colonel) and several other officers of that rank and above became alleged accomplices.
- The FMG alleged that Bisalla gave Dimka operational orders for the coup, such as which officers should be in charge of eliminating key figures in the regime. However, under interrogation Dimka stated that it was Major Rabo that gave these instructions — not Bisalla.
- The FMG alleged that the aim of the coup plotters was to return Gowon to power and that Gowon urged Dimka to coordinate activities with Bisalla. However, several members of the SMC subsequently cast great skepticism on the veracity of Dimka's testimony against Gowon. If it is accepted that Dimka's testimony against Gowon was unreliable, then it also casts serious doubt on his linked testimony regarding the alleged involvement of Bisalla. There was no explanation regarding how Bisalla (Defense Minister of the regime that deposed Gowon) came to be the "leader" of a coup started by a group of Majors who did not want senior officers involved, and whose aim was to restore Gowon to power. No one has ever explained what Bisalla had to gain from organizing the murder of his friend Murtala and restoring Gowon to power.
- One of the plotters' primary grievances was the proposed program of army demobilization. However, Isa Bukar in the past spoke in favor of demobilization, and Bisalla was one of the conceptual architects of the demobilization program. It appears incoherent that an officer closely allied to the FMG's policy on demobilization would become the arrowhead for a coup with the stated aim of preventing demobilization.

---

1 *This Day*, Sunday June 20, 2008.

- The "evidence" against many of the suspects and those interrogated consisted of hearsay evidence from other co-accused, and hazy family, regional, and ethnic linkages with other suspects. For example the ethnicity of Angas officers such as Gowon, his brothers, and Gomwalk played a key role in the suspicion against them. If the January 1966 coup was an Igbo coup, then this one was perceived as an "Angas coup" or "middle belt" coup. Angas officers were deemed suspect for sharing ethnicity with Dimka. Bisalla was Pyem but his wife was Angas. Gowon's other circumstantial links to Dimka have already been discussed above. Middle belt officers from other ethnicities were also investigated. Major Victor Malu, Yohanna Madaki and Chris Alli were all investigated (all three were exonerated). Malu was interrogated on the basis that he was a friend of some of the suspects.
- Dimka was drinking beer even while he was being interrogated.

It is not beyond the realms of possibility that, knowing he was a condemned man living on borrowed time, Dimka decided to take other people with him. As a member of the Special Military Tribunal that sentenced many of the convicts to death, then Colonel Domkat Bali agreed with this view:

> Probably if Dimka decided to keep his mouth shut, many of those who were executed would in all probability have been saved except of course those who were caught in the act. But many of those killed were implicated by Dimka.[1] . . . If probably Dimka had kept quiet and just decided to take the punishment and go, many lives would have been saved. But it appears as if he had made up his mind that he would have to go with as many people as possible.[2]

In his letter to the new head of state Lt-General Obasanjo dated 31 March, 1976, Gowon wrote, "I believe that Lieutenant-Colonel Dimka is only trying to implicate innocent people while the real culprits get away with it."[3] Among the convictions whose reliability was later questioned, the name of Colonel A.D.S. Wya has frequently been mentioned. Wya's grief-stricken Irish wife later died in a car crash. The case of Major Ola Ogunmekan may also warrant further scrutiny. He was one of the few non-middle belt soldiers executed. His former NDA course mate Chris Alli cryptically observed that before the coup Ogunmekan "was to challenge the Chief of Army Staff, Lt-General Danjuma, on some equity issues later in 1975. . . . An independent inquiry into our past can establish the justice of his final fate and exit from this earth."[4]

The former ADC to Shehu Musa Yar'Adua and Muhammadu Buhari, Mustapha Haruna Jokolo went further and categorically stated that innocent men were executed in the aftermath of the February 1976 coup:

> Do you know there were people killed innocently during the coup attempt? . . . There were some of these officers who really did not take part . . . But they were shot. . . . I'll give you an example like Colonel A.D.S. Waya [sic]. Nobody was sure of his involvement. There was no proof of it. Like Colonel A.B. Umar. Nobody was sure of his involvement. No definite certainty. Why is it that they didn't make the proceedings public?[5]

---

1 Femi Ahmed, *Domkat: A Biography of General Domkat Bali*, page 127.
2 Ibid., page 129.
3 Text reproduced in Elaigwu — *Gowon, The Biography of a Soldier-Statesman*, page 264.
4 Chris Alli, *The Federal Republic of Nigeria Army: The Siege of a Nation*, page 41.
5 *The Sun*, Saturday, May 31, 2008.

Life After Murtala

The violence of the coup and the executions that followed it shattered the SMC's innocence and low profile outlook. The coup demonstrated that the demons of 1966 had not been entirely exorcized, and that the army still contained officers who had no qualms about murdering their superiors in order to pursue political objectives or settle professional rivalries. It also led to the adoption of reinforced security measures. To avoid being ambushed while travelling from home to work, senior SMC members travelled to their offices escorted by armored personnel carriers. Obasanjo later took the security precaution further by moving into Dodan Barracks (then the location of Nigeria's Ministry of Defense). To avoid identification of their official cars, SMC members were sometimes ferried to meetings by bus.

Command of security and intelligence formations were also reshuffled with potentially subversive elements being replaced by officers loyal to senior figures in the regime. This led to power being consolidated in mid-ranking civil war veteran officers who went on to dominate Nigeria's military and political life for the next two decades. Remnants of the Brigade of Guards from Gowon's home state were flushed out and the unit's commander Lt-Colonel Sani Sami[1] was replaced by Lt-Colonel Mamman Vatsa. Sami had been strangely incommunicado while the coup was in progress. Under Vatsa the Brigade of Guards moved its headquarters from Dodan Barracks to Victoria Island. Vatsa was to feature prominently in subsequent military regimes and coup plots. The Lagos Garrison Organization was upgraded to a full division and became the 4th infantry division under the command of Brigadier M.I. Wushishi. Years later Wushishi became the Chief of Army Staff. Murtala's relative Brigadier Abbas Wali was recalled from London (where he was working as the military adviser at Nigeria's High Commission) and appointed the new Adjutant-General. Another redeployment saw Colonel Buhari moved from his job as military governor of Borno state to become Commissioner for Petroleum and a member of the SMC. Buhari was succeeded as Borno State military governor by Lt-Colonel Tunde Idiagbon.[2] Membership of the SMC was enlarged by the addition of Colonel Buhari, Brigadier Jalo (commandant of the NDA), Brigadier Wushishi, Colonel Abdullahi Mohammed (head of army intelligence), Captain Oduwaiye, Alhaji Buba Fika of the police and Lt-Commander Ogoh Ebitu Ukiwe of the navy. Most of these men served at the top echelon of the military well into the 1980s. One of the few senior officers to retain his post was the Quartermaster-General Brigadier Olu Bajowa.

The intelligence failure that allowed the conspirators to plan and execute their plot without detection proved embarrassing and led to the creation of a new intelligence agency called the National Security Organization (NSO) under Colonel Abdullahi Mohammed. Mohammed is regarded as the godfather of modern Nigerian military intelligence. The Inspector-General of police M.D. Yusuf lost jurisdiction over the "E" department (Special Branch) of the police which was incorporated into the NSO. Although Yusuf was blamed in some quarters for not detecting the plot, in fairness it should be recalled that he was dissuaded from taking pre-emptive action against the 1975 coup plot that brought the regime to power. The movement of the Special Branch away from the police weakened the police as it had to rely on an external agency for its intelligence. A decade later the NSO was split into three different

---

1 Headed a coup special investigation panel in 1985 which investigated an alleged coup involving his successor Vatsa.
2 Later became Chief of Staff, Supreme Headquarters.

bodies: (i) the Defense Intelligence Agency (DIA), which is responsible for intra-military intelligence (first headed by Babatunde Elegbede) (ii) the National Intelligence Agency (NIA), which is responsible for overseas intelligence, and (iii) the State Security Service (SSS), which is responsible for domestic intelligence and subsequently proved to be the most feared and brutal of the intelligence organizations.

Obasanjo eventually returned the country to civilian democratic rule on October 1, 1979 as Murtala had promised. The new democratic constitution and federal government with a powerful executive President (Shehu Shagari) was modeled on the United States, with a two chamber legislature consisting of a Senate and House of Representatives, states and governors, in a federal republic. As a lasting symbol of his legacy, Nigeria's largest international airport at Ikeja in Lagos was renamed the "Murtala Muhammed International Airport." In a remarkable irony, the same airport which he had taken over by force was named after him a decade later. This airport is the entry point for most visitors to Nigeria, and is Africa's busiest airport. The bullet riddled black Mercedes Benz car in which Murtala was killed is today on museum display in Nigeria, and Murtala's image appears on the Nigerian twenty Naira bank note. A hospital in Kano is also named the Murtala Muhammed hospital. Murtala's brief rule of six months is nostalgically recalled as a golden age in Nigeria's history. He ruled for the same length of time as Aguiyi-Ironsi but left a vastly different legacy. Aguiyi-Ironsi was Nigeria's first military leader at a time when the army had no political experience, and he was opposed by every faction in the army. By the time Murtala came to power, the army had bloated in size by a factor of twenty and had become so politicized that it was seen by some as an armed political party. Murtala governed under much more favorable conditions than his predecessors. His legacy may have been very different had he encountered the crises that confronted his predecessors and successors (ethnic and religious polarization, communal violence, declining oil prices, pro democracy activism).

MURTALA'S FAMILY

Murtala was survived by his wife Ajoke (a dentist) and five children: Aisha (12) Zakari (10), Fatima (9), Risqua Abba (8), Zeliha (2) and Jumai — a baby less than one year old. Ajoke is half Yoruba. His eldest daughter Aisha is a law graduate of Kings College, University of London. She also has a Masters Degree in Business Administration from Imperial College, University of London, and runs an asset management company. Fatima is a horticulturist (although she is also a qualified accountant). Risqua is now Murtala's only surviving son since his elder brother Zakari was shot dead in 1994 in an incident that has not been resolved to the satisfaction of some members of Murtala's family. Risqua undertook a business career after his graduation with a degree in Business Administration from the University of Lagos, and a postgraduate degree from the University of Cardiff. Risqua was subsequently appointed as President Olusegun Obasanjo's Special Assistant on Privatization. Zeliha is a graduate of Economics from Nottingham University in the UK, and works for a real estate survey firm in Lagos. Murtala's youngest child Jumai studied Economics at the University of London. Murtala's widow and family launched the Murtala Muhammed Foundation in his memory, and the organization's board of trustees includes his children Aisha and Risqua, his widow Ajoke, as well as prominent retired Nigerian army Generals such as Olusegun Obasanjo, Ibrahim Babangida and T.Y. Danjuma. Murtala died as a man of great contradictions. The former secessionist firebrand who fought to prevent a secessionist movement and became a nationwide hero. He departed from Nigeria's political scene in the same manner he entered it: in a hail of bullets.

The "Coup Widows"

Being convicted of coup plotting usually brings instant and complete ostracization of the coup plotter's name and family. The wives and children of the condemned men are usually left to fend for themselves in undeclared purgatory while their properties are routinely confiscated without compensation. Some families changed their names to escape the notoriety. However, the Dimka family remains prominent in the police force. Captain Samuel Wakias' widow Cecilia is still alive, as are three of his sons, Hercules, Sheridan and Wungak. Another son, named Success, died aged only eight months. In March 1976 a group of soldiers arrived at Wakias' house and asked him to report to 1 division headquarters in Kaduna. Mrs. Wakias never saw her husband alive again after he reported. Major Gagara was from the same Local Government Area as Major-General Iliya Bisalla (Mangu Local Government Area in Plateau State). Gagara's younger brother Nehemiah is still alive and works as a civil servant. His daughters, Tapin and Tahari, and sons Chamsan and Pirwit, are also still alive. Pirwit is a basketball player in Greece.[1] Joseph Gomwalk's wives Hannatu and Azuma are still alive but have refused to speak to the press since the execution of their husband. Gomwalk's sister-in-law Helen (who was also convicted) was freed and became active in local politics. Gomwalk's cousin is Professor Nenfort Gomwalk, the renowned academic who was once the Administrator of the University of Nigeria.

A number of lessons can be learnt from the tragedies of the decade chronicled in this book. Most of the coups that established the military regimes of this era were carried out by the same cabal of officers. The first lesson to be learnt from these tragedies is that an unpunished coup will be followed by a bloodier coup, and that unpunished coup plotters will re-offend. The coup plotters behind Nigeria's military regimes were repeat offenders — often with fatal consequences for themselves. They were men who lived life on the edge, snacked on danger and dined on death. For them coup plotting was in the blood; it was a compulsive urge. Major Ifeajuna executed a coup in January 1966 but was released in March 1967. Within four months of his release he was at it again, this time plotting against Ojukwu. Unpunished coup plotters inevitably revolt against the person that had the power to punish them but declined to do so. The NCOs and Lieutenants that shot Gowon to power graduated into the Colonels that overthrew him exactly nine years later. A different but also unpunished faction of the northern soldiers from the July 1966 mutiny rose up again and murdered Murtala Muhammed in February 1976. As brigadiers and major-generals, the surviving July 1966 mutineers overthrew the elected civilian government of Shehu Shagari on the last day of 1983, and removed Major-General Buhari from power in a palace coup in August 1985. Not punishing coup plotters gives them no incentive to change their ways or devote themselves to non-political matters. It took over thirty years for the Nigerian government to learn these lessons when belatedly in 1999, all serving army officers that had held political office for six or more months were compulsorily retired. This retirement exercise swept away many of the hardened coup plotters in the army and the politicized officers who if left in the army, could be a danger to the sustenance of a civilian democracy. Those who do not heed history are doomed to repeat it.

---

1 *The Nation*, January 15, 2008.

APPENDIX 1

Table 1: Nigerian Military High Command as of January 14, 1966.

Name	Position	Background
Major-General Johnson Thomas Umunankwe Aguiyi-Ironsi	General Officer Commanding (GOC) — Nigerian Army	East: Igbo
Commodore Joseph Edet Akinwale Wey	Commanding Officer, Nigerian Navy — Lagos	Mixed Yoruba/ eastern minority heritage
Brigadier Samuel Adesujo Ademulegun	Commander, 1 Brigade — Kaduna	West: Yoruba
Brigadier Zakariya Maimalari	Commander, 2 Brigade — Lagos	North: Kanuri
Brigadier Babafemi Olatunde A. Ogundipe	Overseas: in London	West: Yoruba
Colonel W. Timming	Commanding Officer, Nigerian Air Force — Kaduna	German expatriate officer
Brigadier M.R. Varma	Commandant, Nigerian Defense Academy — Kaduna	Indian expatriate officer
Colonel Robert Adeyinka Adebayo	Attending a course at the Imperial Defense College in London	West: Yoruba

Colonel Kur Mohammed	(Acting) Chief of Staff at Army Headquarters — Lagos (in place of Colonel Robert Adebayo)	North: Kanuri
Colonel Ralph Adetunji Shodeinde	Deputy-Commandant, Nigerian Defense Academy and Commandant, Nigerian Military Training College — Kaduna	West: Yoruba
Lt-Colonel David Akpode Ejoor (Had just been posted to take over command from Lt-Colonel Francis Fajuyi who was posted to command the Abeokuta garrison. Fajuyi was on leave during the coup)	Commanding Officer, 1st Battalion — Enugu	Mid-West: Urhobo
Lt-Colonel Hilary Njoku (was about to hand over command to Lt-Colonel Gowon who had just returned from a course overseas at the Joint Services Staff College in the UK)	Commanding Officer, 2nd Battalion — Lagos	East: Igbo
Lt-Colonel George Kurubo	Commanding Officer, 3rd Battalion — Kaduna	East: Ijaw
Lt-Colonel Abogo Largema	Commanding Officer, 4th Battalion — Ibadan	North: Kanuri
Lt-Colonel Chukwuemeka Odumegwu Ojukwu	Commanding Officer, 5th Battalion — Kano	East: Igbo
Lt-Colonel James Yakubu Pam	Adjutant-General of the Nigerian Army — Lagos	North: Birom
Lt-Colonel Arthur Chinyelu Unegbe	Quartermaster-General of the Nigerian Army — Lagos	East: Igbo
Lt-Colonel Ogere Umo Imo[1]	Commanding Officer — Lagos Garrison (Abalti Barracks)	East: Igbo
Major Hassan Usman Katsina	Commanding Officer, 1st Reconnaissance squadron — Kaduna	North: Fulani
Major John Ikechukwu Obienu	Commanding Officer, 2nd Reconnaissance squadron — Abeokuta	Mid-West: Igbo
Lt-Colonel Wellington Umoh "Duke" Bassey[2]	Commanding Officer, Depot — Zaria	East: Efik

Lt-Colonel Yakubu "Jack" Gowon	Preparing to take over command of the 2nd battalion from Lt-Colonel Hilary Njoku	North: Angas
Major Donatus Okafor	Commander, Federal Guards — Lagos (Dodan Barracks)	(East: Igbo)
Lt-Colonel Victor Banjo	Director — Electrical and Mechanical Engineers	West: Yoruba
Lt-Colonel Rudolph Trimnell	Director of Signals and Transport	Mid-West: Itsekiri
Lt-Colonel Phillip Efiong	Director of Ordnance Services	East: Ibibio
Lt-Colonel Conrad Nwawo	Nigerian military attaché in London (preparing to take over the soon to be formed 6th battalion)	Mid-West: Igbo
Colonel Austen-Peters	Director — Medical Corps	West: Yoruba

[1] This officer was court-martialled in 1964 but the proceedings did not result in his dismissal.

[2] A veteran of the Korean war, this officer was affectionately known as "Baba", and was the oldest and longest serving soldier in the Nigerian army at that time. He conducted Gowon's interview for admission into the army.

* The last five officers were in charge of technical or non-combat posts.

Nigerian Army Hierarchy, January 14, 1966

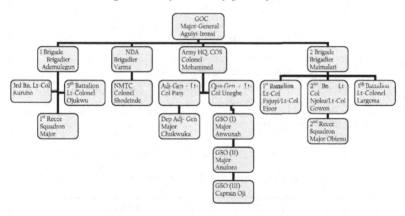

Table 2: Senior posts in Nigerian Ministry of Defense as of January 14, 1966.

Name	Position	Background/ Party
Alhaji Inuwa Wada	Minister of Defense	North: NPC
Alhaji Ibrahim Tako Galadima	Minister of State (Army)	North: NPC
Alhaji Sule Kolo	Permanent Secretary	North
Alhaji Ahmadu Kurfi	Deputy Permanent Secretary	North

Table 3: Nigerian police hierarchy as of January 14, 1966.

Name	Position	Background
Louis Edet	Inspector-General of Police (On Leave)	East: Efik
Alhaji Kam Selem	(Acting) Inspector-General of Police*	North
Hamman Maiduguri	Commissioner of Police — Lagos	North
Alhaji Mohammed Dikko Yusuf	Commissioner of Police — Northern Region	North: Fulani
Patrick Okeke	Commissioner of Police — Eastern Region	East: Igbo
Timothy Omo-Bare	Commissioner of Police — Mid-West Region	Mid-West: Edo
Odofin Bello[1]	Commissioner of Police –Western Region	West: Yoruba

[1] Later convicted of corruption.
*Deputizing for Louis Edet

Table 4: Military Redeployments after January 15, 1966 Coup

Position	Holder Before January Coup	Holder After January Coup
GOC — Nigerian Army	Major-General Johnson Aguiyi-Ironsi (East: Igbo)	N/A
Commanding Officer — Nigerian Navy	Commodore Joseph Wey (Mixed Yoruba/eastern minority heritage)	No Change

Commanding Officer, 1 Brigade — Kaduna	Brigadier Samuel Ademulegun (West: Yoruba)	Lt-Colonel Duke Bassey (East: Efik)
Commanding Officer, 2 Brigade — Lagos	Brigadier Zakariya Maimalari (North: Kanuri)	Lt-Colonel Hilary Njoku (East: Igbo)
Commanding Officer — Nigerian Air Force	Colonel Timming (German expatriate officer)	Lt-Colonel George Kurubo (East: Ijaw)
Commandant, Nigerian Defense Academy — Kaduna	Brigadier M.R. Varma (Indian expatriate officer)	No Change
Deputy Commandant, Nigerian Defense Academy — Kaduna	Colonel Ralph Shodeinde (West: Yoruba)	Lt-Colonel Ogere Imo (East: Igbo)
Commandant, Nigerian Military Training College — Kaduna	Colonel Ralph Shodeinde (West: Yoruba)	Major Ogbugo Kalu (East: Igbo)
Chief of Staff at Army Headquarters — Lagos	Colonel Kur Mohammed (North: Kanuri)	Lt-Colonel Yakubu Gowon (North: Angas)
Commanding Officer, 1st Battalion — Enugu	Lt-Colonel David Ejoor (Mid-West: Urhobo)	Major David Sunday Ogunewe (Mid-West: Igbo)
Commanding Officer, 2nd Battalion — Lagos	Lt-Colonel Hilary Njoku (East: Igbo)	*Major Henry Igboba (Mid-West: Igbo)
Commanding Officer, 3rd Battalion — Kaduna	Lt-Colonel George Kurubo (East: Ijaw)	*Major Israel Okoro (East: Igbo)
Commanding Officer, 4th Battalion — Ibadan	Lt-Colonel Abogo Largema (North: Kanuri)	Major Joseph Akahan (North: Tiv)
Commanding Officer, 5th Battalion — Kano	Lt-Colonel Chukwuemeka Ojukwu (East: Igbo)	Major Mohammed Shuwa (North: Kanuri)
Adjutant-General	Lt-Colonel James Pam (North: Birom)	Major Mike Ivenso (East: Igbo)
Quartermaster-General	Lt-Colonel Arthur Chinyelu Unegbe (East: Igbo)	Major Oluwole Rotimi
Commanding Officer, Lagos Garrison (Abalti Barracks)	Lt-Colonel Ogere Imo (East: Igbo)	Major Tony Eze (East: Igbo)
Commanding Officer, Abeokuta Garrison	Lt-Colonel Francis Fajuyi (West: Yoruba)	Major Gabriel Okonweze (Mid-West: Igbo)
Commanding Officer, 1st Reconnaissance squadron — Kaduna	Major Hassan Usman Katsina (North: Fulani)	Captain Ukpo Isong* (East: Ibibio)

Commanding Officer, 2nd Reconnaissance squadron — Abeokuta	Major John Obienu (Igbo: Mid-West)	No change
Commander, Federal Guards — Lagos (Dodan Barracks)	Major Donatus Okafor (East: Igbo)	Major Ben Okechukwu Ochei (Mid-West: Igbo)
Chief Ordnance Officer[1]	Lt-Colonel Phillip Efiong (East: Ibibio)	Major Ibrahim Bala Migul Haruna (North)

[1] The former title of this post was "Director of Ordnance Services".

*The officers in the above table with asterisks beside their names (Majors Igboba and Okoro and Captain Isong) were not appointed as such by Aguiyi-Ironsi but were already the deputy commanders of their units and thus automatically assumed command of those units on the departure or death of the previous commander.

Nigerian Army Hierarchy, following post-January 1966 redeployments

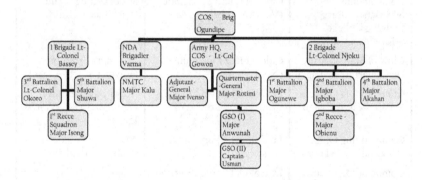

Table 5: Decimation of Military High Command after the Two Coups of 1966

Name	Position As At January 1966	Position As At August 1966
Major-General Johnson Aguiyi-Ironsi	General Officer Commanding–Nigerian Army	Murdered.
Brigadier Samuel Ademulegun	Commander — 1 Brigade — Kaduna	Murdered.
Brigadier Zakariya Maimalari	Commander — 2 Brigade — Lagos	Murdered.
Brigadier Babafemi Ogundipe	Overseas	Forced out of post.
Colonel W. Timming	Commanding Officer — Nigerian Air Force	Resigned

Brigadier M.R. Varma	Commandant — Nigerian Defense Academy	No Change
Colonel Kur Mohammed	(Acting) Chief of Staff at Army Headquarters — Lagos (in place of Colonel Robert Adebayo)	Murdered.
Colonel Ralph Shodeinde	Deputy-Commandant, Nigerian Defense Academy. Commandant, Nigerian Military Training College: Kaduna	Murdered.
Colonel Robert Adebayo	Attending a course in London	Drafted to become the Military Governor of the Western Region.
Lt-Colonel David Ejoor	Commanding Officer, 1st Battalion — Enugu	Drafted to become Military Governor of the Mid-West Region.
Lt-Colonel Hilary Njoku	Commanding Officer, 2nd Battalion — Lagos	Forced out of post.
Lt-Colonel George Kurubo	Commanding Officer, 3rd Battalion — Kaduna	Forced out of post.
Lt-Colonel Abogo Largema	Commanding Officer, 4th Battalion — Ibadan	Murdered.
Lt-Colonel Chukwuemeka Ojukwu	Commanding Officer, 5th Battalion — Kano	Drafted to become Military Governor of the Eastern Region.
Lt-Colonel James Pam	Adjutant-General of the Nigerian Army	Murdered.
Lt-Colonel Arthur Unegbe	Quartermaster-General of the Nigerian Army	Murdered.
Lt-Colonel Francis Fajuyi	Commanding Officer — Abeokuta Garrison	Murdered.
Lt-Colonel Ogere Ume Imo	Commanding Officer, Lagos Garrison (Abalti Barracks)	Forced out of post.
Major Hassan Usman Katsina	Commanding Officer, 1st Reconnaissance squadron — Kaduna	Drafted to become Military Governor of the Northern Region.
Major John Obienu	Commanding Officer, 2nd Reconnaissance squadron — Abeokuta	Murdered.
Major Donatus Okafor	Commander, Federal Guards — Lagos (Dodan Barracks)	Murdered
Major Chukwuma Kaduna Nzeogwu	Chief Instructor, Nigerian Military Training College	Imprisoned.

Lt-Colonel Wellington Umoh "Duke" Bassey	Commanding Officer, Depot — Zaria	Forced out of post.
Lt-Colonel Yakubu Gowon	Preparing to take over command of the 2nd battalion from Lt-Colonel Hilary Njoku	Head of State.
Lt-Colonel Victor Banjo	Director — Electrical and Mechanical Engineers	In detention.
Lt-Colonel Ruddy Trimnell	Director of Signals and Transport	Forced out of post.
Lt-Colonel Phillip Efiong	Director of Ordnance Services	Forced out of post.

Sample of Northern Participants in January 15, 1966 Coup

Captain John Swanton
Second-Lieutenant John Atom Kpera
Sergeant Husa Kanga
Sergeant Musa Manga
Sergeant Yakubu Adebiyi
Sergeant Daramola Oyegoke
Private Bello Mbulla
Lance Corporal Danyo Mbulla
Private Lekoja Gidan-Jibrin
Corporal Bako Lamundo
Private Joseph Wadu Goji
Private Lagwin Goshit
Corporal Tunana Bangir
Private Uguman Monogi
Corporal Yakubu Kaje
Lance Corporal Mamis Hundu
Lance Corporal Thaddens Thamyil Tsenyil
Lance Corporal Issnam Tayapa
Lance Corporal Ali Shendam
Private Usuman Gabure
Private Erastus Nakito
Private I. Onoja
Lance Corporal N. Noji

Speech of Major Nzeogwu — Declaration of Martial
Law in Northern Nigeria, January 15, 1966

In the name of the Supreme Council of the Revolution of the Nigerian armed
forces, I declare martial law over the northern provinces of Nigeria. The Constitution is suspended and the regional government and elected assemblies are
hereby dissolved. All political, cultural, tribal and trade union activities, together with all demonstrations and unauthorized gatherings, excluding religious
worship, are banned until further notice. The aim of the Revolutionary Council
is to establish a strong united and prosperous nation, free from corruption and
internal strife. Our method of achieving this is strictly military but we have no
doubt that every Nigerian will give us maximum cooperation by assisting the
regime and not disturbing the peace during the slight changes that are taking
place. I am to assure all foreigners living and working in this part of Nigeria that
their rights will continue to be respected. All treaty obligations previously entered into with any foreign nation will be respected and we hope that such nations will respect our country's territorial integrity and will avoid taking sides
with enemies of the revolution and enemies of the people.

My dear countrymen, you will hear, and probably see a lot being done by certain
bodies charged by the Supreme Council with the duties of national integration,
supreme justice, general security and property recovery. As an interim measure
all permanent secretaries, corporation chairmen and senior heads of depart-
ments are allowed to make decisions until the new organs are functioning, so
long as such decisions are not contrary to the aims and wishes of the Supreme
Council. No Minister or Parliamentary Secretary possesses administrative or
other forms of control over any Ministry, even if they are not considered too
dangerous to be arrested. This is not a time for long speech-making and so let
me acquaint you with ten proclamations in the Extraordinary Orders of the
Day which the Supreme Council has promulgated. These will be modified as
the situation improves.

You are hereby warned that looting, arson, homosexuality, rape, embezzlement,
bribery or corruption, obstruction of the revolution, sabotage, subversion, false

alarms and assistance to foreign invaders, are all offenses punishable by death sentence.

Demonstrations and unauthorized assembly, non-cooperation with revolutionary troops are punishable in grave manner up to death.

Refusal or neglect to perform normal duties or any task that may of necessity be ordered by local military commanders in support of the change will be punishable by a sentence imposed by the local military commander.

Spying, harmful or injurious publications, and broadcasts of troop movements or actions, will be punished by any suitable sentence deemed fit by the local military commander.

Shouting of slogans, loitering and rowdy behavior will be rectified by any sentence of incarceration, or any more severe punishment deemed fit by the local military commander.

Doubtful loyalty will be penalized by imprisonment or any more severe sentence.

Illegal possession or carrying of firearms, smuggling or trying to escape with documents, valuables, including money or other assets vital to the running of any establishment will be punished by death sentence.

Wavering or sitting on the fence and failing to declare open loyalty with the revolution will be regarded as an act of hostility punishable by any sentence deemed suitable by the local military commander.

Tearing down an order of the day or proclamation or other authorized notices will be penalized by death.

This is the end of the Extraordinary Order of the Day which you will soon begin to see displayed in public.

My dear countrymen, no citizen should have anything to fear, so long as that citizen is law abiding and if that citizen has religiously obeyed the native laws of the country and those set down in every heart and conscience since 1st October, 1960. Our enemies are the political profiteers, the swindlers, the men in high and low places that seek bribes and demand 10 percent, those that seek to keep the country divided permanently so that they can remain in office as ministers or VIPs at least, the tribalists, the nepotists, those that make the country look big for nothing before international circles, those that have corrupted our society and put the Nigerian political calendar back by their words and deeds. Like good soldiers we are not promising anything miraculous or spectacular. But what we do promise every law abiding citizen is freedom from fear and all forms of oppression, freedom from general inefficiency and freedom to live and strive in every field of human endeavour, both nationally and internationally. We promise that you will no more be ashamed to say that you are a Nigerian.

I leave you with a message of good wishes and ask for your support at all times, so that our land, watered by the Niger and Benue, between the sandy wastes and gulf of Guinea, washed in salt by the mighty Atlantic, shall not detract Nigeria from gaining sway in any great aspect of international endeavour.

My dear countrymen, this is the end of this speech. I wish you all good luck and I hope you will cooperate to the fullest in this job which we have set for ourselves of establishing a prosperous nation and achieving solidarity.

Thank you very much and goodbye for now.[1]

---

1 Broadcast on Radio Kaduna, January 15, 1966.

Major-General Aguiyi-Ironsi's Inaugural Speech as Head of State, January 16, 1966

Suspension of Certain Parts of the Constitution

The Federal Military Government hereby decrees:

a. the suspension of the provisions of the Constitution of the Federation relating to the office of President, the establishment of Parliament, and of the office of Prime Minister;

b. the suspension of the provisions of the Constitutions of the Regions relating to the establishment of the offices of Regional Governors, Regional Premiers and Executive Councils, and Regional

Legislatures.

Appointment of regional military governors

The Federal Military Government further decrees:

a) that there shall be appointed a military governor in each Region of the Federation, who shall be directly responsible to the Federal Military Government for the good government of the Region;

b) the appointment as adviser to the military governor of the Region, of the last person to hold the office of Governor of the Region under the suspended provisions of the Constitution.

The Judiciary, The Civil Service and the Police

The Federal Military Government further decrees:

a) that the Chief Justice and all other holders of judicial appointments within the Federation shall continue in their appointments, and that the judiciary generally shall continue to function under their existing statutes;

b) that all holders of appointments in the Civil Service of the Federation and of the Regions shall continue to hold their appointments and to carry out their duties in the normal way, and that similarly the Nigeria Police Force and the Nigeria Special Constabulary shall continue to exercise their functions in the normal way;

c) that all Local Government Police Forces and Native Authority Police Forces shall be placed under the overall command of the Inspector-General.

Internal Affairs Policy

The Federal Military Government announces, in connection with the internal affairs of the Federation:

a) that it is determined to suppress the current disorder in the Western Region and in the Tiv area of the Northern Region;

b) that it will declare martial law in any area of the Federation in which disturbances continue;

c) that it is its intention to maintain law and order in the Federation until such time as a new Constitution for the Federation, prepared in accordance with the wishes of the people, is brought into being.

External Affairs Policy

The Federal Military Government announces, in connection with the external affairs of the country:

a) that it is desirous of maintaining the existing diplomatic relations with other States; and

b) that it is its intention to honor all treaty obligations and all financial agreements and obligations entered into by the previous government.

Citizens to Co-Operate

The Federal Military Government calls upon all citizens of the Federation to extend their full co-operation to the government in the urgent task of restoring law and order in the present crisis, and to continue in their normal occupations.[1]

PRESIDENT AZIKIWE'S STATEMENT TO THE PRESS: REACTION TO NIGERIA'S FIRST MILITARY COUP, JANUARY 1966

Violence has never been an instrument used by us, as founding fathers of the Nigerian Republic, to solve political problems. In the British tradition, we talked the Colonial Office into accepting our challenges for the demerits and merits of our case for self-government. After six constitutional conferences in 1953, 1954, 1957, 1958, 1959, and 1960, Great Britain conceded to us the right to assert our political independence as from October 1, 1960. None of the Nigerian political parties ever adopted violent means to gain our political freedom and we are happy to claim that not a drop of British or Nigerian blood was shed in the course of our national struggle for our place in the sun. This historical fact enabled me to state publicly in Nigeria that Her Majesty's Government has presented self-government to us on a platter of gold. Of course, my contemporaries scorned at me, but the facts of history are irrefutable. I consider it most unfortunate that our 'Young Turks' decided to introduce the element of violent revolution into Nigerian politics. No matter how they and our general public might have been provoked by obstinate and perhaps grasping politicians, it is an unwise policy. I have contacted General Aguiyi-Ironsi, General Officer Commanding the Nigerian armed forces, who I understand, has now assumed the reins of the Federal Government. I offered my services for any peace overtures to stop further bloodshed, to placate the mutinous officers, and to restore law and order. As soon as I hear from him, I shall make arrangements to return home. As far as I am concerned, I regard the killings of our political and military leaders as a national calamity.

INAUGURAL SPEECH OF LT-COLONEL YAKUBU GOWON AS HEAD OF STATE, AUGUST 1, 1966

This is Lt-Colonel Y. Gowon, Army Chief of Staff, speaking to you.

My fellow countrymen, the year 1966 has certainly been a fateful year for our beloved country, Nigeria. I have been brought to the position today of having to shoulder the great responsibilities of this country and the armed forces with the consent of the majority of the members of the Supreme Military Council as a result of the unfortunate incident that occurred on the early morning of 29th July 1966.

However, before I dwell on the sad issue of 29th July 1966, I would like to recall to you the sad and unfortunate incidents of 15th January 1966 which bear relevance. According to certain well-known facts, which have so far not been disclosed to the nation and the world, the country was plunged into a national disaster by the grave and unfortunate action taken by a section of the army

---

1 Federal Ministry of Information Release and Government Notice No. 148/1966.

against the public. By this I mean that a group of officers, in conjunction with certain civilians, decided to overthrow the legal government of the day. But their efforts were thwarted by the inscrutable discipline and loyalty of the great majority of the army and the other members of the armed forces and the police. The army was called upon to take up the reins of government until such time that law and order had been restored. The attempt to overthrow the government of the day was done by eliminating political leaders and high-ranking army officers, a majority of whom came from a particular section of the country. The Prime Minister lost his life during this uprising. But for the outstanding discipline and loyalty of the members of the army who are most affected, and the other members of the armed forces and the police, the situation probably could have degenerated into a civil war.

There followed a period of determined effort of reconstruction ably shouldered by Major-General J. T. U. Aguiyi-Ironsi but, unfortunately, certain parties caused suspicion and grave doubts of the government's sincerity in several quarters. Thus, coupled with the already unpleasant experience of the 15th January still fresh in the minds of the majority of the people, certain parts of the country decided to agitate against the military regime which ad hitherto enjoyed country-wide support. It was, unfortunately, followed by serious rioting and bloodshed in many cities and towns in the north.

There followed a period of uneasy calm until the early hours of 29th July 1966, when the country was once again plunged into another very serious and grave situation, the second in seven months. The position on the early morning of 29th July was a report from Abeokuta garrison, that there was a mutiny and that two senior and one junior officer from a particular section of the country were killed. This soon spread to Ibadan and Ikeja. More casualties were reported in these places. The Supreme Commander was by this time at Ibadan attending the natural rulers' conference and was due to return on the afternoon of 29th July. The government lodge was reported attacked and the last report was that he and the West military governor were both kidnapped by some soldiers. Up till now, there is no confirmation of their whereabouts. The situation was soon brought under control in these places. Very shortly afterward, at about the same time, there was a report that there were similar disturbances among the troops in the north, and that a section of the troops had taken control of all military stations in the north as well. The units of Enugu and the garrison at Benin were not involved. All is now quiet and I can assure the public that I shall do all in my power to stop any further bloodshed and to restore law, order and confidence in all parts of the country with your co-operation and goodwill.

I have now come to the most difficult part, or the most important part, of this statement. I am doing it, conscious of the great disappointment and heartbreak it will cause all true and sincere lovers of Nigeria and of Nigerian unity both at home and abroad, especially our brothers in the Commonwealth. As a result of the recent events and the other previous similar ones, I have come to strongly believe that we cannot honestly and sincerely continue in this wise, as the basis of trust and confidence in our unitary system of government has not been able to stand the test of time. I have already remarked on the issues in question. Suffice to say that, putting all considerations to test-political, economic, as well as social-the base for unity is not there or is so badly rocked, not only once but several times. I therefore feel that we should review the issue of our national standing and see if we can help stop the country form drifting away into utter destruction. With the general consensus of opinion of all the military governors and other members of the Supreme and Executive Council, a Decree will soon be issued to lay a firm foundation of this objective. Fellow countrymen, I sincerely hope we shall be able to resolve most of the problems that have disunited us in the past and really come to respect and trust one another in accordance with an all-round code of good conduct and etiquette.

All foreigners are assured of their personal safety and should have no fear of being molested. I intend to continue the policy laid down in the statement by the Supreme Commander on 16th January 1966 published on 26th January 1966. We shall also honor all international treaty obligations and commitments and all financial agreements and obligations entered into by the previous government. We are desirous of maintaining good diplomatic relationships with all countries. We therefore consider any foreign interference in any form will be regarded as an act of aggression. All members of the armed forces are requested to keep within their barracks except on essential duties and when ordered from Supreme Headquarters. Troops must not terrorise the public, as such action will discredit the new National Military Government. Any act of looting or sabotage will be dealt with severely. You are to remember that your task is to help restore law and order and confidence in the public in time of crisis.

I am convinced that with your co-operation and understanding, we shall be able to pull the country out of its present predicament. I promise you that I shall do all I can to return to civil rule as soon as it can be arranged. I also intend to pursue most vigorously the question of the release of political prisoners. Fellow countrymen, give me your support and I shall endeavour to live up to expectations. Thank you.

INAUGURAL SPEECH OF BRIGADIER MURTALA MUHAMMED AS HEAD OF STATE, JULY 30, 1976

Fellow Nigerians. Events of the past few years have indicated that despite our great human and material resources, the government has not been able to fulfill the legitimate expectations of our people. Nigeria has been left to drift. This situation, if not arrested, would inevitably have resulted in chaos and even bloodshed.

In the endeavor to build a strong, united and virile nation, Nigerians have shed much blood. The thought of further bloodshed, for whatever reasons must, I am sure, be revolting to our people. The armed forces, having examined the situation, came to the conclusion that certain changes were inevitable. After the civil war, the affairs of state, hitherto a collective responsibility, became characterized by lack of consultation, indecision, indiscipline and even neglect. Indeed, the public at large became disillusioned and disappointed by these developments. This trend was clearly incompatible with the philosophy and image of a corrective regime. Unknown to the general public, the feeling of disillusionment was also evident among members of the armed forces whose administration was neglected but who, out of sheer loyalty to the nation, and in the hope that there would be a change, continued to suffer in silence.

Things got a stage where the head of administration became virtually inaccessible even to official advisers; and when advice was tendered, it was often ignored. Responsible opinion, including advice by eminent Nigerians, traditional rulers, intellectuals, et cetera, was similarly discarded. The leadership, either by design or default, had become too insensitive to the true feelings and yearnings of the people. The nation was thus plunged inexorably into chaos. It was obvious that matters could not, and should not, be allowed in this manner, and in order to give the nation a new lease of life, and sense of direction, the following decisions were taken:

1. The removal of General Yakubu Gowon as Head of the Federal Military Government and Commander in Chief of the Armed Forces.

2. The retirement of General Yakubu Gowon from the Armed Forces in his present rank of General with full benefits, in recognition of his past services to the
nation.

3. General Gowon will be free to return to the country as soon as conditions
permit; he will be free to pursue any legitimate undertakings of his choice in
any part of the country. His personal safety and freedom and those of his family
will be guaranteed.

4. The following members of the Armed Forces are retired with immediate
effect:

Vice Admiral J.E.A, Wey - Chief of Staff, Supreme Headquarters

Major-General Hassan Katsina - Deputy Chief of Staff, Supreme
Headquarters

Major-General David Ejoor - Chief of Staff (Army)

Rear Admiral Nelson Soroh - Chief of Naval Staff

Brigadier EE Ikwue - Chief of Air Staff, and

all other officers of the rank of Major-General (or equivalent) and above.

Alhaji Kam Salem - Inspector General of Police,

Chief T.A. Fagbola - Deputy Inspector General of Police

5. Also with immediate effect, all the present military governors, and the Administrator of East Central State, have been relieved of their appointments and
retired.

6. As you are already aware, new appointments have been made as follows:

Brigadier T.Y. Danjuma - Chief of Army Staff

Colonel John Yisa Doko - Chief of Air Staff

Commodore Michael Adelanwa - Chief of Naval Staff

Mr. M.D. Yusuf - Inspector General of Police

New military governors have also been appointed for the States as follows:

Lt-Colonel Muhammadu Buhari - North East

Colonel George Innih – Mid-West

Lt-Colonel Sani Bello - Kano

Captain Adekunle Lawal (Navy) - Lagos

Lt-Colonel Paul Omu - South East

Colonel Ibrahim Taiwo - Kwara

Captain Akin Aduwo (Navy) - West

Colonel Anthony Ochefu - East Central

Lt-Colonel Usman Jibrin - North Central

Colonel Abdullahi Mohammed - Benue-Plateau

Lt-Colonel Umaru Mohammed - North West

Lt-Colonel Zamani Lekwot - Rivers

The structure of government has been reorganized. There will now be three
organs of government at the federal level namely (i) The Supreme Military

Council (ii) The National Council of States (iii) The Federal Executive Council. There will of course continue to be Executive Councils at the State level. The reconstituted Supreme Military Council will comprise the following:

The Head of State and Commander-in-Chief of the Armed Forces

Brigadier Olusegun Obasanjo - Chief of Staff, Supreme Headquarters

Brigadier T.Y. Danjuma - Chief of Army Staff

Commodore Michael Adelanwa - Chief of Naval Staff

Colonel John Yisa Doko - Chief of Air Staff

Mr. M.D. Yusuf - Inspector-General of Police

GOCs:

1st Division - Brigadier Julius Akinrinade

2nd Division - Brigadier Martin Adamu

3rd Division - Brigadier Emmanuel Abisoye

Lagos Garrison Organization - Brigadier John Obada

Colonel Joseph Garba

Lt-Colonel Shehu YarAdua

Brigadier James Oluleye

Brigadier Iliya Bisalla

Colonel Ibrahim Babangida

Lt-Colonel Muktar Mohammed

Colonel Dan Suleiman

Captain Olufemi Olumide (Navy)

Captain Hussaini Abdullahi (Navy)

Mr. Adamu Suleiman - Commissioner of Police

Lt-Colonel Alfred Aduloju

Lt-Commander Godwin Kanu (NN)

All the civil commissioners in the Federal Executive Council are relieved of their appointments with immediate effect. The composition of the new Executive Council will be announced shortly.

We will review the political programme and make an announcement in due course. In the meantime, a panel will be set up to advise on the question of new states. A panel will also be set up to advise on the question of the federal capital. With due regard to the 1973 population census, it is now clear that whatever results are announced will not command general acceptance throughout the country. It has, therefore, been decided to cancel the 1973 population census. Accordingly, for planning purposes, the 1963 census figures shall continue to be used.

A panel will be set up to advise on the future of the Interim Common Services Agency (ICSA) and the Eastern States Interim Assets and Liability Agency (ESIALA). The Second World Black and African Festival of Arts and Culture is postponed in view of the obvious difficulties in providing all the necessary facilities. Consultations will be held with other participating countries with a view to fixing a new date.

Finally, we reaffirm this country's friendship with all countries. Foreign nationals living in Nigeria will be protected. Foreign investments will also be protected. The government will honour all obligations entered into by the previous Governments of the Federation. We will also give continued support to the Organization of African Unity, the United Nations Organization, and the Commonwealth.

Fellow Countrymen, the task ahead of us calls for sacrifice and self discipline at all levels of our society. This government will not tolerate indiscipline. The government will not condone abuse of office. I appeal to you all to cooperate with the government in our endeavour to give this nation a new lease of life. This change of government has been accomplished without shedding any blood; and we intend to keep it so. Long live the Federal Republic of Nigeria.

Appendix 3. Casualties of the 1966 Coups

Casualties of January 15, 1966 Coup

Civilians	Soldiers And Police
Alhaji Sir Ahmadu Bello, Sardauna of Sokoto	Brigadier Sam Ademulegun
Alhaji Sir Abubakar Tafawa Balewa	Brigadier Zakariya Maimalari
Chief Festus Okotie-Eboh	Colonel Ralph Shodeinde
Chief Samuel Akintola	Colonel Kur Mohammed
Ahmed Ben Musa[1]	Lt-Colonel Abogo Largema
Hafsatu Bello	Lt-Colonel Yakubu Pam
Mrs. Latifat Ademulegun	Lt-Colonel Arthur Unegbe
Zarumi Sardauna	Sergeant Daramola Oyegoke[2]
Ahmed Pategi[3]	PC Yohana Garkawa
	Lance Corporal Musa Nimzo
	PC Akpan Anduka
	PC Hagai Lai

[1] Senior Assistant Secretary for Security.
[2] He was one of the officers that assisted Nzeogwu in the attack on the Sardauna's lodge.
[3] A government driver.

Officers Killed During July/August 1966 Counter-Coup*

	Name	Unit
1	Major-General Johnson Aguiyi-Ironsi	Head of State, Supreme Commander, Nigerian Armed Forces
2	Lt-Colonel Francis Fajuyi	Military Governor, Western Region
3	Lt-Colonel Gabriel Okonweze	Commanding Officer, Abeokuta Garrison
4	Lt-Colonel Israel Okoro	Commanding Officer, 3rd Battalion, Kaduna
5	Major Christian Anuforo	N/A (abducted from prison and killed)
6	Major Alister Drummond	
7	Major Ibanga Essien Ekanem	Provost-Marshal, Nigerian Army
8	Major Christopher Chukwuike Emelifonwu	Deputy Adjutant and Quartermaster General, 1 Brigade, Kaduna
9	Major Joseph Ihedigbo	5th Battalion, Kano
10	Major Ukpo Isong	Commanding Officer, 1st Reconnaisance Squadron, Kaduna
11	Major Bernard Nnamani	Company Commander, 2nd Battalion, Ikeja
12	Major Theophilus E. Nzegwu (Air Force)	Staff Officer, Supreme Headquarters, Lagos
13	Major Peter C. Obi	Nigerian Air Force
14	Major John Obienu	Commanding Officer, 2nd Reconnaisance Squadron, Abeokuta
15	Major David V.A. Ogunro	NMTC
16	Major Donatus Okafor	N/A (abducted from prison and killed)
17	Captain R.I. Agbazue	Army Workshop
18	Captain A.O. Akpet	Staff Captain, 1 Brigade, Kaduna
19	Captain H.A. Auna	5th Battalion, Kano
20	Captain John Chukwueke	Education Officer, 2nd Battalion, Ikeja, Lagos
21	Captain Lawrence C. Dilibe	1 Brigade Headquaters, Kaduna
22	Captain Jonathan U. Egere	2nd Battalion, Ikeja, Lagos
23	Captain I.U. Idika	Nigerian Army Headquarters, Lagos
24	Captain H.A. Iloputaife	1 Brigade Headquaters, Kaduna
25	Captain Tom Iweanya	4th Battalion, Ibadan
26	Captain S.E. Maduabam	5th Battalion, Kano
27	Captain P.C. Okoye	Nigerian Army Headquarters — Lagos
28	Captain Godwin N.E. Ugoala	2nd Battalion, Ikeja, Lagos

29	Lieutenant Eleazar C.N. Achebe	4th Battalion, Ibadan
30	Lieutenant A.D.C. Egbuna	5th Battalion, Kano
31	Lieutenant P.D. Ekedingyo	4th Battalion, Ibadan
32	Lieutenant Zacchareus Idowu	Quartermaster, 2nd Battalion, Ikeja, Lagos
33	Lieutenant F.P. Jasper	4th Battalion, Ibadan
34	Lieutenant Godson Mbabie	2nd Battalion, Ikeja, Lagos
35	Lieutenant S.A. Mbadiwe	4th Battalion, Ibadan
36	Lieutenant S. Onwukwe	4th Battalion, Ibadan
37	Lieutenant E.B. Orok	2nd Reconnaissance Squadron, Abeokuta
38	Lieutenant J.D. Ovueziri	5th Battalion, Kano
39	Lieutenant J.U. Ugbe	1 Brigade Transport Company
40	Lieutenant Dag Waribor	3rd Battalion, Kaduna
41	Second-Lieutenant F.M. Agbonaye	2nd Battalion, Ikeja, Lagos
42	Second-Lieutenant Patrick Ogeogbunam Ibik	First Field Squadron, Nigerian Army Engineers, Kaduna
43	Second-Lieutenant A.R.O. Kasaba	2nd Reconnaissance Squadron, Abeokuta
44	Second-Lieutenant A.O. Olaniyan	2nd Field Battery, Abeokuta
45	Second-Lieutenant Pius K. Onyeneho	2nd Battalion, Ikeja, Lagos

*List excludes approximately 200–250 NCOs also killed.

Appendix 4.

Table 1: Fate of January 15, 1966 Coup Participants

Name	Post	Fate
Major Adewale Ademoyega	Nigerian Military Training College, Abeokuta	Survived the counter-coup and the Nigerian civil war. Imprisoned after the war until October 24, 1974, and dismissed from the army upon his release. Wrote his own inside account of the coup entitled Why We Struck." Died in 2007.
Major Christian Anuforo*	General Staff Officer (Grade II), Army Headquarters, Lagos	Abducted from prison at Ilesha (where he was detained for his part in the January 1966 coup) by northern soldiers in August 1966, and killed.
Major Humphrey Iwuchukwu Chukwuka	Deputy Adjutant-General, Army Headquarters, Lagos.	Alive. He survived the Nigerian civil war and was imprisoned along with other surviving January 1966 coup executors. He was released from detention in August 1975. Many years later, he met Lt-Colonel Pam's widow Elizabeth Pam who told Chukwuka that she had forgiven him for the role he played in abducting her husband during the coup.[1]

Major Emmanuel Arinze Ifeajuna	Brigade Major: 2 Brigade, Lagos	Executed in 1967 during the Nigerian civil war after planning a rebellion against Lt-Colonel Ojukwu. Despite his athletic exploits and Commonwealth gold medal, his coup exploits led to him being excluded from Nigeria's sports hall of fame.
Major Chukwuma Kaduna Nzeogwu*	Chief Instructor, Nigerian Military Training College, Kaduna	Killed in 1967 during the early days of the Nigerian civil war while fighting for Biafra. It is a mark of Nzeogwu's popularity that when his body was discovered during the Nigerian civil war by federal soldiers, they took his body away for burial with full military honors on the orders of Gowon (but not before his eyes had been plucked out). He was buried in the Kaduna military cemony. Although one account claims that a northern soldier swore at the minister that performed Nzeogwu's burial ceremony[2]. Despite his death early on in the war, army officers kept up the pretence that he was alive to his mother who was not informed of her son's death till years later. During the civil war the Nzeogwu family changed their name to Nwanze due to the notoriety that the coup brought to the Nzeogwu family name. They reverted back to the Nzeogwu name following the war.
Major Donatus Okafor	Commander, Federal Guards, Lagos	Abducted from Abeokuta prison (where he was detained for his part in the January 1966 coup) by northern soldiers in August 1966, and killed.
Major Timothy Onwuatuegwu	Instructor, Nigerian Military Training College, Kaduna	Killed soon after the end of the Nigerian civil war in 1970. The circumstances of his death remain obscure. Some accounts say he was killed close to the Cameroon border, others that he was tricked into being murdered by a friend.[3]
Captain Ben Gbulie	Commander, Army Engineers, Kaduna	Alive. Wrote the first inside account of the coup entitled "*Nigeria's Five Majors.*"
Captain Emmanuel Nwobosi*	Officer Commanding, 2 Field Battery, Abeokuta	Alive.

Captain Ogbonna Oji	Army Headquarters, Lagos	Status unknown. Some accounts erroneously claim he was killed in February 1968 during the Nigerian civil war. He survived the Nigerian civil war and was imprisoned along with other surviving January 1966 coup executors. He was released from detention in August 1975. If he is still alive, he has kept a scrupulously low profile and remained out of the limelight.
Captain Emmanuel Udeaja	Nigerian Army Engineers — Kaduna	Alive.
Lieutenant Juventus Chijioke Ojukwu[4]	1 Reconnaissance Squadron, Kaduna	Survived the counter-coup and the Nigerian civil war. Imprisoned after the war until October 24 1974, and retired from the army with four years' benefits upon his release. Alive.
Lieutenant Amechi Okaka	Ordnance Ammunition Depot, Lagos	Killed in action during the Nigerian civil war.
Lieutenant Edwin Okafor	First Field Squadron, Nigerian Army Engineers, Kaduna	Killed in action during the Nigerian civil war.
Lieutenant Fola Oyewole	2 Brigade Transport Company — Lagos	Alive. Fought on the side of Biafra during the Nigerian civil war. Wrote a book entitled "The Reluctant Rebel."
Second-Lieutenant Cyril Augustine Azubuogu	Artillery, Kaduna	Alive.
Second-Lieutenant Harris Otadafeuwerha Eghagha	Second Field Squadron, Nigerian Army Engineers — Kaduna	Alive. Later became commander of the Nigerian army's engineers unit and Military Administrator of Ogun state.
Second-Lieutenant Godfrey Ezedigbo	Federal Guards, Lagos	Killed in action during the Nigerian civil war.
Second-Lieutenant Ozoemena Igweze	Federal Guards, Lagos	Survived the counter-coup and the Nigerian civil war. Imprisoned after the war until October 24 1974, and retired from the army with one year's benefits upon his release.

Second-Lieutenant Patrick Ogeogbunam Ibik	First Field Squadron, Nigerian Army Engineers, Kaduna	Killed in 1966 during the northern counter-coup.
Second Lieutenant 'Bob' Ikejiofor	Signals, Lagos	Survived the counter-coup and the Nigerian civil war. Imprisoned after the war until October 24 1974, and dismissed from the army upon his release. Alive.
Second-Lieutenant John Atom Kpera	First Field Squadron, Nigerian Army Engineers, Kaduna	Alive. Later served as Military Governor of Benue and Anambra states.[5]
Second-Lieutenant Emmanuel Nweke	Signals, Lagos	Killed in action during the Nigerian civil war.
Second-Lieutenant Samson Emeka Omeruah	C Company, 3rd Battalion — Kaduna	Later joined the air force, rising to the rank of Air Commodore. Also served as Military Governor of Anambra State, Chairman of the Nigerian Football Association and Minister of Youth and Sports. Deceased. Died in December 2006.
Second-Lieutenant Dag Waribor	C Company, 3rd Battalion, Kaduna	Killed in 1966 during the northern counter-coup.

[1] Mrs Pam also served as a member of the Human Rights Violations Investigation Panel in 2001.

[2] see Luckham, The Nigerian Military: A Sociological Analysis of Authority and Revolt.

[3] An eyewitness informed the author that Onwuatuegwu was badly beaten up and detained before being taken out and killed.

[4] This officer is not related to Emeka Odumegwu Ojukwu and it is not clear why he was detained as he was not among the conspirators.

[5] Kpera earned himself a degree of infamy by commenting, at the end of his tenure as Benue state Military Governor, that he left behind an empty treasury because the treasury was empty when he was first appointed to the post!

*Major Nzeogwu, Major Anuforo and Captain Nwobosi were all former students together at St John's school in Kaduna.

The key plotters that survived the counter-coup and the civil war who were imprisoned after the civil war are Majors Ademoyega and Chukwuka, Captains Adeleke, Gbulie, Oji, Udeaja, Goddy Ude, Lieutenants Akpuaka, Amuchienwa, Anyafulu, Igweze, Ikejiofor, Ngwuluka, J.C. Ojukwu, Okocha, Olafimihan, Oyewole, Wokocha, and Second Lieutenants Azubuogu, Egbikor and Onyefuru.[1]

1 Gbulie, *The Fall of Biafra*, and Efiong *Nigeria and Biafra: My Story*, page 366.

Table 2: Fate of July 1966 Coup Participants

Name	Unit	Positions Achieved (Rank Achieved)	Fate
Second-Lieutenant Mohammed Sani Abacha	3rd Battalion, Kaduna	Head of State (Four Star General)	Died of a heart attack on June 8, 1998. Took part in further coups in 1983 and 1985, and possibly again in 1993.
Lieutenant D.S. Abubakar	Abeokuta Garrison	Military Administrator of Anambra State (Colonel)	Alive
Major Martin Adamu	2nd Battalion, Lagos	GOC, 2 Mechanized Division Member, Supreme Military Council (Major-General)	Deceased
Lt-Colonel Joseph Akahan	Commander, 4th Battalion, Kaduna	Chief of Staff (Army)	Died in a helicopter crash in 1967.
Major Shittu Alao	Nigerian Air Force Headquarters, Lagos	Commander of the Nigerian Air Force (Colonel)	Died on a solo flight in 1969 when he ran into bad weather and crash landed. The aircraft in which he died is on display at the National War Museum in Umuahia.
Lieutenant Ibrahim Babangida	1st Reconnaissance Squadron, Kaduna	Head of State (Four Star General)	Alive. Took part in further coups in 1975, 1983 and 1985.
Lieutenant Ibrahim Bako	4th Battalion, Ibadan	(Brigadier)	Killed on January 1, 1984 while taking part in a coup.
Lieutenant Muhammadu Buhari	2 Brigade, Lagos	Head of State (Major- General)	Alive. Took part in further coups in 1975 and 1983.
Captain Isa Bukar	Federal Guards, Lagos	(Colonel)	Convicted of treason in 1976 and executed by a firing squad for his alleged role in a coup.

Lieutenant Yakubu Dambo	3rd Battalion, Kaduna	(Lieutenant)	Killed in action during the Nigerian civil war.
Lieutenant Garba .A. Dada ("Paiko")	Adjutant, 4th Battalion, Ibadan	Later became a Senator in the second republic during the presidency of Shehu Shagari. (Brigadier)	Deceased
Major Theophilus Yakubu Danjuma	Principal Staff Officer, Army Headquarters, Lagos	Chief of Army Staff Defense Secretary (Lt-General)	Alive
Sergeant Paul Dickson	Lagos	(Major)	Deceased
Lieutenant Bukar Suka Dimka	Nigerian Military Training College, Kaduna	Head of Army Physical Training Corps (Lt-Colonel)	Convicted of treason in 1976 and executed by a firing squad.
Lieutenant Garba Duba	1 Reconnaissance Squadron, Kaduna	Military Governor — Bauchi State Military Governor — Sokoto State GOC, 2 Mechanized Division GOC, 3 Armored Division Commandant, Nigerian Defense Academy (Lt-General)	Alive
Captain Joseph Nanven Garba	Federal Guards, Lagos	Commandant of the Nigerian Defense Academy Member, Supreme Military Council Foreign Minister Nigeria's representative to the United Nations Director-General of Nigeria's National Institute for Policy and Strategic Studies (Major-General)	Died on June 1, 2002.

Lieutenant Mohammed Balarabe Haladu	4th Battalion, Ibadan	Minister of Industries (Lt-General)	Deceased. Died in 1998.
Major Abba Kyari	Artillery, Kaduna	Military Governor of North-Central State (Brigadier)	Alive
Sergeant Sabo Kwale	Abeokuta Garrison	(Lieutenant)	Convicted of treason in 1976 and executed by a firing squad for his alleged role in a coup.
Lt-Colonel Murtala Ramat Muhammed	Inspector of Signals, Lagos	Head of State (Four Star General)	Murdered on Friday 13 February 1976 during an unsuccessful coup.
Second-Lieutenant Muhammadu Gado Nasko	Artillery, Kaduna	Minister of the Federal Capital Territory Minister of Trade, Agriculture and Water Resources (Lt-General)	Alive
Lieutenant Malami Mahe Nassarawa	2nd Battalion, Lagos	Commandant, Infantry School: Jaji (Brigadier)	Deceased. Tried for his alleged role in a coup in 1986 and dismissed from the army as a result.
Lieutenant James Onoja	4th Battalion, Ibadan	Chief of Staff - United Nations peacekeeping forces in Lebanon (Brigadier)	Shot and wounded in 1981 when his vehicle was ambushed by Palestinian guerrillas while on peacekeeping duty in Lebanon in 1981. Survived that attack but now deceased.
Corporal John Nanzip Shagaya	2nd Reconnaissance Squadron, Abeokuta	Internal Affairs Minister ECOMOG Commander (Brigadier)	Alive. Current Senator, Plateau South.
Lieutenant Abdullahi Shelleng	Company Commander, 4th Battalion, Ibadan	Military Governor of Benue State (Major-General)	Alive
Captain Ibrahim Taiwo	Lagos Garrison, Yaba	Military Governor of Kwara State (Colonel)	Murdered on Friday 13 February 1976 during an unsuccessful coup.

Lieutenant Paul Chabri Tarfa	Federal Guards — Lagos	Military Administrator of Oyo State (Major-General)	Alive
Captain Baba Usman	GSO (Grade II), Army Headquarters, Lagos	(Brigadier)	Alive
Major Musa Usman	Nigerian Air Force, Lagos	Military Governor of North-Eastern State (Brigadier)	Deceased
Lieutenant William .G. Walbe	2nd Battalion, Lagos	ADC to General Gowon (Colonel)	Alive
Lieutenant Mamman Jiya Vatsa	4th Battalion, Ibadan	Minister of the Federal Capital Territory (Major-General)	Deceased. Convicted of treason in 1986 and executed by a firing squad for his alleged role in a coup.
Captain Abdul D.S. Wya	3rd Battalion, Kaduna	(Colonel)	Convicted of treason in 1976 and executed by a firing squad for his alleged role in a coup.

Table 3: List of those Executed for Their Role in the Coup of February 13, 1976

	Name	State of Origin	Post
1	Commissioner of Police Joseph Dechi Gomwalk	Plateau	Former Military Governor of Benue-Plateau State
2	Mr. Abdulakarim Zakari	Kaduna	Civilian Radio Broadcaster
3	Major General Iliyasu D. Bisalla	Plateau	Commissioner of Defense and Member of the Supreme Military Council
4	Colonel Isa Bukar	Borno	Commanding Officer, 4th Infantry Brigade, Benin
5	Colonel A.D.S. Wya	Kaduna	Corps Commandant, Artillery
6	Lt-Colonel K. Adamu	Plateau	Commandant, 1 Division School of Infantry, Kaduna
7	Lt-Colonel Alfa R. Aliyu	Plateau	Commandant, 5 Infantry Brigade, Onitsha
8	Lt-Colonel Bukar Suka Dimka	Plateau	Director, Army Physical Training Corps

9	Lt-Colonel Ayuba Tense	Plateau	Commandant, 44 Engineers Brigade
10	Lt-Colonel Adamu .B. Umaru	Kaduna	Chief Instructor, Nigerian Defense Academy, Kaduna
11	Major J. Kola Afolabi	Kwara	
12	Major Clement D. Dabang	Plateau	Commanding Officer, 1 Guards Battalion
13	Major Kefas Kolo Gagara	Plateau	Commandant, 2 Division School of Infantry
14	Major Joe W. Kasai	Gongola	Commanding Officer, 4 Provost Battalion
15	Major M.M. Mshelia	Gongola	Commandant, Anti-Aircraft Regiment, Ikeja, Lagos
16	Major Olasebikan Ogunmekan	Osun	Supply and Transport Headquarters, Lagos
17	Major Ibrahim B. Rabo	Kaduna	Regimental Commandant, Nigerian Army Engineers
18	Captain A.A. Aliyu	Kaduna	4 Armed Regiment, Badagary, Lagos
19	Captain Augustine Dawurang	Plateau	1 Armed Regiment, Kaduna
20	Captain J. Idi Fadah	Plateau	Army Headquarters, Lagos
21	Captain McDonald R. Gotip	Plateau	Brigade of Guards, Dodan Barracks, Lagos
22	Captain Malaki Parwang	Plateau	Instructor, School of Artillery
23	Captain Samuel Wakias	Plateau	AA Regiment, Nigerian Army Artillery
24	Lieutenant Peter Cigari	Plateau	
25	Lieutenant Lawrence Garba	Plateau	
26	Lieutenant Sabo Kwale	Gongola	
27	Lieutenant Mohammed	Kaduna	Physical Training Corps, Offa
28	Lieutenant William Seri	Plateau	CC Administration Company, 4 Infantry Brigade
29	Lieutenant E.L.K. Shelleng	Plateau	Paymaster, 1 Artillery Brigade, Kaduna
30	Lieutenant S. Wayah	Kaduna	
31	Lieutenant O. Zagmi	Gongola	
32	Warrant Officer Edward Bawa	Plateau	
33	Warrant Officer Monday Monchong	Plateau	

34	Warrant Officer (II) Sambo Pankshin	Plateau	Physical Training Corps, Offa
35	Warrant Officer Emmanuel Dakup Seri	Plateau	Physical Training Corps, Offa
36	Staff Sergeant Richard Dungdang	Plateau	
37	Sergeant Bala Javan	Plateau	Physical Training Corps, Offa
38	Sergeant Sale Pankshin	Plateau	
39	Sergeant Amadu Rege	Plateau	Physical Training Corps, Offa
40	Police Sergeant H.Shaiyen	Plateau	

Table 4: List of those Imprisoned for Their Role in the Coup of February 13, 1976

Name	Term Of Imprisonment
Major A.K. Abang	Life
Captain A.A. Maidobo	Life
Captain Peter Temlong	Life
Captain C.Wuyep	Life
Second-Lieutenant A.Walbe	Life
Mrs Helen Gomwalk	Life
Mr. S.Anyadofu	Life
Mr. D.Gontu (police)	Life
Gyang Pam (police)	Life
Mr. S.K. Dimka (police)	Life
Warrant Officer (II) E.Izah	Life
Sgt J.Bupwada	Life
Lt-Colonel J.S. Madugu	2 years
Captain Isaiah Gowon[1]	15 years
Mr. J.Tuwe	10 years

[1] Younger brother of General Gowon.

NIGERIAN CHIEFS OF ARMY STAFF SINCE AUGUST 1966

	Name	Dates Of Incumbency	Origin
1	Lt-Colonel Joseph Akahan	August 1966–July 1967	North
2	Colonel Hassan Katsina	July 1967–1972	North
3	Major-General David Ejoor	1972–July 28, 1975	South
4	Brigadier Theophilus Yakubu Danjuma	July 29, 1975 –September 30, 1979	North
5	Lt-General Alani Akinrinade	October 1, 1979–April 1980	South
6	Lt-General Gibson Jalo	April 2, 1980–October 1981	North
7	Lt-General Mohammed Inuwa Wushishi	October 1981–December 31, 1983	North
8	Major-General Ibrahim Babangida	January 1, 1984–August 26, 1985	North
9	Major-General Sani Abacha	August 27, 1985–September 26, 1990	North
10	Lt-General Salihu Ibrahim	September 27, 1990–August 26, 1993	North
11	Lt-General Aliyu Mohammed	August 27, 1993–November 1993	North
12	Major-General Chris Alli	November 1993–August 1994	North
13	Major-General Alwali Kazir	August 1994–March 1996	North

14	Major-General Ishaya Rizi Bamaiyi	March 1996–May 1999	North
15	Major-General Samuel Victor Leo Malu	May 1999–April 2001	North
16	Major-General Alexander Oderuduo Ogomudia	April 2001–June 2003	South
17	Lt-General Martin Luther Agwai	June 2003–May 2006	North
18	Major-General Owoye Andrew Azazi	May 2006–June 6, 2007	South
19	Lt-General Luka Nyeh Yusuf	June 6, 2007–August 27, 2008	North
20	Major-General Abdulrahman Bello Dambazau	August 28, 2008 — Present	North

*Major I.D. Bisalla was briefly appointed acting Chief of Staff after the death of Akahan.

Glossary

ADC: Aide de Camp — A military officer acting as secretary and confidential assistant to a superior officer.

AG: Action Group

Battalion: A group of approximately 750–800 soldiers. A battalion is normally commanded by a Lt-Colonel, and is usually composed of 4–6 companies.

Brigade: A brigade is usually composed of 2–3 battalions and supporting units. A brigade is usually commanded by a Brigadier.

Company: A group of approximately 150 soldiers. A company is normally commanded by a Major, with a Captain as second in command. A company is usually composed of 3–5 platoons.

CDC: Constitution Drafting Committee.

Council of Ministers: The cabinet ministers of the Nigerian federal government (until January 1966).

Coup d'état: The sudden overthrow, often violent, of an existing government by a group of conspirators.

Division: A division is usually composed of 2–3 brigades. A division is usually commanded by a Major-General.

ECN: Electricity Corporation of Nigeria.

FEC: Federal Executive Council (the federal cabinet).

FMG: Federal Military Government.

GOC: General Officer Commanding.

GSO: General Staff Officer.

Infantry: infantry soldiers are the army's "foot soldiers" who engage in combat operations.

LGO: Lagos Garrison Organization.

NCNC: National Council of Nigerian Citizens.

NCO: Non-Commissioned Officer. These are soldiers who, while enlisted in the army, are below the officer corps in the chain of command. They usually perform administrative and training functions, but can become (commissioned) officers through promotion.

NDA: Nigerian Defense Academy.

NMTC: Nigerian Military Training College.

NNA: Nigerian National Alliance.

NPC: Northern Peoples Congress.

OPEC: Organization of Petroleum Exporting Countries.

Platoon: a group of approximately 35 soldiers. A platoon is normally commanded by a Lieutenant.

Recce: Reconnaissance.

ROSTS: Regular Officers Special Training School.

RSM: Regimental Sergeant Major.

RWAFF: Royal West African Frontier Force.

SMC: Supreme Military Council.

UNESCO: United Nations Educational, Scientific and Cultural Organization.

UPGA: United Progressive Grand Alliance.

Nigerian Military Officer Ranks (in order of decreasing seniority)

Army Rank	Air Force Equivalent Rank	Navy Equivalent Rank
Field-Marshal[1]	Marshal of the Air Force	Admiral of the Fleet
General (Four Star)	Air Chief Marshal	Admiral
Lieutenant-General	Air Marshal	Vice-Admiral
Major-General	Air Vice Marshal	Rear-Admiral
Brigadier (Also referred to as "Brigadier-General")	Air Commodore	Commodore
Colonel	Group Captain	Captain
Lieutenant-Colonel	Wing Commander	Commander
Major	Squadron Leader	Lieutenant-Commander
Captain	Flight Lieutenant	Lieutenant
Lieutenant	Flying Officer	Sub-Lieutenant
Second-Lieutenant	Pilot Officer	Midshipman

[1] No person has ever achieved the rank of Field-Marshal in the history of the Nigerian army. The rank is usually deployed in times of war.

Nigerian Military NCO Ranks (in order of decreasing seniority)

Army NCO Rank	Air Force Equivalent Rank	Navy Equivalent Rank
N/A	Air Warrant Officer	Warrant Petty Office
Warrant Officer Class I	Master Warrant Officer	Chief Petty Officer
Warrant Officer Class II	Warrant Officer	N/A
Staff Sergeant	Flight Sergeant	Petty Officer
Sergeant	Sergeant	N/A
Corporal	Corporal	Leading Rating
Lance Corporal	Lance Corporal	Able Rating
Private	Aircraftsman	Ordinary Rating

BIBLIOGRAPHY

BOOKS

Adebo, Simeon. *Our Unforgettable Years*, Macmillan Nigeria, 1984.

Adekunle, Abiodun. *The Nigeria–Biafra War Letters (A Soldier's Story)*. Phoenix Publishing, 2004.

Ademoyega, Wale. *Why We Struck: The Story of the First Nigerian Coup*. Evans Brothers: Ibadan, 1981.

Adetowun, Ogunsheye, F. *A Break in the Silence: Lt-Colonel Victor Adebukunola Banjo*. Spectrum Books, 2001.

Afrifa, A.A. *The Ghana Coup*. Cass, 1967.

Agbese, Dan. *Fellow Nigerians (Turning Points in the Political History of Nigeria)*. Umbrella Books, 2000.

Ahmed, Femi. *Domkat, A Biography of General Domkat Bali*, 1993.

Akinola, Richard. *Fellow Countrymen — The Story of Coup d'Etats in Nigeria*. Rich Konsult, 2000.

Akpan, Ntieyoug U. *The Struggle for Secession, 1966–1970: A Personal Account of the Nigerian Civil War*. Routledge: London. 1976.

Alaoma, Godwin, Onyegbula. *The Nigerian–Biafran Bureaucrat: An Account of Life in Biafra and Within Nigeria*. Spectrum Books, 2005.

Alli, Chris. *The Federal Republic of Nigeria Army: The Siege of a Nation*. Malthouse Press, 2002.

Alli, Sidi. *Murtala Muhammed, A Betrayed Revolutionary*.

Anthony, Douglas. *I Need to Get to Kano: The Unmaking and Remaking of an Igbo Migrant Community in Northern Nigeria, 1966–1986*. Northwestern University, 1996.

Anthony, Douglas. *Poison and Medicine: Ethnicity, Power, and Violence in a Nigerian City, 1966 to 1986*. Heinemann, 2002.

Anwunah, Patrick. *The Nigeria–Biafra War (1967–1970): My Memoirs.* Spectrum Books, 2007.

Austin, Dennis and Luckham, Robin. *Politicians and Soldiers in Ghana.* Frank Cass: London, 1975.

Azikiwe, Nnamdi. *My Odyssey: An Autobiography.* Hurst: London, 1970.

Barrett, Lindsay. *Danjuma: The Making of A General.* Fourth Dimension Publishers: Enugu, 1979.

Bhandari, P.L. *Top Secret and All That.* Sangam Books: New Delhi, 1974.

Burji, Badamasi Shuaibu. *Tributes to a Man of the People — General Hassan Usman Katsina.*

Clark, Trevor. *A Right Honorable Gentleman: The Life and Times of Alhaji Sir Abubakar Tafawa Balewa.* Hudahuda Publishing, 1991.

Dassah, Edward. *Shagaya : The Will to Excel.* Echo Communications, 1994.

Davies, Hezekiah Oladipo Olagunju, *Memoirs.* Evans Brothers, 1989.

Dudley, Billy J. *Instability and Political Order: Politics and Crisis in Nigeria.* Ibadan University Press, 1973.

Dudley, Billy J. *An Introduction to Nigerian Government and Politics.* Bloomington: Indiana University Press, 1982.

Dudley, Billy J. *Parties and Politics in Northern Nigeria.* Cass: London, 1968.

Efiong, Philip. *Nigeria and Biafra: My Story.* Sungai Books, 2003.

Ejoor, David Akpode, *Reminiscences.* Malthouse Press: Lagos, 1990.

Ejueyitchie, Jane.O. *H.A. Ejueyitchie — Portrait of a Civil Servant.* Shaneson Ltd, Nigeria, 1988.

Elaigwu, J. Isawa. *Gowon: The Biography of a Soldier-Statesman.* West Books: Ibadan, 1986.

Elias, Taslim Olawale and Richard Akinjide, *Africa and the Development of International Law.* Martinus Nijhoff Publishers: Leiden, 1988.

Elias, T.O. *Nigeria: The Development of its Laws and Constitution.* Stevens: London, 1967.

Enonchong, Charles. *I Know Who Killed Major Nzeogwu! An Investigation Into the Most Secret Cover-up of the Nigerian Civil War.* Century Books, 1991.

Eghosa E. Osaghae. *Crippled Giant: Nigeria Since Independence.* Indiana University Press, 1998.

Feinstein, Alan. *African Revolutionary — The Life and Times of Nigeria's Aminu Kano.* Lynne Rienner, 1987.

Forsyth, Frederick. *The Biafra Story — The Making of an African Legend,* Penguin: Baltimore, 1969.

Forsyth, Fredrick. *Emeka.* Spectrum Books, 1991.

Garba, Joseph Nanven. *Diplomatic Soldiering: Nigerian Foreign Policy, 1975–1979.* Spectrum Books, 1987.

Garba, Joseph Nanven. *Revolution in Nigeria: Another View.* Africa Books Limited, 1982.

Gbulie, Ben. *The Fall of Biafra.* Benlie Nigeria Publishers, 1989.

Gbulie, Ben. *Nigeria's Five Majors: Coup d'Etat of 15th January 1966, First Inside Account.* Africana Educational Publishers, 1981.

Gutteridge, William. *The Military in African Politics.* Methuen & Co, 1969.

Haywood, Colonel A, and Clarke, Brigadier F.A.S. *The History of the Royal West African Frontier Force.* Gale and Polden, Aldershot, 1964.

Ihonde, Moses. *First Call: An Account of the Gowon Years.* Diamond Publications, 2004.

Ikeazor, C. *Nigeria 66: The Turning Point.* New Millennium, 1997.

Ikegwuoha, Bernard Thompson O. *Nigeria, an Endless Cycle of Coup d'Etat,* 1994, Europress, 1989.

Iloegbunam, Chuks. *Ironside.* Press Alliance Network, 1999.

Isichei, Elizabeth. *A History of the Igbo People.* Palgrave Macmillan: London, 1976.

Isichei, Elizabeth. *A History of Nigeria,* Longman, 1983.

Jemibewon, David. *A Combatant in Government.* Heinemann Educational Books, 1998.

Jemibewon, David. *The Military, Law and Society: Reflections of a General.* Spectrum Books, 1998.

Kayode, M.O. and Otobo, Dafe. *Allison Akene Ayida: Nigeria's Quintessential Public Servant.* Malthouse Press, 2005.

Kankara, Kadani. *The March to Megiddo: a Detailed Narrative of the 1966 Military Coups in Nigeria.* 2002.

Kirk-Greene, Anthony Hamilton Millard. *Crisis and Conflict in Nigeria — A Documentary Sourcebook (2 volumes).* Oxford University Press: London, 1971.

Kirk-Greene, Anthony, Diamond, Larry, Oyediran, Oyeleye. *Transition Without End: Nigerian Politics and Civil Society Under Babangida.* Lynne Rienner Publishers, 1997.

Kurfi, Ahmadu. *The Nigerian General Elections, 1959 and 1979 and the Aftermath.* MacMillan Nigeria, 1983.

Ladigbolu, A.G.A. *A Great Hero: Lieutenant-Colonel Francis Adekunle Fajuyi, 1926–1966.* Lichfield Nigeria: Lagos, 1992.

Lai, Hassan Mamman. *The Infantryman in the Regiment.* 2001.

Luckham, Robin. *The Nigerian Military: A Sociological Analysis of Authority and Revolt: 1960–67.* Cambridge University Press, 1971.

Mackintosh, John P. (ed.). *Nigerian Government and Politics.* Allen and Unwin: London, 1966.

Madiebo, Alexander. *The Nigerian Revolution and the Biafran War.* Fourth Dimension Publishers: Enugu, 1980.

Maier, Karl. *This House Has Fallen: Midnight in Nigeria.* Public Affairs Books: New York, 2000.

Mainasara, A.M. *The Five Majors: Why They Struck.* Hudahuda Publishing: Zaria, 1982.

Mbadiwe, Kingsley Ozumba. *Rebirth of a Nation.* Fourth Dimension Publications: Enugu, Nigeria, 1991.

Melson, Robert, and Howard Wolpe (eds.). *Nigeria: Modernization and the Politics of Communalism.* Michigan State University Press: East Lansing, 1971.

Miners, N.J. *The Nigerian Army 1956–1966.* Methuen & Co, 1971.

Mohammed, Dantsoho. *Kumasi — Portrait of a Model RSM.* Nigerian Army Education Corps and School.

Momoh, Hafiz (editor). *The Nigerian Civil War 1967–1970: History and Reminiscences.* Sam Bookman Publishers: Ibadan, Nigeria, 2000.

Muffett, DJM. *Let Truth Be Told: The Coups d'etats of 1966.* Hudahuda Publishing: Zaria, 1982.

Nigerian Army Education Corps and School, *History of the Nigerian Army.*

Nigerian Army Education Corps and School, *History of the Nigerian Army (2ⁿᵈ ed).*

Njoku, Hilary. *A Tragedy Without Heroes.* Fourth Dimension Publishers: Enugu, 1987.

Njoku, Rose. *Withstand the Storm: War Memoirs of a Housewife.* Heinemann Educational Books, 1986.

Nwankwo, Arthur Agwuncha and Ifejika, Samuel Udochukwu. *Biafra: The Making of A Nation.* Praeger: New York (1970)

Nwankwo, Arthur. *Nigeria: The Challenge of Biafra.* R.Collings, 1972.

Nzeogwu, Okeleke Peter. *Major C.K.Nzeogwu: Fighting the Illusive Nigerian Enemy from Childhood to Death.* Spectrum Books, 2003.

Obasanjo, Olusegun. *An Intimate Portrait of Chukwuma Kaduna Nzeogwu.* Spectrum Books: Enugu, 1987.

Obasanjo, Olusegun. *My Command.* Heinemann: London, 1980.

Obasanjo, Olusegun. *Not My Will.* University Press Ltd, Nigeria, 1990.

Ogbemudia, Samuel. *Years of Challenge.* Heinemann Educational Books, 1991.

Ojiako, James. *Nigeria: Yesterday, Today and ?,* Africana Educational Publishers, 1981.

Ojiako, James. *Thirteen Years of Military Rule, 1966–1979.* Daily Times of Nigeria.

Ojukwu, C.O. Biafra: *Random Thoughts of C. Odumegwu Ojukwu,* Harper & Row, 1969.

Oluleye, James. *Architecturing a Destiny.* Spectrum Books, 2001.

Oluleye, James J. *Military Leadership in Nigeria, 1966–1979.* Ibadan University Press, 1985.

Omoruyi, Omo. *The Tale of June 12: The Betrayal of the Democratic Rights of Nigerians.* Press Alliance Network, 1999.

Onigbinde, Akinyemi. *The Road to Lalupon: Tribute to Gallantry.* Frontline Books, 2001.

Osuntokun, Akinjide. *Chief S.Ladoke Akintola — His Life and Times.* Frank Cass, 1984.

Osuntokun, Akinjide. *Power Broker: A Biography of Sir Kashim Ibrahim.* Spectrum Books, 1987.

Ottah, Nelson. *Rebels Against Rebels.* Manson, 1981.

Oyeweso, Siyan. *Perspectives on the Nigerian Civil War.* Campus Press Ltd: Lagos, 1992.

Oyewole, Fola. *Reluctant Rebel.* R.Collings, 1975.

Oyinbo, John. *Crisis and Beyond.* Charles Knight, 1971.

Paden, John N. Ahmadu Bello, *Sardauna of Sokoto: Values and Leadership in Nigeria.* Hodder and Stoughton: London, 1986.

Panter-Brick, S.K. (ed.) *Nigerian Politics and Military Rule: Prelude to the Civil War,* Athlone Press: London, 1970.

Panter-Brick, S.K. *Soldiers and Oil: The Political Transformation of Nigeria.* Cass: London, 1978.

Post, K. and Vickers, M. *Structure and Conflict in Nigeria, 1960–1966*, Heinemann Educational: London, 1973.

Schwarz, Walter *Nigeria*. Pall Mall: London, 1968.

Sharwood-Smith, Bryan. *But Always as Friends. Northern Nigeria and the Cameroons, 1921–1957*. George Allen & Unwin: London, 1969.

Sharwood-Smith, Joan. *Diary of a Colonial Wife: An African Experience*, Radcliffe Press: London, 1992.

Smart, Emmanuel Unya. *The History of Coups in Nigeria*. Gaek Moke, Nigeria, 1998.

St. Jorre, John de. *The Brothers' War: Biafra and Nigeria*. Houghton Mifflin: London, 1972

Umoden, Gabriel. *The Babangida Years: The First Authoritative Biography of Nigeria's Most Visionary Leader*. Gabumo Publishing, Lagos, Nigeria (1992).

Usman, Yusufu Bala and Kwanashie, George Amale. *Inside Nigerian History, 1950–1970: Events, Issues and Sources*. Ibadan, Nigeria, 1995.

Williams, Ebenezer. *My Great Ordeal*. Kwara State Printing and Publishing, 1976.

Zdenek, Cervenka. *A History of the Nigerian War, 1967–1970*. Onibonoje Press, 1972.

OTHER PUBLICATIONS

Newspapers and Periodicals

"Conscience Is The Most Independent Judge One Can Have," *This Day*, November 12, 2007.

"Facts and Fantasies of Nzeogwu Revolution," *This Day*, November 16, 2004, by Emma Okocha.

"Festival of Death," *Time* Magazine, March 22, 1976.

"Igbo in the Enterprise Called Nigeria," *This Day*, January 26, 2001, by Nwokolo, J.S.P.C.

"Massacre in Kano," *Time Magazine*, October 14, 1966.

"Nigerian Federalism Under Military Regimes," by J. Isawa Elaigwu, *Publius, The Journal of Federalism* 18 (Winter 1988).

"Penny-Ante Putsch," *Time Magazine*, March 1, 1976.

"The Men of Sandhurst," *Time Magazine*, January 28, 1966.

"What You did not know about Fajuyi" by Adeyinka Adebayo, *Guardian*, July 31, 2001.

Official Memoranda and Publications

Airgram from US Embassy in Nigeria to the Department of State: Lagos A-419, February 11th, 1968.

Constitution (Suspension and Modification) Decree.

Decree 34 of 1966.

Fabian Colonial Bureau. Venture: Socialism and the Developing World, volume 24, 1972.

Federal Military Government (Supremacy and Enforcement of Powers) Decree.

January 15: Before and After, Eastern Region Ministry of Information

Memorandum From Robert W Komer of the National Security Council Staff to the President's Special Assistant for National Security Affairs, Washington, January 2, 1965.

Memorandum from Samuel E Belk of National Security Council Staff to the President's Special Assistant for National Security Affairs, Washington, December 30, 1964.

Memorandum from Ulric Haynes of the National Security Council Staff to the president's Special Assistant: Foreign Relations of the United States 1964–68, Volume XXIV, Africa.

Military Rebellion of January 15th 1966 — Special Branch Police Report on coup of January 15, 1966.

Nigerian Crisis 1966. Nigeria, Eastern Region Ministry of Information.

Treason and Other Offenses (Special Military Tribunal) Decree

Quick Kill in Slow Motion: The Nigerian Civil War, by Michael Stafford, Marine Corps Command and Staff College, 1984.

Top secret memorandum from Major-General Welby-Everard to Permanent Secretary dated 14 September 1964.

The Verbatim Report of the Meeting of the Supreme Military Council, Aburi, Accra, Ghana. 4–5 January, 1967. Published in 1967 by ENIS.

INDEX